WORK WITH TEXT FILES (SEE CHAPTER 8)

How Do I	Use This Command	Example
Compare two sorted files and view the differences between them with surrounding context?	**diff**	`diff -i first-draft.txt second-draft.txt`
Number the lines in a text file?	**nl**	`nl magic.txt > magic-numbered.txt`
Convert a Portable Document Format (PDF) file to PostScript?	**pdf2ps**	`pdf2ps resume.pdf resume.ps`
Translate all the uppercase characters in a text file to lowercase?	**tr**	`cat uppercase.txt	tr '[A-Z]' '[a-z]'`

WORK WITH SOUND AND GRAPHIC FILES (SEE CHAPTER 9)

How Do I	Use This Command	Example
Create a thumbnail index of all the graphic files in the working directory?	**convert**	`convert 'vid:*.jpg' catalog.jpg`
Create a printed jewel case label for a CD-ROM that I've just burned?	**cdlabelgen**	`cdlabelgen -c 'My Favorites' -s '2000' -i 'Blues%Jazz%Rock% Alternative Rock%Techno% Industrial' -e images/mp3.eps > cover.ps`
Create a composite image of two or more graphic files using special effects?	**combine**	`combine -compose bumpmap image1.jpg image2.jpg combined.jpg`

CONFIGURE AND USE NETWORKS AND THE INTERNET (SEE CHAPTER 13)

How Do I	Use This Command	Example
Display information about all the TCP/IP sockets currently in operation?	**netstat**	`netstat -a`
Copy a file to a remote server for which I have appropriate permissions?	**rpc**	`rcp essay1.doc essay1.bak@lothlorien:/home/ suzanne/Documents/Backup`
View available NFS shares?	**showmount**	`showmount -a`
Mount a Samba share on a remote system?	**smbmount**	`smbmount //lothlorien/suzanne /home/suzanne/lothlorien`
Connect to a remote Telnet service?	**telnet**	`telnet lothlorien.mynetwork.org`

Linux Command

INSTANT REFERENCE

Linux Command

INSTANT REFERENCE

Bryan Pfaffenberger

SYBEX

San Francisco   Paris
Düsseldorf   Soest   London

Publisher: Jordan Gold

Contracts and Licensing Manager: Kristine O'Callaghan

Acquisitions and Developmental Editor: Ellen Dendy

Editors: Raquel Baker, Suzanne Goraj

Production Editor: Jennifer Campbell

Technical Editors: Don Hergert, Elizabeth Zinkann

Book Designer: Kate Kaminski

Electronic Publishing Specialist: Maureen Forys, Happenstance Type-O-Rama

Proofreaders: Erika Donald, Amey Garber, Camera Obscura, Laurie O'Connell, Nancy Riddiough

Indexer: Rebecca Plunkett

Cover Design: Design Site

Cover Illustration: Sergie Loobkoff, Design Site

Library of Congress Card Number: 00-101810

ISBN: 0-7821-2748-7

Contents at a Glance

Contents

CHAPTER 3   **Learning Shell Fundamentals**   **49**

Introduction

Welcome to *Linux Command Instant Reference*!

This is the first Linux command reference to be written *from scratch* for today's Linux user. This book isn't a compilation of man (manual) pages or old, out-of-date, how-to documents. Every word of this book is original, and it's been professionally written to ensure the highest degree of readability and technical accuracy.

Who This Book Is For

The organization of this book is also unique, making this book the perfect reference for today's Linux user.

It's Organized by Task Not Tradition

Most Linux command references organize commands in the old, traditional Unix way—that is, they begin with all the commands available to users and then proceed with those that are accessible only to system and network administrators. This organization doesn't make sense for today's Linux users, who are running Linux on single-user systems. Linux users wear two hats—the user's *and* the system administrator's—so it no longer makes sense to categorize Linux commands in the old, Unix-influenced way. Instead, this book is organized by the *tasks* you want to perform, such as navigating the file system, finding elusive files, dealing with disks, burning CD-ROMs, and more. For more information on what's covered and where, see the section "A Guide to This Book's Contents."

It's about Linux Not Unix

Unlike most works of this type, this book isn't a rehash of ages-old Unix documentation. It's the first Linux command reference to deal with today's Linux distributions, today's Linux utilities, and today's users' needs. To be sure, you'll find detailed coverage of the classic utilities that have made their way to the Linux environment, including the **bash** shell (Chapter 3), text-processing utilities such as **gawk** and **sed** (Chapter 8), and text editors such as **vi** and **emacs** (Chapter 11). This book also covers the new commands that make Linux such an exciting and rewarding operating system to use, such as the latest utilities for using and manipulating MP3 music files and burning your own CD-R or CD-RW discs (see Chapter 9), the most recent version of Windows networking software for Linux systems (see Chapter 13), and the software needed to get TrueType fonts working on your system (see Chapter 10). This is *the* book for today's Linux user.

It's for Users Not Hackers

Millions of people are installing Linux and learning how to use this exciting operating system successfully. Very few of them have the time or inclination to become programmers. And that's new. Until very recently, almost all Linux users were hackers, a term I'm using in its positive sense. (Among computer enthusiasts, the term *hacker* refers to a programmer who enjoys writing software and especially "tweaking" this software to extract the maximum possible performance.) Unlike other works of its type, *Linux Command Instant Reference* is aimed squarely at the needs of non-programming users. As a result, this book doesn't attempt to cover utilities that are of interest only to Linux hackers and software developers. These utilities would make sense only if you possessed a great deal of background knowledge and programming expertise. Instead, this book provides quick, informative reference information about the utilities needed by today's Linux *users*.

To use your Linux system effectively, keep this book next to your computer; you'll use it every day.

Why Learn Linux Commands?

This book doesn't attempt to document X Window System, KDE, and GNOME utilities and applications. Instead, it cuts straight to the heart of the matter: the commands and utilities you use when you're faced with the Linux prompt, which you'll see when you run Linux in its text-only mode or in an X Session's terminal window.

To be sure, desktop environments such as KDE and GNOME are increasingly able to hide the complex, command-line environment from users. So why bother learning Linux commands?

Here are some darned good reasons:

- Most of the X, KDE, and GNOME utililities are pretty-looking *front-end* programs that drive the underlying, text-mode utilites. (A front-end program provides a GUI interface to a command-line utility.) However, most front-end programs offer only a fraction of the underlying utility's capabilities. For example, there's no easy way with the KDE and GNOME file managers to change the owner-ship of file *recursively* (that is, throughout an entire directory and all of its associated subdirectories). With the **chmod** command (Chapter 5), you can accomplish this feat very quickly. An accomplished Linux user knows when to use the graphical utilities—and when to switch to the command-line interface.

- Once you've learned to deal with command-line syntax, the text-mode utilities are *faster*. On the command line, an accomplished Linux user can get done in minutes tasks that would take much longer if you had to deal with window after window in a graphical environment. There's nothing wrong with using the graphical util-ities if they do the job for you. All too often, though, you'll find that you can't get the job done expeditiously working in the graph-ical environment. It's *so* much faster and easier to look for files, translate fonts, work with file permissions, and a myriad of other tasks when you're using the command-line environment. And sometimes, there's no alternative!

- There's no better way to come to a full understanding of your Linux system than going mano-a-mano with the text-mode utilities.

Thanks to its Unix heritage, Linux is intrinsically a text-mode environment—and that's a good thing indeed. For example, Linux adheres to the Unix dictum that all system-configuration files should be written in plain, accessible text, so that they can be read and altered with ease. As you delve into text-mode utilities and learn more about the way your Linux system is configured, you'll gradually build a more accurate picture of the way this complex, powerful operating system actually works. This knowledge will prove invaluable when it comes to solving the problems that arise as you're using Linux and Linux applications.

The pathway to Linux mastery lies in a judicious combination of graphical utilities and powerful, text-mode utilities. As you'll quickly discover, this isn't a drawback of Linux. On the contrary, it's precisely the strength of this amazingly powerful operating system. You can use the graphical utilities for day-to-day work, and that's fine. But, when you're ready to unlock the incredible power of Linux, open a terminal window, flip open this book, and step into the technology that's lurking under your system's pretty face. You won't be disappointed!

A Guide to This Book's Contents

Linux Command Instant Reference organizes the world of Linux commands by task. Here's a quick overview of the book's organization:

Chapter 1, "Logging In and Managing Sessions"   In this chapter, you'll learn about the commands and utilities that you'll use to create, establish, and exit user sessions on your Linux system.

Chapter 2, "Getting Help and Finding Your Bearings"   This chapter covers the commands and utilities that provide on-screen help when you're lost or confused.

Chapter 3, "Learning Shell Fundamentals"   This chapter focuses on **bash**, the command-line interface (*shell*) that's installed by default on most versions of Linux. Although the bash shell superficially resembles MS-DOS, it's far more powerful and useful. This chapter covers all the bash commands and utilities that users need to understand in order to use their systems effectively.

Chapter 4, "Navigating the Filesystem and Finding Files" In this chapter, the focus turns to the GNU Project's file-management utilities, which are installed by default on most Linux distributions. You'll learn how to get around the filesystem and locate files in ways that enable you to pinpoint the data you're looking for.

Chapter 5, "Managing Files and Directories" Continuing this book's treatment of the GNU Project's file-management utilities, this chapter focuses on the file-management tasks you perform every day, including copying, moving, and deleting files. You'll learn how to take full advantage of the capabilities accessible only by using these utilities in their text-only mode.

Chapter 6, "Archiving, Encoding, Compressing, and Encrypting Files" This chapter covers the panoply of utilities that are available for performing all of these file-management tasks, including archiving and compressing files in a way that you can easily exchange them over the Internet and even with Windows and Macintosh users.

Chapter 7, "Managing Disks and Tape Drives" In this chapter, the focus shifts to floppy disks, CD-ROMs, and tape drives. You'll learn how to perform tasks such as formatting disks and backing up your data.

Chapter 8, "Working with Text Files" This chapter explores the amazing world of Linux text-processing utilities, which enable you to perform automated text-processing tasks in hundreds of ways. You'll learn how to search for files containing text that you specify, sort files in a variety of ways, prepare text files for attractive printing, and even generate a key-word-in-context (KWIC) concordance, in which every word in a document is printed in an alphabetized list that shows its context.

Chapter 9, "Working with Sound and Graphics Files" This chapter turns to the exciting world of Linux multimedia utilities. You'll learn how to "rip" files from audio music CD-ROMs, translate them into an amazing variety of sound formats, play them on your computer, and "burn" CD-R discs containing audio or computer data. You'll also learn how to use the full range of ImageMagick graphics processing utilities, which can transform graphic images in an amazing variety of ways.

Chapter 10, "Working with Fonts"   Continuing the theme of dealing with the needs of today's Linux users, this chapter discusses the commands and utilities you can use to get fonts working correctly on your system, including TrueType fonts. You'll learn how to install fonts, translate fonts from one format to another, and deal with on-screen font problems.

Chapter 11, "Using Text Editors"   This chapter turns to a subject that often proves confusing to new Linux users: text editors. The default Linux text editors, such as **emacs** and **vi**, were designed for use by programmers, and they're not terribly user-friendly. If you'd like to try these programs, you'll find full coverage of all aspects of their use. You'll also learn about easier text editors, such as **joe**; and you'll learn how to change your system's defaults so that an easy-to-use editor is launched by default.

Chapter 12, "Configuring and Managing Your System"   Turning to system administration commands and utilities, this chapter presents the core knowledge that Linux users need in order to run a single-user workstation effectively (as distinguished from the more complex, esoteric commands that are required to manage multi-user Unix systems).

Chapter 13, "Configuring and Using Networks and the Internet"   This chapter surveys the commands and utilities that Linux users need in order to connect a single-user workstation to the Internet and share files and printers with other computer users on a local area network (LAN). Here again, the focus is on the user's needs, rather than on those of a professional network administrator. For example, the coverage of Windows networking with Samba assumes that you're interested in learning how to exchange files with Windows users rather than implementing a full-scale, complex imitation of Windows NT Server.

Special Features of This Book

Each chapter of this book is organized in the same, helpful way. You'll find three sections: the At a Glance section, the essential background information section, and the Alphabetical Command Reference.

At a Glance

Located at the beginning of each chapter, this section presents the heart of the chapter's coverage, assembled and summarized for instant reference purposes. In the left column, titled "How Do I," you'll find the tasks you want to perform. In the middle column, you'll find the names of the commands and utilities you can use to accomplish this task in case you'd like to look them up. But you probably won't need to because the right column provides an example that will often serve your exact needs.

Essential Background Information

Following the At a Glance table, you'll find a section that presents essential background information on the topics covered in the chapter. For example, in Chapter 1, this section, titled "Linux Fundamentals," contains a section titled "Essential Typing and Editing Skills." This section assembles and conveys the information you need to use Linux successfully—information that's almost impossible to find assembled in the useful, handy way that you'll find in this book.

The Alphabetical Command Reference

Following the background section, you'll find the reference information that you need to use Linux commands and utilities effectively. Each command is presented with a brief description that focuses on the command's purpose.

Hey! That Command's Not on My System!

If you see the message "Command not found" after trying out one of the utilities discussed in this book, make sure that it really isn't installed. If the command is not on the current *path* (the list of directories that the shell searches by default), you'll get this message even if the command is actually installed. To find out where the command is located, type **whereis** followed by the command's name, and press Enter.

If the command isn't present on your system, you may be able to install it from your Linux distribution's CD-ROM. Check your Linux distribution's documentation to find out how to install software that wasn't installed during the normal installation process.

Some of the commands discussed in this book aren't often distributed with Linux. Where appropriate, the individual entries contain tips on Internet archives where you can obtain these commands. In general, you can find almost anything you're looking for on Freshmeat at http://www.freshmeat.net, on Metalab at http://www.metalab .unc.edu, on Linuxberg at http://linux.tucows.com, or on RPM-find at http://www.rpmfind.org. Also, check your Linux distribution's home page for contributed commands and utilities that aren't part of the standard distribution.

Using This Book's Conventions

So that you can get the most out of this book, please take a moment to study this section. You'll learn how to use the information that you'll find in the "Alphabetical Command Reference" sections. This book uses certain typographical conventions to tell you what to type.

Why are these conventions needed? To use Linux commands successfully, you must follow a few rules, called *syntax*. These rules specify just where certain parts of the command have to go. They also tell you how to type the command so that Linux can recognize what you've typed and process the command correctly.

Here's an example. In Chapter 4, you'll learn about the **ls** command, which is described as follows:

ls [option] [*shell pattern*]

In brief, here's what this convention tells you:

Bold   Whenever you see anything in boldface type, you should type this exactly. To use the **ls** command, you type **ls**.

Brackets   Anything within square brackets is optional. You can leave it out, and the command will still run. In this example, the first item within the bracket is *option*. Here, you can place one or more *command options,* which change the way the command works. Most commands have one or more options, which often are available in a short form and a long form. In the short form, you type a hyphen followed by the options letter (such as –l or –a). Most commands let you combine the options in a list (such as –la). In the long form, you type two hyphens followed by the spelled-out version of the option (such as - –**help**). Note that not all commands follow this practice, but it's widely used.

Italics   When you see something in italic (such as [*shell pattern*] in the previous example), you're supposed to substitute something that makes sense in the command.

Conventions Used in Tables

This Type of Entry	Means This
bold	Type this item literally.
italic	Replace this item with the appropriate value.
[item]	This item is optional. If you use it, do not type the brackets.

This Type of Entry	Means This
[option]	This command has options that you can use, but they are not required. Most options are single letters preceded by a dash, such as **–a** or **–x**. Some commands enable you to use lengthier option names, which must be preceded by two dashes (for example, **– –help** or **– –version**).
[item-1 | item-2]	These items are optional. You can use item-1 or item-2, but not both. Do not type the brackets or bar character.
< item-1 | item-2 >	These items are required. You must use item-1 or item-2, but not both. Do not type the angle brackets or bar character.
[item-1 [item-2]]	These items are optional. You can use item-1. If you do use item-1, you can optionally use item-2, but item-2 is not required. Do not type the brackets.
< item-1 [item-2] >	Item-1 is required. You can optionally use item-2, but it is not required. Do not type the brackets.
Example	This is an example that illustrates how to use the command. It is not meant to be typed literally, but you can adapt the example for your own use.

Conventions Used in Example Tables

Command	Example	Description
ls [option] [*shell pattern*]	ls	Lists all the files in the current directory. Note that the use of an option and shell pattern are not required.
	ls –R	Lists all the files in the current directory and all associated directories.

Command	Example	Description
	`ls -R *.jpg`	Lists all the files with the specified shell pattern (`*.jpg`) in the current directory and all of its associated subdirectories.
rmdir [option] *directory*	`rmdir junk`	Removes the specified directory. Note that you must specify a directory.
dirs [**+**N	−N] [option]	`dirs`	Displays all the directories in the current list of remembered directories.
	`dirs +5`	Displays the fifth directory from the top of the list of remembered directories. Note that you can specify + (from the top of the list) or − (from the bottom of the list) when typing the number.
	dirs −5 −I	Displays the fifth directory from the end of a list of remembered directories and shows a long listing (−**I**).

Sybex Technical Support

If you have questions or comments about this book (or other Sybex books) you can contact Sybex directly.

For the Fastest Reply

E-mail us or visit the Sybex Web site! You can contact Sybex through the Web by visiting http://www.sybex.com and clicking Support. You may find the answer you're looking for on this site in the FAQ (Frequently Asked Questions) file.

When you reach the support page, click `support@sybex.com` to send Sybex an e-mail. You can also e-mail Sybex directly at `support @sybex.com`.

Make sure that you include the following information in your e-mail:

Title   The complete title of the book in question. For this book, it is *Linux Command Instant Reference.*

Page number   Include the page number where you have a problem.

ISBN number   The ISBN that appears on the bottom-right corner of the back cover of the book. This number looks like this:

0-7821-2478-7

Printing   The printing of the book. You can find this near the front of the book at the bottom of the copyright page. You should see a line of numbers as in the following:

10 9 8 7 6 5 4 3 2 1

Tell us what the lowest number is in the line of numbers. This is the printing number of the book. The example here indicates that the book is the first printing.

NOTE   The ISBN number and printing are very important for Technical Support because it indicates the edition and reprint that you have in your hands. Changes may occur between printings. Don't forget to include this information!

For a Fast Reply

Call Sybex Technical Support and leave a message. Sybex guarantees that they will call you back within 24 hours, excluding weekends and holidays.

Technical Support can be reached at (510) 523-8233 ext. 563.

After you dial the extension, press 1 to leave a message. Sybex will call you back within 24 hours. Make sure you leave a phone number where you can be reached!

Other Ways To Reach Sybex

You can reach Sybex through the mail at the following address:

SYBEX Inc.
Attention: Technical Support
1151 Marina Village Parkway
Alameda, CA 94501

Again, it's important that you include all the following information to expedite a reply:

Title The complete title of the book in question.

ISBN number The ISBN that appears on the bottom-right corner of the back cover of the book and looks like this:

0-8721-2478-7

Printing The printing of the book. You can find this near the front of the book at the bottom of the copyright page. You should see a line of numbers as in the following:

10 9 8 7 6 5 4 3 2 1

Tell us what the lowest number is in the line of numbers. This is the printing number of the book. The example here indicates that the book is the first printing.

Page number Include the page number where you have a problem.

No matter how you contact Sybex, Technical Support will try to answer your question quickly and accurately.

CHAPTER 1

Logging In and
Managing Sessions

This chapter introduces the fundamentals of Linux so that you will understand what you're seeing when you log in for the first time. It covers the commands and utilities you use to create, establish, and exit user sessions on your Linux system. You will also learn how to restart or halt your computer.

WARNING   Before using Linux to run applications, create an ordinary user account for your use (see Chapter 12). You should not run applications or use Linux for other day-to-day uses when you are logged in as the root user. When you work as the root user, Linux does not prevent you from overwriting system configuration and other vital files. If you damage one of these files without knowing how to repair the damage, your system may become unstable or unusable.

AT A GLANCE

How Do I	See This Entry	Example
Log in to the system?	**login**	`login suzanne`
Log out? (In RedHat6, also prompts to log in again.)	**logout**	`logout`
Log into another computer on the local area network?	**rlogin**	`rlogin -l suzanne 192.168.100.10`
Halt my computer?	**shutdown**	`shutdown -h now`
Restart my computer?	**shutdown**	`shutdown -r now`
Display the identification number of the terminal I'm using?	**tty**	
Start an X session?	**startx**, **xdm**	`startx -- --bpp32`

AT A GLANCE *(CONT.)*

How Do I	See This Entry	Example
Gain the root user's privileges without logging out of my user account?	**su**	su
Configure the X Window System on my computer or change an existing configuration?	**Xconfigurator** (for Red Hat systems), **XF86Setup** (for other distributions)	XF86Setup

Linux Fundamentals

This section introduces the following:

- Linux fundamentals
- Linux distributions
- Users and the system administrator
- Logging in
- What you'll see after you log in
- Essential typing and editing skills
- Virtual consoles
- The X Window System

For more information on the Linux boot and initialization processes, see Chapter 12, "Configuring and Managing Your System."

Linux Distributions

Linux is typically made available by means of *Linux distributions*. A Linux distribution assembles the many components of a functioning Linux operating system into a cohesive package.

Distributions are available by FTP download; however, it is more convenient to obtain a distribution on a CD-ROM. Most of the software included with a Linux distribution, including the Linux kernel, is licensed under the terms of the GNU Project's *General Public License* (GPL). This license grants users the freedom to view, alter, and redistribute the source code, as long as subsequent distributions do not deny these freedoms to others (for more information, see http://www.gnu.org). The first table in this section covers the major Linux distributions, while the second table defines the individual components that make up a Linux distribution.

LEADING LINUX DISTRIBUTIONS

Name	Description and Download Site
Caldera OpenLinux	Features an easy-to-use graphical installation utility; defaults to the KDE desktop. Includes trial or personal versions of several applications, including WordPerfect 8.0 and StarOffice 5.1. Supported platforms: Intel x86. Download site: http://www.calderasystems.com.
Corel Linux	Based on Debian, this smoothly engineered distribution defaults to the KDE desktop and features a user-friendly installation utility; this distribution is a good choice for new Linux users migrating from Microsoft Windows or Mac OS. Not suitable for older PCs, Corel Linux's minimum system requirement is a Pentium-class machine with at least 16MB of RAM. Supported platforms: Intel Pentium and higher, SPARC, Motorola 680x0, Alpha. Download site: http://linux.corel.com.
Debian GNU/Linux	The hacker's version of Linux. Requires previous Linux experience and system administration expertise to install and configure. Supported platforms: Intel x86, SPARC, Motorola 680x0, Alpha. Download site: http://www.debian.org.
Linux Mandrake	Version of Red Hat Linux that defaults to the KDE desktop. Supported platform: Intel x86. Download site: http://www.linux-mandrake.com.

LEADING LINUX DISTRIBUTIONS *(CONT.)*

Name	Description and Download Site
LinuxPPC	A version of Linux for PowerPC systems, including iMacs. Supported platforms: PCI-based Apple Power Macintoshes and some IBM/Motorola PReP workstations. Download site: `http://www.linuxppc.org`.
Red Hat Linux	Well-supported distribution that offers an easy-to-use graphical installation utility and defaults to the GNOME desktop. (KDE is available as an option.) Supported platforms: Intel x86, Alpha, SPARC. Download site: `http://www.redhat.com`.
Slackware	A technically challenging distribution best suited to knowledgeable users and developers. It aims to be the most "UNIX-like" distribution. Supported platforms: Intel x86. Download site: `http://www.slackware.org`.
SuSE	Market-leading Linux distribution in Europe; defaults to the KDE desktop. Supported platforms: Intel x86. Download site: `http://www.suse.com`.
TurboLinux	Emphasizes multilingual support and is a market leader in Asia. Supported platforms: Intel x86 and PowerPC. Download site: `http://www.pht.com`.

LINUX SYSTEM COMPONENTS

Component	Description
Kernel	The core of the Linux operating system. The *kernel* is like a digital master of ceremonies. It receives requests (called *system calls*) from programs and initiates processes that carry out these requests. In addition, the kernel manages system resources so that running processes do not overwhelm each other or the system's capabilities. The Linux kernel is a *multiuser operating system* that is capable of supporting more than 1,000 simultaneous users. It is also a *multitasking operating system* that fully protects each running process from intrusions into its assigned memory space.

LINUX SYSTEM COMPONENTS *(CONT.)*

Component	Description
Shell	The interface between the user and the kernel. The *shell* functions as a *command interpreter* in that it accepts and processes user commands. It is also a programming language in its own right; users can write *scripts* that automate system functions. Users can choose the shell they prefer.
Filesystem	The hierarchical organization of files into a pyramid-like structure of *directories*. The top-level directory, called the *root directory*, contains all the others. File *ownership* and *permissions* enable users and system administrators to prevent unauthorized access to sensitive data.
Utilities	A wide variety of useful programs, many of which were developed by the GNU Project (`http://www.gnu.org`). Also called *commands*. Most of the commands discussed in this book are utilities; they are designed to enable users and system administrators to configure and maintain the system.
Console applications	Application programs designed to run in the text-only console mode or in a terminal emulation utility.
X applications	Application programs that require the X Window System, which is defined later in this chapter.
Window manager	An X Window System application that enables users to control window position and size.
Desktop environment	Software that runs on top of the X Window System and window manager, providing these with the interface features familiar to Microsoft Windows and Mac OS users, such as a drag-and-drop–enabled desktop, dockable toolbars, and a full range of desktop utilities. The leading desktop environments are GNOME and KDE.
GNOME and KDE applications	Application programs that require the GNOME or KDE desktops. Many GNOME programs will run under KDE, and many KDE programs will run under GNOME.

Users and the System Administrator

Linux is a multiuser operating system that distinguishes between users and the system administrator.

Users   Also called *ordinary users*, users possess ownership of the files in their *home directories* (the portion of the filesystem that is assigned to their use), but they generally may not view or alter other users' files. In addition, they may not alter *system configuration files*, which are vital to the system's proper functioning.

System administrator   Also called the *root user* or *superuser*, the administrator possesses read and write privileges throughout the entire system and is responsible for system configuration and maintenance. On a single-user system, Linux users switch hats between these two roles. For day-to-day work, they log on and work as ordinary users; doing so prevents them from inadvertently altering or deleting files that are crucial for the system's smooth functioning. For system administration purposes, they log on as root users.

Logging In

When Linux starts, you will see a number of messages on-screen. Typically, these fly by so quickly that you cannot read them. (You can review these messages using the **dmesg** command, discussed in Chapter 12.) When the boot and initialization processes terminate, you will be prompted to supply your *username* and *password*. This process is called *logging in*.

Some of the newer Linux distributions enable you to set up a user account during system installation. If you did so, type your username and press Enter. If you did not create a user account at installation, you must log on as the root user. To do so, type **root** and press Enter.

You must then supply the password; type the password carefully and press Enter. As a security measure, the password is not visible on-screen. Be aware that Linux login names and passwords are case sensitive; you must type the exact capitalization pattern you used when you created your password. Once you have successfully logged in to your Linux system, you should create a user account for day-to-day use (see **adduser** in Chapter 12).

What You'll See After You Log In

Your Linux system can be configured to run several different types of user interfaces:

Console mode   If you see a text-mode login prompt when you start Linux, your system has been configured to run in the *console mode* by default. This is a text-only environment. In the console mode, you interact with your Linux system by means of the shell (see the Linux System Components table in this chapter). Although you can use Linux with a variety of shells (see the Linux Shells table in this section), the most common is the Bourne Again Shell (bash). From the shell, you can also run *console* programs, which are designed to work in the text-mode environment. You can also start the X Window System and, optionally, a desktop environment, such as KDE or GNOME.

LINUX SHELLS

Name	Description and Download Location
bash	Based on the Bourne shell, this shell is the *de facto* standard shell on most Linux systems. It provides an unprecedented level of functionality, including keyboard macros, command history, easy-to-use command-line editing tools, a simple and elegant programming language, job control, and much more.
csh	Short for C shell, this shell draws its inspiration from the C programming language, so naturally, it is preferred by C programmers. Offering somewhat fewer features than bash, it is nevertheless preferred by some because it runs csh scripts.
tcsh	An enhanced version of csh.
ksh	Short for Korn shell, this shell is (like bash) another derivative of the Bourne shell.

X Window System   Your system may have been configured to start the *X Window System* by default. If so, you will see a *graphical user interface* (GUI) on-screen, in which applications appear within windows. In brief, X (as it is commonly abbreviated) is a graphical user interface that provides windowing capabilities for X-compatible applications. Many applications require X in order to run. To use X, you must run a *window manager*. A window manager is an application that enables you to launch X applications and position windows on-screen. If your system has been configured to start X by default, you will see a GUI-based window manager (see the Linux Window Managers table in this chapter). However, your system may have been configured to start a desktop environment, such as KDE or GNOME, in addition to X. Desktop environments add features to the X environment that are not available with the X Window System alone.

Desktop environment   A *desktop environment* supplements the X Window System by providing features that are missing or poorly implemented in X. These include application panels, consistent look and feel for compatible applications, dockable toolbars, integrated foreign language support, multiple drag-and-drop formats, 3D support, system-level support for fonts and printing, and customizable menus. There are several competing desktop environments, including the K Desktop Environment (KDE) and GNOME, which are shown in the next table, Linux Desktop Environments. Both require X in order to run. Your system may have been configured to run KDE or GNOME automatically. For information on configuring your system to run a desktop environment automatically, see the "Understanding Run Levels" section in Chapter 12.

LINUX DESKTOP ENVIRONMENTS

Name	Description and Download Site
GNOME	A desktop environment that relies on the GTK+ toolkit, which is available under the terms of the GPL (General Public License). Works with a variety of window managers but works especially well with WindowMaker and Enlightenment. Emphasizes configurability. Offers fewer applications than KDE. Download site: http://www.gnome.org.

LINUX DESKTOP ENVIRONMENTS *(CONT.)*

Name	Description and Download Site
KDE	A desktop environment that relies on the Qt toolkit. Although KDE works with some window managers, it is easiest and best to use the default KDE window manager. Currently offers as many as twice the number of compatible applications as GNOME. Download site: `http://www.kde.org`.

At installation, your Linux system was configured to run in one of these interface modes by default. If the system starts in the console mode, you can use **startx** to start the X Window System.

You can still use the text-only console mode even if you are running the X Window System. To do so, you launch a *terminal emulation program*. Such a program provides a window in which the shell prompt appears. You can then use Linux as if you were working in the console mode. The table that follows provides a list of commonly available terminal emulators.

LINUX TERMINAL EMULATION UTILITIES

Name	Description
eterm	VT102 terminal emulator designed to work with the Enlightenment window manager.
gnome–terminal	GNOME-compatible implementation of xterm with VT102 compatibility.
kterm	Multilingual and color version of xterm.
kvt	KDE-compatible implementation of rxvt.
rxvt	Color-enabled version of xterm that consumes less memory by deleting Tektronix 4014 compatibility. Can use an XPM graphic as a window background.
xterm	Monochrome. Emulates DEC VT102/VT220 and Tektronix 4014 and compatible terminals.

Essential Typing and Editing Skills

If you are working in the console mode or in a terminal emulation utility (explained in the previous section), you see the *system prompt*. The system prompt informs you that the shell is running and ready to accept your commands.

On most Linux systems, the bash shell is the default for console mode. If your system is running the bash shell and you are logged in as an ordinary user, the system prompt is $. It is # if you're logged in as the root user.

To use your system in console mode, you will type commands. You will find the following editing and control shortcuts helpful. Chapter 3 fully details the keyboard shortcuts you can use with bash.

EDITING AND CONTROL SHORTCUTS

Use This Keyboard Shortcut	To Do This
Backspace Ctrl + h	Delete previous character
Delete Ctrl + d	Delete current character
Ctrl + u	Delete entire line
Ctrl + c	Cancel command
Ctrl + d	Log out
Return Enter	Execute command

Using Virtual Consoles

Because Linux is a multiuser system, it's possible to establish more than one user session at the same time. This feature dates back to the time when computers were very expensive. To cut down costs, one computer could be used by several people at once, with each user accessing the system by means of a *remote terminal* (an input-output device featuring a keyboard and display but lacking any data processing or storage capabilities). Although few Linux users implement multiuser systems using remote terminals, you can still make use of the system's capability to run more than one user session at a time. For example, your system is preconfigured to run two or more *virtual consoles*, which are like separate computers. Your system starts in the default console, which is called the *system console*. Your system may have been configured with five or more virtual consoles.

To switch to the first virtual console while you are using X, press Ctrl + Alt + F1. To view the second virtual console, press Ctrl + Alt + F2, and so on to view successive virtual consoles. Just how many virtual consoles are available depends on how your system was configured. On Red Hat and Red Hat-derived systems, Ctrl + Alt + F7 returns to the system console. You can also switch virtual consoles using the **chvt** command.

In most of the consoles, you will see a login prompt. You can log in to one of these consoles and start a separate user session. This capability provides a convenient way to switch from X to the console mode. If you are running X in the default console, you can switch to a virtual console to start a console mode session. Some systems are configured so that you can start a second X session in one of the virtual consoles, but this is not recommended unless your system is equipped with lots of memory (128MB or 256MB).

The X Window System

The *X Window System* provides a graphical user interface for Linux systems. Called X for short, the system is divided into two components: the *X server*, which responds to requests for interface services and controls the display hardware; and *X clients*, the X-compatible applications that request services from the X server. X servers are designed to work with specific brands and models of hardware, including video adapters, mice, keyboards, and monitors. For Intel-based Linux distributions, the default X server is XFree86 (available for download at http://www .xfree86.org), a series of X servers that are designed to work with popular video adapters and monitors. The following table provides you with some handy Xfree86 keyboard shortcuts.

XFREE86 KEYBOARD SHORTCUTS

Use This Keyboard Shortcut	To Do This
Ctrl + Alt + Backspace	Kill the X server. **Caution**: You will lose work in any open applications.
Ctrl + Alt + Keypad plus	Change to the next video mode specified in the XFree86 configuration file.
Ctrl + Alt + Keypad minus	Change to the previous video mode specified in the XFree86 configuration file.
Ctrl + Alt + Fn	Switch to the nth virtual terminal; for example, Ctrl + Alt + F3 switches to the third virtual terminal.

Chances are that X is already installed on your system; most Linux distributions use an installation utility that configures X automatically. If not, you can configure X by using the **XF86Setup** or **Xconfigurator** utilities discussed in this chapter.

A *window manager* is a special type of X client. It enables you to control the size and position of application windows. Most window managers offer additional features, including some that resemble those of desktop environments. The table that follows lists the most common Linux window managers.

LINUX WINDOW MANAGERS

Name	Description and Download Site
AfterStep	A window manager that emulates the NeXT desktop using fvwm code. Its features include application docking, themes, pinnable menus, gradient-rendered window decorations, virtual desktops, GNOME compliance, KDE compliance, and integrated support for GNUStep applications. Download site: http://www.afterstep.org.

LINUX WINDOW MANAGERS *(CONT.)*

Name	Description and Download Site
Enlightenment	This is the default window manager for current Red Hat Linux and Mandrake distributions. It is highly compatible with GNOME. It includes all the features of Window-Maker and AfterStep, plus sound support, TrueType support with anti-aliasing, and advanced graphics features. Download site: `http://www.enlightenment.org/`.
fvwm	Widely available on Linux distributions, this is a highly configurable window manager with advanced features, such as drag-and-drop compatibility, virtual desktops, workplace switchers, and application icons. Download site: `http://www.fvwm.org/`.
fvwm '95	This is a version of fvwm that is modified to look like Microsoft Windows 95, including the taskbar. Download site: `ftp://mitac11.uia.ac.be/html-test/fvwm95.html`.
IceWM	This is a GNOME-compatible window manager that offers several default themes, including Motif, GTK, OS/2 Warp, and Windows 95. Features include virtual desktops, a taskbar, drag-and-drop, workspace switchers, themes, application icons, and window list menus. Download site: `http://icewm.sourceforge.net/`.
WindowMaker	A window manager that emulates the NeXT desktop, but without using fvwm code. Its features include application docking, themes, pinnable menus, gradient-rendered window decorations, virtual desktops, GNOME compliance, excellent configuration menu system, and integrated support for GNUStep applications. Download site: `http://www.windowmaker.org/`.

Alphabetical Command Reference

In this section, you will find commands for performing the following tasks:

- Logging in, logging out, rebooting, and shutting down your system (**login, logout, rlogin, shutdown**)

- Using virtual terminals while in console mode (**chvt, tty**)

- Configuring the X Window System (**Xconfigurator, XF86Setup**)

- Starting graphical user interfaces (**startx, xdm**)

- Using terminal emulation programs (**xterm, rxvt**)

- Switching to the superuser so that you can perform tasks requiring root-level access (**su**)

chvt

chvt *terminal*

Switches the display to the specified virtual *terminal* (a number from 1–35).

See also **dellocvt, tty.**

login

login [*username*]

Prompts the user to supply a username and password and establishes a new user session on the current terminal. In addition, the command checks to see whether the user has received new mail, starts the shell specified for this user in the /etc/passwd file (the default shell is bash), and executes startup shell scripts associated with the user's account. This command should be used in text mode sessions only. Do not use it when X is running.

logout

logout

Exits the current session and displays login. This command should be used in text mode sessions only. Do not use it when X is running.

rlogin

rlogin [option] [*hostname*]

Enables you to establish a user session on another computer connected to the local area network or the Internet, provided that the remote computer is configured to accept remote logins.

OPTION

Use This Option	To Do This
–l *username*	Log in with a specific username

EXAMPLE

This Command	Does the Following
`rlogin -l suzanne lothlorien .pfaffenberger.org` or `rlogin -l suzanne 192.168.100.10`	Establishes a remote terminal session on lothlorien.pfaffenberger.org for the user named suzanne.

rxvt

rxvt [option]

Starts the **rxvt** terminal emulation program. Requires the X Window System. Certain **rxvt** options are toggles. To switch the option on, precede the option with a plus sign (+). To turn it off, precede the option with a minus sign (−).

See also **xterm.**

OPTIONS

Use This Option	To Do This
−bd *color*	Specify the color to use for window borders
−bg *color*	Specify the color to use for the background
−cr *color*	Specify the cursor color
−fb *fontname*	Specify the font to be used for bold
−fg *color*	Specify the foreground color
−fm *fontname*	Specify the font to be used for multicharacter text
−fn *fontname*	Specify the font for normal text
−grk *mode*	Enable Greek keyboard translation
+|−ip	Enable inheritance of parent window's background pixmap
−pixmap *filename*	Specify the filename of an XPM graphic to use as the background
−pr *color*	Specify the mouse pointer color
+|−rv	Simulate reverse video by swapping the foreground and background colors
+|−sb	Save all lines scrolled off the top and display scroll bar
−sf	Enable Sun function keys
+|−si	Finish output at the bottom of the window
+|−sk	Enable automatic repositioning of window when scrolling
−sl *n*	Specify the number (*n*) of lines to save that are scrolled off the top of the screen
+|−sr	Place scroll bar on left
+|−st	Display normal scroll bar without a trough
+|−ut	Inhibit utmp log entries
+|−vb	Enable the visual rather than audible bell

shutdown

shutdown [options] *time* [*message*]

Shuts down your Linux system in a way that prevents damage to the filesystem. Do not use this command when the X Window System is running; exit X first. To shut down your system with GNOME or KDE, log out of your current session and use the menu options available with the GNOME or KDE Display Manager to halt or restart your system. If you're using X, you should exit before shutting down. Use **shutdown** only when X is not running and you are using your Linux system in its text-only mode. On most systems, you need root user status to use this command (see **su**). The options enable you to specify whether the system halts or restarts. If other users are logged on to the system, you may wish to specify a delay by typing a plus sign followed by the number of minutes until shutdown (for example, +5). You can also type **now**, which is equivalent to +0. You can also specify a message, which will appear on the terminals of all the users connected to the system.

OPTIONS

Use This Option	To Do This
–f	Reboot quickly without checking filesystem integrity.
–h	Halt the system after shutdown. On most recent PCs, this option turns the system off automatically.
–k	Send the warning message without actually shutting down.
–r	Restart the system.

EXAMPLES

This Command	Does the Following
shutdown –r now	Restarts the system without delay.
shutdown –h +2	Halts the system in two minutes.

startx

startx [– –option]

This shell script, typically supplied with X11 distributions, enables you to start an X session from the current user account. It is a front end to the **xinit** utility. To determine which window manager or desktop environment to use, **startx** looks for a file called .xinitrc in the user's home directory. The last line of this file should contain the name of your preferred window manager (such as Enlightenment or fvwm). If there is no such file in the user's home directory, X uses the defaults specified in the default configuration file (typically, /etc/xinitrc). To specify an option with **startx**, you must also type two dashes (– –) followed by a space. If your system has been configured with a default runlevel that starts X automatically, as specified in the file /etc/inittab (see Chapter 12), you won't need to use **startx**.

OPTIONS

Use This Option	To Do This
–allow MouseOpenFail	Start the server even if the mouse cannot be detected or initialized.
–bgamma *value*	Set the server's blue gamma correction to the specified value. Must fall within the range 0.1 to 10. The default is 1.0.
–bpp *n*	Start the X server with the pixel bit depth specified by *n*. Legal values are 8, 15, 16, 24, and 32.
–gamma *value*	Set the server's gamma correction for all colors to the specified value. Must fall within the range 0.1 to 10. The default is 1.0.
–ggamma *value*	Set the server's green gamma correction to the specified value. Must fall within the range 0.1 to 10. The default is 1.0.
–probeonly	Probe the device but quit after the probe is executed.
–rgamma *value*	Set the server's red gamma correction to the specified value. Must fall within the range 0.1 to 10. The default is 1.0.

OPTIONS *(CONT.)*

Use This Option	To Do This
–showconfig	Display the server's configuration information.
–vt *n*	Use *n*th virtual terminal instead of the next available one.
–xf86config *filename*	Read the configuration from the specified filename instead of from the default configuration file.

EXAMPLES

This Command	Does the Following
`startx – – –bpp 32`	Starts the X server in 32-bit display mode. Requires a video card and monitor capable of 32-bit color depth.

su

su [*username*]

Creates a new shell session with a different user's ID and privileges. If you run **su** without specifying a username, you create a shell for the superuser; that is, a user who has gained the root user's privileges. You'll be prompted to specify the user's password. To exit the superuser shell, type **exit** and press Enter.

tty

tty

Displays the number of the terminal device that is currently in use.

See also **chvt**.

Xconfigurator

Xconfigurator [option]

Launches a menu-driven utility that configures XFree86 for use on a Red Hat Linux system. This utility can also be used in kickstart mode, which suppresses the interactive menus; however, you must specify the monitor type using the – –**monitor** option.

OPTIONS

Use This Option	To Do This
– –**help**	Display available options, including a list of available video card and monitor types.
– –**expert**	Enable manual control of configuration options that are otherwise set automatically.
– –**kickstart**	Enable the non-interactive mode.
– –**card** *name*	Install the specified video card. Use – –**help** to see a list of valid video card names.
– –**server** *name*	Configure the specified server. Use – –**help** to see a list of valid server names.
– –**monitor** *name*	Configure the specified monitor. Use – –**help** to see a list of valid monitor names.
– –**hsynch** *frequency*	Configure the server using the specified horizontal frequency.
– –**vsynch** *frequency*	Configure the server using the specified vertical frequency.

xdm

xdm

Starts the X Display Manager (xdm), which provides a graphical login shell and launches the X Window System. Unlike **startx, xdm** consults a file named .xsession to determine user preferences, including the default window manager. The last line of this file should contain the name of your preferred window manager (such as Enlightenment or fvwm). The utility first looks for an .xsession file in the user's home directory. If no such file exists, **xdm** uses the defaults specified by the system administrator.

XF86Setup

XF86Setup [option]

Launches a menu-driven utility that configures an XFree86 server. This utility can be used to install a server for the first time or to change the default configuration. A change is needed if you change your video adapter, mouse, keyboard, or monitor. To use XF86Setup, you may need some or all of the following information: the brand and model of your video adapter, the amount of video RAM (VRAM) installed on the video adapter, the brand and model of your monitor, and the type of keyboard you are using (such as 102-key U.S.).

See also **Xconfigurator.**

OPTIONS

Use This Option	To Do This
–sync	Enable synchronization for all communications with the X server
–name *appname*	Use *appname* as the name for the configuration window
–display *n*	Use the *n*th display instead of the next available one
–nodialog	Suppress the menu-based interactive system
–geometry *specification*	Use the specified geometry for the window
–script	Run the specified script

xterm

xterm [option]

Starts the xterm terminal emulation program. Requires the X Window System. Certain **xterm** options are toggles. Precede this option with a plus sign (+) to turn it on or a minus sign (–) to turn it off.

OPTIONS

Use This Option	To Do This
+|–132	Enable 132 column mode.
+|–ah	Always highlight the cursor, even when the window is inactive.
+|–ai	Disable active icon support.
+|–aw	Enable text word-wrapping.
–b *n*	Specify the width of the border in *n* pixels.
–bd *color*	Specify the color to use for window borders.
+|–bdc	Disable bold characters.
–bw *n*	Specify the window border width in *n* pixels.
–C	Enable the window to receive console output.
+|–cb	Set the VT100 variable *cutToBeginningOfLine* to false.
+|–cm	Disable ANSI color changes.
+|–cn	Disable cutting new lines in line-mode selections.
–cr *color*	Specify the text cursor color.
+|–cu	Work around bugs in **more** program (see Chapter 8) that display lines incorrectly when the line equals the window width.
+|–dc	Disable dynamic colors.
–e *command*	Run the specified command in an xterm window.
–fb *font*	Use the specified font.
–fg *color*	Specify the foreground color.
–fi *fontname*	Set the font for active icons.

OPTIONS *(CONT.)*

Use This Option	To Do This
–fn *font*	Specify the font to be used for normal text.
–hc *color*	Set the color to be used for the foreground.
+|–ie	Enable detection of the **stty** *erase* value.
+|–im	Enable the insert mode.
+|–j	Enable jump scrolling.
–leftbar	Force the scroll bar to the left of the window.
+|–ls	Start the shell as a login shell.
+|–mb	Ring the margin bell when the user types near the right border.
–mc *time*	Specify the maximum time (in milliseconds) between multi-click selections.
–ms *color*	Specify the default pointer color.
–nb *n*	Specify the number of characters (*n*) from the right border at which the margin bell rings if the bell is enabled.
+|–nul	Enable the display of underlining.
+|–pc	Enable bold colors.
–rightbar	Force the scroll bar to the right window border.
–rv	Simulate reverse video by swapping the foreground and background colors.
+|–rw	Enable reverse wrap-around.
+|–s	Enable asynchronous scrolling.
+|–sb	Save all lines scrolled off the top and display scroll bar.
+|–sf	Enable Sun function keys.
+|–si	Finish output at the bottom of the window.
+|–sk	Enable automatic repositioning of window when scrolling.
–sl *n*	Specify the number (*n*) of lines to save that are scrolled off the top of the screen.

OPTIONS *(CONT.)*

Use This Option	To Do This
+|–sp	Enable Sun keyboard mapping.
+|–t	Start in Tektronix rather than VT102 mode.
–title *string*	Use the specified string for the window title.
–tm *keyword*	Indicate the terminal setting that should be used, which is specified by *keyword*. Options include **intr, quit, erase, kill, eof, eol, swtch, start, stop, brk, sup, dsup, rprnt, flush, weras,** and **lnext**.
–tn *name*	Specify the name of the terminal type to be used.
+|–ulc	Disable the display of underlining with color.
+|–ut	Skip making entries in system log.
+|–vb	Enable the visual rather than audible bell.
+|–wf	Wait for window to be mapped before enabling subprocesses.
–ziconbeep *percentage*	Sound bell at the specified percentage of full volume.

CHAPTER 2

Getting Help and Finding Your Bearings

In this chapter, you'll learn the commands you can use to get help with Linux. You'll also learn the commands that can help you get your bearings. The latter category includes commands that remind you where you're positioned in the Linux filesystem, what user groups you belong to, and much more—including a command that displays or prints nicely-formatted calendars for the current month or year (or for any month or any year).

AT A GLANCE

How Do I	See This Entry	Examples
Find out which man page has the information I'm looking for?	**apropos**, **man**	`apropos fonts`
Display or print a calendar?	**cal**	`cal -y 2003	lpr`
See the current system date and time?	**date**, **rdate**	`date`
Find out who else is using computers on the network?	**finger**, **rwho**	`finger suzanne`
Find out what the various bash shell commands do?	**help**	`help cd`
Display this system's IP address?	**hostname**	`hostname -i`
Change the system date and time?	**hwclock**	`hwclock - -set - - date='05/21/03 12:56'`
Find out my user and group names and IDs?	**id**, **groups**, **whoami**	`id`
Get information about GNU utilities?	**info**	`info emacs`
Get detailed information about a command?	**man**	`man cdrecord`
See the full path name of the current directory?	**pwd**	`pwd`
Set the time zone correctly?	**tzselect**	`tzselect`

AT A GLANCE *(CONT.)*

How Do I	See This Entry	Examples
Find out which version of the Linux kernel I'm running?	**uname**	uname
Find out how long I've been using Linux during this session?	**uptime**	uptime
Find out who else is using this system?	**w, who**	w

Getting Help with Linux

This section introduces the following:

- Getting help with Linux
- Getting help online

For getting help on Linux commands, the star of the show is the **man** command, which displays command documentation on-screen. Almost all Linux commands and utilities have manual pages, called *man pages*. These documents provide information about the command in a standard format. Less useful is the **info** command, which provides a text-based, and rather confusing hypertext environment for information concerning GNU utilities; and the **help** command, which provides brief, one- or two-sentence descriptions of the bash shell's built-in commands. In general, the information available within **info** is also available in man pages. Similarly, you'll find information on built-in bash commands—much more information than is available with the **help** command—in the bash man page. You may also try browsing the /usr/doc directory, which contains additional documents for installed application programs.

TIP If you've forgotten which options you can use with a command, type the command name followed by a space and **– –help**, as in the following example: **cal – –help**. This option isn't available with all commands, but it works with most of them.

In addition to the commands available while you are using Linux, you can get help online. The "Where to Get Help Online" table provides some excellent sources for Internet-based help with Linux. See the Leading Linux Web Sites table for the latest Linux news, information, and tips.

WHERE TO GET HELP ONLINE

Web Site	URL	Description
CNET Linux Help	`http://searchlinux.com/`	Provides a search interface to thousands of Usenet messages concerning Linux.
Linux Frequently Asked Questions with Answers	`http://metalab.unc` `.edu/mdw/FAQ/Linux-FAQ` `.html`	Entry-level FAQ (Frequently Asked Questions) for beginning Linux users.
Linux Gazette search page	`http://www.linuxgazette` `.com/wgindex.html`	Provides a search interface to hundreds of online *Linux Gazette* articles.
Linux Hardware Database	`http://lhd.datapower` `.com/start.html`	Provides information about compatibility of hardware and peripherals with Linux.
Linux HOWTO Index	`http://metalab.unc` `.edu/mdw/HOWTO/` `HOWTO-INDEX.html`	Index to online HOWTO documents.
Linux Information Sheet	`http://metalab.unc` `.edu/mdw/HOWTO/` `INFO-SHEET.html`	Facts and information about the Linux operating system.
Linux Online!	`http://www.linux.org/` `help/irc.html`	Lists dozens of Linux-related Internet Relay Chat (IRC) channels.
Linux Knowledge Base	`http://linuxkb.cheek` `.com`	Provides a search interface to moderated discussions concerning Linux.

WHERE TO GET HELP ONLINE *(CONT.)*

Web Site	URL	Description
Linux Online! Mailing Lists	`http://www.linux.org/help/lists.html`	Lists dozens of Linux-related mailing lists.
Linux Online! Project Guides	`http://www.linux.org/help/projectguide.html`	Provides access to online versions of full-text books concerning Linux.
Linux Software Map	`http://www.execpc.com/lsm/`	Provides a search interface to a database of Linux software.

LEADING LINUX-RELATED WEB SITES

Web Site	URL	Description
Linux Today	`http://www.linuxtoday.com`	Latest news concerning Linux, including links to Linux-related news articles.
Freshmeat	`http://www.freshmeat.net`	Fast-breaking news concerning the latest Linux applications and utilities.
Linux v2 Information HQ	`http://www.linuxHQ.com`	Information about the latest Linux kernel.
Linux International	`http://www.li.org`	Home page of Linux International, the premier non-profit organization devoted to advancing Linux.
Linux Journal	`http://linuxjournal.com`	The Web site of the leading Linux print-based magazine. Its features include industry briefs and online articles.

Web Site	URL	Description
Linux.com	`http://www.linux.com`	Major Linux portal site. It features news, chat groups, press releases, featured articles, links, and much more.
LinuxMall.com	`http://www.linuxmall.com`	Shopping site for Linux distributions and Linux goodies.
Slashdot	`http://slashdot.org`	News and discussion site for Linux-oriented hackers.

Alphabetical Command Reference

In this section, you will find commands for performing the following tasks:

- Reading program documentation on-line (**apropos, help, info, man, whatis, who, whoami**)

- Displaying and setting the date and time (**cal, date, hwclock, rdate, tzselect**)

- Providing information about yourself to other users (**chfn, finger**)

- Displaying information about users (**groups, id, rwho, users, w**)

- Getting information about your system and getting your bearings (**hostname, pwd, uname, uptime**)

apropos

apropos *string*

Searches a database of man (manual) page titles and descriptions and returns a list of the man pages that contain the specified *string* anywhere in the page's entry, including the description, as well as the title. Use **whatis** to return only those pages that match the specified title exactly. For example, **apropos lookup** returns a list of all the man pages that contain *lookup* in their titles or descriptions.

EXAMPLE

This Command	Does the Following
apropos fonts	Displays a list of man pages that contain the word *fonts* in their titles or brief descriptions.

---

cal

cal [option] [*month*] [*year*]

When typed without options, displays a formatted calendar for the current month. The available options enable you to display and print calendars in a variety of formats.

OPTIONS

Use This Option	To Do This
−j	Display the calendar using Julian dates, with the days numbered from 1 (January 1) sequentially to the end of the year
−y	Display a calendar for the entire year

EXAMPLES

This Command	Does the Following
cal	Displays a calendar for the current month.
cal −y	Displays a calendar for the entire current year.
cal −y 2005	Displays a calendar for the entire year 2005.
cal 06 2003	Displays a calendar for June 2003.
cal −y 2003 | lpr	Prints a calendar for the year 2003.

chfn

chfn [option]

When typed without options, **chfn** prompts you to provide the information made available by **finger** (described later in this chapter), including full name, office room number, office phone, and home phone. You can use the options to specify one or more of these at the command line. To ensure that a field is blank, such as home phone number, use the keyboard "none."

See also **finger.**

OPTIONS

Use This Option	To Do This
--full-name *full name*	Specify your full name
--office *office number*	Specify your office room number
--home-phone *home phone number*	Specify your home phone number
--office-phone *office phone number*	Specify your office phone number
--help	List available options
--version	Display version number

EXAMPLES

This Command	Does the Following
chfn	Enters **chfn** in its interactive mode so that you can supply all the information in response to the utility's queries.

date

date [option] [*date*]

When typed without options, displays the current date and time as tracked by the *system clock*, a utility within the Linux kernel. To get the date and time from another computer on the local area network or the Internet, see **rdate**.

WARNING   Do not use **date –s** to change the system clock. Always use **hwclock**, which is described in this chapter, and then reboot your system to synchronize the system clock and hardware clock. If you change the system clock while time-dependent processes are running, your system could crash.

OPTIONS

Use This Option	To Do This
–u, –utc	Display the date and time in Universal Coordinated Time (UTC), also known as Greenwich Mean Time (GMT).
–s *date*	Set the date (requires root user status). Do not use this option; see **hwclock**, described later in this chapter.

EXAMPLES

This Command	Does the Following
date	Displays the current date and time.
date –u	Displays Universal Coordinated Time (UTC).

finger

finger [options] *username*

Displays data about the user indicated in *username*, including the user's full name, office room number, phone numbers, e-mail status (whether the user has received unread e-mail), and information stored in the user's .plan and .project files. In a local area network and the Internet, information on remote users may be obtainable by specifying *username* using the format user@remote-host (such as mike1@frodo.pfaffenberger.org or mike1@192.168.10.14). The **finger** utility relies on the finger daemon, which many system administrators disable by default, both to protect users' privacy and to close a potential entry point for unauthorized intruders. To fill out basic **finger** information for yourself, see **chfn** (described earlier in this chapter). You may also wish to create and save .plan and .project files in your home directory. The .plan file contains your meeting schedule, while your .project file contains a list of the projects you're working on.

TIP Some organizations use **finger** to make specialized information available. Type **finger quake@gldfs.cr.usgs.gov** to see a list of recent earthquakes (including exact time, exact location, depth, magnitude, and brief comments).

OPTION

Use This Option	To Do This
–l	List available information in the long (verbose) format

---

groups

groups [*username*]

When typed without a username, **groups** displays the user groups to which the current user belongs. To see all the user and group ID information about yourself, use **id**.

help

help [*command name*]

Displays help for commands made available by the default Linux shell, bash. When typed without a command name, displays a list of all the bash commands for which help is available. You'll find much more information about these commands by typing **man bash**.

hostname

hostname [option] [*host name*]

When typed without options, **hostname** displays the system's network identification name (host name). If you have root privileges, you can change the host name by specifying a valid host name.

OPTIONS

Use This Option	To Do This
–a, – –alias	Display the host name's alias
–i, – –ip-address	Display the host's Internet (IP) address
–d, – –domain	Display the name of the domain to which the host belongs
–h, – –help	List all options

EXAMPLES

This Command	Does the Following
hostname –i	Finds out your system's current Internet address (IP address).
hostname –a	Finds out your system's host name alias.

hwclock

hwclock [options]

Displays or sets the system's *hardware clock*, the time-keeping circuitry that keeps track of the date and time when your system is switched off. When typed without options (or with the – –show option), this command displays the current time and date settings. The hardware clock differs from the *system clock*, a time-keeping routine that is part of the Linux kernel. Although the two are synchronized when you start your system, variations and anomalies in both time-keeping mechanisms can introduce variations between the system and hardware clock settings. To reset the date and time, use **hwclock**—do *not* use date with the –s switch—and then restart your system to synchronize the hardware and system clocks. You'll need root user privileges to use this command to change time (see **su** in Chapter 1).

See also **date, rdate,** and **tzselect.**

OPTIONS

Use This Option	To Do This
– –hctosys	Set the system clock to the current hardware clock. **Caution**: Do not use this option; instead, set the hardware clock (using – –set – –date =*datestring*) and reboot your system.
– –set – –date=*datestring*	Change the hardware date and time. Express the datestring using the following syntax:
	MM/DD/YY hh:mm:ss
	where **MM** is the month (expressed as a number from 01 to 12), **DD** is the day (expressed as a number from 01 to 31), YY is the last two digits of the year, **hh** is the hour (expressed as a number from 01 to 24), and **mm** is the minute (expressed as a number from 01 to 60). Optionally, you can express seconds, too.
– –show	Display the current hardware clock setting. The date and time shown are the local time.

OPTIONS *(CONT.)*

Use This Option	To Do This
– –systohc	Set the hardware clock to the current system time.
– –utc	Specify that the hardware clock should track the time in Universal Coordinated Time (GMT).
– –version	Display the version number.

EXAMPLES

This Command	Does the Following
hwclock	Displays the current hardware clock setting.
hwclock – –set – –date='05/21/03 12:56'	Sets the hardware clock local time to 12:56, May 21, 2003.

id

id [option] [*username*]

When typed without an option or arguments, **id** displays user ID information about yourself, including your user and group ID name and number. Use **groups** if you're interested only in group IDs.

OPTIONS

Use This Option	To Do This
–g, – –group	Display the group ID only
–G, – –groups	Display the supplementary groups
– –help	List all options
–u, – –user	Print only the user ID
– –version	Display the version number

EXAMPLE

This Command	Does the Following
id	Shows all information for the current user, including user ID, group ID, and supplemental group IDs.

info

info [options] [*node*]

Displays a text-based hypertext help system for GNU utilities, including the bash shell; the cpio archiver; the emacs text editor; the GNU file utilities; and GNU programming languages, such as gcc and awk. Unless you are familiar with the emacs text editor, you may find **info** counterintuitive and somewhat difficult to use. Almost all of the available information can also be accessed using **man,** which is easier to use. See the Commands table for the command keys you can use in the interactive mode.

OPTIONS

Use This Option	To Do This
–d *directory*, **– –directory** *directory*	Add the specified directory to the list of directories for which **info** should search for info files
–f *filename*, **– –file** *filename*	Display the specified info file
– –help	List all options
–n *nodename*, **– –node** *nodename*	Display the specified node within an **info** file
–o *filename*, **– –output** *filename*	Route output to the specified file instead of displaying it on-screen
– –subnodes	Display a list of subtopics
– –version	Display the version number

COMMANDS

Press This Key	To Do This
?	Display all commands
b	Go to the beginning of the node
Ctrl + A	Go to the beginning of the line
Ctrl + Already	Cancel the previous command
Ctrl + B	Move back one character
Ctrl + E	Go to the end of the line
Ctrl + F	Go to the beginning of the line
Ctrl + H	Display the Help window
Ctrl + N	Go to the next line
Ctrl + P	Go to the previous lines
Ctrl + R	Search up within a list
Ctrl + S	Search down within a list
Ctrl + X, B	Show the history list
d	Display the top-level directory
Delete	Scroll up
e	Go to the end of the node
Esc + s	Search up within the current node
f	Follow a cross-reference
i	Search for a string in the index
l	Go back in the history list
m	Choose a menu item
n	Move to the next node
p	Move to the previous node
q	Quit **info**
s	Search down within the current node
Spacebar	Scroll down
t	Move to the top node
Tab	Skip to the next hyperlink
u	Move up

EXAMPLES

This Command	Does the Following
info	Starts info and displays the top-level menu.
info file	Displays the top-level menu of File Utilities.
info file disk	Displays the Disk Usage node within File Utilities.

man

man [options] [*section*] [*title*]

Displays text-only manual (man) pages using the **less** text reader (see Chapter 8). Adhering to a standard heading format, man pages provide a quick way to get information on most of the utilities installed on your system. Man pages also include information of interest to programmers, including details concerning system and library calls. Man pages are organized into separate directories, called *sections* (see the Sections table). To use man, type **man** followed by the title of the man page you're looking for. You can also use several command options. When you're searching with the **–K** option, be sure to limit the scope of the search by specifying the section you want (for example, for utilities and shell commands, use Section 1).

See also **info, less** (Chapter 8).

SECTIONS

Section Number	Topic
1	Utilities and shell commands
2	System calls
3	Library calls
4	Device and other special files
5	File formats
6	Games

SECTIONS *(CONT.)*

Section Number	Topic
7	Macro packages
8	System administration commands
9	Kernel routines

OPTIONS

Use This Option	To Do This
–a *title*	List all the man pages that match the specified title
–d	Display debugging information
–f *title*	List short descriptions of all the man pages that match the specified title
–h	List all options
–k *string*	List short descriptions of all the man pages that match the specified string
–K *string*	Find and display all pages containing the specified string
–M *directory*	Look for man pages in the directory instead of in the default man directories
–P *program*	Use the specified program to display the man page

EXAMPLES

This Command	Does the Following
`man du`	Displays the du (disk usage) man page.
`man -a less`	Displays all the man pages that match the title *less*.
`man -f file`	Displays a list containing brief descriptions of all the man pages that match the title *file*.
`man 1 -K file`	Displays all the man pages from Section 1 (executable commands and utilities) that contain the word *file*.

pwd

pwd

Displays the full path name of the current directory. If you've forgotten which directory is current, type **pwd** and press Enter to see the directory's path name.

rdate

rdate [option] *host name*

Obtains the date and time from another computer on the local area network or Internet. For *host name,* specify the computer's name (such as frodo.pfaffenberger.org) or IP address (192.168.100.14). If you have root user privileges, you can use the –s switch to set your system's date and time using the imported information.

See also **date.**

OPTIONS

Use This Option	To Do This
–s	Set the date and time using the information obtained from another computer on the network

EXAMPLES

This Command	Does the Following
rdate frodo.pfaffenberger.org	Obtains the date and time from another computer on the local area network or Internet.
rdate –s frodo.pfaffenberger.org	Sets the current system's date and time using information imported from the specified computer (requires root user privileges).

rwho

rwho [option]

Lists the usernames of other active users of the local area network. This information may not be available if it has been disabled by system or network administrators for security or privacy reasons.

OPTIONS

Use This Option	To Do This
–a	Display all users, including those who have been idle for more than one hour

tzselect

tzselect

Launches an interactive utility that enables you to specify your time zone.

uname

uname

Provides a wealth of information about the system you're using. Typed by itself, **uname** returns the name of the operating system (Linux). Use options to view additional types of information.

OPTIONS

Use This Option	To Do This
–a, – –all	Display all available information
– –help	List all options
–m, – –machine	Display the type of processor in use
–n, – –nodename	Display the computer's host name

OPTIONS *(CONT.)*

Use This Option	To Do This
–p, – –processor	Display the name of the processor in use
–r, – –release	Display the version number of the operating system
– –version	Display the utility's version number

uptime

uptime

Displays the current time, the amount of time that the system has been running in the current login session, the number of users currently logged in to the system, and the average CPU load.

users

users

Displays a brief list of the users currently logged in to the system. To get more detailed information, use **who**.

See also **id, w.**

w

w [*username*]

When typed without an argument, **w** displays detailed information about all the users currently logged in to the system, including which terminal they're using, when they logged on, their amount of idle time, and information about their CPU usage. To see information about just one user, type **w** followed by a username.

See also **users, who.**

whatis

whatis *title*

Searches the database of man pages and lists brief descriptions for each man (manual) page that has a title matching the specified title. For example, type **whatis finger** to see a brief description of man pages with the title *finger*. Use **apropos** to match words in the man page to brief descriptions, as well those in the list of man page titles.

who

who [option]

Displays a list of the users currently logged in to the system. If you type **who** without an option, you'll see the user's name, the terminal they're using, and the time they logged on. For a less verbose report, see **user**.

See also **w**.

OPTIONS

Use This Option	To Do This
–H, – –heading	Display column headings
– –help	List available options

whoami

whoami

Displays the username of the user currently logged in to this terminal session.

CHAPTER 3

Learning Shell Fundamentals

T he shell acts as an intermediary between you and the Linux *kernel*, the heart of the operating system. With knowledge of the shell, you can perform many tasks far more quickly than you could with graphical utilities. In addition, the shell provides the only means available for tasks that are not supported by graphical utilities. For these reasons, knowledge of the shell is essential for all Linux users.

Linux enables you to work with more than one shell. By far the most popular is the *GNU Bourne Again Shell* (bash), which is the default shell for most Linux distributions. Some users prefer the *C Shell* (csh), which uses the syntax of the C programming language. Still others prefer *tcsh*, an extended version of the C Shell. All three of these commonly used shells resemble each other so closely that many of the basic shell commands and the essentials of shell syntax work the same way in all three. This chapter covers the fundamentals of bash shell use.

TIP You can tell which shell you're using by looking at the default prompt in a terminal window; bash uses $, while csh and tcsh use %. Alternatively, type **echo $SHELL** and press Enter; you'll see the current shell's name on the next line.

AT A GLANCE

How Do I	See This Entry	Example
Create simple aliases (nicknames) for complex commands that are tedious to type?	**alias**	`alias newfiles='ls -tl'`
Type more than one command on a single line?	The "Command Sequences and Groups" section later in this chapter	`gunzip ballistic.tar.gz; tar -xvf ballistic.tar`

AT A GLANCE *(CONT.)*

How Do I	See This Entry	Example
Save information about the path to a command so that I don't have to type the full path name every time?	**hash**	`hash cdrecord bladeenc`
Redirect output to another command via a pipe?	The "Input/Output Redirection" section later in this chapter	`cat readme.txt	less`
Redirect command output to a file?	The "Input/Output Redirection" section later in this chapter	`dir > listing.txt`
Record a keyboard macro?	The "Shell Keyboard Shortcuts" section later in this chapter	`Ctrl + x(` *keystrokes* `Ctrl +x`
Play back the keyboard macro I just recorded?	The "Shell Keyboard Shortcuts" section later in this chapter	`Ctrl + xe`
Assign a keyboard macro to a key?	**bind**	`bind '"\cb" : "/home/suzanne/books"'`
Complete filenames, usernames, host names, and variables without having to type the entire name?	The "Shell Keyboard Shortcuts" section later in this chapter	`Tab`
Repeat the last command I gave without having to retype it?	The "Shell Keyboard Shortcuts" section later in this chapter, **history, fc**	`Up arrow, fc -s`

AT A GLANCE *(CONT.)*

How Do I	See This Entry	Example
Kill a process that no longer responds to my input?	**kill, killall**	`kill 5076`

Create my own variables and use them in my commands?	The "Parameter Expansion" section later in this chapter	`docsdir=/home/suzanne/` `creative-stuff/documents`
		
		`cd $docsdir`

View a list of running processes?	**ps**	`ps -a`
Find out which processes are hogging the most memory or CPU time?	**ps, top**	`ps -el - -sort - -size`
Choose shell modes, including one called noclobber, which prevents the overwriting of files when I use output redirection?	**set**	`set -o noclobber`
Redirect command output to a file, as well as show it on-screen?	**tee**	`dir	tee > listing.txt`
Enter my home directory or the current directory without typing the whole path name?	See the "Tilde Expansion" section later in this chapter	`cd ~` `cd ~/mp3s`
Export a variable that is needed by an application?	**export**	`export MYFILES=/home/` `suzanne/essays`
Run an executable program or script in the working directory, even if this directory isn't on the path?	The Special Characters table later in this chapter	`./cdrecord`
Add a directory to the path without wiping out the existing path?	**export**	`export PATH=$PATH:/home/` `suzanne/essays`

Shell Fundamentals

This section discusses the following topics:

- What the shell does
- Shell configuration files
- Shell keyboard shortcuts
- Overview of shell command syntax
- Special characters and quoting
- Command sequences and groups
- Input/output redirection
- Brace expansion
- Tilde expansion
- Command substitution
- History expansion
- Parameter expansion
- Shell functions
- Job control
- Signals

What the Shell Does

The Linux shell enables you to perform the following tasks:

Issue commands   When you type a command and press Enter, the shell processes the command by interpreting special characters. It then executes the command. You use the shell to launch the utilities and programs discussed throughout this book. You can also use the shell to launch the shell's *built-in utilities*, a set of commands that are always available when the shell is running. For more information on the built-in utilities, see the "Alphabetical Command Reference" section later in this chapter.

Control processes   A running program is called a *process*. Each process has an identification number, called a *process ID*. With the shell, you can control running processes in several ways, including running several processes simultaneously, running processes in the background, suspending running processes, and killing comatose processes that no longer respond to commands.

Customize your session   When you log in to your user account, Linux starts bash. In turn, bash consults a file in your home directory called .bash_profile. You can modify this file to change bash's behavior and on-screen appearance.

Create shell scripts   A *shell script* is a simple program containing shell and other Linux commands. With the programming capabilities built into Linux shells, you can create shell scripts that automate tasks that would otherwise be quite tedious.

This chapter covers the bash knowledge needed to issue commands and control processes. Shell capabilities relevant to customization, programming, and shell scripts are discussed in Chapter 12.

Shell Configuration Files

Bash relies on a number of *startup files*, which contain bash commands. The shell executes these commands just as if they had been typed at the keyboard. These files include the following (note that the tilde [~] stands for your home directory):

/etc/profile   This file is executed every time you log in to a bash shell. It contains commands that are made available to all users in the system.

~/.bash_profile, ~/.bash_login, and ~/.profile   These files are executed every time you log in to your user account. It contains commands that are made available only to the current user.

~/.**bashrc** This file is executed only when you start an interactive non-login shell; you do so, for instance, when you start a terminal emulation program after logging in using X.

~/.**bash_logout** This file is executed when you log out of a bash session.

In addition to the previous files, bash also consults the following:

/**etc/inputrc** This file contains the default key bindings (see **bind**) that are made available to all users.

~/.**inputrc** This file contains the key bindings that are made available to the current user only.

Order of Execution of Startup Files

If you start bash as an interactive login shell, the following files are executed in the order shown in the following list:

1. /etc/profile

2. ~/bash.profile

3. ~/.bash_login

4. ~/.profile

If you start bash as an interactive non-login shell, bash consults ~/.bashrc.

TIP When you start bash as an interactive non-login shell, as you do when you launch a terminal emulation program after logging in, bash consults only one startup file: ~/.bashrc. However, most Linux distributions are configured so that the commands placed in ~/.bashrc are executed no matter how the shell is started. This is accomplished by placing the following command in ~/.bash_profile, which forces the shell to load ~/.bashrc and execute the file:

```
export ENV=~/.bashrc
if [ -f ~/.bashrc ] ; then source ~/.bashrc; fi
```

Shell Keyboard Shortcuts

By default, bash uses keyboard shortcuts that resemble those used by the emacs text editor (see Chapter 11, "Using Text Editors"). However, these shortcuts can be changed using the **bind** command; if you're using a system other than your own, the system administrator may have altered the keyboard bindings (see **bind**). If the shortcuts listed in this section don't work, try the **vi** shortcuts (see Chapter 11).

In the following tables, you'll find the default bash shortcuts for the following:

- Moving the cursor

- Editing text on the command line

- Automatically completing command names, filenames, host names, and other names known to the system

- Re-entering previous commands from the *history list* (a list of stored commands that you have previously entered)

- Creating and using keyboard macros (recorded keystrokes)

- Executing commands once you have finished typing them

TIP   Many of these shortcuts use what is known as the *meta key*. The meta key is a generic descriptor designed to facilitate the use of Linux on a variety of systems. For Intel hardware, Linux distributions map the Alt key to meta. For example, to use the meta + b keyboard shortcut on an Intel-based system, press Alt + b.

MOVING THE CURSOR

Use This Keyboard Shortcut	To Do This
Left arrow Ctrl + b	Go back one character

MOVING THE CURSOR *(CONT.)*

Use This Keyboard Shortcut	To Do This
Meta + b	Go back one word
Ctrl + f	Go forward one character
Meta + f	Go forward one word
Home Ctrl + a	Go to the beginning of line
End Ctrl + e	Go to the end of the line

EDITING TEXT ON THE COMMAND LINE

Use This Keyboard Shortcut	To Do This
Meta + l	Convert a word to lowercase
Meta + u	Convert a word to uppercase
Delete Ctrl + d	Delete the current character
Ctrl + u	Delete a word
Ctrl + k	Delete from the cursor to the end of the line
Meta + \	Delete all the horizontal space around a word
Backspace Ctrl + h	Delete the previous character
Meta Ctrl + h	Delete the previous word
Ctrl + x, Ctrl + v	Display the version number
Meta + c	Capitalize the first character of a word
Ctrl + t	Transpose characters
Meta + t	Transpose words
Ctrl + x, Ctrl + u	Undo the last change

USING COMPLETION SHORTCUTS

Use This Keyboard Shortcut	To Do This
Esc, {	Complete braces
Esc, Tab	Complete the line from the history list
Esc, !	Complete the name of an existing command
Tab Ctrl + i	Complete the name of an existing file, directory, variable, host, or command after typing enough characters to identify it
Esc, /	Complete the name of an existing filename
Esc, @	Complete the name of an existing host
Esc, ~	Complete the name of an existing user
Esc, $	Complete the name of an existing variable
Esc, ?	Show the possible completions
Ctrl + x/	Show the possible filename completions
Ctrl + x@	Show the possible host name completions
Ctrl + x~	Show the possible username completions
Ctrl + x$	Show the possible variable completions

USING THE HISTORY LIST

Use This Keyboard Shortcut	To Do This
Down arrow Ctrl + n	Go to the next item in the history list
Up arrow Ctrl + p	Go to the previous item in the history list
Ctrl + r	Search backward in the history list
Meta + <	Go to the beginning of the history list
Meta + >	Go to the end of the history list

USING KEYBOARD MACROS

Use This Keyboard Shortcut	To Do This
Ctrl + xe	Replay last keyboard macro
Ctrl + x(	Start a keyboard macro
Ctrl + x	Stop a keyboard macro

EXECUTING COMMANDS

Use This Keyboard Shortcut	To Do This
Ctrl + g	Cancel the command
Ctrl + l	Clear the screen
Return	Execute the command
Ctrl + j	
Ctrl + m	

Overview of Shell Command Syntax

You can enter most commands by typing the command's name, followed by a space and the options and arguments you want to use. To create more complex commands, you need to learn the fundamentals of bash's *syntax*, the rules that specify precisely how such commands are constructed:

Special characters and quoting   Certain characters have a special meaning to bash. If you want to use these characters in a way other than how bash interprets them, you must enclose them in quotation marks. For example, you may wish to begin a filename with a hash mark (#). However, bash interprets this character to represent the beginning of a non-executing comment. If you wish to use the hash mark for a purpose other than beginning a comment, you must enclose the hash mark in quotation marks.

Metacharacters   A *metacharacter* is a special character that functions as a *word separator*, as if it were a blank space. However, not all special characters are metacharacters. Some special characters will not serve their intended function unless you place a space before them.

Command sequences and groups   You can type more than one command on a single line so that they are executed together in the specified sequence from left to right. To alter the default execution sequence, you can arrange commands in groups so that the commands enclosed by parentheses or brackets are executed first.

Input/output redirection   By default, bash reads from the *standard input* (the keyboard) and writes output to the *standard output* (the display); or, in the case of an error, to the *standard error* (again, the display). With input/output redirection, you can redirect output to another command or to a file. You can also tell a command to take input from a file.

You should also understand how bash uses *expansion*, a method of generating a lengthier entry from a shorthand expression. To use expansion, you use special expansion characters. After you press Enter, bash reads (*parses*) your command, detects the expansion characters, and generates the lengthier command in accordance with your instructions. You can use the following types of expansion:

Brace expansion   This shell capability enables you to generate several output patterns from a single entry.

Tilde expansion   This shell capability gives you quick ways to enter directory names.

Command substitution   This shell capability enables you to construct commands by inserting a command's output. A common use of this capability is &pwd, a command substitution that inserts the output of the **pwd** command (see Chapter 2). This command's output is the current directory.

History expansion   The shell keeps track of the commands you have entered by creating a *history list*. By means of *history expansion,* you can re-use commands you previously entered.

Parameter expansion   *Parameters* are named entities, such as variables. You can define your own variables and insert their values using parameter expansion. In addition, you can make use of a number of built-in variables.

Shell functions   With *shell functions*, you can group two or more commands and assign them to a name of your choosing.

Job control   You can use the shell to place lengthy processes in the background, as long as they can operate without intervention. An example of such a job is compiling a large program. Background programs have a *job ID* and can be brought back to the foreground or suspended by means of bash commands.

Special Characters and Quoting

Some characters have special meaning for bash. If you wish to use them for purposes other than those indicated here, you must protect them with quotation characters. Note that some of these special characters are *metacharacters*, which separate words even if you omit spaces; however, other characters do not perform a word separation function. For example, parentheses are metacharacters, but curly braces are not. If you create a command using curly braces and fail to type a space before and after each curly brace, the command will not work.

TIP   When quoting, it is safest to use single quotation marks rather than double quotation marks, unless you have a special reason to use double quotation marks. Double quotation marks preserve the special meaning of several characters, such as *, $, and '.

The following tables detail information concerning special characters and quoting:

- The Special Characters table shows all the characters that have special meaning to bash.

- The Quotation Characters table shows the punctuation you can use to prevent bash from processing special characters.

- The Metacharacters table shows special characters that also function as word separators.

SPECIAL CHARACTERS

Special Character	Purpose
' '	Quotes all of the enclosed text, preventing all expansions or substitutions.
!	A logical NOT in a command sequence.
" "	Quotes the enclosed text with the exception of variable expansion and command substitution.
#	Inserts a comment; bash ignores the rest of the line.
$	Inserts a named variable. It is also used for command and arithmetic substitution.
&	When appended to a command name, executes a command in the background.
&&	A logical AND in a command sequence.
( )	Groups commands for execution by a subshell. It is also used to identify a function.
*	Stands for zero or any characters in a shell pattern.
./	When placed at the beginning of a line, executes a command in the working directory that is not on the current path.
:	A null command.
?	Stands for any one character in a shell pattern.
[ ]	Defines a character class in a shell pattern.
\	Quotes the following character.
' '	Indicates a command substitution.
{ }	Groups commands. These are also used for brace expansion.
|	Redirects the command output to a second command.
||	A logical OR in a command sequence.
<	Takes input from a file rather than from the keyboard.
<<	Uses the standard input but only up to the specified text.
>	Redirects the command output to a file.
>>	Appends the command output to a file.
%	Indicates a job number.

QUOTATION CHARACTERS

Quotation Character	Purpose
\	This character is called the *escape character*. It preserves the literal meaning of the following character, except newline characters.
' ' (single quotes)	Preserves the literal meaning of all characters within the single quotes.
" " (double quotes)	Preserves the literal meaning of all the characters within the quotes, with the exception of those that initiate variable expansion ($) and command substitution (`).

METACHARACTERS

Metacharacter	Purpose
|	Pipeline
&	Command substitution
;	Command separator
( )	Command grouping for execution in a subshell
< >	Redirection operators

EXAMPLES

This Command	Does the Following
cat 'income $ expenses.doc'	Displays the text of income $ expenses.doc. If single quotes were not used, the shell would interpret the dollar sign ($) as a variable substitution.
dir "$pwd/chapter (overview)"	Specifies a directory to be displayed using command substitution ($pwd). The double quotation marks protect the parentheses from interpretation by the shell but enable the use of command substitution.

EXAMPLES

This Command	Does the Following
`gunzip essay1.tar.gz;tar -xvf essay1.tar`	Unzips `essay1.tar.gz` and extracts the files from the archive. Spaces are not needed around the semicolon because it is a metacharacter.
`{ find essay* ; find paper* ; }|less`	Locates all the files that start with *essay* and *paper*, and pipes the output to the **less** command (see Chapter 8). Spaces are needed before the curly braces but not before the vertical bar character. Unlike the curly braces, the vertical bar character is a metacharacter.

Command Sequences and Groups

With *command sequences and groups*, you can type more than one command on a single command line. The following table outlines the various ways you can create command sequences and groups.

COMMAND FORMS

Command Form	Meaning
command1 ; *command2*	Execute *command1*, then execute *command2*.
(*command1* ; *command2*)	In a subshell, execute *command1*, then execute *command2*.
{ *command1* ; *command2* }	In the current shell, execute *command1*, then execute *command2*.
command1 **&&** *command2*	Execute *command2* only if *command1* succeeds.
command1 **||** *command2*	Execute *command2* only if *command1* fails.

EXAMPLES

This Command

This Command	Does the Following
`gunzip ballistic.tar.gz;` `tar -xvf ballistic.tar`	Decompresses `ballistic.tar.gz` and extracts the files from the archive.
`find readme.txt && cat` `readme.txt`	Displays `readme.txt` only if the **find** command succeeds (see Chapter 4).
`find readme.bak || cp` `readme.txt readme.bak`	Makes a backup of `readme.txt` only if the **find** command fails (see Chapter 4).

Input/Output Redirection

With *input/output redirection*, you can redirect output from the standard output (the display) to a file. You can write a new file or append the output to an existing file. You can also tell a command to accept input from a file rather than from the standard input (the keyboard).

COMMAND FORMS

Command Form	Meaning
command1 | *command2*	Pipe output from *command1* to *command2*.
command > *filename*	Direct output from *command* to the file specified by *filename*.
filename < *command*	Use *filename* as the input for *command*.
command >> *filename*	Append output from *command* to the file specified by *filename*; create the file, if necessary.
command <> *filename*	Use *filename* as both the input and the output for *command*.
command >| *filename*	Direct output from *command* to the file specified by *filename*, and overwrite the file if it exists.
command << *text*	Use the standard input for *command*, but only up to the specified *text*.

EXAMPLES

This Command	Does the Following
dir > listing.txt	Directs output from the **dir** command (see Chapter 4) to the specified file (listing.txt).
cat readme.txt | less	Reads the file readme.txt and pipes the output to the less utility.
dir | lpr	Directs output from the **dir** command to the printer (see Chapter 4).
dir >> listing.txt	Appends output from the **dir** command to the specified file (listing.txt).
listing.txt < less	Uses listing.txt as the input for the **less** command (see Chapter 8).

Brace Expansion

With *brace expansion*, you can generate two or more commands from a single typed command. When bash encounters a brace character, it reads the comma-separated list inside the braces from left to right. One by one, it uses the strings within the braces to form a series of commands. For example, suppose you type this command:

```
mkdir expenses/{Jan,Feb,Mar}
```

This is equivalent to typing this:

```
mkdir expenses/Jan
mkdir expenses/Feb
mkdir expenses/Mar
```

Tilde Expansion

With *tilde expansion*, you can quickly enter directory names. The following table, Tilde Prefixes, lists the ways you can use tildes to enter directory names.

TILDE PREFIXES

Use This Prefix	To Do This
~	Insert the current user's home directory
~/*subdirectory*	Insert a path name that begins with the user's home directory and includes *subdirectory*
~+	Insert the name of the current directory
~-	Insert the name of the previous directory

EXAMPLES

This Command	Does the Following
`dir ~`	Displays the contents of the current user's home directory.
`dir ~+`	Displays the contents of the current directory.

Command Substitution

With *command substitution*, you can insert the output of a command within a command that you are creating. You can use either of two alternative forms of command substitution syntax shown in the following table.

COMMAND SUBSTITUTION SYNTAX

Command Form	Meaning
&*command*	Insert the output of *command*
`command`	Insert the output of *command*

EXAMPLES

This Command	Does the Following
dir &pwd	Displays the contents of the current directory.
dir `pwd`	Displays the contents of the current directory.

History Expansion

The shell keeps track of the commands you have entered. It does so by creating a *history list* in which each command is given a unique identifying number. Although this capability is most useful in shell scripts, you can use history list expansion to insert commands from the history list. This table shows the history expansion command forms you can use.

HISTORY EXPANSION SYNTAX

Command Form	Meaning
!*n*	Enter the *n*th command in the history list.
!!	Enter the previous command.
!–*n*	Enter the *n*th command back from the current command.
!*string*	Enter the most recent command that starts with *string*.
!?*string?*	Enter the most recent command that contains *string*.
!?*string%*	Enter the most recent argument that contains *string*.
!$	Enter the last argument of the previous command.
!!*string*	Enter the previous command and append *string*.
!*n string*	Enter the *n*th command in the history list and append *string*.
!(*string1*)*string2*	Enter the most recent command that starts with *string1* and append *string2*.
^*string1*^*string2*^	Change *string1* from the previous command to *string2*, and execute command.

Parameter Expansion

A *shell parameter* is an entity that stores a value (which can be null). Among the various types of shell parameters are *variables*. You can create your own variables and assign values to them (see the Creating and Using Variables table in this section). You can also make use of several built-in variables (see the Built-In Variables table). By convention, local variables are typed with lowercase letters. In contrast, exported variables (see **export**) are typed with uppercase letters.

CREATING AND USING VARIABLES

Command Form	Meaning
name **=** *value*	Create a variable called *name* and assign *value* to this variable.
$*name*	Insert the value of *name*.

BUILT-IN VARIABLES

Variable	Value
$BASH	The location of bash
$BASH_ENV	The location of the current `.bashrc` file in use
$BASH_VERSION	The version number of bash
$CDPATH	The paths to search when CD is used
$DIRSTACK	An array variable containing the current contents of the directory stack (see **dirs** in Chapter 4)
$EUID	The numeric effective user ID of the current user
$FCEDIT	The text editor used by default for the **fc** command
$FIGNORE	A colon-separated list of suffixes to ignore when performing filename completion
$GLOBIGNORE	A colon-separated list of filenames to be ignored when performing filename completion

BUILT-IN VARIABLES *(CONT.)*

Variable	Value
$GROUPS	An array variable listing the groups to which the current user belongs
$HISTFILE	The location of the bash history file in current use
$HISTFILESIZE	The maximum size of current history file
$HOME	The current user's home directory
$HOSTNAME	The system's host name
$HOSTTYPE	The type of computer
$LANG	The current default language
$MAIL	The location of the current user's mailbox
$MAILCHECK	The mail-checking interval in minutes
$OLDPWD	The previous directory
$PATH	The directories used to search for executables
$PS1	The values and text used to define the bash prompt
$PWD	The current directory
$RANDOM	A random number
$SECONDS	The number of seconds since bash was started
$SHELL	The current shell
$SHELLOPTS	A colon-separated list of enabled shell options (see **set**)
$SHLVL	The number of times new shells have been started
$UID	The current user's numerical ID number
$USER	The current user's name

Shell Functions

A *shell function* is a new command with the name you specify. The shell function executes all the *commands* listed within the curly braces. The Shell Function Syntax tables shows command forms used to create functions. Note that you must insert a space before and after each curly brace, and you must end the command list with a semicolon.

SHELL FUNCTION SYNTAX

Command Form	Meaning
[function] *name* **{** *command1;* *command2; ... ;* **}**	Create a function called *name* that includes the specified commands.
name **()** **{** *command1;* *command2; ... ;* **}**	Create a function called *name* that includes the specified commands.

EXAMPLES

This Command	Does the Following
`list () { ls -Ssh	less; }`	Creates a shell function called *list* that executes the **ls** command and pipes its output to less.
`detar () { gunzip *doc.tar .gz ; tar -xvf *.doc.tar }`	Creates a shell function that unzips all the `*.doc.tar.gz` files and extracts the files from the decompressed `*.doc.tar` archives.

Job Control

Normally, processes execute in the *foreground*, which means that they take over the current shell session while running. If you begin an especially time-consuming process, such as compiling a lengthy program, you may wish to place a job in the *background*. By doing this, you regain control of the shell session, and the process executes invisibly. To place a job in the background, you use the **bg** command. You must also give the job a *job ID*, using the syntax discussed in the following table.

SPECIFYING JOB IDS

Use This Job ID	To Refer to This Job
%*n*	Job *n*
%*string*	The job that uses a command with a name starting with *string*
%?*string*	The job that uses a command with a name containing *string*
%%	The current job
%+	
%−	The previous job

EXAMPLES

This Command	Does the Following
make &	Begins compiling a program and places the process in the background.
stop %%	Suspends the current process.
Ctrl + z	

Signals

Linux processes can send *signals* to each other, and each signal has both an identifying number and a fixed message. For example, to kill a process, you use the **kill** command, which sends the SIGKILL signal (identified by number 9) to the process. The following table lists the available signals, their ID numbers, and a brief description of the message that each signal sends.

AVAILABLE SIGNALS

Signal	Number	Message
EXIT	0	Exit from shell.
SIGHUP	1	Keep executing even after logout.
SIGINT	2	Interrupt processing (same as Ctrl + z).
SIGQUIT	3	Quit.
SIGILL	4	Illegal instruction.
SIGTRAP	5	Trace trap.
SIGIOT	6	Abort.
SIGBUT	7	Unused.
SIGFPE	8	Floating-point exception.
SIGKILL	9	Kill process.
SIGUSR1	10	User-defined message.
SIGSEGV	11	Invalid memory.
SIGUSR2	12	User-defined message.
SIGPIPE	13	Write to a pipe.
SIGALRM	14	Alarm timeout.
SIGTERM	15	Terminate.
SIGJUNK	16	Coprocessor stack fault.
SIGCHILD	17	Terminate child process.
SIGCONT	18	Continue processing.
SIGSTOP	19	Stop.
SIGTSTP	20	Stop typed at terminal.
SIGTTIN	21	Background process has tty input.
SIGTTOU	22	Background process has tty output.
SIGURG	23	Input/output error.
SIGXCPU	24	CPU time limit exceeded.
SIGXFSZ	25	File size limit exceeded.
SIGVTALRM	26	Virtual alarm clock.
SIGPROF	27	Profile.

AVAILABLE SIGNALS *(CONT.)*

Signal	Number	Message
SIGWINCH	28	Window resize.
SIGIO	29	Input/output event occurs.
SIGPWR	30	Power is failing.

Alphabetical Command Reference

This section covers the bash commands and Linux utilities relevant to issuing commands, controlling processes, and managing the history list. Note that the commands listed here are *built-in commands*, unless the entry specifically indicates that the command is an ordinary utility (that is, one that is executed from a file). Built-in utilities are made available in memory by the shell.

In this section, you will find commands for doing the following:

- Working more conveniently with commands (**alias, chroot, fc, function, hash, history, script, source, tee, unalias**).

- Managing processes (**bg, jobs, kill, killall, nice, nohup, ps, renice, suspend, times, top, trap, type**).

- Customizing your environment (**bash, bind, chsh, export, set, ulimit**).

- Creating and working with variables (**declare, echo, env, printenv, readonly, set**).

alias

alias *name=command*

Creates an alternative name for a command. To create an alias, type the name of your choice followed by an equals sign (=) and the name of an executable command or program, plus options or arguments if you wish (use quotes so that bash processes the options and arguments correctly). If you type **alias** without an argument, you see a list of all the aliases you have defined, if there are any.

See also **unalias.**

EXAMPLES

This Command	Does the Following
`alias bigfiles='ls -Shl'`	Lists files sorted by size, showing the largest files first.
`alias newfiles='ls -tl'`	Lists files sorted by the time of the last modification, showing most recently modified files first.
`alias oldfiles='ls -Rtlr'`	Using reverse chronological order (oldest files first), lists all the files in the current directory and all associated subdirectories.

bash

bash [option] [*filename*]

Starts the bash shell. If you specify a filename, bash reads commands from the specified file.

OPTIONS

Use This Option	To Do This
–c *string*	Read commands from the specified string.
–i	Start bash as an interactive shell
–login	Start bash by reading all the startup files that are consulted when bash is started after you log in
–nobracexpansion	Disable brace expansion
–nolineediting	Disable line editing
–noprofile	Do not execute the login startup files

OPTIONS *(CONT.)*

Use This Option	To Do This
–norc	Do not execute the non-login startup file
–p	Do not execute any of the current user's startup files
–posix	Enable POSIX compatibility
–rc *filename*	Execute the specified filename instead of `~/.bashrc`.
–s	Read commands from the standard input (default)
–version	Show the version number and exit

bg

bg [*job ID*]

Places the process specified by *job ID* in the background, as if you had launched the process by appending an ampersand (&).

bind

bind [option]

Displays or adjusts the default key bindings used for bash, which uses the readline program to specify key bindings. To determine the key bindings, bash reads a configuration file named /etc/inputrc when it starts. When you log in to your user account, it reads ~/.inputrc (a file in your home directory called .inputrc). You can change the default key bindings by adding entries to etc/inputrc (so that the changes are available to all users) or to ~/.inputrc (so that the changes are available only to the user to whom the directory belongs). You must specify the key bindings using the keymap codes, and you must link the keymap codes to one of the readline functions. For a list of these functions, see the Default Key Bindings table in this section. Examples of keymap codes are \c (Ctrl), \M (Meta), and \e (Escape). To see the keymap code for any key on your keyboard, press Ctrl + qv and type the key for which you want to view the code. You can also use **bind** to assign keys to functions and macros. See the examples in this section for the correct syntax to use when adding entries to these files.

TIP   On Intel-based systems, most Linux distributions are configured to map Esc key bindings (signified by the \e code) to the Meta key, which in turn is mapped to the Alt key. To determine the keymap code for any of the keys on your keyboard, use Ctrl + q, Ctrl + v, and press the key.

OPTIONS

Use This Option	To Do This
–m *keymap*	Change the default keymap for the remainder of the session. Alternatives include the following: emacs, emacs-standard, emacs-meta, emacs-ctlx, vi, vi-move, vi-command, and vi-insert.
–l	Display the names of all the readline functions.
–v	Display current key bindings.
–f *filename*	Read key bindings from the specified filename.
–q *function*	Show the keys, if any, that are bound to the specified function.

DEFAULT KEY BINDINGS

Readline Function	Default Key Binding
abort	\C-g \C-x\C-g \e\C-g
accept-line	\C-j \C-m
backward-char	\C-b \eOD \e[D

DEFAULT KEY BINDINGS *(CONT.)*

Readline Function	Default Key Binding
backward-delete-char	\C-h
	\C-?
backward-kill-line	\C-x\C-?
backward-kill-word	\e\C-h
	\e\C-?
backward-word	\e0d
	\eb
beginning-of-history	\e<
	\e[5~
beginning-of-line	\C-a
	\e[1~
	\e[h
call-last-kbd-macro	\C-xe
capitalize-word	\ec
clear-screen	\C-l
complete	\C-i
	\e\C-[
complete-command	\e!
complete-filename	\e/
complete-hostname	\e@
complete-into-braces	\e{
complete-username	\e~
complete-variable	\e$
delete-char	\C-d
	\e[3~
delete-horizontal-space	\e\\
digit-argument	\e-
	\e1
	\e2
	\e3
	\e4

DEFAULT KEY BINDINGS *(CONT.)*

Readline Function	Default Key Binding
display-shell-version	\C-x\C-v
do-lowercase-version	\C-xA
	\C-xB
	\C-xC
	\C-xD
	\C-xE
downcase-word	\el
dynamic-complete-history	\e\C-i
end-kbd-macro	\C-x)
end-of-history	\e>
	\e[6~
end-of-line	\C-e
	\e[4~
	\e[f
forward-char	\C-f
	\eOC
	\e[C
forward-search-history	\C-s
forward-word	\e0c
	\ef
history-expand-line	\e^
insert-last-argument	\e.
	\e_
kill-line	\C-k
kill-word	\ed
next-history	\C-n
	\eOB
	\e[B
non-incremental-forward-search-history	\en
non-incremental-reverse-search-history	\ep
operate-and-get-next	\C-o

DEFAULT KEY BINDINGS *(CONT.)*

Readline Function	Default Key Binding
possible-command-completions	\C-x!
possible-completions	\e?
possible-filename-completions	\C-x/
possible-host name-completions	\C-x@
possible-username-completions	\C-x~
possible-variable-completions	\C-x$
previous-history	\C-p
	\eOA
	\e[A
quoted-insert	\C-q
	\C-v
	\e[2~
re-read-init-file	\C-x\C-r.
reverse-search-history	\C-r
revert-line	\e\C-r
	\er
self-insert	! \ # $ ...
shell-expand-line	\e\C-e
start-kbd-macro	\C-x(
tilde-expand	\e&
transpose-chars	\C-t
transpose-words	\et
undo	\C-x\C-u
	\C-_
unix-line-discard	\C-u
unix-word-rubout	\C-w
upcase-word	\eu

EXAMPLES

This Command	Does the Following
`"\em\er" : start-keyboard-macro`	Assigns Alt + m, Alt + r to the specified readline function (start-keyboard-macro) in `/etc/inputrc` or `~/.inputrc`. Add this line to one of these files with a text editor.
`bind '"\em\er" : start-keyboard-macro'`	Assigns Alt + m, Alt + r to the specified readline function (start-keyboard-macro) for the duration of the session. Note the single quote punctuation around the entire argument.
`bind '"\cb" : bigfiles'`	Assigns Ctrl + b to the specified function.
`bind ' "\cp" : "/home/suzanne/documents/pix"'`	Assigns Ctrl + p to the specified macro (inserts the quoted text).

chroot

chroot *path name* [*command*]

This utility executes the specified command with a root directory other than the default for the current session. Requires superuser status (see **su** in Chapter 1).

chsh

chsh [option] [*username*]

Changes the login shell. To see a list of available shells, use the –l option.

OPTIONS

Use This Option	To Do This
–l, – –list-shells	Display a list of available shells
–s *shell*, **– –shell** *shell*	Switch to the specified shell
–u, – –help	Display available options
–v, – –version	Show the version number

---

declare

> **declare** [options] [*name* [= *value*]]

Displays or changes variables. When used without options or arguments, prints a list of all the currently assigned variables and their values. To create or reset a variable, specify the name and value.

OPTIONS

Use This Option	To Do This
–f	Show function names only
–r	Create variable as read-only
–x	Mark variables for export
–l	Restrict value to integers

EXAMPLES

This Command	Does the Following
declare	Shows the current variables and values.
declare docs='/home/ bryan/Documents'	Creates the specified variable (docs) and assigns the value */home/bryan/ Documents*.

echo

echo [option] [*string*]

Displays the specified string on the display. This command can also be used to show the values of variables and functions.

OPTIONS

Use This Option	To Do This
–n	Not add a newline character to the output
–e	Enable interpretation of escape characters
–E	Disable interpretation of escape characters

EXAMPLE

This Command	Does the Following
echo $USER	Shows the current user's name.

env

env [option] [*variable=value*] [*command*]

This utility displays or sets the specified *variable*. When you type this command without options or arguments, it displays all the current variables and their values. If you specify a command, the command is executed in the altered environment.

OPTIONS

Use This Option	To Do This
–u *variable*, **– –unset** *variable*	Unset the specified variable
–i, **– –ignore-environment**	Ignore the current environment

EXAMPLES

This Command	Does the Following
env	Displays the current variables and values.
env mood=bad	Sets the variable mood to the value *bad*.
env mood=bad joy	Executes the program called joy in the environment in which mood is bad.
env -u mood	Unsets the specified variable (mood).

export

export [option] [*variable*] [*name* = [*value*]

Makes the specified variable available throughout the current bash environment. When used without an argument, this command lists the variables that are currently exported by the shell. If the variable does not exist, you can create it by specifying a name and assigning a value. By convention, exported variables are typed with uppercase letters.

OPTIONS

Use This Option	To Do This
--	Define all the following strings as arguments not options
-f	Export functions, not variables
-n	Unexport specified variable
-p	List variables exported by the shell

EXAMPLES

This Command	Does the Following
export	Displays the variables that are currently exported to the shell.

EXAMPLES *(CONT.)*

This Command	Does the Following
export PATH=$PATH:/usr/local/ Office51/bin	Exports a new directory to the path without erasing the previous PATH value. Note that the existing variable's value is incorporated into the new variable definition.
export PATH=$PATH:/usr/sbin:/ usr/local/bin:/usr/local/ Office51/bin:/usr/local/ ballistic/bin	Exports all of the specified directories. Note that they are separated by colons.

---

fc

fc –l [option] [*first item*] [*last item*] [*command*]

fc –s [*old-string=new string*] [command]

This command has two forms. The first displays a range of commands in the history list, starting with *first item* and ending with *last item*. To enter the item numbers, use the command number in the history list.

You can also type a string as the *first item* and *last item*. If you do, fc performs a substring search and returns a list of all the commands. If you omit *first item* and *last item*, you see the last 16 commands. The second form of the command re-executes the specified command after substituting *new string* for *old string*. When used without an argument, **fc –s** re-executes the last command you gave.

OPTIONS

Use This Option	To Do This
–e [*editor name*]	Open the default editor (or the editor specified by *editor name*) so that you can edit the history list directly
–n	Suppress history item numbering
–r	Reverse the order of the history list

EXAMPLES

This Command	Does the Following
fc -1	Displays the most recent 16 commands in a numbered list, with the oldest at the top.
fc -s	Re-executes the last command you gave.

function

> **function** *name* {
> *command1*
> *command2*
> *command3*...}

Defines a shell function with the specified name. After typing the opening curly brace, press Enter and type each command on its own line. Finish the function by typing the closing curly brace, and press Enter.

EXAMPLE

This Command	Does the Following
function untar { gunzip *tar.gz; tar -xvf *.tar}	Creates a function named untar, which decompresses all the .tar.gz files in the current directory and extracts the files from the **tar** archives (see Chapter 6).

hash

> **hash** [option] *command*

Creates an association between the specified command name and the command's location so that the shell no longer needs to search the path to locate the command. Used without an option or argument, this command lists the current hashed commands, if any.

OPTION

Use This Option	To Do This
–r	Remove the hashed command

EXAMPLES

This Command	Does the Following
hash ttmkfdir cdrecord bladeenc	Creates hash entries for the specified commands.
hash	Displays the current list of hashed commands.

---

history

history [option] [*lines*]

Displays a numbered list of the commands you have used in this and previous sessions. You can specify the maximum number of *lines* to display. If the history list contains more lines than you specified, you see the most recently used commands.

OPTIONS

Use This Option	To Do This
–a	Write current session's commands to .bash_history
–n	Add to .bash_history any commands that are not yet listed in the history list
–r	Use .bash_history as the history list, discarding commands used in the current session
–w	Overwrite .bash_history with the commands used in this session

EXAMPLES

This Command	Does the Following
history | less	Displays the current history list and pipe to **less** for convenient reading.
history -n	Adds this session's new commands to **.bash_history**.

jobs

jobs [option] [*job ID*]

Lists all running or suspended jobs.

OPTIONS

Use This Option	To Do This
-l	List job IDs and process IDs
-n	List only those jobs that have been altered since the last time this command was used
-p	List process IDs only
-x *command*	Replace the command being used with the specified command

kill

kill [option] *id*

Terminate the process specified by *id*. To kill the process, you must be the owner or have superuser status (see **su** in Chapter 1). For a list of signals and signal IDs, see the "Signals" section in this chapter.

OPTIONS

Use This Option	To Do This
–signal *n*	Use the signal specified by *n*. To see a list with numbers, use **kill –l**.
–l	List the available signal names and numbers.
–s *signal*	Specify the signal by name.

EXAMPLE

This Command	Does the Following
`kill 5047`	Kills the specified process.

---

killall

killall [option] [*name*]

This utility kills processes by name or filename rather than by ID number (see **kill**). In the command, *name* can refer to a command or, if preceded by a slash mark, to a file. In either case, this command kills all processes that use the specified name or file.

OPTIONS

Use This Option	To Do This
–signal	Send the specified signal to the process. For a list, see the "Signals" section in this chapter.
–e	Require an exact match for long names (those longer than 15 characters). By default, **killall** will kill every process that has a name matching within 15 characters.
–i	Ask for confirmation before killing processes.
–l	List signal names and ID numbers.
–q	Hide program messages.
–v	Show all program messages.
–w	Wait for killed processes to die before exiting.

nice

> **nice** [option] [*command* [*argument*]]

Displays or adjusts the scheduling priority of a job. When used without specifying a command, **nice** displays the current scheduling priority. The range extends from the highest priority (–20) to the lowest (19). If you specify a command with the –**ADJUST** option, nice executes the command with a priority of 10. You will need super-user privileges to use negative priorities.

See also **renice**.

OPTIONS

Use This Option	To Do This
–ADJUST	Execute the specified command with a priority of 10
–n	Execute the specified command with a priority of *n*

nohup

> **nohup** *command*

This utility executes the specified command so that it ignores SIGHUP (hang up) signals. The command can continue executing in the background even after you log out of your current user session.

printenv

> **printenv** [*variable*]

When used without specifying a variable, this utility displays the values of all variables in the current environment. To view this utility's value, specify a variable.

ps

ps [option] [*sort key*] [*output field*]

Displays a list of running processes. To make the command output easier to read, you can specify one of the sort keys listed in the Sort Keys table. You can also use one of the output fields listed in the Output Fields table.

OPTIONS

Use This Option	To Do This
–a	Show all processes on the current terminal, including those of other users.
–A	Show all processes (same as **–e**).
–C *name*	Show process specified by *name*.
–d	Show all but omit session leaders.
–e	Show all processes (same as **–A**).
–f	Use the full listing.
–G *group ID*	Show processes owned by the specified group ID (name or number).
–g *name*	Show processes owned by the session leader or group name specified by *name*.
–H	Show the process hierarchy.
– –help	Show the available commands.
–j	Use the jobs format.
–l	Use the long format.
–p *process ID*	Show the process specified by *process ID*.
–r	Restrict the output to running processes.
– –sort [–]*key*	Sort the output using the specified sort key (see the Sort Keys table). Use the long form of the sort key. Specify a minus sign before the key to reverse the default sort order.
–s *session ID*	Show the processes specified by *session ID*.

OPTIONS *(CONT.)*

Use This Option	To Do This
–T	Show all the processes on this terminal.
–t *tty*	Show processes running on the specified tty.
–U *user* ID	Show processes owned by the specified user ID (name or number).
–V	Display the version number.
–w	Use wide output.
–x	Show processes running without a terminal.

SORT KEYS

Short Form	Long Form	Description
p	pid	The process ID number
c	cmd	The name of the executable
C	cmdline	The flags
g	pgrp	The group owner ID of the process
G	tpgid	The group owner ID of the controlling tty process
j	cutime	The cumulative user time
J	cstime	The cumulative system time
k	utime	The user time
K	stime	The system time
m	min_flt	The number of minor page faults
M	maj_flt	The number of major page faults
n	cmin_flt	The cumulative minor page faults
N	cmaj_flt	The cumulative major page faults
o	session	The session ID
P	ppid	The process ID of the parent process
r	rss	The resident set size
R	resident	The resident pages
s	size	The memory usage in K (kilobytes)

SORT KEYS *(CONT.)*

Short Form	Long Form	Description
S	share	The number of shared memory pages
t	tty	The ID number of the tty device
T	start_time	The time the process was started
U	uid	The ID number of the process owner
u	user	The username of the process owner
v	vsize	The virtual memory usage in K (kilobytes)
y	priority	The kernel scheduling priority

OUTPUT FIELDS

Field	Description
F	Displays one of the following process flags:
	001 Alignment warning.
	002 Being created.
	004 Shutting down.
	010 Being traced.
	020 Tracing system calls.
	040 Forked but did not exec.
	100 Run by superuser.
	200 Dumped core.
	400 Killed.
S, STAT	Displays the state codes:
	< Higher-priority process.
	D Uninterruptible sleep.
	L Pages locked in memory.
	N Lower-priority process.
	R Runnable.
	S Sleeping.
	T Traced or stopped.
	W No resident memory pages.
	Z Zombie process (stalled).
UID	Displays the user ID.

OUTPUT FIELDS *(CONT.)*

Field	Description
PPID	Displays the parent process ID.
PRI	Displays the process scheduling priority.
NI	Displays the **nice** value.
SZ	Displays the amount of physical memory used.
VSZ	Displays the amount of virtual memory used.
RSS	Displays the size of resident set memory.
WCHAN	Displays the related kernel function.
TTY	Displays the name of the terminal in use for this process.
TIME	Displays the cumulative time of execution.
CMD	Displays the name of the executable.

EXAMPLES

This Command	Does the Following
ps	Displays a list of every running process on the current terminal.
ps −e	Displays a list of all running processes.
ps −eH	Displays a list of all running processes and shows the relationship between parent and child processes.
ps −el − −sort −size	Displays a verbose list of all running processes, sorted by the amount of memory used. The biggest memory hogs are listed first.

readonly

readonly [*variable*]

Makes the specified variable read-only so that its value cannot be changed. When used without a variable name, displays all current read-only variables.

renice

renice [*priority*] [option] [*target*]

Specifies the scheduling priority of the specified target. When using this utility from an ordinary user account, the priority must range from 0 (medium priority) to 20 (low priority). The root user or super-user may specify a higher priority using a negative number (to −20, depending on the system's configuration). The target can be a process ID, a process group ID, or a user.

OPTIONS

Use This Option	To Do This
−g	Set the priority of a process group ID.
−p	Set the priority of a process ID. This is the default option.
−u	Set the priority of a user.

script

script [option] [*filename*]

This utility writes all output from the terminal to the file specified by *filename*. If you do not specify a filename, the output is written to a file named typescript. To stop writing to the file, press Ctrl + d.

OPTION

Use This Option	To Do This
−a	Append to the file rather than overwriting if the file exists

set

set [option] [*argument 1, argument 2, argument 3, ...*]

Used without any options or arguments, this command displays a list of all current variables. This command is often used in scripts to assign values to *positional parameters*. For example, if you specify a value for *argument 1*, bash assigns this value to $1. You can also use this command to choose *shell modes* for the current operating environment, including *noclobber*, which prevents bash from overwriting files when you use output redirection.

OPTIONS

Use This Option	To Do This
−o *shell mode* **+o** *shell mode*	Enable one of the following shell modes (**−o**) or disable a shell mode (**+o**). (The preceding is *not* a misprint; you use **−** to turn the option on and **+** to turn it off.) The following lists the available shell modes. The typical default settings are indicated in parentheses.

allexport(off)   Automatically export variables.

braceexpand (on)   Enable brace expansion.

emacs (on)   Use emacs as the default editor.

errexit (off)   Exit if a command encounters an error.

histexpand (on)   Enable history expansion.

ignoreeof (off)   Do not exit on end of file.

interactive-comments (on)   Treat # as a comment character.

monitor (on)   Enable job control.

noclobber (off)   Do not overwrite files when using output redirection.

noexec (off)   Do not execute commands.

noglob (off)   Do not use filename expansion.

nohash (off)   Do not use command hashing.

notify (off)   Show message about background jobs at termination.

nounset (off)   Treat unset variables as errors in substitutions.

physical (off)   Print absolute path names in response to **pwd**.

posix (off)   Use POSIX standards.

privileged (off)   Start as the superuser; do not process the user's profile.

verbose (off)   Show each shell command when read.

vi (off)   Use **vi** as the default editor.

xtrace (off)   Show commands and arguments as they are executed.

OPTIONS *(CONT.)*

Use This Option	To Do This
–a	Same as **–o allexport**
–b	Same as **–o notify**
–C	Same as **–o noclobber**
–d	Same as **–o nohash**
–e	Same as **–o errexit**
–f	Same as **–o noglob**
–h	Same as **+o nohash**
–k	Enable assignment of variables no matter where they appear on the command line
–l	Restore a variable's original value after a **for** command uses the variable
–m	Same as **–o monitor**
–n	Same as **–o errexit**
–p	Same as **–o privileged**
–t	Exit after one command is executed
–u	Same as **–o errexit**
–v	Same as **–o verbose**
–x	Same as **–o xtrace**
–H	Enable **!** and **!!** commands (on by default)
–P	Same as **–o physical**

EXAMPLES

This Command	Does the Following
`set`	Displays all the current variables.
`set -o`	Displays the current settings for the shell modes.
`set -o noclobber`	Turns the noclobber shell mode on.
`set +o noclobber`	Turns the noclobber shell mode off.

source

source *filename*

Reads commands from the text file specified by *filename*.

suspend

suspend

Suspends a command (same as Ctrl + z).

tee

command | **tee** [option] *filename*

Used in a pipe, this utility accepts output from the specified command and "splits" the output to the standard output (the terminal) and the specified filename.

OPTIONS

Use This Option	To Do This
–a, – –append	Append to the file rather than overwriting it, if the file exists
– –help	Show available options
–i, – –ignore-interrupts	Ignore interrupt signals
– –version	Show current version

times

times

Displays the accumulated process running times for the system and the current user.

top

top [option]

Launches an interactive program that enables you to track running processes. See the Interactive Commands table for the commands you can use once **top** is running. This utility highlights the processes that are consuming the greatest amount of CPU time and provides a wealth of additional information. See the Output Fields table in this section for an explanation of the **top** command's column headers.

OPTIONS

Use This Option	To Do This
–c	Display entire command line not just the command name
–d *n*	Specify the delay between refreshes in *n* seconds
–l	Do not show idle or zombie processes
–q	Refresh without any delay
–s	Disable dangerous commands
–S	Display cumulative CPU times
–n *n*	Refresh the display *n* times and then exit

INTERACTIVE COMMANDS

Use This Command	To Do This
c	Toggle the display of the command name or the full command line.
Ctrl + l	Redraw the screen.
h, ?	Show available commands.
k	Kill a process. You will be prompted for the process ID.
l	Toggle display of idle and zombie processes.
n, #	Specify the number of processes to show. You will be prompted for the number. By default, **top** shows as many processes as will fit on the display.

INTERACTIVE COMMANDS *(CONT.)*

Use This Command	To Do This
q	Quit **top**.
r	Re-**nice** a process. You will be prompted to enter a **nice** value (see **nice**).
S	Toggles cumulative mode.
s	Change the delay between updates. You will be prompted to enter a delay time in seconds. Enter 0 (zero) to force continuous updates. The default is 5 seconds.
f, F	Add or remove fields from the display.
o, O	Change the order of displayed fields.
l	Toggle the display of load average and uptime information.
m	Toggle the display of memory information.
t	Toggle the display of processes and CPU state information.
N	Sort tasks by process ID.
A	Sort tasks by age, showing the newest first.
P	Sort tasks by CPU usage. This is the default sort order.
M	Sort tasks by resident memory usage.
T	Sort tasks by cumulative time.
W	Write the current setup to the top configuration file.

OUTPUT FIELDS

Field	Description
PID	Displays the process ID.
USER	Displays the username of the task's owner.
NI	Displays the **nice** value.

OUTPUT FIELDS *(CONT.)*

Field	Description
SIZE	Displays the size of the code, plus data, plus stack space, in K (kilobytes).
RSS	Displays the total amount of physical memory in K (kilobytes).
SHARE	Displays the amount of shared memory in K (kilobytes).
STAT	Displays one of the following state codes: **<** Higher-priority process. **D** Uninterruptible sleep. **L** Pages locked in memory. **N** Lower-priority process. **R** Runnable. **S** Sleeping. **T** Traced or stopped. **W** No resident memory pages. **Z** Zombie process (stalled).
LIB	Displays the size of the library pages used in K (kilobytes).
%CPU	Displays the percentage of total CPU time used by this process.
%MEM	Displays the percentage of total physical memory used by this process.
TIME	Displays the total CPU time used by this process since it was started.
COMMAND	Displays the command name of the process.

EXAMPLES

This Command	Does the Following
`top -is`	Starts **top** so that zombie and idle processes are hidden, and dangerous commands are disabled.
`M`	In interactive mode, sorts by memory usage so that the biggest memory hogs are shown first.

trap

trap [option] [*command*] *signal*]]

Executes *command* if the specified signal is received.

OPTION

Use This Option	To Do This
–l	List available signals

type

type [option] *command*

Display the absolute path name of the specified command and indicate whether the command has been hashed.

See also **hash**.

OPTIONS

Use This Option	To Do This
–a, – –all	Display all instances of the specified command
–p, – –path	Display the hashed value of the specified command
–t, – –type	Indicate the type of the specified file

typeset

See **declare**.

ulimit

ulimit [option] [*n*]

Display a resource limit. If *n* is specified, set the limit.

OPTIONS

Use This Option	To Do This
–a	Show all the current limits
–H	Set a hard limit
–S	Set a soft limit (default)
–c	Display or set size the limit for core files in K (kilobytes)
–d	Display or set size the limit for processes' data segments in K (kilobytes)
–f	Display or set the size limit of the shell-created files in K (kilobytes)
–m	Display or set the maximum resident set size in K (kilobytes)
–s	Display or set the maximum stack size in K (kilobytes)
–t	Display or set the maximum amount of CPU time in seconds
–u	Display or set the maximum number of user processes
–v	Display or set the maximum size of virtual memory in K (kilobytes)

unalias

unalias [option] [*name*]

Removes an alias that you have created (see **alias**). If you use the –a option without a name, bash removes all of the aliases you have created.

CHAPTER 4

Navigating the Filesystem
and Finding Files

$\mathbf{T}$his chapter provides the reference information you need to navigate the Linux filesystem and locate files quickly. For information on finding information within files, see Chapter 8, "Working with Text Files."

AT A GLANCE

How Do I	See This Entry	Example
List files sorted by size, showing the largest files first?	**dir, ls**	`ls -Sl`
List files sorted by the time of their last modification, showing the most recently modified files first?	**dir, ls**	`ls -cl`
Display all the files within a directory and its associated subdirectories that match a specified pattern?	**dir, ls**	`ls -R *.jpg`
Find all the files that have been changed in the last two hours?	**find**	`find /home/suzanne -ctime -2`
List all the files in the current directory that belong to a certain user?	**find**	`find /home/suzanne -user 'mike'`
Find a file in the current directory that has been changed since you last made changes to another file?	**find**	`find /home/suzanne -newer 'essay1.doc'`
Locate a file in the current directory that you saved a few minutes ago?	**find**	`find /home/suzanne -cmin -10`
Display all the files in a directory that have a specified permission setting, such as 755?	**find**	`find /home/suzanne -perm 755`

AT A GLANCE

How Do I	See This Entry	Example
Search the entire filesystem for a file containing a specified word?	**find**	`find / -print0 | xargs -0 grep -1 happiness`
Quickly locate all the files on your system that have the `.doc` extension?	**locate, slocate**	`slocate doc`
Create a database of filenames so that files can be located quickly?	**slocate**	`slocate -u`
Switch back and forth between two directories so that you don't have to keep typing the same names over and over?	**pushd**	`pushd /home/suzanne/essays` or `pushd /home/suzanne/poetry` or `pushd`

The Linux Filesystem

This section discusses the following topics:

- Filenames
- Directories and the standard directory structure
- Shell patterns

Filenames

In the standard Linux filesystem, the Second Extended Filesystem (e2fs), you can create filenames of up to 255 characters in length. Note that Linux filenames are case sensitive: `essay-1.DOC` and `essay-1.doc` are two different files. When naming files, avoid the illegal characters listed in the following Illegal Characters table. It is best to use only the letters *a–z* (or *A–Z*), the numbers *0–9*, and underscores (_). Certain utilities and applications may experience problems processing filenames that contain spaces.

Linux does not require the use of suffixes, also called extensions. A *suffix* is the portion of the filename after the period. If you use suffixes, use those that conform to standards or prevailing practices (see the Commonly Used Suffixes table in this section). Filenames that begin with a period are called *hidden files* and do not appear in the default **ls** directory listings. Use **ls –a** to see all files, including hidden files.

TIP If a file lacks a suffix, type **file** followed by a space and the filename, and press Enter. You will see a brief description of the type of data contained in the file.

ILLEGAL CHARACTERS

Character	Function
#	Inserts a comment; bash ignores the rest of the line.
&	Inserts a named variable.
* ? [ ] ~ !	Constructs shell patterns.
< >	Redirects input and output.
`	Inserts the output of the specified command.
;	Begins new command on the same line.
( )	Groups commands for execution in a subshell. The grouped commands execute before other commands.
{ }	Groups commands so that they execute before other commands.

COMMONLY USED SUFFIXES

Extension	Description
.afm	Type1 font metric file
.aif, .aiff	Amiga or Macintosh audio file
.arj	File compressed with **arj** utility
.au	Sun/NeXT audio file

COMMONLY USED SUFFIXES

Extension	Description
`.avi`	Windows AVI video file
`.bak`	Backup file
`.bmp`	Windows bitmap graphics file
`.c`	C source code
`.cf, .cfg, .cong, .confg`	Configuration file
`.cgi`	Common Gateway Interface script
`.cgm`	Computer Graphics Metafile graphics file
`.chr`	Character map
`.cron`	Configuration file for cron utility
`.dat`	Data file
`.db`	Database file
`.doc`	Document file
`.dot`	Microsoft Word template file
`.elm`	Elm text file
`.err`	Error log
`.fli`	FLI animation
`.gif`	GIF graphics file
`.gz`	Gzip compressed file
`.h`	C header file
`.hqx`	BINHEX encoded file
`.htm, .html`	Web page
`.icb`	Targa bitmapped graphics file
`.idf`	MIDI instrument drivers file
`.img`	Bitmapped graphics file
`.jpg, .jpeg, .jpe, .jfif`	JPEG graphics file
`.js`	JavaScript source code
`.kar`	Karoake MIDI file
`.lock`	Lock file that prevents access to executable while it is running
`.log`	Log file
`.mid, .midi`	MIDI file

COMMONLY USED SUFFIXES

Extension	Description
.mod	MOD sound file
.mov	QuickTime movie
.mp3	Mp3 audio file
.mpg, .mpeg	MPEG video file
.o	Object code
.pbm	X portable bitmap graphic file
.pcm	CD audio file
.pdf	Portable Document Format (Adobe Acrobat) file
.pfa	Type 1 ASCII printer font
.pfb	Type 1 ASCII printer font
.pfm	Type 1 printer font metrics file
.pgm	X portable grayscale graphic file
.pid	Process ID file
.png	Portable Network Graphics graphics file
.pnm	X portable-anymap graphic file
.ps	Postscript file
.qt	QuickTime video
.ra, .ram	RealAudio file
.rpm	Red Hat Package Manager package
.rtf	Rich Text Format file
.sda	StarOffice drawing
.sdc	StarOffice spreadsheet
.sdd	StarOffice presentation
.sds	StarOffice chart
.sdw	StarOffice text
.snd	Macintosh sound file
.tar	**Tar** archive
.tgz, .tar.gz	**Tar** archive compressed with **gzip**
.tif, .tiff	Tagged Image Format file

COMMONLY USED SUFFIXES

Extension	Description
.tmp	Temporary file
.ttf	TrueType font
.txt	Text file
.vcf	VCard file
.vcs	VCalendar file
.vrml	VRML world
.wav	Windows WAV sound file
.wp	WordPerfect file
.xbm	X bitmap graphic file
.xpm	X pixmap graphic file
.Z	File compressed with **compress** utility
.zip	File compressed with **pkzip** compression utility

Directories and the Standard Directory Structure

The Linux filesystem is organized into a hierarchical structure of directories, with the *root directory* (/) positioned at the top. The directory structure is not tied to a specific storage device. It may span two or more physical disk drives, and it can also include directories from other computers on the network. Only one directory, the *working directory*, is current at any given time. This directory's location within the directory structure is specified by its *absolute path name*, such as /home/suzanne/Documents/Essays. See the "Directory Names and Symbols" table in this section for the standard nomenclature.

In the working directory, you can also use relative path names. For example, in /home/suzanne/Documents, you can type **cd Essays** to change to the /home/suzanne/Documents/Essays directory. Standards-conformant Linux systems use a standard method of organizing top-level directories (see the Standard Directory Structure table in this section).

DIRECTORY NAMES AND SYMBOLS

Example	Description
.	The current or working directory
..	The parent directory
~	The home directory of the current user
/	The root directory (*not* /**root**)
../directory	Refers to another directory of the same parent
/home/suzanne/Documents/Essays	The absolute path name
Essays	The relative path name

STANDARD DIRECTORY STRUCTURE

Directory	Purpose
/	The root directory. Stores essential start-up files and serves as the top-level directory for the entire directory structure. Do not confuse with /**root**.
/bin	Startup programs and commands used in single-user mode.
/boot	Files used to start the system.
/dev	Special files representing system devices and device drivers.
/etc	System-level configuration files and scripts.
/home	The users' home directories.
/lib	Shared library files.
/mnt	The mount point for temporary filesystems.
/opt	The installation directory for commercial software.
/proc	The virtual filesystem for kernel and process information.
/root	The home directory for the root user. Do not confuse with the root directory (/).
/sbin	Essential system utilities that are used for booting the system.
/tmp	The storage space for temporary files.

STANDARD DIRECTORY STRUCTURE

Directory	Purpose
/usr	The storage space for files that need to be made available sys-temwide, including user utilities and programs (/usr/bin); documentation (/usr/doc); libraries used by user-installed programs (/usr/lib); software installed by users (/usr/local); man pages (/usr/man); non-essential system admin-istration utilities (/usr/sbin); and other shared items, such as fonts and icons (/usr/share).
/var	Data files of variable length, including spool directories for mail and printing.

Shell Patterns

Shell patterns are useful when you are displaying the contents of directories (see **dir, ls**) or searching for files (see **find, locate**). See the Shell Pattern Characters table in this section for the wildcard and other expressions you can use in shell pattern searches.

SHELL PATTERN CHARACTERS

Use This Pattern	To Do This
*	Match one or more characters
?	Match any single character
[characters]	Match any of the characters
[character1-character2]	Match any of the characters within the range character1 to character2.
[!characters]	Do not match any of the characters

EXAMPLES

*.jpg	Matches any file with the .jpg extension.
essay?.doc	Matches essay1, essayB, etc.

EXAMPLES

essay[0-9].doc	Matches essay1.doc, essay2.doc, essay3.doc, etc.
[Aa]utobiography.doc	Matches Autobiography.doc or autobiography.doc.

Alphabetical Command Reference

In this section, you will find commands for doing the following:

- Working with directories (**cd, dir, dirs, ls, popd, pushd, vdir**)
- Working with Macintosh files (**hcd, hdir, hls, hmkdir, hpwd, hrmdir**)
- Finding files (**find, locate, slocate, updatedb, xargs**)
- Determining the amount of free memory in your system (**free**)
- Determining the content of a file (**file**)

cd

cd [*directory* | *path name*]

Changes the current directory. If you type **cd** without specifying an argument, this command changes to the current user's home directory. This is one of the shell's built-in commands rather than a disk-based utility.

EXAMPLES

This Command	Does the Following
cd	Switches to user's home directory.
cd ..	Switches to the parent directory (the next directory up).
cd documents	Switches to a subdirectory in the current directory named documents.
cd /usr/share/pixmaps	Switches to the directory specified by the path name.

dir

dir [options] [*pattern*]

Lists the files in the current directory in case-sensitive, alphabetical order, using a columnar format. If you specify a pattern, this command lists only the files that match a shell pattern (see Chapter 3). In the GNU file utilities commonly provided with Linux distributions, this command is identical to **ls**.

See also **vdir.**

OPTIONS

Use This Option	To Do This
–1	List entries using one line for each filename.
–a, – –all	Show all files, including hidden files, those that have names beginning with a period.
–A, – –almost-all	List all files in the directory, including hidden files, but hide the display of the current directory (.) and parent directory (..) symbols.
–B, – –ignore-backups	Hide backup files, those with filenames beginning with ~.
–c	List files sorted by the time of the last modification to the file's status. Use **–cl** to display the times. Same as **– –sort=ctime**.
–C	List entries using columns.
– –color	Display file types using distinctive colors if the current terminal supports color output.
–d, – –directory	List the names of subdirectories but not their contents.
–F	Display the file type with a character appended to the filename output: * Executable file. / Directory. = Socket. | Named pipe FIFO (/). @ Symbolic link.

OPTIONS

Use This Option	To Do This
–h, – –human-readable	Display file sizes in kilobytes (KB), megabytes (MB), or gigabytes (GB), using base 2 calculations (1K = 1,024 bytes). Use with **–l**.
–H, – –si	Display file sizes in kilobytes (KB), megabytes (MB), or gigabytes (GB), using base 10 calculations (1K = 1,000 bytes). Use with **–l**.
– –help	Display available options.
–I=pattern, **– –ignore=**pattern	Ignore files with names matching the specified pattern.
–i, – –inode	Display the file inode number.
–l, – –format=long, **– –format=verbose**	List entries using the verbose (long) display format.
–L, – –dereference	For symbolic links, show information for the files to which symbolic links are linked.
–m, – –format=commas	List files in a comma-separated list.
–p, – –file-type	Display the file type with a character appended to the filename output. Same as **–F**, except executables are not marked.
–R, – –recursive	List the contents of subdirectories.
–r, – –reverse	Reverse the sort order.
–s	Show the size of each file in blocks.
–S, – –sort=size	List files sorted by size, with the lengthiest items shown first. Use **–Sl** to display the file sizes.
– –sort=sort type	List files sorted by any of the following types: extension, size, time, version, status, atime (time of last access), access (time of last access), or use.
–t, – –sort=time	List files sorted by the time of last their modification. Use **–tl** to display the times. Same as **–c**.

OPTIONS

Use This Option	To Do This
–T *cols*, **– –tabsize=***cols*	For columnar output, specify the column width (*cols*) in characters.
– –time=*time type*	List files sorted by any of the following types: atime, access, use, ctime, or status.
–u, **– –sort=atime**	List files sorted by the time of the last access. Use **–ul** to list the times.
–v	List files sorted by version.
– –version	Display version number.
–w *cols*, **– –width=***cols*	Specify the screen width (*cols*) in characters.
–x	List entries line by line instead of by columns.
–X	Sort by extension. Same as **– – sort=extension**.

EXAMPLES

This Command	Does the Following
`dir`	Lists files and directories in the current directory in case-sensitive, alphabetical order.
`dir *.doc`	Lists only those files with the `.doc` extension.
`dir –R *.jpg`	Lists all the files with the `*.jpg` extension in the current directory and all associated subdirectories.
`dir –Sl`	Lists files sorted by size, showing the largest files first.
`dir –Shl`	Lists files sorted by size, showing the largest files first, and shows the sizes in a human-readable form.
`dir –tl, dir –cl`	Lists files by the time of the last modification, showing the most recently modified files first.
`dir –Rtlr *.doc`	Using reverse chronological order (oldest files first), lists all the files in the current directory and all associated subdirectories that have the `*.doc` extension.
`dir –F`	Displays filenames with appended characters that indicate the file type, such as executable (*) or directory (/).

dirs

dirs [option]

Displays the directories you have added to the *directory stack*, a list of remembered directory names. To add directories to the stack, use **pushd**. To remove directories from the stack, use **popd**.

OPTIONS

Use This Option	To Do This
+*n*	Display the name of the *n*th directory in the stack, starting from zero
−n	Display the name of the *n*th directory from the end of the list
−l	Display entries with absolute path names

file

file [option] *filename*

Displays the type of content (text, executable, or data) that a file contains. For some data files, this utility can provide detailed information, including the name of the utility that created the data.

OPTIONS

Use This Option	To Do This
−b	Display the results concisely, omitting the filenames
−f *filename*	Obtain the names of the files to be examined from the specified filename
−L	Follow symlinks to their targets
−m *filename*	Obtain a list of *magic numbers* (codes representing various data types) from the specified filename
−s	Read block or character special files
−v	Show the version number
−z	Process compressed files

find

find *pattern*

find [*path name*] [option] [*test*] [*action*]

In its simple form (**find** *pattern*), this command searches the current directory for files with names that match the specified shell pattern (see Chapter 3). If you specify a path name, **find** starts searching at the specified directory and searches all associated subdirectories if there are any. You can also perform a more advanced search by specifying a test and an action. The default test is –**name**, while the default action is –**print** (displays the name of the files that meet the specified test). When you specify tests that call for a numerical specification (*n*), you can type **+n** to indicate *n* or more than *n*, **–n** to indicate *n* or less than *n*, or **n** to indicate exactly *n*. For example, the test –**ctime –1** searches for files that were changed one or fewer hours ago. When you specify a path name, you cannot specify the test using the command's short form; you must use –**text** '*filename*.'

See also **locate**.

OPTIONS

Use This Option	To Do This
–**daystart**	When used with the various time tests (–**amin**, –**atime**, –**cmin**, –**ctime**, –**min**, and –**mtime**), measure time from the start of the current day rather than 24 hours ago.
–**depth**	Process each directory's contents before processing the directory itself.
–**follow**	Display the files to which symbolic links point rather than the links themselves.
–**help**, – –**help**	Display available options, tests, and actions.
–**maxdepth** *levels*	Specify the number of levels to descend down a directory tree from the current level. Use an integer (a whole number) other than zero to specify *levels*.

OPTIONS *(CONT.)*

Use This Option	To Do This
–mindepth *levels*	Begin processing tests and actions at the specified level below the current directory. Use an integer (a whole number) other than zero to specify *levels*.
–mount, –xdev	Do not search directories on other mounted filesystems.
–noleaf	Use this option when searching non-Unix file-systems, such as CD-ROMs or MS-DOS disks.
–version, – –version	Display the version number.

TESTS

Use This Test	To Do This
–amin *n*	Match files that were last accessed *n* minutes ago
–anewer *filename*	Match files that have been accessed since the specified filename was modified
–atime *n*	Match files that were last accessed *n* hours ago
–cmin *n*	Match files that were last changed *n* minutes ago
–cnewer *filename*	Match files that have been changed since the specified filename was modified.
–ctime *n*	Match files that were last changed *n* hours ago
–empty	Match files with 0 bytes of content.
–fstype *type*	Match files stored on the specified type of filesystem, such as msdos or vfat.
–gid *n*	Match files owned by the numeric group ID specified by *n*.
–ilname *shell pattern*	Match symbolic links with the specified shell pattern. Enclose the shell pattern in quotation marks. This search ignores case.

TESTS *(CONT.)*

Use This Test	To Do This
–iname *shell pattern*	Match files with the filename specified in *shell pattern*. Enclose the shell pattern in quotation marks. This search ignores case.
–lname *shell pattern*	Match symbolic links with the specified shell pattern. Enclose the shell pattern in quotation marks.
–name *shell pattern*	Match files with the filename specified in shell pattern. Enclose the shell pattern in quotation marks. This search is case sensitive.
–inum *n*	Match files with the specified inode number *n*.
–ipath *shell pattern*	Match the path with the specified shell pattern. Enclose the shell pattern in quotation marks. This search ignores case.
–iregex *regular expression*	Match the files with the filename specified in *regular expression*. This search ignores case.
–links *n*	Match files that have *n* symbolic links.
–mmin *n*	Match files that were last modified *n* minutes ago.
–mtime *n*	Match files that were last modified *n* hours ago.
–newer *filename*	Match files that are newer than the file specified in *filename*.
–nouser	Match files that have no assigned owner.
–nogroup	Match files that have no assigned group owner.
–path *shell pattern*	Match the path with the specified shell pattern. Enclose the shell pattern in quotation marks.

TESTS *(CONT.)*

Use This Test	To Do This
–perm *permissions*	Match files with the specified permissions (octal or symbolic).
–regex *regular expression*	Match the files with the filename specified in *regular expression*.
–size *n* [**b**	**c**	**k**	**w**]	Match files with the size specified by *n*. By default, *n* refers to the file size in 512-byte blocks (**–size** *n*b). You can also specify bytes (**–size** *n*c), kilobytes (**–size** *n*k), or 2-byte words (**–size** *n*w).
– type [**b**	**c**	**d**	**f**	**l**	**p**	**s**]	Match files of the specified type:
	b Buffered block.
	c Unbuffered character.
	d Directory.
	f Regular file (default).
	l Symbolic link.
	p Named pipe (FIFO).
	s socket.
–uid *n*	Match files belonging to the user whose numerical ID is specified by *n*.
–used *n*	Match files last accessed *n* days after any of its attributes were last changed.
–user *username*	Match files belonging to the user specified by *username*.
–xtype [**b**	**c**	**d**	**f**	**l**	**p**	**s**]	Match symbolic links of the specified type:
	b Buffered block.
	c Unbuffered character.
	d Directory.
	f Regular file (default).
	l Symbolic link.
	p Named pipe (FIFO).
	s Socket.

ACTIONS

Use This Option	To Do This
–exec *command* **'{}' ';'**	Run the utility specified by *command*. Use '{}' to echo the filename specified in the test you are using. Use ';' to terminate the command. Note that '{}' and ';' must be enclosed in single quotation marks so that the shell does not interpret them.
–fls *filename*	Write the contents of retrieved file(s) to the file specified by *filename*.
–fprint *filename*	Write the names of retrieved file(s) to the file specified by *filename*.
–ls	Display the names of retrieved file(s) using **ls –dils**.
–print	Display the names of retrieved file(s). This is the default action.
–print0	Display the names of retrieved files(s) in a format that enables **xargs** to work with filenames containing spaces.

EXAMPLES

This Command	Does the Following
`find *.jpg`	Finds all the files in the current directory with the `.jpg` extension.
`find /home/suzanne -name '*.doc'`	Finds all the files in the specified directory (/home/**suzanne**) and all associated subdirectories that have the **.doc** extension.
`find /home/suzanne -ctime -2`	Finds all the files in the specified directory (/home/**suzanne**) that have been changed within the past two hours.
`find /home/suzanne -newer 'essay1.doc'`	Finds all the files in the specified directory (/home/**suzanne**) that are newer than **essay1.doc**

EXAMPLES

This Command	Does the Following
`find /home/suzanne -size +1000k`	Finds all the files in the specified directory (**/home/suzanne**) that are larger than 1,000 kilobytes.
`find /home/suzanne -user 'bryan'`	Finds all the files in the specified directory (**/home/suzanne**) that are owned by the user named bryan.
`find -name 'proposal.txt' -exec less '{}' ';'`	Finds **proposal.txt** and displays the file using the **less** command (see Chapter 8).
`find -amin +5 -amin -10`	Finds all the files in the current directory that were last accessed 5 or more minutes ago but less than 10 or fewer minutes ago.
`find / -name '*.doc' -ctime -24`	Searches the entire filesystem to find all the files with the extension **.doc** that have been created or altered in the past 24 hours.
`find -name '*.doc' -ctime -24 -print0 | xargs -0 cp /home/suzanne/backup`	Locates all the files in the current directory with the **.doc** extension that were created or altered in the past 24 hours and copies them to **/home/suzanne/backup** (see **xargs**).
`find / -name '*.doc' -print0 | xargs -0 grep -l proposal`	Search the entire filesystem for files with the **.doc** extension that contain the word *proposal* (see **xargs** and **grep** in Chapter 8).

free

free [option]

Displays the following figures (in kilobytes) concerning available RAM memory: total memory available, memory currently in use, free memory, shared memory, memory used by kernel buffers, cached memory, size of the swap file, swap file currently in use, and free swap file.

OPTIONS

Use This Option	To Do This
–b	Display memory sizes in bytes instead of in kilobytes
–k	Display memory sizes in kilobytes (default)
–m	Display memory sizes in megabytes
–o	Do not display the buffer adjusted line
–s *n*	Check memory use every *n* seconds
–t	Display a line of totals at the bottom of the output
–V	Show the current version number

EXAMPLES

This Command	Does the Following
`free`	Shows available and used memory in kilobytes.
`free –m`	Shows available and used memory in megabytes.
`free –mot`	Shows available and used memory in megabytes, hides the buffer adjusted line, and displays a line of totals at the bottom.

hcd

hcd *directory*

Changes directories in a mounted Macintosh (HFS) filesystem (see **hmount** in Chapter 7). This command is part of the macutils package, which can be downloaded at `ftp://sunsite.unc.edu/pub/Linux/distributions/debian/source/otherosfs`.

See also **hdir, hls, hmkdir, hpwd, hrmdir.**

hdir

hdir [*directory*]

Displays the contents of a directory in a mounted Macintosh (HFS) filesystem (see **hmount** in Chapter 7). This command is equivalent to **hls** with the **–l** option. It is part of the macutils package, which can be downloaded at `ftp://sunsite.unc.edu/pub/Linux/distributions/debian/source/otherosfs`.

See also **hcd, hpwd.**

hls

hls [option] [*directory*]

Displays the contents of a directory in a mounted Macintosh (HFS) filesystem (see **hmount** in Chapter 7). This command is part of the macutils package, which can be downloaded at `ftp://sunsite.unc.edu/pub/Linux/distributions/debian/source/otherosfs`.

See also **hdir, hpwd.**

OPTIONS

Use This Option	To Do This
–1	Display the output line-by-line.
–a	Show all files and directories, including invisible ones.
–b	Display special characters with escape (backslash) notation rather than with a question mark.
–c	Sort entries by file creation date rather than by file modification date.
–C	Display entries in columnar format with entries sorted vertically.
–d	List directory entries but not their contents.
–f	Do not sort directory contents.

OPTIONS *(CONT.)*

Use This Option	To Do This
–F	Show type of entry. Directories are followed by a colon. Applications are followed by an asterisk.
–i	Show the catalog IDs for each entry.
–l	Display the entries in long format.
–m	Display the entries in a comma-separated list.
–N	Display filenames verbatim without escape characters or question marks.
–q	Replace special and non-printable characters with question marks (default).
–Q	Enclose all filenames in double quotation marks.
–r	Show entries in reverse order.
–R	Show contents of the working directory and all associated subdirectories (recursive display).
–s	Display file sizes in 1K units.
–t	Sort entries by the time of the last modification instead of by name.
–U	Do not sort directory contents.
–w *n*	Set the output width to *n* characters.
–x	Display entries in columnar format, sorted horizontally by rows.

hmkdir

hmkdir [*directory*]

Creates a directory in a mounted Macintosh (HFS) filesystem. This command is part of the macutils package, which can be downloaded at `ftp://sunsite.unc.edu/pub/Linux/distributions/debian/source/otherosfs`.

See also **hrmdir**, **hmount** (Chapter 7).

hpwd

hpwd

Displays the full path to the current directory in a mounted Macintosh (HFS) filesystem (see **hmount** in Chapter 7). This command is part of the macutils package, which can be downloaded at ftp://sunsite .unc.edu/pub/Linux/distributions/debian/source/otherosfs.

See also **hcd, hdir, hls, hmkdir, hrmdir.**

hrmdir

hrmdir [*directory*]

Removes an empty directory in a mounted Macintosh (HFS) filesystem. This command is part of the macutils package, which can be downloaded at ftp://sunsite.unc.edu/pub/Linux/distributions/ debian/source/otherosfs.

See also **hmkdir, hmount** (Chapter 7).

locate

locate [option] [*shell pattern*]

Quickly locates files by searching a database of filenames rather than the actual directory tree. To create the database, use **locatedb**. Unlike **slocate, locate** is not secure because it enables users to view files belonging to other users. For this reason, most distributions now provide **slocate** and symbolically link this command to its newer, more secure alternative. By default, **locate** uses a substring search, so it is not necessary to use wildcards to search for one or more files that contain the specified shell pattern in their filenames. Note that the database does not reflect filesystem changes that have occurred since the system administrator last updated the database. You can use **cron** (see Chapter 12) to update the database automatically at specified intervals.

See also **updatedb.**

NOTE On most Linux distributions, **locate** is a symbolic link to **slocate**, which is a more secure version of this program. Try typing **slocate** at the command prompt to determine whether the more secure version is installed. If so, ignore the command syntax and options discussed here; see **slocate** instead.

OPTIONS

Use This Option	To Do This
–u	Create the **locate** database starting at the root directory (/). You must be logged in as the root user to use this option.
–U *directory*	Create the **locate** database starting at the specified directory. You must be logged in as the root user to use this option.
–e *directory1,directory2,...*	Exclude the specified directories from the **locate** database. You must be logged in as the root user to use this option.
–f *type*	Exclude the specified filesystem type (such as msdos or vfat) from the **locate** database. You must be logged in as the root user to use this option.
–l < **0** | **1** >	Specify the security level: **0** Turns security checks off. **1** Turns security checks on (default).
–n *n*	Limit the number of results displayed to *n* (an integer).
q	Hide nonessential messages.
–r *regular expression*	Search the database using the specified regular expression.

EXAMPLES

This Command	Does the Following:
locate -u	Creates a **slocate** database beginning at the root directory. Requires superuser status (see **su** in Chapter 1).
locate -U /home/suzanne	Creates a **slocate** database beginning at the specified directory. Requires superuser status (see **su** in Chapter 1).
locate jpg	Locates all the files in the **slocate** database that contain the characters *jpg*.

ls

ls [option] [*pattern*]

Lists the files in the current directory in case-sensitive alphabetical order, using a columnar format. If you specify a pattern, this command lists only the files that match a shell pattern (see Chapter 3). In the GNU file utilities commonly provided with Linux distributions, this command is identical to **dir**.

See also **vdir.**

See **dir.**

EXAMPLES

This Command	Does the Following
ls	Lists files and directories in the current directory in case-sensitive alphabetical order.
ls *.doc	Lists only those files with the **.doc** extension.
ls -R *.jpg	Lists all the files with the ***.jpg** extension in the current directory and all associated subdirectories.
ls -Sl	Lists files sorted by size, showing the largest files first.
ls -Shl	Lists files sorted by size, showing the largest files first, and shows sizes in a human-readable form.

EXAMPLES *(CONT.)*

This Command	Does the Following
`ls -tl`, `ls -cl`	Lists files sorted by the time of the last modification, showing most recently modified files first.
`ls -Rtlr *.doc`	Using reverse chronological order (oldest files first), lists all the files in the current directory and all associated subdirectories that have the `*.doc` extension.
`ls -F`	Displays filenames with appended characters that indicate the file type, such as executable (*) or directory (/).

popd

popd [option]

When used without an option, this command removes the top directory from the directory stack (see **dirs**) and makes this directory current. When used with an option, this command removes the specified directory from the stack and makes it current.

OPTIONS

Use This Option	To Do This
+*n*	Cycle the directory stack so that the *n*th directory is at the top
−*n*	Cycle the directory stack so that the *n*th directory from the bottom of the stack is at the top

pushd

pushd [option] [*directory*]

When used without an option or directory specification, this command switches the top two directories on the stack and makes the new top directory current. Specify a directory to add a directory to the top of the stack and make this directory current.

See also **dirs, popd.**

OPTIONS

Use This Option	To Do This
+*n*	Cycle the directory stack so that the *n*th directory is at the top
−*n*	Cycle the directory stack so that the *n*th directory from the bottom of the stack is at the top

EXAMPLES

This Command	Does the Following
pushd /home/suzanne/essays	Adds the specified directory to the top of the stack and switches to this directory.
pushd	Switches the position of the top two directories on the stack and switches to the top directory. You can use this command to switch back and forth between two directories at the top of the stack.

slocate

slocate [option] [*shell pattern*]

Quickly locates files by searching a database of filenames rather than the actual directory tree. Unlike **locate, slocate** is secure because it does not enable users to view files belonging to other users. By default, **slocate** uses a substring search, so it is not necessary to use wildcards to search for one or more files that contain the specified shell pattern in their filenames.

Note that the database does not reflect filesystem changes that have occurred since the system administrator last updated the database. You can use **cron** (see Chapter 12) to update the database automatically at specified intervals.

OPTIONS

Use This Option	To Do This
–u	Create the **locate** database starting at the root directory (/). You must be logged in as the root user to use this option.
–U *directory*	Create the **locate** database starting at the specified directory. You must be logged in as the root user to use this option.
–e *directory1,directory2,...*	Exclude the specified directories from the **locate** database. You must be logged in as the root user to use this option.
–f *type*	Exclude the specified filesystem type (such as msdos or vfat) from the **locate** database. You must be logged in as the root user to use this option.
–l < **0** | **1** >	Specify the security level: **0** Turns security checks off. **1** Turns security checks on (default).
–n *n*	Limit the number of results displayed to *n* (an integer).
–r *regular expression*	Search the database using the specified regular expression.

EXAMPLES

This Command	Does the Following
slocate -u	Creates a **slocate** database beginning at the root directory. Requires superuser status (see **su** in Chapter 1).
slocate -U /home/suzanne	Creates a **slocate** database beginning at the specified directory. Requires superuser status (see **su** in Chapter 1).
slocate jpg	Locates all the files in the **slocate** database that contain the characters *jpg*.

updatedb

updatedb

Updates the **locate** database. If **slocate** is installed, this command is a symbolic link to the **slocate -u** command.

vdir

vdir [option] [*pattern*]

When used without an option or argument, lists the files in the current directory in case-sensitive alphabetical order with a detailed columnar display (equivalent to **dir -l** or **ls -l**). For available options, see **dir**.

See also **ls**.

xargs

xargs [option] [*command* [*initial arguments*]]

Used primarily with piped output from **find**, **xargs** (pronounced "X-args") accepts a list of filenames and runs the specified command on each one. To enable **xargs** to work with filenames containing spaces, be sure to use **find** with the –**print0** option and use **xarg** with the –**0** option.

OPTIONS

Use This Option	To Do This
–**0**, – –**null**	Handle input filenames that contain spaces.
–**x**, – –**exit**	Stop processing if the size specified by the –**s** option is exceeded.
– –**version**	Display the version number.
–**t**, – –**verbose**	Display each command before executing it.
–**P** *n*	Run up to *n* processes simultaneously. The default is 1.
–**l** *n*	Use *n* nonblank input lines per command line. The default is 1.
–**n** *n*	Use *n* arguments per command line. The default is 1.
–**p**, – –**interactive**	Prompt the user to confirm each command before it is executed.
–**r**	Do not run the command if the input is blank.
–**s** *n*	Use no more than *n* characters per command line. The default limit is set to 20K characters.
–**i** *string*	Replace occurrences of *string* in the initial arguments with names read from the standard input. The default is '{} (any name is used for replacement).
– –**help**	Display command options.

EXAMPLES

This Command	Does the Following
`find /usr/doc/ballistic -name *README* -print0	xargs -0	less`	Searches the `/usr/doc/ballistic` directory for all files that contain the string "README" in their filenames, and displays them using **less**.

CHAPTER 5

Managing Files and Directories

$\mathbf{T}$his chapter details the commands used to manage files and directories, including copying, moving, renaming, and deleting files or directories. The commands used to change file ownership and set permissions are also covered.

AT A GLANCE

How Do I	See This Entry	Example
Make sure my files cannot be altered by other users?	**chmod**	chmod o-w
Assign ownership of a file to a different user group?	**chgrp**	chgrp authors proposal.doc
Set the ownership of a file to numeric per-mission mode 755?	**chmod**	chmod 755 welcome.html
Modify a file so that it executes with the set user ID (SUID) bit set?	**chmod**	chmod u+s ballistic
Set the permissions of all the files in the working directory so that the user has read and write privi-leges, group owners have read privileges, and others have no privileges?	**chown**	chmod u=rw,g=r
Change the owner of a file?	**chown**	chown suzanne proposal.doc
Change the owner-ship of all of the files in an entire directory?	**chown**	chown -R suzanne *

AT A GLANCE *(CONT.)*

How Do I	See This Entry	Example
Copy one or more files?	**cp**	`cp -ivb essay1.doc essay1.bak`
Copy an entire directory and all associated subdirectories?	**cp**	`cp -ivbR /home/suzanne/ docs /home/suzanne/backup`
Copy files as symbolic links?	**cp**	`cp -ivbs essay?.doc /home/ suzanne/essays`
Create an alias name (*symbolic link*) for a file that I can place in a different directory?	**ln**	`ln -s essay1.doc /home/ suzanne/essays/first- essay.doc`
View a file's permissions and other attributes?	**ls, stat**	`stat essay1.doc`
Create a new directory?	**mkdir**	`mkdir essays`
Remove an existing empty directory?	**rmdir**	`rmdir big-ideas`
Rename a file?	**mv**	`mv essay1.doc new- essay1.doc`
Move a file to a new location?	**mv**	`mv essay1.doc /home/ suzanne/dead-stuff/ essay1.doc`
Delete a file?	**rm**	`rm essay1.doc`
Delete all the files in the working directory and all associated directories that conform to the specified shell pattern?	**rm**	`rm -R *.tmp`
Delete files so that they can be recovered if the deletion is in error?	**safedelete**	`safedelete essay1.doc`

How Do I	See This Entry	Example
Change a file's time of last access and modification to December 15, 2000?	**touch**	`touch -t 1215073500 essay1.doc`
Change the system default permissions that are automatically assigned to new files?	**umask**	`umask 022`
Find out how many words are in a file?	**wc**	`wc essay1.doc`

File Management Fundamentals

This section provides essential background and reference information for the following topics:

- Block sizes
- File ownership
- Permissions
- Links
- File types
- Date and time expressions

Block Sizes

Several file utilities enable you to select *block size* (file size) display preferences. When viewed in a human-readable form, the following suffixes are used to denote block size multiples.

SPECIFYING BLOCK SIZES

Suffix	Meaning
c	1 character
w	1 word (2 bytes)
b	512-byte block
kD	1,000 bytes
k	Kilobyte (1,024 bytes)
MD	1,000,000 bytes
M	Megabyte (1,048,576 bytes)
GD	1,000,000,000 bytes
G	Gigabyte (1,073,741,824 bytes)
TD	1,000,000,000,000 bytes
T	Terabyte (1,099,511,627,776 bytes)
PD	1,000,000,000,000,000 bytes
P	Petabyte (1,125,899,906,842,624 bytes)
ED	1,000,000,000,000,000,000 bytes
E	Exabyte (1,152,921,504,606,846,976 bytes)
ZD	1,000,000,000,000,000,000,000 bytes
Z	Zettabyte (1,180,591,620,717,411,303,424 bytes)
YD	1,000,000,000,000,000,000,000,000 bytes
Y	Yottabyte (1,208,925,819,614,629,174,706,176 bytes)

File Ownership

Any user who wishes to access a file belongs to one of the four user classes shown in the following table, File Owner Types. By default, the user who creates a file is the file's *owner*. Since most users belong to groups, the file also belongs to the user's group. Members of the group are, in turn, *group owners*. Two other user types are implied: *others* (any user who is neither the owner nor a member of the owner's group) and *all* (all users, including the owner, other members of the owner's group, and others). When working with commands that involve ownership (such as **chown** and **chmod**), you will use the abbreviations shown in the following table.

FILE OWNER TYPES

Abbreviation	Meaning
u	Owner (user)
g	Group
o	Others
a	All

Permissions

Permissions specify the access privileges of the different types of users: owners, groups, and others.

Types of Permissions

The three fundamental permission types are *read* (the file can be read but not altered or deleted), *write* (the file can be altered or deleted), and *execute* (the file can be executed, if it is a program or script).

Permissions can vary for file owners, group users, and others. For example, the file owner may have read and write permission, while group users are restricted to read permission, and others are denied access completely.

Permissions for Directories

For directories, the meaning of permissions differs from that of files: the execute bit (x) controls whether the specified user can list and search the filenames within the directory. To access the contents of a directory, a given user must possess read *and* execute permission. Write permission is required to alter or delete files within the directory.

Setting Permissions

For new files, default permissions are specified systemwide by the **umask** command. These settings can be altered by the system administrator.

To change a file's permissions, you must be the file's owner or the superuser (see **su** in Chapter 1); use the **chown** command to change the permissions. To specify permissions for a given file or group of files, you can use the **chmod** command, which requires that you specify permissions using either of two possible permission description modes: *symbolic* and *numeric*.

Symbolic mode   Permissions use abbreviations to specify permission levels. To set permissions using the symbolic mode, you use abbreviations that stand for the type of owner (see the File Owner Types table in the previous section), the type of permission you are changing (see the Permission Types table in this section), and the action you are performing (see the Actions table in this section). You can add to the existing permissions (chmod o+rw), set the permissions (chmod a=rw), or take away from the existing permissions (chmod o−w).

Numeric mode   Permissions (also called *absolute mode permissions*) use a type of notation in which permission levels are independently specified by each digit of a four-digit number (such as 4755). The right-most digit (0005) specifies the permissions available for others. The next digit (0050) specifies the permissions available for group users, while the third digit from the right (0700) specifies the owner's permissions. The left-most digit (4000) specifies special permissions, including *set user ID* (sets the user's privileges to those of the file's owner upon execution) and set *group user ID* (sets the user's privileges to those of the file's group user upon execution). A third type of special permission saves an image of the program on the system's swap device so that it loads more quickly when it is run. This permission is called the *sticky bit*. For an overview of the basic numeric modes, see the Numeric Mode Overview table. See the Permission Mode Reference table for the symbolic and numeric mode specifications for all possible permission modes, excluding special permissions.

NOTE When specifying permissions using numeric mode, it is not necessary to type leading zeroes.

PERMISSION TYPES

Abbreviation	Type of Permission
r	Read
w	Write
x	Execute
X	Execute only if the file is a directory
s	Set user or group ID on execution (suid or guid)
t	Save program text on swap (sticky bit)
u	Existing user's permissions
g	Existing group users' permissions
o	Existing other users' permissions

ACTIONS

Abbreviation	Action
+	Add the specified permission to the existing permissions
=	Set the permission to the specified level, erasing all existing permissions
−	Remove the specified permission from the existing permissions

NUMERIC MODE OVERVIEW

Use This Mode	To Indicate This Permission
1	Other users may execute (o=x).
2	Other users may write (o=w).
4	Other users may read (o=r).
6 (2 + 4)	Other users may write and read (o=wr).

NUMERIC MODE OVERVIEW *(CONT.)*

Use This Mode	To Indicate This Permission
7 (1 + 2 + 4)	Other users may execute, write, and read (o=xwr).
10	Group users may execute (g=x).
20	Group users may write (g=w).
40	Group users may read (g=r).
60 (20 + 40)	Group users may write and read (g=wr).
70 (10 + 20 + 40)	Group users may write, read, and execute (g=wrx).
100	The file's owner may execute (u=x).
200	The file's owner may write (u=w).
400	The file's owner may read (u=r).
600 (200 + 400)	The file's owner may write and read (u=wr).
700 (100 + 200+ 400)	The file's owner may write, read, and execute (u=wrx).
1000	Save the text image on a swap device.
2000	Set the group ID on execution (g=s).
4000	Set the user ID on execution (u=s).

PERMISSION MODE REFERENCE

Numeric Mode	Symbolic Mode	Permissions as Displayed in File Listings		
		Owner	Group	Others
1	o=x	– – –	– – –	– –x
2	o=w	– – –	– – –	–w–
4	o=r	– – –	– – –	r– –
5	o=rx	– – –	– – –	r–x
6	o=rw	– – –	– – –	rw–
7	o=rwx	– – –	– – –	rwx
10	g=x	– – –	– –x	– – –
11	go=x	– – –	– –x	– –x

PERMISSION MODE REFERENCE *(CONT.)*

Numeric Mode	Symbolic Mode	Permissions as Displayed in File Listings		
12	g=x,o=w	− − −	− −x	−w−
14	g=x,o=r	− − −	− −x	r− −
15	g=x,o=rx	− − −	− −x	r−x
16	g=x,o=rw	− − −	− −x	rw−
17	g=x,o=rwx	− − −	− −x	rwx
20	g=w	− − −	− −w	− − −
21	g=w,o=x	− − −	− −w	− −x
22	go=w	− − −	− −w	−w−
24	g=w,o=r	− − −	− −w	r− −
25	g=w,o=rx	− − −	− −w	r−x
26	g=w,o=rw	− − −	− −w	rw−
27	g=w,o=rwx	− − −	− −w	rwx
40	g=r	− − −	r− −	− − −
41	g=r,o=x	− − −	r− −	− −x
42	g=r,o=w	− − −	r− −	−w−
44	go=4	− − −	r− −	r− −
45	g=r,o=rx	− − −	r− −	r−x
46	g=r,o=rw	− − −	r− −	rw−
47	g=r,o=rwx	− − −	r− −	rwx
50	g=rx	− − −	r−x	− − −
51	g=rx,o=x	− − −	r−x	− −x
52	g=rx,o=w	− − −	r−x	−w−
54	g=rx,o=r	− − −	r−x	r− −
55	go=rx	− − −	r−x	r−x
56	g=rx,o=rw	− − −	r−x	rw−
57	g=rx,o=rwx	− − −	r−x	rwx
60	g=rw	− − −	rw−	− − −
61	g=rw,o=x	− − −	rw−	− −x

PERMISSION MODE REFERENCE *(CONT.)*

Numeric Mode	Symbolic Mode	Permissions as Displayed in File Listings		
62	g=rw,o=w	– – –	rw–	–w–
64	g=rw,o=r	– – –	rw–	r– –
65	g=rw,o=rx	– – –	rw–	r–x
66	go=rw	– – –	rw–	rw–
67	g=rw,o=rwx	– – –	rw–	rwx
70	g=rwx	– – –	rwx	– – –
71	g=rwx,o=x	– – –	rwx	– –x
72	g=rwx,o=w	– – –	rwx	–w–
74	g=rwx,o=r	– – –	rwx	r– –
75	g=rwx,o=rx	– – –	rwx	r–x
76	g=rwx,o=rw	– – –	rwx	rw–
77	go=rwx	– – –	rwx	rwx
100	u=x	– –x	– – –	– – –
101	uo=x	– –x	– – –	– –x
102	u=x,o=w	– –x	– – –	–w–
104	u=x,o=r	– –x	– – –	r– –
105	u=x,o=rx	– –x	– – –	r–x
106	u=x,o=rw	– –x	– – –	rw–
107	u=x,o=rwx	– –x	– – –	rwx
110	ug=x	– –x	– –x	– – –
111	a=x	– –x	– –x	– –x
112	ug=x,o=w	– –x	– –x	–w–
114	ug=x,o=r	– –x	– –x	r– –
115	ug=x,o=rx	– –x	– –x	r–x
116	ug=x,o=rw	– –x	– –x	rw–
117	ug=x,o=rwx	– –x	– –x	rwx
120	u=x,g=w	– –x	– –w	– – –
121	g=w,ou=x	– – x	– –w	– –x

PERMISSION MODE REFERENCE *(CONT.)*

Numeric Mode	Symbolic Mode	Permissions as Displayed in File Listings		
122	u=x,go=w	--x	--w	-w-
124	u=x,g=w,o=r	--x	--w	r--
125	u=x,g=w,o=rx	--x	--w	r-x
126	u=x,g=w,o=rw	--x	--w	rw-
127	u=x,g=w,o=rwx	--x	--w	rwx
140	u=x,g=r	--x	r--	---
141	u=x,g=r,o=x	--x	r--	--x
142	u=x,g=r,o=w	--x	r--	-w-
144	u=x,go=r	--x	r--	r--
145	u=x,g=r,o=rx	--x	r--	r-x
146	u=x,g=r,o=rw	--x	r--	rw-
147	u=x,g=r,o=rwx	--x	r--	rwx
150	u=x,g=rx	--x	r-x	---
151	uo=x,g=rx	--x	r-x	--x
152	u=x,g=rx,o=w	--x	r-x	-w-
154	u=x,g=rx,o=r	--x	r-x	r--
155	u=x,go=rx	--x	r-x	r-x
156	u=x,g=rx,o=rw	--x	r-x	rw-
157	u=x,g=rx,o=rwx	--x	r-x	rwx
160	u=x,g=rw	--x	rw-	---
161	uo=x,g=rw	--x	rw-	--x
162	u=x,g=rw,o=w	--x	rw-	-w-
164	u=x,g=rw,o=r	--x	rw-	r--
165	u=x,g=rw,o=rx	--x	rw-	r-x
166	u=x,go=rw	--x	rw-	rw-
167	u=x,g=rw,o=rwx	--x	rw-	rwx
170	u=x,g=rwx	---	rwx	---
171	u=x,g=rwx,o=x	---	rwx	--x

PERMISSION MODE REFERENCE *(CONT.)*

Numeric Mode	Symbolic Mode	Permissions as Displayed in File Listings		
172	u=x,g=rwx,o=w	--x	rwx	-w-
174	u=x,g=rwx,o=r	--x	rwx	r--
175	u=x,g=rwx,o=rx	--x	rwx	r-x
176	u=x,g=rwx,o=rw	--x	rwx	rw-
177	u=x,go=rwx	--x	rwx	rwx
200	u=w	-w-	---	---
201	u=w,o=x	-w-	---	--x
202	uo=w	-w-	---	-w-
204	u=w,o=r	-w-	---	r--
205	u=w,o=rx	-w-	---	r-x
206	u=w,o=rw	-w-	---	rw-
207	u=x,o=rwx	-w-	---	rwx
210	u=w,g=x	-w-	--x	---
211	u=w,go=x	-w-	--x	--x
212	uo=w,g=x	-w-	--x	-w-
214	u=w,g=x,o=r	-w-	--x	r--
215	u=w,g=x,o=rx	-w-	--x	r-x
216	u=w,g=x,o=rw	-w-	--x	rw-
217	u=w,g=x,o=rwx	-w-	--x	rwx
220	u=w,g=w	-w-	--w	---
221	ug=w,o=x	-w-	--w	--x
222	a=w	-w-	--w	-w-
224	ug=w,o=r	-w-	--w	r--
225	ug=w,o=rx	-w-	--w	r-x
226	ug=w,o=rw	-w-	--w	rw-
227	ug=w,o=rwx	-w-	--w	rwx
240	u=w,g=r	-w-	r--	---
241	u=w,g=r,o=x	-w-	r--	--x

PERMISSION MODE REFERENCE *(CONT.)*

Numeric Mode	Symbolic Mode	Permissions as Displayed in File Listings		
242	u=w,g=r,o=w	–w–	r– –	–w–
244	u=w,go=r	–w–	r– –	r– –
245	u=w,g=r,o=rx	–w–	r– –	r–x
246	u=w,g=r,o=rw	–w–	r– –	rw–
247	u=w,g=r,o=rwx	–w–	r– –	rwx
250	u=w,g=rx	–w–	r–x	– – –
251	u=w,g=rx,o=x	–w–	r–x	– –x
252	uo=w,g=rx,o=w	–w–	r–x	–w–
254	u=w,g=rx,o=r	–w–	r–x	r– –
255	u=w,go=rx	–w–	r–x	r–x
256	u=w,g=rx,o=rw	–w–	r–x	rw–
257	u=w,g=rx,o=rwx	–w–	r–x	rwx
260	u=w,g=rw	–w–	rw–	– – –
261	uo=w,g=rw	–w–	rw–	– –x
262	uo=w,g=rw	–w–	rw–	–w–
264	u=w,g=rw,o=r	–w–	rw–	r– –
265	u=w,g=rw,o=rx	–w–	rw–	r–x
266	u=w,go=rw	–w–	rw–	rw–
267	u=w,g=rw,o=rwx	–w–	rw–	rwx
270	u=w,g=rwx	–w–	rwx	– – –
271	u=w,g=rwx,o=x	–w–	rwx	– –x
272	uo=w,g=rwx	–w–	rwx	–w–
274	u=w,g=rwx,o=r	–w–	rwx	r– –
275	u=w,g=rwx,o=rx	–w–	rwx	r–x
276	u=w,g=rwx,o=rw	–w–	rwx	rw–
277	u=w,go=rwx	–w–	rwx	rwx
400	u=r	r– –	– – –	– – –
401	u=r,o=x	r– –	– – –	– –x

PERMISSION MODE REFERENCE *(CONT.)*

Numeric Mode	Symbolic Mode	Permissions as Displayed in File Listings		
402	u=r,o=w	r– –	– – –	–w–
404	uo=r	r– –	– – –	r– –
405	u=r,o=rx	r– –	– – –	r–x
406	u=r,o=rw	r– –	– – –	rw–
407	u=r,o=rwx	r– –	– – –	rwx
410	u=r,g=x	r– –	– –x	– – –
411	u=r,go=x	r– –	– –x	– –x
412	u=r,g=x,o=w	r– –	– –x	–w–
414	u=r,g=x,o=r	r– –	– –x	r– –
415	u=r,g=x,o=rx	r– –	– –x	r–x
416	u=r,g=x,o=rw	r–	– –x	rw–
417	u=r,g=x,o=rwx	r– –	– –x	rwx
420	u=r,g=w	r– –	– –w	– – –
421	u=r,g=w,o=x	r– –	– –w	– –x
422	u=r,go=w	r– –	– –w	–w–
424	ug=w,o=r	r– –	– –w	r– –
425	ug=w,o=rx	r– –	– –w	r–x
426	ug=w,o=rw	r– –	– –w	rw–
427	ug=w,o=rwx	r– –	– –w	rwx
440	ug=r	r– –	r– –	– – –
441	ug=r,o=x	r– –	r– –	– –x
442	ug=r,o=w	r– –	r– –	–w–
444	ugo=r	r– –	r– –	r– –
445	ug=r,o=rx	r– –	r– –	r–x
446	ug=r,o=rw	r– –	r– –	rw–
447	ug=r,o=rwx	r– –	r– –	rwx
450	u=r,g=rx	r– –	r–x	– – –
451	u=r,g=rx,o=x	r– –	r–x	– –x

PERMISSION MODE REFERENCE *(CONT.)*

Numeric Mode	Symbolic Mode	Permissions as Displayed in File Listings		
452	u=r,g=rx,o=w	r−−	r−x	−w−
454	uo=r,g=rx	r−−	r−x	r−−
455	u=r,go=rx	r−−	r−x	r−x
456	u=r,g=rx,o=rw	r−−	r−x	rw−
457	u=r,g=rx,o=rwx	r−−	r−x	rwx
460	u=r,g=rw	r−−	rw−	−−−
461	u=r,g=rw,o=x	r−−	rw−	−−x
462	u=r,g=rw,o=w	r−−	rw−	−w−
464	u=r,g=rw,o=r	r−−	rw−	r−−
465	u=r,g=rw,o=rx	r−−	rw−	r−x
466	u=r,go=rw	r−−	rw−	rw−
467	u=r,g=rw,o=rwx	r−−	rw−	rwx
470	u=r,g=rwx	r−−	rwx	−−−
471	uo=r,g=rwx	r−−	rwx	−−x
472	u=r,g=rwx,o=w	r−−	rwx	−w−
474	uo=r,g=rwx	r−−	rwx	r−−
475	u=r,g=rwx,o=rx	r−−	rwx	r−x
476	u=r,g=rwx,o=rw	r−−	rwx	rw−
477	u=r,go=rwx	r−−	rwx	rwx
500	u=rx	r−x	−−−	−−−
501	u=rx,o=x	r−x	−−−	−−x
502	u=rx,o=w	r−x	−−−	−w−
504	u=rx,o=r	r−x	−−−	r−−
505	uo=rx	r−x	−−−	r−x
506	u=rx,o=rw	r−x	−−−	rw−
507	u=rx,o=rwx	r−x	−−−	rwx
510	u=rx,g=x	r−x	−−x	−−−
511	u=rx,go=x	r−x	−−x	−−x

PERMISSION MODE REFERENCE *(CONT.)*

Numeric Mode	Symbolic Mode	Permissions as Displayed in File Listings		
512	u=rx,g=x,o=w	r–x	– –x	–w–
514	u=rx,g=x,o=r	r–x	– –x	r– –
515	uo=rx,g=x	r–x	– –x	r–x
516	u=rx,g=x,o=rw	r–x	– –x	rw–
517	u=rx,g=x,o=rwx	r–x	– –x	rwx
520	u=rx,g=w	r–x	– –w	– – –
521	u=rx,g=w,o=x	r–x	– –w	– –x
522	u=rx,go=w	r–x	– –w	–w–
524	u=rx,g=w,o=r	r–x	– –w	r– –
525	uo=rx,g=w	r–x	– –w	r–x
526	u=rx,g=w,o=rw	r–x	– –w	rw–
527	u=rx,g=w,o=rwx	r–x	– –w	rwx
540	u=rx,g=r	r–x	r– –	– – –
541	u=rx,g=r,o=x	r–x	r– –	– –x
542	u=rx,g=r,o=w	r–x	r– –	–w–
544	u=rx,go=r	r–x	r– –	r– –
545	uo=rx,g=r	r–x	r– –	r–x
546	u=rx,g=r,o=rw	r–x	r– –	rw–
547	u=rx,g=r,o=rwx	r–x	r– –	rwx
550	ug=rx	r–x	r–x	– – –
551	ug=rx,o=x	r–x	r–x	– –x
552	ug=rx,o=w	r–x	r–x	–w–
554	ug=rx,o=r	r–x	r–x	r– –
555	a=rx	r–x	r–x	r–x
556	ug=rx,o=rw	r–x	r–x	rw–
557	ug=rx,o=rwx	r–x	r–x	rwx
560	u=rx,g=rw	r–x	rw–	– – –
561	u=rx,g=rw,o=x	r–x	rw–	– –x

PERMISSION MODE REFERENCE *(CONT.)*

Numeric Mode	Symbolic Mode	Permissions as Displayed in File Listings		
562	u=rx,g=rw,o=w	r–x	rw–	–w–
564	u=rx,g=rw,o=r	r–x	rw–	r– –
565	uo=rx,g=rw	r–x	rw–	r–x
566	u=rx,go=rw	r–x	rw–	rw–
567	u=rx,g=rw,o=rwx	r–x	rw–	rwx
570	u=rx,g=rwx	r–x	rwx	– – –
571	u=rx,g=rwx,o=x	r–x	rwx	– –x
572	u=rx,g=rwx,o=w	r–x	rwx	–w–
574	u=rx,g=rwx,o=r	r–x	rwx	r– –
575	uo=rx,g=rwx	r–x	rwx	r–x
576	u=rx,g=rwx,o=rw	r–x	rwx	rw–
577	u=rx,go=rwx	r–x	rwx	rwx
600	u=rw	rw–	– – –	– – –
601	u=rw,o=x	rw–	– – –	– –x
602	u=rw,o=w	rw–	– – –	–w–
604	u=rw,o=r	rw–	– – –	r– –
605	uo=rx	rw–	– – –	r–x
606	uo=rw	rw–	– – –	rw–
607	u=rw,o=rwx	rw–	– – –	rwx
610	u=rw,g=x	rw–	– –x	– – –
611	u=rw,go=x	rw–	– –x	– –x
612	u=rw,g=x,o=w	rw–	– –x	–w–
614	u=rw,g=x,o=r	rw–	– –x	r– –
615	u=rw,o=rx,g=x	rw–	– –x	r–x
616	uo=rw,g=x	rw–	– –x	rw–
617	u=rw,g=x,o=rwx	rw–	– –x	rwx
620	u=rw,g=w	rw–	– –w	– – –
621	u=rw,g=w,o=x	rw–	– –w	– –x

PERMISSION MODE REFERENCE *(CONT.)*

Numeric Mode	Symbolic Mode	Permissions as Displayed in File Listings		
622	u=rw,go=w	rw–	– –w	–w–
624	u=rw,g=w,o=r	rw–	– –w	r– –
625	u=rw,g=w,o=rx	rw–	– –w	r–x
626	uo=rw,g=w	rw–	– –w	rw–
627	u=rw,g=w,o=rwx	rw–	– –w	rwx
640	u=rw,g=r	rw–	r– –	– – –
641	u=rw,g=r,o=x	rw–	r– –	– –x
642	u=rw,g=r,o=w	rw–	r– –	–w–
644	u=rw,go=r	rw–	r– –	r– –
645	u=rw,g=r,o=rx	rw–	r– –	r–x
646	uo=rw,g=r	rw–	r– –	rw–
647	u=rw,g=r,o=rwx	rw–	r– –	rwx
650	u=rw,g=rx	rw–	r–x	– – –
651	u=rw,g=rx,o=x	rw–	r–x	– –x
652	u=rw,g=rx,o=w	rw–	r–x	–w–
654	u=rw,g=rx,o=r	rw–	r–x	r– –
655	a=rx	rw–	r–x	r–x
656	ug=rx,o=rw	rw–	r–x	rw–
657	ug=rx,o=rwx	rw–	r–x	rwx
660	ug=rw	rw–	rw–	– – –
661	u=rw,g=rw,o=x	rw–	rw–	– –x
662	u=rw,g=rw,o=w	rw–	rw–	–w–
664	ug=rw,o=r	rw–	rw–	r– –
665	ug=rw,o=rx	rw–	rw–	r–x
666	a=rw	rw–	rw–	rw–
667	ug=rw,o=rwx	rw–	rw–	rwx
670	u=rw,g=rwx	rw–	rwx	– – –
671	u=rw,g=rwx,o=x	rw–	rwx	– –x

PERMISSION MODE REFERENCE *(CONT.)*

Numeric Mode	Symbolic Mode	Permissions as Displayed in File Listings		
672	u=rw,g=rwx,o=w	rw–	rwx	–w–
674	u=rw,g=rwx,o=r	rw–	rwx	r– –
675	uo=rx,g=rwx	rw–	rwx	r–x
676	uo=rw,g=rwx	rw–	rwx	rw–
677	u=rw,go=rwx	rw–	rwx	rwx
700	u=rwx	rw–	– – –	– – –
701	u=rwx,o=x	rwx	– – –	– –x
702	u=rwx,o=w	rwx	– – –	–w–
704	u=rwx,o=r	rwx	– – –	r– –
705	uo=rx	rwx	– – –	r–x
706	u=rwx,o=rw	rwx	– – –	rw–
707	uo=rwx	rwx	– – –	rwx
710	u=rwx,g=x	rwx	– –x	– – –
711	u=rwx,go=x	rwx	– –x	– –x
712	u=rwx,g=x,o=w	rwx	– –x	–w–
714	u=rwx,g=x,o=r	rwx	– –x	r– –
715	u=rwx,o=rx,g=x	rwx	– –x	r–x
716	u=rwx,o=rw,g=x	rwx	– –x	rw–
717	uo=rwx,g=x	rwx	– –x	rwx
720	u=rwx,g=w	rwx	– –w	– – –
721	u=rwx,g=w,o=x	rwx	– –w	– –x
722	u=rwx,go=w	rwx	– –w	–w–
724	u=rwx,g=w,o=r	rwx	– –w	r– –
725	u=rwx,g=w,o=rx	rwx	– –w	r–x
726	u=rwx,g=w,o=rw	rwx	– –w	rw–
727	uo=rwx,g=w	rwx	– –w	rwx
740	u=rwx,g=r	rwx	r– –	– – –
741	u=rwx,g=r,o=x	rwx	r– –	– –x

PERMISSION MODE REFERENCE *(CONT.)*

Numeric Mode	Symbolic Mode	Permissions as Displayed in File Listings		
742	u=rwx,g=r,o=w	rwx	r– –	–w–
744	u=rwx,go=r	rwx	r– –	r– –
745	u=rwx,g=r,o=rx	rwx	r– –	r–x
746	u=rwx,o=rw,g=r	rwx	r– –	rw–
747	uo=rwx,g=r	rwx	r– –	rwx
750	u=rwx,g=rx	rwx	r–x	– – –
751	u=rwx,g=rx,o=x	rwx	r–x	– –x
752	u=rwx,g=rx,o=w	rwx	r–x	–w–
754	u=rwx,g=rx,o=r	rwx	r–x	r– –
755	u=rwx,go=rx	rwx	r–x	r–x
756	u=rwx,g=rx,o=rw	rwx	r–x	rw–
757	u=rwx,g=rx,o=rwx	rwx	r–x	rwx
760	u=rwx,g=rw	rwx	rw–	– – –
761	u=rwx,g=rw,o=x	rwx	rw–	– –x
762	u=rwx,g=rw,o=w	rwx	rw–	–w–
764	u=rwx,g=rw,o=r	rwx	rw–	r– –
765	u=rwx,g=rw,o=rx	rwx	rw–	r–x
766	u=rwx,go=rw	rwx	rw–	rw–
767	uo=rwx,g=rw	rwx	rw–	rwx
770	ug=rwx	rwx	rwx	– – –
771	ug=rwx,o=x	rwx	rwx	– –x
772	ug=rwx,o=w	rwx	rwx	–w–
774	ug=rwx,o=r	rwx	rwx	r– –
775	ug=rwx,o=rx	rwx	rwx	r–x
776	ug=rwx, o=rw	rwx	rwx	rw–
777	a=rwx	rwx	rwx	rwx

Viewing Permissions

In verbose directory listings (such as that produced by **ls –l**), permissions are shown using a nine-digit symbolic expression, such as the following:

```
rwx r-x r- -
```

From the left, each group of three symbols specifies, respectively, the owner's permissions (read, write, and execute), the group owner's permissions (read and execute), and others' permissions (read). See the Permissions Types table for a complete list of permission types.

See the Permissions Mode Reference table for a complete list of all possible permissions, including their symbolic, numeric, and list display equivalents.

WARNING   Be wary of using the set permissions action (specified by the equals sign) in symbolic mode, as in `chmod o=rw myfile.txt`. This command gives others read and write permission, but it erases all existing permissions and gives the file's owner no access at all!

Links

You can use *links* to create an alias for a file. Linux enables you to use two types of links: hard links and symbolic links. (Symbolic links are also called soft links and symlinks.) Both types of links refer to a destination, called the *target*.

A *hard link* is simply another directory entry for the same underlying file. If two hard links exist for the same underlying file, they are indistinguishable. Should you remove one, the other disappears, as well. You cannot create a hard link to a directory. Also, hard links cannot cross filesystem boundaries.

A *symbolic link* is a file in itself, albeit a very small one. It points to a second file. Symbolic links are safer to use than hard links. If you delete a symbolic link, the deletion does not affect the second file. Soft links are also more convenient because they can cross filesystem boundaries.

File Types

In verbose directory listings (such as those generated by **ls –l**), you will see the following file type symbols, as shown in the File Type Symbols table.

FILE TYPE SYMBOLS

Symbol	Description
–	Plain file
*	Executable (program or script)
/	Directory
equals	Socket
|	FIFO (named pipe)
@	Symbolic link

Date and Time Expressions

Some commands require you to specify a date or time. You can use the following conventions to describe calendar dates, days of the week, and times of day, as shown in the Calendar Dates table.

CALENDAR DATES

Use Any of These Strings	To Specify This Date
2002–09–21 9/21/02 21 September 2002 21 Sept 02 21 Sep 02 Sep 21, 2002 21–sep–02 21sep02	September 21, 2002

DAY OF THE WEEK

Use Any of These Strings	To Indicate
monday, mon	Monday
tuesday, tue	Tuesday
wednesday, wed	Wednesday
thursday, thu	Thursday
friday, fri	Friday
saturday, sat	Saturday

TIME OF DAY

Use Any of These Strings	To Specify This Time
20:02:0	8:02 P.M.
20:02	
8:02pm	
20:02-0500	8:02 P.M. EST

Alphabetical Command Reference

This section details commands for the following purposes:

- Viewing and modifying ownership, permissions, and other file attributes (**chgrp, chmod, chown, mc, lsattr, stat, touch, umask, wc**)

- Copying, moving, renaming, and deleting files (**cp, dd, mc, mv, rm, safedelete, undelete**)

- Creating and maintaining hard and symbolic links (**ln, mc, symlinks**)

- Creating and removing directories (**mc, mkdir, rmdir**)

- Creating special files (**mkfifo, mknod**)

chgrp

chgrp [option] *group file*

Change the ownership of the specified file to the specified group. To specify the group owner, you can supply group names or ID numbers. This command requires superuser status (see **su**, in Chapter 1).

See also **chown.**

OPTIONS

Use This Option	To Do This
–c, – –changes	Display messages only when changes are made
–f, – –silent, – –quiet	Hide messages
–h, –no-dereference	Change symbolic links, not the file to which the symbolic links point
– –help	Display available options
–R, – –recursive	Change ownership in the current directory and all associated subdirectories
– –reference=*filename*	Use the group of the specified reference filename
–v, – –verbose	Display messages concerning all processed files
– –version	Display the version number

EXAMPLES

This Command	Does the Following
`chgrp games puzzle`	Makes the specified group (games) the owner of puzzle.
`chgrp –R authors *.doc`	Makes the specified group (authors) the group owner of all files with the **.doc** extension located in the current directory and all of its associated directories.

chmod

chmod [option] *mode filename*

Changes the permissions settings of the filename to the mode. To specify the mode, you can use symbolic or numeric modes. For more information on mode specifications, see the "Setting Permissions" section. To change permissions for other users' files, superuser status is required (see **su**, in Chapter 1). To view a file's current permissions, use **stat**. To change ownership, use **chown**.

OPTIONS

Use This Option	To Do This
–c, – –changes	Display messages only when changes are made
–f, – –silent, – –quiet	Hide messages
–v, – –verbose	Display messages concerning all processed files
–R, – –recursive	Change permissions in the current directory and all of its associated subdirectories
– –reference=*filename*	Use the mode of the specified reference filename
– –help	Display the available options
– –version	Display the version number

EXAMPLES

This Command	Does the Following
chmod 755 welcome.html	Sets the permissions of the specified file (welcome.html) to numeric permission mode 0755.
chmod u+x ballistic	Increases the permissions of the specified file (ballistic) so that the user can execute the file.
chmod o–w my–doctoral–thesis.doc	Decreases the permissions of the specified file (my–doctoral–thesis.doc) so that others cannot write to the file.

EXAMPLES *(CONT.)*

This Command	Does the Following
chmod u=rw,go=r info.txt	Sets the permissions of the specified file (info.txt) so that the file owner (user) may read and write, but group owners and others are restricted to reading the file.
chmod a=rw *.doc	Sets the permissions of all the files that conform to the specified shell pattern (see Chapter 4) so that all users may read and write to the file.
chmod −R u+rw *	Increases the permissions of all files in the specified directory and, if necessary, in all of its associated subdirectories so that the user has both read and write privileges.
chmod u+s ballistic	Adds the set user ID special permission to the specified executable (ballistic).
chmod u−s ballistic	Removes the set user ID special permission from the specified executable (ballistic).
chmod o+t ballistic	Saves a copy of the program on the swap device so that it loads more quickly.

chown

chown [option] *user* [*.group*] *file*

Change the ownership of the specified file to the specified user. To change the group ownership, type a period after the user name and type the group name or ID with no intervening spaces. To specify owners or groups, you can supply user or group names or ID numbers. This command requires superuser status (see **su** in Chapter 1).

See also **chgrp.**

OPTIONS

Use This Option	To Do This
–c, **– –changes**	Display messages only when changes are made
– –dereference	Change the target's ownership rather than the symbolic link's ownership
–f, **– –silent**, **– –quiet**	Hide messages
–h, –no-dereference	Change symbolic links, not the file to which the symbolic links point
– –help	Display available options
–R, **– –recursive**	Change ownership in the current directory and all of its associated subdirectories
– –reference=_filename_	Use the specified filename's owner and group
–v, **– –verbose**	Display messages concerning all processed files
– –version	Display the version number

EXAMPLES

This Command	Does the Following
`chown suzanne autobiography.doc`	Makes the specified user (suzanne) the owner of **auto-biography.doc**.
`chown suzanne.authors essay1.doc`	Makes the specified user (suzanne) and the specified group (authors) the owners of **essay1.doc**.
`chown -R mike.games *`	Makes the specified user (mike) and the specified group (games) the owners of all files in the current directory and all of its associated subdirectories.

---

cp

cp [option] [_source_] [_destination_]

Copies one source file (_source_) to a destination file (_destination_) or copies multiple source files to a destination that must be an existing directory. When you copy multiple files, you can use a shell pattern to specify the source (see the section "Shell Patterns" in Chapter 4).

See also **dd.**

OPTIONS

Use This Option	To Do This
−a, − −archive	Create archive copies of the files specified by *source* (same as **−dpR**).
−b, − −backup	Make a backup copy of existing destination files that will be deleted by the copying operation.
−d, − −no-dereference	Copy symbolic links as symbolic links rather than copying the files that they point to.
−f, − −force	Remove existing destination files without prompting for conformation.
− −help	Display available options.
−i, − −interactive	Prompt before overwriting existing destination files.
−l, − −link	Create hard links instead of destination files.
−p, − −preserve	Preserve file attributes if possible.
−P *path name*, **− −parents=***path name*	Add the specified directory information to the destination directory for each destination file and create the required subdirectories if necessary.
−r *directory*	Copy the specified directory recursively from the current directory and all of its associated subdirectories. This option attempts to copy FIFOs and special files, as well as regular files. If necessary, this option creates subdirectories in the destination directory.

OPTIONS *(CONT.)*

Use This Option	To Do This
−R	Copy the specified directory recursively, which means copying the current directory and all of its associated subdirectories. This option does not attempt to copy FIFOs and special files. If necessary, this option creates subdirectories in the destination directory.
−s, − −symbolic-link	Create symbolic links instead of copying the files.
−S *extension*, **− −suffix=***extension*	Use the specified extension instead of the default backup suffix, ~, which is appended to filenames.
− −sparse=*type*	Remove blank data from binary files with the specified type of removal: **Auto** Create sparse files if the source file contains sufficient sequences of zero bytes. **Always** Always create sparse files. **Never** Never create sparse files.
−u, − −update	Create the copy only when the source file is newer than the destination file or when the destination file is missing.
−v, − −verbose	Show messages explaining what the command is doing.
− −version	Display the version number.
−V *type*, **− −version-control=***type*	Specify the type of backup suffix to use. Available types are **t, numbered** Numbered backups. **nil, existing** Numbered if numbered backups exist. **never, simple** Always use ~.
−x, − −one-file-system	Perform operations only on the current filesystem.

EXAMPLES

This Command	Does the Following
cp —ivb essay1.doc essay1.bak	Copies the source file named essay1.doc to the destination file named essay1.bak.
cp —ivb *.doc /home/suzanne/backup	Copies all the files in the current directory with the .doc extension to the /home/suzanne/backup directory.
cp —ivbR /home/suzanne/docs /home/suzanne/backup	Copies the specified source directory (/home/suzanne/docs) and all of its associated subdirectories, if any, to the specified destination directory (/home/suzanne/backup).
cp —ivRu /home/suzanne/docs /home/suzanne/backup	Copies the specified source directory (/home/suzanne/docs) and all of its associated subdirectories, if any, to the specified destination directory (/home/suzanne/backup), but only if the source files are newer than the destination files.

dd

dd [option]

Copies a file and performs various conversions at the same time. By default, this command accepts input from the standard input and produces output on the standard output. You must use the **–if** and **–of** options to read from a file and write to a file. To specify bytes in options, such as **–bs**, you can use block size suffixes (see the section "Block Sizes" in this chapter).

See also **cp, install** (Chapter 12).

OPTIONS

Use This Option	To Do This
bs=_bytes_	Specify the size of the input and output bit streams in bytes.
cbs=_bytes_	Specify the number of bytes to convert at a time.
conv=_type_	Perform one or more of the following types of conversions: **ascii** From EBCDIC to ASCII. **ebcdic** From ASCII to EBCDIC. **ibm** From ASCII to alternate EBCDIC. **block** Pad newline-terminated records to the block size specified by **cbs**. **unblock** Replace blank space in **cbs**-sized records with a newline character. **ucase** Convert from lowercase to uppercase. **lcase** Convert from uppercase to lowercase. **notrunc** Do not truncate the output file. **swab** Swap every pair of input bytes. **noerror** Continue even if an error is encountered. **sync** Pad every input block to the size specified by **ibs**.
count=_n_	Copy only _n_ input blocks.
ibs=_bytes_	Read specified bytes at a time.
if=_filename_	Read data from _filename_.
obs=_bytes_	Write specified bytes at a time.
of=_filename_	Write to the file specified by _filename_.
seek=_n_	Skip _n_ **obs**-sized blocks at the start of the output.
skip=_n_	Skip _n_ **ibs**-sized blocks at the start of the input.
– –help	Display available options.
– –version	Display the version number.

EXAMPLE

This Command	Does the Following:
`dd if-message.txt of-` `message-lc.txt conv-ucase`	Converts lowercase text to uppercase.

ln

ln [option] *target* [*link name*]

Creates a hard link to the specified target file. When used with the –s option, this command creates a soft link to the specified target file. If you specify two filenames, this command creates the second file (the *link name*) and links it to the first file (the *target*). If you specify a directory name for the link name, this command creates a link to each file in the specified directory that matches the pattern given in *target*. Note that you cannot create hard links to directories. In addition, you cannot create hard links to files outside the current filesystem. However, you can create symbolic links to directories or files outside the current filesystem. To view and repair symbolic links, use **symlinks**.

WARNING Be aware that different Linux shells handle symbolic links to directories differently. If you create a symbolic link to a directory using bash and then **cd** to the link (instead of the actual directory), **pwd** displays the link name instead of the actual directory. In tcsh, by contrast, **pwd** displays the target directory's name.

OPTIONS

Use This Option	To Do This
–b, – –backup	Make a backup copy of any file that would be overwritten or removed by this command.
–d, –F, – –directory	Create hard links to directories. Requires superuser status.
–f, – –force	Remove existing destination files.
– –help	Show the available options.
–i, – –interactive	Prompt before removing destination files.

OPTIONS *(CONT.)*

Use This Option	To Do This
−n, − −no-dereference	When creating a symlink to a target that is, in turn, a symlink to a directory, treat the target as an ordinary file.
−s, − −symbolic	Create a symbolic link instead of a hard link, which is the default.
−S *extension*, **− −suffix=***extension*	Use the specified extension instead of the default backup suffix, ~, which is appended to filenames.
−v, − −verbose	Display the name of each target before creating the link.
−V *type*, **− −version-control=***type*	Specify the type of backup suffix to use. The available types are **t, numbered** Numbered backups. **nil, existing** Numbered if numbered backups exist. **never, simple** Always use ~.
−x, − −one-file-system	Perform operations only on the current filesystem.
−v, − −version	Show the version number.

EXAMPLES

This Command	Does the Following

`ln /home/suzanne/`
`dissertation.doc /home/`
`suzanne/backup/copy-of-`
`dissertation.doc`
	Creates a hard link between the target file (**/home/suzanne/dissertation**.doc) and the link name (**/home/suzanne/copy-of-dissertation**.doc). These are two names for the same, underlying file. The file is not deleted until *both* filenames are deleted.

EXAMPLES *(CONT.)*

This Command	Does the Following

`ln -s /user/share/icons/`
`icon.xpm /home/suzanne/`
`icon.xpm`
	Creates a symbolic link between the target file (`/usr/share/icons/icon.xpm`) and the link name (`/home/suzanne/icon.xpm`). The link name file is created by this command.

`ln -s /user/share/icons /` `home/suzanne/icons`	Creates a symbolic link between the target directory (`/usr/share/icons`) and the link name (`/home/suzanne/icons`). The link name file is created by this command.

lsattr

lsattr [option] [*file*]

Displays the attributes of files on a second Linux extended filesystem.

See also **stat**.

OPTIONS

Use This Option	To Do This
-a	Show all files, including hidden files
-d	Show directories as if they were files, without showing their contents
-R	List the attributes of directories and all of their associated subdirectories
-V	Display the program version
-v	List file versions

mc

mc [option] [*dir1*] [*dir2*]

Launches Midnight Commander, a text-mode file management utility that is reminiscent of similar utilities developed for MS-DOS. Midnight Commander is easy to use and enables novice Linux users to gain control over all aspects of Linux file management in short order. If you specify *dir1*, the program shows the specified directory in the left panel of the two-panel display. If you specify *dir2*, the program displays the specified directory in the right panel. Its features include mouse support, a two-panel display, shortcut keys (see the Midnight Commander Keyboard Shortcuts table in this section), direct access to a shell command line, command menus, a built-in file viewer, a built-in file editor, and a virtual filesystem (VFS) that enables you to browse **tar** archives, FTP sites, and Samba filesystems.

OPTIONS

Use This Option	To Do This
–a	Disable graphic characters for line drawing.
–b	Display Midnight Commander in black and white.
–c	Force the color mode.
–C *color setting*	Use the specified color setting.
–d	Disable mouse support.
–f	Show search paths for Midnight Commander files.
–k	Reset softkeys to the default on HP terminals when the function keys do not work.
–l *filename*	Save the FTP log to the specified filename.
–P	Quit by printing the last working directory.
–s	Enable the slow terminal mode. Do not use line drawing characters.
–t	Use the value of the TERMCAP variable, if available.
–u	Disable the use of the concurrent shell if this support was compiled into the program.

OPTIONS *(CONT.)*

Use This Option	To Do This
–U	Enable the use of the concurrent shell if this support was compiled into the program.
–v *filename*	Display the specified filename in the file viewer.
–V	Display the current version number.
–x	Force **xterm** mode.

MIDNIGHT COMMANDER KEYBOARD SHORTCUTS

Press This Key	To Do This
\	Untag files in the working directory
Alt + !	Filter the view
Alt + ?	Search for a file
Alt + >	Move the selection bar to the first entry in the panel
Alt + b	In an input field or the command line, move the cursor one word to the left
Alt + c	Change directories
Alt + Enter	Copy the selected entry to the command line
Alt + f	In an input field or the command line, move the cursor one word to the right
Alt + h	Show the history for the current input line
Alt + n	Show the next item in the command history
Alt + p	Show the previous item in the command history
Alt + s	Search for a file in the working directory
Alt + t	Show the next directory listing mode
Alt + Tab	Perform filename, command, variable, username, or host name completion on the command line
Alt + u	Move to the next directory in the history list
Alt + v	Move the selection bar one page up
Alt + v	Move the selection bar to the previous page in the panel
Alt + y	Change to the previous directory in the history list

MIDNIGHT COMMANDER KEYBOARD SHORTCUTS *(CONT.)*

Press This Key	To Do This
Backspace	Delete the previous character
Ctrl + @	Set the mark for cutting
Ctrl + \	Show the directory hotlist
Ctrl + 1	Move the selection bar to the first entry in the panel
Ctrl + a	In an input field or on the command line, move the cursor to the beginning of the line
Ctrl + b	In an input field or on the command line, move the cursor one character to the left
Ctrl + d	Delete the current character
Ctrl + e	In an input field or on the command line, move the cursor to the end of the line
Ctrl + Enter	Copy the selected entry to the command line
Ctrl + f	In an input field or on the command line, move the cursor one character to the right
Ctrl + h	Delete the previous character
Ctrl + i	Switch to the next panel
Ctrl + k	Delete from the cursor to the end of the line
Ctrl + l	Refresh the display
Ctrl + n	Move the selection bar down to the next entry
Ctrl + o	Show the output of the previous command
Ctrl + p	Move the selection bar up to the previous entry
Ctrl + PgDn	Change to the selected directory
Ctrl + PgUp	Change to the parent directory
Ctrl + s	Search for a file in the working directory
Ctrl + t	Tag a file or untag a tagged file
Ctrl + v	Move the selection bar down one page
Ctrl + w	Delete the text between the cursor and the mark (set with Ctrl + @) and store the deletion in the kill buffer
Ctrl + x, c	Change the permissions of the selected file
Ctrl + x, h	Add the working directory to the hotlist

MIDNIGHT COMMANDER KEYBOARD SHORTCUTS *(CONT.)*

Press This Key	To Do This
Ctrl + x, i	Show information related to the selected file in the other panel
Ctrl + x, l	Create a hard link to the selected file
Ctrl + x, o	Change the ownership of the selected file
Ctrl + x, p	Copy the current path name to the command line
Ctrl + x, q	Show a quick view of the selected file in the other panel
Ctrl + x, s	Create a soft link to the selected file
Ctrl + x, t	Copy the tagged files to the command line
Ctrl + y	Yank the deletion back from the kill buffer
Delete	Delete the current character
Down arrow	Move the selection bar down
End	Move the selection bar to the last entry in the panel
F1	Show help for Midnight Commander
F10	Quit Midnight Commander
F2	Activate the menu bar
F3	View the selected file
F4	Edit the selected file
F5	Copy the selected file
F6	Rename or move the selected file
F7	Create a directory
F8	Delete the selected file
Home	Move the selection bar to the first entry in the panel
Insert	Tag a file or untag a tagged file
Keypad +	Tag files in the working directory
PgDn	Move the selection bar to the next page in the panel
PgUp	Move the selection bar to the previous page in the panel
Tab	Switch to the next panel
Up arrow	Move the selection bar up

mkdir

mkdir [option] *directory*

Creates the specified directory. To remove a directory, use **rmdir**.

OPTIONS

Use This Option	To Do This
– –help	Show the available options.
–m *mode*, **– –mode=***mode*	Create the directory with the specified permissions. For information on modes, see the section "Permissions" in this chapter.
–p, **– –parents**	Make parent directories as needed.
– –verbose	Print a message for each directory that is created.
– –version	Show the version number.

EXAMPLES

This Command	Does the Following
mkdir essays	Creates the specified directory (**essays**) within the current directory. If the current directory is /**home/ suzanne**, the created directory is /home/suzanne/**essays**.
mkdir –p essays/english101	Creates the specified directory (**english101**) within the essays directory. If the **essays** directory (the parent directory of **english101**) does not exist, this command creates it.

mkfifo

mkfifo [option] *name*

Creates a pipe with the specified name.

OPTIONS

Use This Option	To Do This
– –help	Show the available options.
–m *mode*, – –**mode**=*mode*	Create the directory with the specified permissions. For information on modes, see the section "Permissions" in this chapter.
– –version	Show the version number.

mknod

mknod [option] *name type*

Creates a special file with the specified name and type, where *type* is p (FIFO), b (block special file), or c (character special file). When this command is used to create a block or character special file, the major and minor device numbers must be supplied. This command is used by system administrators when the system is first set up.

OPTIONS

Use This Option	To Do This
– –help	Show the available options.
–m *mode*, – –**mode**=*mode*	Create the directory with the specified permissions. For information on modes, see the section "Permissions" in this chapter.
– –version	Show the version number.

mv

mv [option] [*source*] [*destination*]

Renames or moves one source file to a destination file or moves multiple source files to a destination that must be an existing directory. When you move multiple files, you can use a shell pattern to specify the source (see the section "Shell Patterns" in Chapter 4).

OPTIONS

Use This Option	To Do This
–b, – –backup	Make a backup copy of the source file before removing it.
–f, – –force	Remove existing destination files without prompting for confirmation.
– –help	Display available options.
–i, – –interactive	Prompt before overwriting existing destination files.
–S *extension*, **– –suffix=***extension*	Use the specified extension instead of the default backup suffix ~, which is appended to filenames.
–u, – –update	Create the copy only when the source file, and not a directory, is newer than the destination file.
–v, – –verbose	Show messages explaining what the command is doing.
– –version	Display the version number.
–V *type*, **– –version-control=***type*	Specify the type of backup suffix to use. The available types are **t, numbered** Numbered backups. **nil, existing** Numbered if numbered backups exist. **never, simple** Always use ~. **none, off** Never make backups.
–x, – –one-file-system	Perform operations only on the current filesystem.

EXAMPLES

This Command	Does the Following
mv –ivb essay1.doc essay1.bak	Renames the source file (`essay1.doc`) to `essay1.bak`.
mv –ivb essay1.doc /home/ suzanne/backup/	Moves the source file (`essay1.doc`) to `/home/suzanne/backup`.

EXAMPLES *(CONT.)*

This Command	Does the Following
mv -ivb essay1.doc /home/suzanne/backup/essay1.bak	Moves the source file (essay1.doc) to /home/suzanne/backup and renames it to essay1.bak.
mv -ivb *.doc /home/suzanne/backup	Moves all the files in the current directory with the .doc extension to the /home/suzanne/backup directory.
mv -iub *.doc /home/suzanne/backup	Moves all the files in the current directory with the .doc extension to the /home/suzanne/backup directory, but only if the source files are newer than the destination files or the destination files do not exist.

rm

rm [option] [*file*]

Removes the specified file. When you copy multiple files, you can use a shell pattern to specify the file (see the section "Shell Patterns" in Chapter 4). When used with the –**R** option, removes directory contents recursively (deletes files in the current directory and all of its associated subdirectories).

OPTIONS

Use This Option	To Do This
–**d**, – –**directory**	Unlink the directory even if it is non-empty. Requires superuser status.
–**f**, – –**force**	Ignore nonexistent files and do not prompt.
– –**help**	Display available options.
–**i**, – –**interactive**	Prompt before overwriting existing destination files.
–**r**, –**R**, – –**recursive**	Remove the contents of the current directory and all associated subdirectories.

OPTIONS *(CONT.)*

Use This Option	To Do This
–v, – –verbose	Show messages explaining what the command is doing.
– –version	Display the version number.

EXAMPLES

This Command	Does the Following
rm −iv essay1.doc	Erases essay1.doc.
rm −iv *.doc	Erases all the files in the current directory that have the .doc extension.
rm −iv *	Erases all the files in the current directory.
rm −R /home/suzanne/junk	Erases the specified directory and all of its associated subdirectories, including any files that these directories contain.

rmdir

rmdir [option] *directory*

Removes the specified directory, but only if it is empty. To remove a directory that contains files, see **rm**.

OPTIONS

Use This Option	To Do This
– –ignore-fail-on-n on-empty	Continue processing even if one or more of the specified directories contains files
–p, – –parents	Remove associated parent directories if they are emptied by the current command
– –verbose	Display messages concerning each directory that is processed
– –help	Display available options

EXAMPLE

This Command	Does the Following
`rmdir /home/suzanne/junk`	Removes the specified directory if it is empty.

safedelete

safedelete [option] *file*

Deletes the specified file to the **safedelete** directory, where it is retained for a specified interval before being deleted permanently. You can use a shell pattern to specify the filename (see the section "Shell Patterns" in Chapter 4). You can use **alias** (see Chapter 3) so that **safedelete** is used instead of **rm**. To recover a deleted file, use **undelete**. If this utility is not included in your Linux distribution, you can obtain the source code from `http://metalab.unc.edu/pub/Linux/utils/shell/`.

See also **undelete**.

OPTIONS

Use This Option	To Do This
–i, – –interactive	Prompt the user before deleting a file
–v, – –verbose	Print the name of each file before deleting it
–f, – –force	Ignore nonexistent files and do not prompt the user
–r, –R, – –recursive	Delete all the files in the current directory and all of its associated subdirectories
– –help	Display command options
– –version	Display the command version

EXAMPLES

This Command	Does the Following
`safedelete my-doctoral-thesis.doc`	Deletes the specified file (`my-doctoral-thesis.doc`).

EXAMPLES *(CONT.)*

This Command	Does the Following
safedelete -R *	Deletes all the files in the current directory and all of its associated subdirectories.

stat

stat *file*

Displays all available information about the specified file, including the size, the number of allocated 512K blocks, the type of file, the permissions (in numeric as well as symbolic modes), the owners, the special permissions (set user ID and set group ID), the inode number, the number of links, the time of its last access, the time of its last modification, and the time of its last change.

symlinks

symlinks [options] *directory*

Displays information about the symbolic links in the specified directory or in the working directory if no directory is specified. This utility can determine the following link characteristics:

Relative link   This type of symbolic link is expressed by means of a relative path name, such as ../books/backup.

Dangling link   This type of link no longer has a target.

Absolute link   This type of symbolic link is expressed by means of an absolute path name, such as /home/suzanne/books/backup.

Messy link   Contains unnecessary slashes or dots in the link information.

Lengthy link   Contains unnecessarily convoluted paths to the target.

Other_fs   These links now reside on a filesystem other than the one on which the target originally resided.

OPTIONS

Use This Option	To Do This
−c	Convert absolute path names to relative path names
−d	Remove dangling links
−r	Examine symbolic links within the working directory and all of its associated subdirectories
−s	Shorten lengthy links
−v	Show all symbolic links, including relative links, which are not shown by default

touch

touch [option] *filename*

When used without an option, changes the time of the last access or modification of the specified filename to the current time. You can specify other times by using options. You can specify two or more files by using a shell pattern (see the section "Shell Patterns" in Chapter 4). If the specified filename does not exist, this command creates the file. When you change the date and time with the −t option, use the format *mmddhhmm[yy]*. For example, 0521073002 corresponds to 7:30 AM on May 21, 2002. When you change the date and time with the −d option, you can use any of the valid date and time formats listed in the section "Date and Time Expressions" earlier in this chapter.

OPTIONS

Use This Option	To Do This
−a, **− −time=atime**, **− −time=access**, **− −time=use**	Change the access time but no other times.
−c, **− −nocreate**	Do not create any files.

OPTIONS *(CONT.)*

Use This Option	To Do This
–d *string*, **– –date=***string*	Use the specified string instead of the current time. For *string,* you can use any of the valid date or time formats listed in the "Date and Time Expressions" section in this chapter.
–m, – –time=mtime, – –time=modify	Change the modification time but no other times.
–r *filename,* **– –reference** *filename*	Use the times of the specified filename instead of the current time.
–t *time*	Use the specified time instead of the current time. Specify the time using the format [[cc]yy]mmddhhmm.[ss].
– –time=*type*	Set the specified type of time, using the following types: **access**, **atime** access time **modify**, **mtime** modification time
– –help	Display available options.
– –version	Display the version number.

EXAMPLES

This Command	Does the Following
touch newfile.txt	Creates a file with the specified filename (newfile.txt).
touch –d="05/21/04" newfile.txt	Sets the access and modification times of newfile.txt to May 21, 2004.
touch –t 200405211427 newfile.txt	Sets the access and modification times of newfile.txt to May 21, 2004, 2:27 PM.
touch – –time=atime –t 200405211427 newfile.txt	Sets the access time of newfile.txt to May 21, 2004, but leaves the time of last modification alone.
touch *	Changes the access and modification times of all files in the working directory to the current date and time.

umask

umask [option] [*nnn*]

Displays or sets the *file creation mask*, the permissions that are automatically applied to new files. To determine the file creation mask, you specify a three-digit number, such as 022. This number is subtracted from the highest possible permission level, 777. A umask of 022 generates a permission level of 755, which is equivalent to symbolic mode u=rwx, g=rx, o=rx.

OPTION

Use This Option	To Do This
–S	Display the current file permission list using the symbolic mode

undelete

undelete [option] [*filename*]

Restores files deleted with the **safedelete** command. Undeleted files are returned to their original location, and all original attributes (including permissions and timestamps) are restored. To specify the filename, you can use wildcards (* and ?). When the list of deleted files appears, you can use the commands (For the **undelete** commands, see the Commands table in this section). If this utility is not included in your Linux distribution, you can obtain the source code from http://metalab.unc.edu/pub/Linux/utils/shell/.

See also **safedelete**.

OPTIONS

Use This Option	To Do This
–i, – –info	Display information about the file.
–l, – –list	Display a list of **safedeleted** files that can be restored.

OPTIONS *(CONT.)*

Use This Option	To Do This
–f, – –file	Show the **safedelete** filename of each **safedeleted** file. Must be used with **–l**.
–p *shell pattern*, **– –pattern** *shell pattern*	Search for **safedeleted** files that conform to the specified shell pattern (see the section "Shell Patterns" in Chapter 4). You must enclose the pattern in double quotation marks.
–s, – –subdir	Scan subdirectories for filenames matching the specified pattern. Must be used with **–p**.

COMMANDS

This Command	Does the Following
a	Selects all.
d	Moves the selection bar down.
Down arrow	Moves the selection bar down.
i	Displays information about the selected file.
n	**Undeletes** the selected file to a new filename or directory.
q	Quits **undelete**.
r	Removes the selected file from the display.
s	**Undeletes** the selected file.
u	Moves the selection bar up.
Up arrow	Moves the selection bar up.

WC

wc [option] [*filename*]

Displays line, word, and character counts for the specified filename. You can use a shell pattern (see Chapter 4) to specify more than one file; if you do, you will see a line-by-line listing for each matching file and a total for all the files.

OPTIONS

Use This Option	To Do This
–c, – –bytes, – –chars	Show the character count only
– –help	Show the available options
–L, – –max-line-length	Show the length of the longest line in the file
–l, – –lines	Show the line count only
– –version	Show the version number
–w, – –words	Show the word count only

EXAMPLES

This Command	Does the Following
`wc essay1.txt`	Shows the line, word, and character count for the specified file (`essay1.txt`).
`wc –w essay1.txt`	Shows the word count only for the specified file (`essay1.txt`).
`wc *.txt`	Shows the line, word, and character counts for all the `*.txt` files in the working directory and provides totals.

CHAPTER 6

Archiving, Encoding, Compressing, and Encrypting Files

This chapter describes the Linux utilities you can use to *archive* files (place two or more files into a single file), *compress* files (reduce the size of files so that they take up less disk space), *encode* files (convert binary files to ASCII files so that they can be transmitted over the Internet), and *encrypt* files (scramble file contents so that the files cannot be read by anyone other than their intended recipients).

Some of the utilities included in this chapter may not be installed on your system. See the Introduction for information on obtaining these utilities from Internet download sites.

AT A GLANCE

How Do I	See This Entry	Example
Compress a file using a compression method that yields the maximum reduction in size?	**bzip2**, **gzip**, **zip**	gzip --best massivefile.txt, bzip2 -9 massivefile.txt, zip -9 massivefile.txt
Extract from a backup archive only those files that meet a shell pattern that I specify?	**cpio**	cpio -iv '*.doc' < archive.cpio
Extract files from a backup archive and write them to their original locations in the directory structure?	**cpio**	cpio- ivd < archive.cpio
Make a backup copy of all the files in my home directory?	**cpio**	find /home/suzanne -print -depth | cpio -ov > home-directory.cpio
Make a backup archive of all the files in the working directory?	**cpio**	ls | cpio -ov > this_directory

AT A GLANCE *(CONT.)*

How Do I	See This Entry	Example
Create a key pair (public key and secret key) for encrypting files and e-mail messages?	**gpg**	`gpg --gen-key`
Compress all the files in the specified directory and all its associated subdirectories?	**gzip**	`gzip -r /home/suzanne/ documents`
Encrypt a file so that no one can read it unless they know the pass-phrase and compress it so that it takes up the least possible storage space?	**mcrypt**	`mcrypt -uz mysecrets.txt`
Create a **tar** archive containing all the files in my home directory that have the `*.sdw` extension?	**tar**	`find /home/suzanne -name '*.sdw' -print	xargs tar -cvf backup.tar`
Update an existing **tar** archive by adding only those files that are not already present in the archive?	**tar**	`tar -uvf backup.tar /home/suzanne`
Extract files from a compressed tarball (`*.tgz` or `*.tar.gz`) that I downloaded from the Internet?	**tar**	`tar -xvzf kdebase.tgz`

Determining Which Utility to Use

This section discusses the following:

- Selecting a utility for archiving, compressing, encoding, or encrypting files
- Selecting a utility for decoding, decompressing, decrypting, or extracting files

Selecting the Right Utility for Input Files

The following table lists the preferred utilities for archiving, compressing, encoding, or encrypting your files. Where two utilities are listed, the first has the edge in users' preferences.

UTILITIES FOR INPUT FILES

Purpose	Preferred Utility
Make a file available to Macintosh users.	**binhex**
Encode a file so that it can be transferred on an ASCII-only network, such as the Internet.	**mimencode, uuencode**
Compress files to their smallest possible size.	**bzip2**
Archive files for backup purposes.	**cpio, tar**
Encrypt a file for exchange via the Internet or e-mail.	**gpg**
Encrypt a file for local storage and retrieval.	**mcrypt, gpg**
Archive files for easy exchange.	**tar, cpio**
Make a compressed file available for MS-DOS or Windows users.	**zip**

Selecting the Right Utility for Output Files

To work with archived, compressed, encoded, or encrypted files, you need to use a utility that knows how to deal with these file types. Generally, you can determine the file type by examining the file's suffix (extension). The following table lists the suffixes that utilities automatically append to files after processing. You can also use the **file** command (see Chapter 4) to determine the content of a file.

DEFAULT SUFFIXES

To Work with Output Files with This Suffix	Use This
.bin	**macunpack**
.bz2	**bunzip2**
.enc	**mdecrypt**
.gpg	**gpg**
.hqx	**hexbin**
.tar	**tar**
.tar.gz	**gunzip, tar**
.tgz	**gunzip, tar**
.uue	**uudecode**
.z	**gunzip**
.Z	**uncompress**
.zip	**unzip**

Alphabetical Command Reference

This section details commands for the following tasks:

- Archiving files (**cpio, tar**)

- Compressing and decompressing files (**bzip2, bzip2recover, bunzip2, compress, gunzip, gzexe, gzip, unarj, uncompress, unzip, zip, zipnote, zipinfo, zipsplit, zforce, znew**)

- Encoding and decoding files (**binhex, hexbin, macunpack, mimencode, uudecode, uuencode**)

- Encrypting and decrypting files (**gpg, mcrypt, mdecrypt**)

binhex

binhex [option] *filename*

Encodes the specified filename using the BinHex format (commonly used on Macintosh systems). If the filename is a directory name, the utility works recursively: It encodes all the files in the specified directory and all of its associated subdirectories. By default, the program routes output to the standard output. Use output redirection to write the output to disk. This utility is part of the Macutils package, available for download at `metalab.unc.edu/pub/linux/utils/compress`.

OPTIONS

Use This Option	To Do This
–c *creator*	Mark the file with the specified creator (used with the **–r**, **–d**, **–v**, or **–V**)
–d	Create Macintosh text files with the creator MACA and the type TEXT
–H	Display available options
–i	Provide information about the files but do not process
–l	List files and directories as they are processed
–q	Confirm each file before processing
–r	Create Macintosh resource files with the creator RSED and the type RSRC
–t *type*	When used with **–d** or **–r**, specify the file type with *type*
–u, **–U**	Create Macintosh text files with the creator MACA and the type TEXT, but do not edit line feed characters
–V	Display the program version

bunzip2

bunzip2 [option] *filename*

Decompresses the specified filename using a sophisticated algorithm that is up to 30 percent faster than that used by **gzip**. For *filename*, you can use a shell pattern (see the section "Shell Patterns" in Chapter 4) or a space-separated list of files. By default, **bunzip2** does not overwrite existing output files. Use the – –**force** option to override this setting. However, the program deletes input files by default (use – –**keep** to override this setting) and writes the compressed file with the .bz2 extension.

Use **bzip2** to compress files using the same algorithm. Use **bzip2recover** to recover data from damaged **bzip2** files.

See also **bzcat** (Chapter 8).

OPTIONS

Use This Option	To Do This
– –	Treat all subsequent arguments as filenames. This option enables you to work with files beginning with a dash.
–c, – –stdout	Route output to the standard output.
–c, – –compress	Force **bunzip2** to compress the file. This is the same as running **bzip2**.
–f, – –force	Force overwrite of output files.
–k, – –keep	Keep the input files. Normally, they are deleted.
–L, – –license, –V, – –version	Display the software version, license terms, and conditions.
–q – –quiet	Suppress most program messages, except those concerning input and output errors.
–s – –small	Minimize memory usage during compression, at the cost of compression speed.
–t, – –test	Test the files to see whether they are valid and decompressable.
–v, – –verbose	Display messages as each file is processed.

EXAMPLES

This Command	Does the Following
bunzip2 kdeapp.tar.bz2	Decompresses the specified file.
bunzip2 --keep kdeapp.tar.bz2	Decompresses the specified file without deleting the input file.

bzip2

bzip2 [option] *filename*

Compresses the specified filename using a sophisticated algorithm that is up to 30 percent faster than that used by **gzip**. For filename, specify the name of the file or files to be archived. You can use a shell pattern (see the section "Shell Patterns" in Chapter 4) or a space-separated list of files. By default, **bzip2** does not overwrite existing output files. (Use the – –**force** option to override this setting.) However, the program deletes input files by default (use – –**keep** to override this setting) and writes the compressed file with the .bz2 extension.

Use **bunzip2** to decompress files compressed with **bzip2**. Use **bzip2recover** to recover data from damaged **bzip2** files.

OPTIONS

Use This Option	To Do This
– –	Treat all subsequent arguments as file-names, which enables you to work with files beginning with a dash.
–1, –2, –3, –4, –6, –7, –8, –9	Set the block size to the specified number times 100,000 bytes. The default is 100,000 bytes. If you have sufficient RAM, try using **–2** or **–3** to improve **bzip2**'s performance.

OPTIONS *(CONT.)*

Use This Option	To Do This
−c, − −stdout	Route output to the standard output.
−d, − −decompress	Force **bzip2** to decompress the file. This is the same as running **bunzip2**.
−f, − −force	Force the overwrite of output files.
−k, − −keep	Keep the input files. Normally, they are deleted.
−L, − −license, −V, − −version	Display the software version, license terms, and conditions.
−q − −quiet	Suppress most program messages, except those concerning input and output errors.
−s − −small	Minimize memory usage during compression, at the cost of compression speed.
−t, − −test	Test the files to see whether they are valid and decompressable.
−v, − −verbose	Display messages as each file is processed.

EXAMPLES

This Command	Does the Following
`bzip2 database.dat`	Compresses the specified file (`database.dat`).
`bzip2 --keep database.dat`	Compresses the specified file (`database.dat`) without overwriting the input file.

bzip2recover

bzip2recover *filename*

Attempts to recover data from a damaged file compressed with **bzip2**. If the file contains any blocks with salvageable data, each block is written to a file with a name such as rec0001file.bz2, rec0002file.bz2, etc.

compress

compress [option] *filename*

Compresses the specified filename using the LZW compression algorithm. You can specify the filename by using a shell pattern (see the section "Shell Patterns" in Chapter 4) or by using a space-separated list. By default, the program replaces each input file with a compressed file that has the .Z suffix. To decompress .Z files, use **uncompress** or **gunzip**. Use of this utility is discouraged because the underlying compression algorithm is patented.

TIP   Use **znew** to recompress .Z files to the patent-free **gzip** format (.gz).

See also **bzip2, zip.**

OPTIONS

Use This Option	To Do This
–f	Overwrite files without asking for confirmation.
–c	Write to the standard output.
–r	Compress files in the working directory and all of its associated subdirectories.
–V	Show the version number.
–b	Specify the maximum number *(n)* of bits to use for compression. The valid range is 9 through 16.

cpio

cpio –o [option] [< *name list*] [> *archive*]

cpio –i [option] [*shell pattern*] [< *archive*]

cpio –p [option] *directory < name-list*

Creates archives or extracts files from archives; an additional mode copies files from one directory tree to another. In contrast to **tar**, this command uses the standard input and standard output by default; therefore, you must use a file or pipe to provide the program with a list of filenames (*name list*) to work with. Use output redirection to specify where the output should go.

This utility has three distinct command modes.

Copy-out mode In the copy-out mode (**cpio –o**), **cpio** creates the specified archive from the name list. Because the program routes output to the standard output (display) by default, you should use output redirection to create the archive, which can be indicated by a file or device name. The **find** command (see Chapter 4) is typically used to generate the name list.

Copy-in In the copy-in mode (**cpio –i**), **cpio** uses the specified archive as input and extracts the files. You can use a shell pattern (see the section "Shell Patterns" in Chapter 4) to extract only those files that match criteria that you specify. The files are restored to their original directory locations, but this works only if the original directories still exist. If they do not, use the **–d** option to make the needed directories. This is not done by default. The utility does not overwrite existing files, or files with the same or newer dates than archived files, unless you use the **–u** option.

Pass-through mode In the pass-through mode (**cpio –p**), the utility copies an entire directory tree to the specified directory. As with the copy-out mode, you can use the **find** command (see Chapter 4) to create the name list.

OPTIONS

Use This Option	To Do This
–a, – –reset-access-time	Do not adjust the files' access timestamps when they are read. Modes: Copy-out, pass-through.
–A, – –append	Append to an existing archive that is a disk file. Use with **–O**. Mode: Copy-out only.
–b, – –swap	Convert data between big-endian and little-endian data representation formats. Mode: Copy-in only.
–B	Set the block size to 5120 bytes. The default is 512 bytes. Modes: Copy-out, copy-in.
– –block-size=n	Set the block size to n, where n is a multiple of 512. Modes: Copy-out, copy-in.
–c	Use the portable ASCII storage format. Modes: Copy-out, copy-in.
–C n, **– –io-size=**n	Set the block size to n bytes. Modes: Copy-out, copy-in.
–d, – –make-directories	Create needed directories. Modes: Copy-in, pass-through.
–E *filename*, **– –pattern-file=***filename*	Read filename patterns from the specified filename. Mode: Copy-in only.
–f, – –nonmatching	Copy only those files that do not match any of the specified patterns. Mode: Copy-in only.
–F *filename*, **– –file=***filename*	Use the specified filename as the archive.
– –force-local	Do not use an archive on a non-local host. Modes: Copy-out, copy-in.

OPTIONS *(CONT.)*

Use This Option	To Do This
–H *string*, **– –format=***string*	Use the archive format specified by *string*. In copy-in mode, the format is automatically detected. In copy-out mode, the default format is **bin**. Modes: Copy-out, copy-in. Available options: **bin** Binary data storage format for **cpio** (obsolete). **crc** SVR4 portable format with CRC checksum. **hpbin** HP–UX cpio binary format (obsolete). **hpodc** HP–UX portable format. **newc** SVR4 portable format. **odc** POSIX.1 portable format (obsolete). **tar** Obsolete **tar** format. **ustar** POSIX.1 **tar** format (compatible with GNU tar).
–i, **– –extract**	Use the copy-in mode.
–I *filename*	Use the specified filename instead of the standard input. Mode: Copy-in.
–l, **– –link**	Create symbolic links instead of copying the files. Mode: Pass-through.
–L, **– –dereference**	Do not copy symbolic links; instead, copy the files they point to. Mode: Pass-through.
–m, **– –preserve-modification-time**	Do not alter the file's modification timestamps. Modes: Copy-out, pass-through.

OPTIONS *(CONT.)*

Use This Option	To Do This
–M *string*, **– –message=***string*	When the end of a media volume is reached, display *string* to prompt the user to insert the next volume. Modes: Copy-out, copy-in.
–n, **– –numeric-uid-gid**	Show the user and group ownership using numeric IDs. Modes: Copy-in, pass-through.
– –no-absolute-filenames	Create all files in the working directory, even if the filenames contain path information. Mode: Copy-in.
– –no-preserve-owner	Do not change the file's ownership. Modes: Copy-in, pass-through.
–o, **– –create**	Use the copy-out mode.
–O *filename*	Use the specified filename instead of the standard output. Mode: Copy-out.
– –only-verify-crc	Verify the cyclic redundancy check results for each file in the archive. Do not extract the files. Mode: Copy-in.
–p, **– –pass-through**	Use the pass-through mode.
– –quiet	Do not display messages. Modes: Copy-in, copy-out, pass-through.
–r, **– –rename**	Rename files interactively. Mode: Copy-in only.
–R [*user*][**:,**][*group*], **– –owner** [*user*][**:,**][*group*]	Change file ownership to the specified user or group, or both. Requires superuser status (see **su** in Chapter 1). You can use a period instead of a colon to separate the user and group. If you use a separator but do not name a group, the group ownership is set to the user's primary group. Modes: Copy-in, pass-through.

OPTIONS *(CONT.)*

Use This Option	To Do This
–s, – –swap–bytes	Swap the bytes of each pair of bytes. Mode: Copy-in.
–S, – –swap-halfwords	Swap the half words of each word. Mode: Copy-in.
– –sparse	Use the sparse file format to reduce the size of files with large blocks of zeroes. Modes: Copy-out, pass-through.
–t, – –list	Display a list of filenames instead of copying the files. Modes: Copy-out, copy-in, pass-through.
–u, – –unconditional	Replace all existing files without confirmation. Modes: Copy-in, pass-through.
–v, – –verbose	Display filenames while they are processed. Modes: Copy-out, copy-in, pass-through.
–V – –dot	Display a progress bar that uses dots to show each file that is processed. Modes: Copy-out, copy-in, pass-through.
– –version	Display the version number. Modes: Copy-in, copy-out, pass-through.

EXAMPLES

This Command	Does the Following
`ls	cpio –ov >` `my_directory`	Creates an archive with the specified filename (`this–directory.cpio`) that contains all the files in the working directory.

EXAMPLES *(CONT.)*

This Command	Does the Following
`find /home/suzanne -print -depth | cpio -ov > home-directory.cpio`	Creates an archive with the specified filename (`home-directory.cpio`) that contains all the files in the specified home directory and all of its associated subdirectories.
`cpio -iv < archive.cpio`	Extracts all the files from the specified archive and writes them to their original directory locations, if those directories still exist; otherwise, the files are placed in the working directory.
`cpio- ivd < archive.cpio`	Extracts all the files from the specified archive and writes them to their original directory locations. If the directories no longer exist, creates them.
`cpio -iv '*.doc' < archive.cpio`	Extracts all the files with the .doc extension from the specified archive.

crypt

See **mcrypt**.

gpg

gpg [option] *command*

Encrypts and decrypts data using GNU Privacy Guard, a patent-free, GPL-licensed version of Pretty Good Privacy (PGP). This program uses public key encryption technology to create a *key pair*, consisting of a *secret key* (which you must safeguard) and a *public key* (which you can give freely to others). Your correspondents can encrypt messages to you using your public key. These messages cannot be decrypted without your secret key. Due to the nature of public-key encryption, you must possess not only your own secret and public keys but also the public keys of others. For this reason, you must maintain a *key ring* that includes the public keys of your correspondents. In addition to its encryption and decryption capabilities, GNU Privacy Guard enables you to create *digital signatures*, which enable your correspondents to determine whether a given message likely originated from you and whether it was altered while en route.

GNU Privacy Guard relies on a *Web of Trust* model, in which you assign confidence levels to others' signatures; although you will most commonly use GUI-based utilities, such as Geheimnis (a KDE front end for GNU Privacy Guard) or GPG-compatible e-mail programs. To use GNU Privacy Guard in the text-only mode, you must specify one of the commands listed in this section (see the Commands table for this entry). To obtain a copy, visit http://www.gnupg.org.

See also **mcrypt**.

OPTIONS

Use This Option	To Do This
−a, − −armor	Create ASCII armored output.
− −always-trust	Skip key validation and trust all keys. Use this option only if you are using an external validation scheme.
− −batch	Do not allow interactive commands.
− −charset *encoding*	Use the specified encoding as the default character set and convert to UTF-8 encoding. Encoding options are iso-8859-1, iso-8859-2, and koi8-r.
− −cipher-algo *algorithm*	Use the specified algorithm. To see a list of supported algorithms, use **gpg − −version**.
− −comment *string*	Include the specified string in cleartext digital signatures.
− −completes-needed *n*	Specify the number (*n*) of trusted users needed to introduce a new signature. The default is 1.

OPTIONS *(CONT.)*

Use This Option	To Do This
– –compress-algo *algorithm*	Use the specified compression algorithm. You can choose from the following options: 1 (zlib version used by PGP) or 2 (RFC 1950 compression). The default is 2.
– –default-comment	Use the default comment instead of the one specified by **– –comment**.
– –default-key *user ID*	Use the specified user ID for digital signatures. Otherwise, the default is the first user found in the secret key ring.
– –default-recipient *user ID*	Use the specified user ID as the default recipient (overridden by **– –recipient**).
– –default–recipient-self	Use the first key in the secret key ring as the default recipient if the **– –recipient** option is not used.
– –digest-algo *algorithm*	Use the specified algorithm for the message digest instead of the default, OpenPGP-compliant 160-bit hash.
– –disable-cipher-algo *algorithm*	Do not use the specified algorithm. To see a list of available algorithms, use **– –version**.
– –disable-pubkey-algo *algorithm*	Do not use the specified algorithm as a public key algorithm. To see a list of available algorithms, use **– –version**.
– –emit-version	Write the version string in cleartext digital signatures.
– –encrypt-to *user ID*	Encrypt the data for the specified user ID but do not perform trust checking.

OPTIONS *(CONT.)*

Use This Option	To Do This
– –escape-from-lines	Keep e-mail programs from making changes in cleartext signatures.
– –fast-list-mode	Improve list mode performance by omitting blank portions.
– –force-v3-sigs	Force version 3 digital signatures.
– –homedir *directory*	Use the specified directory instead of the default (~/.gnupg).
– –honor-http-proxy *URL*	Use the specified URL as a proxy server to access the keyserver.
–i, – –interactive	Prompt before overwriting any files.
– –keyring *filename*	Add the specified filename to the list of key rings.
– –keyserver *URL*	Use the specified URL to access a keyserver. This option is used with **– –send-keys**. To see a list of key-servers, use **host –l pgp.net grep wwwkeys**.
– –load-extension *module name*	Load the extension module with the specified module name.
– –lock-multiple	Release the locks every time a lock is no longer needed.
– –lock-once	Lock the databases the first time a lock is requested and do not release the lock until the process terminates.
– –logger-fd *filename*	Write log output to the specified filename instead of to the standard error output.
– –marginals-needed *n*	Set the number (*n*) of marginally trusted users required to introduce a new key signer. The default is 3.
– –max-cert-depth *n*	Set the maximum depth (*n*) of a certification chain. The default is 5.

OPTIONS *(CONT.)*

Use This Option	To Do This
–N, – –notation-data name=value	Put the name value pair into the digital signature as notation data.
– –no	Answer no to most questions in interactive mode.
– –no-armor	Assume that the input data is not in ASCII armored format.
– –no-batch	Disable batch mode if enabled from the configuration file.
– –no-comment	Skip writing comment packets.
– –no-default-keyring	Do not add the default key rings to the list of key rings.
– –no-default-recipient	Clear **– –default-recipient** and **– –default-recipient-self** if these options were enabled by a config- uration file.
– –no-encrypt-to	Disable the use of all **– –encrypt-to** keys.
– –no-greeting	Suppress the initial copyright message.
– –no-options	Suppress the use of an options file.
– –no-secmem-warning	Suppress the warning about using insecure memory.
– –not-dash-escaped	Use cleartext digital signatures for patch files.
– –no-verbose	Suppress program messages.
– –no-version	Omit the version string in cleartext digital signatures.
–o *filename*, **– –output file** *filename*	Write output to the specified filename.
– –openpgp	Conform to OpenPGP standards.
– –options *filename*	Read options from the specified filename.

OPTIONS *(CONT.)*

Use This Option	To Do This
−q, **− −quiet**	Suppress program messages.
−r *user ID*, **− −recipient** *user ID*	Encrypt for the specified user ID.
− −rfc1991	Conform to PGP 2.*x*.
− −s2k-cipher-algo *algorithm*.	Use the specified *algorithm* to protect secret keys. The default cipher is BLOWFISH.
− −s2k-digest-algo *algorithm*	Use the specified algorithm as the digest algorithm used to mangle the passphrases. The default algorithm is RIPEMD-160.
− −s2k-mode *n*	Use the password mangling method specified by *n*. You can use the following: **0** Plain passphrase. **1** Adds a salt to the passphrase. **3** Iterates the process a couple of times.
− −secret-keyring *filename*	Add the specified filename to the list of secret key rings.
− −set-filename *string*	Use *string* as the name of file stored in messages.
− −skip-verify	Skip the digital signature verification step.
− t,**− −textmove**	Use text mode for PGP.
− −throw-keyid	Do not put the key ID into encrypted packets.
−u, **− −local-user** *user ID*	Use the specified user ID.
− −utf8-strings	Use UTF-8 encoded text for command arguments.
−v, **− −verbose**	Show all available options.
− −version	Show the version number.
− −warranty	Show the license information.

OPTIONS *(CONT.)*

Use This Option	To Do This
– –with-colons	Display key listings delimited by colons.
– –with-key-data	Display key listings delimited by colons and print the public key data.
– –yes	Answer yes to most questions.
–z *n*	Set compression level to *n,* where *n* is a number from 0 (disables compression) to 9 (maximum compression).
– –no-utf8-strings	Use the character encoding specified by the **– –charset** option.

COMMANDS

Use This Command	To Do This
–b, – –detach-sign	Create a detached digital signature.
–c, – –symmetric	Encrypt with a symmetric cipher.
– –check-sigs [*username*]	List and verify the digital signatures of all users or those of the user specified by *username.*
– –clearsign	Create a cleartext signature.
– –decrypt *filename*	Decrypt the specified filename, verfiy the signature (if any), and write it to the standard output. Use the **– –output** option to write the output to a file.
– –delete-key name	Remove key from the public key ring.
– –delete-secret-key name	Remove key from the secret and public key ring.
–e *filename,* **– –encrypt** *filename*	Encrypt the specified filename.
– –edit-key name	Launch an interactive utility that enables you to manage keys.

COMMANDS *(CONT.)*

Use This Command	To Do This
– –export [*user ID*]	Export all key rings or those with of the specified user ID.
– –export-all [*user ID*]	Export all key rings, or those of the specified user ID, including those that are not compatible with OpenPGP.
– –export-ownertrust	Display the assigned owner trust values.
– –export-secret-keys [*user ID*]	Export all secret keys, or those of the specified user ID. This option poses a security risk and should not normally be used.
– –fingerprint [*user ID*]	List all keys with their fingerprints or those with the specified user ID.
– –gen-key	Launch an interactive utility that generates a new key pair.
– –gen-revoke *user ID*	Generate a complete revocation certificate for the specified user's user ID.
–h, – –help	Display available options.
– –import [*filename*] **– –fast-import** [*filename*]	Add the keys in the specified filename to the key ring.
– –import-ownertrust [*filename*]	Update the trust database with the settings specified in *filename.*
– –list-keys [*user ID*] **– –list-public-keys** [*user ID*]	Show the keys on the specified key ring, or just those owned by the specified user ID.
– –list-secret-keys [*user ID*]	Show the keys on the specified secret key ring or just those owned by the specified user ID.
– –list-sigs [*user ID*]	Show the keys and signatures on the specified key ring or just those owned by the specified user ID.

COMMANDS *(CONT.)*

Use This Command	To Do This
– –lsign-key name	Sign a public key with your signature but mark it as unexportable.
–s, – –sign	Create a digital signature.
– –send-keys [*user ID*]	Send all public keys, or just those of the specified user ID, to a keyserver. Specify the keyserver with – –**keyserver**.
– –sign-key *user ID*	Sign a public key with your secret key.
– –verify [*filename*]	Verify the digital signature in the specified filename.
– –version	Show the version number.
– –warranty	Display warranty information.

EXAMPLES

This Command	Does the Following
gpg --gen-key	Generates a new key pair.
gpg --clearsign mysig	Creates a cleartext signature.
gpg -e autobiography.doc	Encrypts the specified file. You will be prompted for a destination user ID.
gpg --list-keys	Shows all the public keys on the current key ring.
gpg --decrypt autobiography.doc.gpg	Decrypts the specified file. You will be prompted for the passphrase.

gunzip

gunzip [option] *filename*

Decompresses the specified filename. For *filename*, you can use a shell pattern (see the section "Shell Patterns" in Chapter 4) or a space-separated list of files. This utility can decompress files created with the following utilities: **compress** (.Z), **gzip** (.gz, .tgz), and **zip** (.zip). By default, **gzip** does not overwrite existing output files. Use the – –force option to override this setting.

See also zcat (Chapter 8).

OPTIONS

Use This Option	To Do This
–c, – –stdout, – –tostdart	Route output to the standard output
–f, – –force	Force overwrite of output files
–h, – –help	Display available options
–L, – –license,	Display the software version and license terms and conditions
–l, – –list	For each compressed file, list the compressed size, uncompressed sized, compression ratio, and name of the uncompressed file
–n, – –noname	Skip saving the original file's name and timestamp
–N, – –name	Save the original file's name and timestamp
–q – –quiet	Suppress most program messages, except those concerning input and output errors
–r, – –recursive	Compress all the specified directories and all of their associated subdirectories
–t, – –test	Test the files to see whether they are valid and decompressable
–v, – –verbose	Display messages as each file is processed
–V, – –version	Show the version number

gzexe

gzexe [*filename*]

Compresses the executable file specified by *filename* so that it auto-matically decompresses and executes when you run it. Although compressing an executable in this way saves disk storage space, the executable takes longer to start. The program automatically backs up the original file with the ~ suffix. You can remove this backup file when you are sure that the compressed executable runs correctly.

OPTION

Use This Option	To Do This
–d	Decompress the executable file

EXAMPLE

This Command	Does the Following
gzexe /usr/local/ Office51/bin/soffice	Compresses the specified executable so that it occupies less disk space.

gzip

gzip [option] *filename*

Compresses the specified filename using a patent-free compression algorithm (LZ77). For *filename*, specify the name of the file or files to be archived. You can use a shell pattern (see the section "Shell Patterns" in Chapter 4), a space-separated list of files, or a directory name. With the –r option, you can quickly compress all the files in a directory tree. By default, **gzip** does not overwrite existing output files (use the – –**force** option to override this setting), but the program replaces input files with compressed files that have the .gz extension. To decompress the files, use **gunzip**.

See also **compress, bzip2**.

OPTIONS

Use This Option	To Do This
–1, **–2**, **–3**, **–4**, **–5**, **–6**, **–7**, **–8**, **–9**	Specify compression performance on a continuum from 1 to 9, with 1 giving the best speed but poorest compression ratio (equivalent to **– –fast)** and 9 giving the slowest speed but best compression ratio (equivalent to **– –best**). The default is **–6**.
– –best	Compress for the smallest possible file size at the cost of execution speed.
–c, **– –stdout**, **– –to-stdout**	Route output to the standard output.
–d, **– –decompress**, **– –uncompress**	Force **gzip** to decompress files. This is the same as running **gunzip**.
–f, **– –force**	Force the overwrite of output files.
– –fast	Compress quickly at the cost of a larger compressed file size.
– –help	Display available options.
–L, **– –license**	Display the license terms and conditions.
–n, **– –noname**	Skip reporting the original file's name and timestamp.
–N, **– –name**	Save the original filename and time-stamp. This is the default.
–q – –quiet	Suppress most program messages, except those concerning input and output errors.
–r, **– –recursive**	Compress the specified directory and all of its associated subdirectories.
–S .*suffix*, **– –suffix** .*suffix*	Use the specified suffix instead of the program default (**.gz**).
–v, **– –verbose**	Display messages as each file is processed.
–V, **– –version**	Show the version number.

EXAMPLES

This Command	Does the Following
gzip massivefile.txt	Compresses the specified file (massivefile.txt).
gzip --best massivefile.txt	Compresses the specified file (massivefile.txt) using the compression method that yields the maximum reduction in size.
gzip -r /home/suzanne/documents	Compress all the files in the specified directory and all of its associated subdirectories.

hexbin

hexbin [option] *filename*

Extracts files from a Macintosh **binhex** (.bin.hqx) archive. By default, the program extracts files from the specified filename and writes the output to the working directory. This utility is part of the Macutils package which is available on the following ftp site: metalab.unc.edu/pub/linux/utils/compress.

See also **macunpack, hexbin.**

OPTIONS

Use This Option	To Do This
–3	Write files in fork format (info, data, and rsrc).
–a	Save in AppleShare format in a valid AppleShare folder.
–c	Skip checking to make sure all lines are of equal length.
–d	Write data forks only.
–f	Write files in fork format but skip empty data and resource forks.
–H	Show available options.

OPTIONS *(CONT.)*

Use This Option	To Do This
–i	Provide information only.
–l	List information about the files being extracted.
–n *filename*	Use the specified filename.
–q	Ask for confirmation before extracting files.
–r	Write resource forks only.
–s	Write extracted files to standard output in MacBinary format.
–u	Write data forks only but use Linux line-feed conventions and name the files with the `.text` suffix.
–U	Write data forks only but use Linux line-feed conventions. No suffix is added.
–v	Show all available messages.
–V	Show the version number.

macunpack

macunpack [option] *filename*

Extracts files from a Macintosh MacBinary archive (generally saved with the `.bin` suffix). By default, the program extracts the files to the working directory and creates subdirectories, if needed, for files saved with path information. This utility is part of the Macutils package, which is available on the following ftp site: `metalab.unc.edu/pub/linux/utils/compress`.

See also **hexbin**.

OPTIONS

Use This Option	To Do This
–3	Write files in fork format (info, data, and rsrc).
–a	Save in AppleShare format in a valid AppleShare folder.
–d	Write data forks only.

OPTIONS *(CONT.)*

Use This Option	To Do This
–f	Write files in fork format but skip empty data and resource forks.
–H	Show available options.
–i	Provide information only.
–l	List information about the files being extracted.
–q	Ask for confirmation before extracting files.
–r	Write resource forks only.
–s	Write extracted files to standard output in MacBinary format.
–u	Write data forks only but use Linux line-feed conventions and name the files with the `.text` suffix.
–U	Write data forks only but use Linux line-feed conventions. No suffix is added.
–v	Show all available messages.
–V	Show the version number.

mcrypt

mcrypt [option] [*filename*]

Encrypts the specified filename. By default, the program creates a new file in the working directory with the `.enc` extension. To delete the original file, use the **–u** option. If no files are specified, the program accepts input from the standard input. You will be asked to supply a valid passphrase (one that uses uppercase as well as lowercase letters and numbers). Do not forget your passphrase! To decrypt the file, see **mdecrypt**. To obtain a copy of this utility, visit `http://mcrypt/hellug.grl`.

OPTIONS

Use This Option	To Do This
–a *algorithm*, **––algorithm** *algorithm*	Use the specified algorithm for encryption. Valid options are ABCFOUR, BLOWFISH-448, BLOWFISH-256, BLOWFISH-192, BLOW-FISH-128, TWOFISH-128, TWOFISH-192, 0.0%-256, DES, DES-COMPAT, 3DES, 3-WAY, GOST, MARS, RC2-128, RC2-256, RC2-1024, RC6-128, RC6-192, RC6-256, RIJDAEL-128, RIJDAEL-192, RIJDAEL-256, SERPENT-128, SERPENT-192, SERPENT-256, IDEA, SAFER-SK64, SAFER-SK128, SAFER+, CAST-128, CAST-256, LOKI97, xTEA, RC4, and WAKE.
–b, **– –bare**	Omit information about the algorithm, mode, bit mode, and checksum.
–c *filename*, **– –config** *filename*	Use the specified filename as a configuration file.
–d, **– –decrypt**	Force decryption. This is the same as **mdecrypt**.
–F, **– –force**	Force output to the standard output rather than to the filesystem.
–f *filename*, **– –keyfile** *filename*	Use the specified filename as a source of keywords.
–h, **– –help**	Display available options.
–h *algorithm*, **– –hash-algorithm** *algorithm*	Use the specified hash algorithm.
– –hashlist	List all the hash algorithms.
– –keymodelist	List all supported keymodes.
–L, **– –license**	Display the program license.
– –list	List all supported algorithms.
–m *mode*, **– –mode** *mode*	Use the specified mode of encryption. Valid options are ECB, CFB, OFB, nOFB, and CBC.
–o *keymode*, **– –keymode** *keymode*	Use the specified keymode.
–p, **– –bzip2**	Compress files with **bzip2** before encrypting.

OPTIONS *(CONT.)*

Use This Option	To Do This
–q, **– –quiet**	Hide program messages.
–r, **– –random**	Use a random number generator (if available) that requires keystrokes or mouse movement.
–s *n*, **– –keysize** *n*	Use the specified key size. Use **– –list** to determine the maximum key sizes.
–u, **– –unlink**	Delete the input file. Before it is deleted it is overwritten with zeroes.
–z, **– –gzip**	Compress files before encrypting with **gzip**.

EXAMPLES

This Command	Does the Following
mcrypt –u mysecret.doc	Encrypts the specified file and then deletes the input file after writing zeroes to the file. You will be prompted for a passphrase.
mcrypt –z mysecret.doc	Compresses the specified file with **gzip** and encrypts the file. You will be prompted for a passphrase.

---

mdecrypt

mdecrypt [option] [*filename*]

Decrypts a filename (with the .enc suffix) that was encrypted by **mcrypt**. By default, the program creates a new file in the working directory with the .enc extension. To delete the original file, use the **–d** option. If no files are specified, the program accepts input from the standard input. You will be asked to supply a valid passphrase (one that uses uppercase as well as lowercase letters and numbers). Do not forget your passphrase! To encrypt the file, see **mcrypt**. To obtain a copy of this utlilty, visit http://mcrypt/hellug.grl.

OPTIONS

Use This Option	To Do This
–c *filename*, – –**config** *filename*	Use the specified filename as a configuration file
–**F**, – –**force**	Force output to the standard output rather than to the filesystem
–**h**, – –**help**	Display available options
–**L**, – –**license**	Display program license
–**q**, – –**quiet**	Hide program messages

EXAMPLE

This Command	Does the Following
`mdecrypt mysecret.doc.enc`	Decrpyts the specified file. You will need to supply the passphrase you used when you created the file.

mimencode

mimencode [option] [*input filename*] [–o *output filename*]

Encodes the binary file specified by *input filename* to one of the ASCII encoding formats defined by the Multipurpose Internet Mail Encoding (MIME) standards. The utility uses base64 encoding by default and writes to the standard output. To write to a file, use the –o option. Use the –u option to decode MIME-encoded input.

See also **uuencode**.

OPTIONS

Use This Option	To Do This
–**q**	Use quoted-principle encoding

OPTIONS *(CONT.)*

Use This Option	To Do This
–u	Decode from the standard input or the input filename if specified
–o *filename*	Write output to the specified filename

EXAMPLE

This Command	Does the Following
mimencode –o interior.mime interior.jpg	Encodes the specified file (interior.jpg) and saves the encoded output to interior.mime.

tar

tar *–required option* [option] [**–f** *archive*] [*filename*]

Places two or more files into a new or existing archive or extracts the files from an existing archive. Archives are made for backup purposes, as well as for convenient file transfer via the network. For *required option*, specify one of the options listed in the Required Options table in this section. For *archive*, specify the name of the archive or tape device. For *filename*, specify the name of the file or files to be archived. To specify the filename, you can use a shell pattern (see "Shell Patterns" in Chapter 4). If you specify a directory name, **tar** archives all of the files in associated directories, as well as those in the specified directory.

REQUIRED OPTIONS

Use This Option	To Do This
–A, **– –catenate**, **– –concatenate**	Append the specified files to an existing archive
–c, **– –create**	Create a new archive
–d, **– –diff**, **– –compare**	Compare the archive to the filesystem

REQUIRED OPTIONS *(CONT.)*

Use This Option

– –delete

–r, – –append

–t, – –list

–u, – –update

–x, – –extract, – –get

To Do This

Delete from the archive. This option cannot be used with magnetic tapes.

Append the specified files to the end of an existing archive.

List the contents of an archive.

Append the specified files to an existing archive, but only if they are newer than the files already in the archive.

Extract files from an existing archive.

OPTIONS

Use This Option

– –atime-preserve

–b, – –block-size *n*

–B, – –read-full-blocks

–C *directory*, **– –directory** *directory*

– –checkpoint

–f *filename* **– –file** *filename*

– –force–local

–*filename*, **– –info-script** *filename*, **– –new-volume-script** *filename*

–G, – –incremental

–g *filename*, **– –listed-incremental** *filename*

To Do This

Keep the existing file access times.

Specify the block size in multiples of 512 bytes. The default is *n*=20.

Reblock during reading (for BSD version 4.2 pipes).

Change to the specified directory.

Print directory names while reading the archive.

Use the specified archive file. You can specify an external location using the form *hostname:filename*.

Use a local archive file even if an external location is specified.

Run script at end of each tape.

Use the old GNU-format incremental backup.

Use the new GNU-format incremental backup.

OPTIONS *(CONT.)*

Use This Option	To Do This
–h, – –dereference	Don't archive symbolic links; instead, archive the files they point to.
–I, – –bzip	Use **bzip2** for compression and decompression.
–i, – –ignore-zeroes	Ignore blocks of zeroes in the archive.
– –ignore-failed-read	Don't exit if an unreadable file is encountered.
–k, – –keep-old-files	Don't overwrite existing files when restoring from the archive.
–K *filename,* **– –starting-file** *filename*	Start with the specified filename in the archive.
–l, – –one–file–system	Stay in the current filesystem.
–L *n,* **– –tape-length** *n*	Change tapes after writing *n* kilobytes of data.
–m, – –modification-time	Don't extract the file modification times.
–M, – –multivolume	Work with a multivolume archive.
–N *date,* **– –after-date** *date,* **– –newer** *date*	Archive only the files that are newer than the specified date.
–O, – –to-stdout	Extract files to the standard output.
–o, – –old-archive, – –portability	Write a V7 format archive rather than the default ANSI format.
–p, – –same-permissions, – –preserve-permissions	Keep the existing permissions.
–P, – –absolute-paths	Don't remove path information from filenames.
– –preserve	Same as **–ps**.
–R, – –record-number	Display the record number in the archive.
– –remove-files	Remove the files after adding them to the archive.

OPTIONS *(CONT.)*

Use This Option	To Do This
–s, – –same-order, – –preserve-order	Sort the list of names of files to extract to match the names in the archive.
– –same-owner	Create extracted files with the same ownership.
– –S, – –sparse	Work with sparse files correctly.
–T *filename,* **– –files-from** *filename*	Consult the specified filename for the names of files to extract.
– –null	Read null-terminated names.
– –totals	Display the total bytes written with **– –create**.
–v, – –verbose	Show the names of files being processed.
–V, – –label *name*	Create the archive with the specified volume label name.
– –version	Show the version number.
–w, – –interactive, – –confirmation	Ask for confirmation for every action.
–W, – –verify	Verify the archive after creating it.
– –exclude *filename*	Exclude the specified filename. You can use a shell pattern (see "Shell Patterns" in Chapter 4).
–X *filename,* **– –exclude-from** *filename*	Exclude the files listed in the specified *filename.*
–Z, – –compress, – –uncompress	Use the compress program to compress or decompress the file.
–z, – –gzip, – –ungzip	Use the **gzip** program to compress or decompress the file.
– –use-compress-program *filename*	Use the specified compression program.
– –block-compress	Do not compress files routed to a tape device.

EXAMPLES

This Command	Does the Following
`tar -cvf backup.tar /home/suzanne/documents`	Creates a new archive with the specified filename (**backup.tar**) and include all the files in **/home/suzanne/documents**, including those in all of the associated subdirectories.
`tar -xvf backup.tar`	Extracts the files from the specified archive. By default, the extracted files will be placed in the directory from which they were archived.
`tar -cvf /dev/ftape /home/suzanne`	Creates a new archive on the specified tape device (**/dev/ftape**). Include all the files in **/home/suzanne**, including those in all associated subdirectories.
`tar -xvzf kdebase.tgz`	Decompresses the specified compressed archive (**kdebase.tgz**) and extract the files.
`tar -uvf backup.tar /home/suzanne`	Updates the specified archive (**backup.tar**) by adding only those files from **/home/suzanne** and all associated subdirectories that are not already present in the archive.
`find /home/suzanne -name '*.sdw' -print | xargs tar -cvf backup.tar`	Finds all the StarWriter (***.sdw**) files in **/home/suzanne** and add them to a new archive named **backup.tar**.

unarj

unarj [option] *archive*

Decompresses or lists the contents of the specified ARJ archive. ARJ is an MS-DOS compression format. When used without an option, **unarj** lists the contents of the archive. It is not necessary to precede the options with a dash.

See also **unzip**.

OPTIONS

Use This Option	To Do This
e	Extract the files from the archive to the working directory
t	Test the archive's integrity
x	Extract the files from the archive to their original location if the needed subdirectories exist

uncompress

uncompress [option] *filename*

Decompresses the **compress** (.Z) compressed file specified by *filename*. You can specify the filename by using a shell pattern (see the section "Shell Patterns" in Chapter 4) or a space-separated list. By default, the program prompts the user before overwriting existing files. You can suppress the confirmations by using the –f option. Use of this utility is discouraged because the underlying compression algorithm is patented. You can use **gunzip** to decompress .Z files.

OPTIONS

Use This Option	To Do This
–c	Write to the standard output
–f	Overwrite files without asking for conformation
–V	Show version number

unzip

unzip [option] [*archive*] [*filename*]

Decompresses and extracts files from archives created by the Linux **zip** utility, PKZIP (MS-DOS), or WinZip (Microsoft Windows). For *archive*, specify the name of the zip archive you want to decompress.

The utility supplies the .zip suffix automatically. You can selectively extract files from the archive by specifying a filename, which can be the name of one of the files in the archive, a shell pattern (see the "Shell Patterns" section in Chapter 4), or a space-separated list of files. By default, **unzip** asks for confirmation before overwriting existing files. To suppress the confirmations, use the –o option. To compress files, use **zip**. To view information about files in a **zip** archive, see **zipinfo**.

TIP   If you use a shell pattern, be sure to enclose the expression in double quotation marks so that the shell does not expand or modify the expression.

See also **compress, bunzip2, gunzip.**

OPTIONS

Use This Option	To Do This
–$	Restore the volume label if the working medium is a removable disk.
–a	Automatically translate MS-DOS and Macintosh text files so that they conform to Linux line-feed conventions.
–b	Treat all files as if they were binary files. Omits automatic conversion of text files.
–c	Extract the files to the standard output and display the name of each file as it is extracted.
–C	Use case-insensitive filename matching.
–d *directory*	Extract the files to the specified directory instead of to the working directory.
–f	Freshen the files in the working directory by extracting only those files from the archive that are newer than the files in the working directory.
–j	Extract all the files in the archive to the working directory. Ignore path name information.
–l	Display the archive contents using the short format.

OPTIONS *(CONT.)*

Use This Option	To Do This
–L	Convert all filenames to lowercase.
–M	Display output on-screen with a text-paging utility.
–n	Skip the confirmation message for existing files. Never overwrites them.
–o	Overwrite existing files without prompting.
–p	Extract the files to the standard output without displaying the filenames.
–q	Hide program messages.
–s	Convert spaces in filenames to underscores.
–T	Set the timestamps on the archived files to that of the newest file in the archive.
–t	Test the integrity of the archived files by performing a checksum.
–u	Update an existing file in the working directory only if the archived file is newer than the one in the archive; also extract any files that are not present in the working directory.
–v	Display all program messages.
–X	Restore file ownership and permissions.
–x *filename*	Extract only the files specified by *filename.* You can use one filename, a space-separated list of filenames, or a shell pattern (see the "Shell Patterns" section in Chapter 4). Place this option at the end of the command.
–z	Display only the archive comment. Do not extract the files.

EXAMPLES

This Command	Does the Following
`unzip documents`	Decompresses all the files in the specified archive (`documents.zip`) and writes them to the working directory, or to the working directory and its associated subdirectories if the archive contains path name information.

EXAMPLES *(CONT.)*

This Command	Does the Following
unzip -j documents	Decompresses all the files in the specified archive (documents.zip) and writes them to the working directory. It ignores path name information in the archive.
unzip -f documents	Freshens the working directory by extracting only those files from the archive that are newer than the ones in the directory.
unzip -u documents	Freshens the working directory by extracting only those files from the archive that are newer than the ones in the directory. It also extracts any files that are not present in the working directory.
unzip documents "*.doc"	Decompresses all the files with the *.doc suffix in the specified archive (documents.zip).
unzip documents -x "*.txt"	Decompresses all the files in the specified archive (documents.zip) except those named with the *.txt suffix.
unzip -L fonts	Decompresses all the files in the specified archive (fonts.zip) and converts all the filenames to lowercase if necessary.

uudecode

uudecode [option] [*filename*]

Decodes the **uuencoded** file specified by *filename*. By default, this utility writes to standard output. Use –o to write the output to a file.

See also **uuencode**.

OPTION

Use This Option	To Do This
–o *filename*	Write to the specified filename instead of standard output.

EXAMPLE

This Command	Does the Following
uudecode –o interior.jpg interior.uue	Decodes the specified file (interior.uue) and saves the encoded output to interior.jpg.

---

uuencode

uuencode [option] [*input filename*] *name > output filename*

Encodes the binary file specified by *filename* so that it can be transferred over a medium that does not support non-ASCII characters. *Name* is the name of the file included in the encoding. By default, this utility writes to standard output. Use output redirection to write to an output filename.

TIP   Don't forget to include a name for the enclosed file; it's required.

See also **mimencode, uudecode.**

OPTION

Use This Option	To Do This
–m	Use base-64 encoding

EXAMPLE

This Command	Does the Following
uuencode interior.jpg interior.jpg > interior.uue	Encodes the specified file (interior .jpg) and saves the encoded output to interior.uue. The uuencoded file indicates that the file is named interior.jpg.

zforce

zforce [*filename*]

Adds the .gz extension to all the files in the working directory, or to the specified filename, that were compressed with **gzip** but lack the .gz extension. This utility prevents **gzip** from compressing files twice.

zip

zip [option] [*archive*] [*filename*]

Archives and compresses files using a format compatible with PKZIP and WinZip, the most popular archiving and compression utilities for MS-DOS and Microsoft Windows. Unlike Linux or UNIX compression and archiving utilities, **zip** combines archiving (combining files into one) and compression (reducing the size of files). For *archive*, specify the name of the zip archive you want to use or create. The utility supplies the .zip suffix automatically. For *filename*, specify the name of the file or files to be archived. You can use a bash shell pattern (see the "Shell Patterns" section in Chapter 4), a space-separated list of files, or a directory name. With the **–R** option, you can quickly compress all the files in the working directory and all of its associated subdirectories. By default, **zip** does not delete input files (to do so, use the – –m option). To decompress the files, use **unzip**.

See also **compress, bzip2, gzip, zipcloak, zipnote, zipsplit**.

OPTIONS

Use This Option	To Do This
–b *path name*	Use the specified path name for the temporary **zip** archive.
–c	Add one-line comments for each file. You will be prompted to add the comments after the file operations are complete.
–d	Delete the specified filenames from an existing archive.

OPTIONS *(CONT.)*

Use This Option	To Do This
–D	Omit directory names from the archive.
–e	Specify a password.
–f	Freshen an existing archive by including only those files that are newer than the files already in the archive. Unlike **–u**, this option does *not* add new files to the archive.
–F	Repair a damaged archive if possible.
–g	Append to the existing archive.
–h	Show available options.
–i *filename*	When used with **–r** or **–R**, include only the files speci-fied by *filename.* You can use one filename, a space-separated list of filenames, or a shell pattern (see the "Shell Patterns" section in Chapter 4). Place this option at the end of the command.
–j	Omit path information from the names of the archived files. Store the filename only.
–J	Strip prepended data from the archive.
–k	Attempt to convert the names and paths to conform to MS-DOS conventions.
–l	In text files, convert the Unix end-of-line character LF so that it conforms to the MS-DOS convention (CR + LF).
–ll	Translate the MS-DOS end-of-line format (CR LF) into the Unix format (LF only). Use this option only on text files.
–L	Display the program license.
–m	Delete the input files after creating the archive. Caution: Use with **–T** to make sure the archive is valid.
–n *suffix*	Archive files with the specified suffix but do not com-press them. To specify more than one suffix, separate the suffixes with colons or semicolons.
–o	Set the time of last modification to the oldest time among the specified filenames.
–q	Hide program messages.

OPTIONS *(CONT.)*

Use This Option	To Do This
–r *directory*	Archive all the files in the specified directory and all of its associated subdirectories.
–R	Archive all the files in the working directory and all of its associated subdirectories.
–t *time*	Skip files modified before the specified time. To specify the time, use the form *mmddyyyy*. For example, May 21, 2002 is 05212002.
–tt *time*	Skip files modified after the specified time. To specify the time, use the form *mmddyyyy*. For example, May 21, 2002 is 05212002.
–T	Verify the validity of the newly created **zip** archive. If the test fails, the existing archive (if any) is not changed. If used with the **–m** option, input files are not deleted.
–u	Update an existing entry in the archive only if the input file is newer than the one in the archive or does not exist in the archive.
–v	Display all program messages.
–x *filename*	When used with **–r** or **–R**, include only the files specified by *filename*. You can use one filename, a space-separated list of filenames, or a shell pattern (see the "Shell Patterns" section in Chapter 4). Place this option at the end of the command.
–X	Omit ownership and timestamp information.
–y	Archive the symbolic links instead of the files they point to.
–z	Prompt the user to supply a multiline comment for the entire archive. Complete the comment by pressing Ctrl + d.
–#	Specify compression performance on a continuum from 1 to 9, with 1 giving the best speed but poorest compression ratio (equivalent to **– –fast**) and 9 giving the slowest speed but best compression ratio (equivalent to **– –best**). The default is –6.
–@	Accept input from the standard input. Place this option at the end of the command.

EXAMPLES

This Command	Does the Following
`zip documents *`	Creates the specified archive (**documents.zip**) containing all the files in the working directory.
`zip documents *.sdw`	Creates the specified archive (**documents.zip**) containing all the *.sdw files in the working directory.
`zip -f documents *`	Freshens the existing archive (**documents.zip**) by adding only those files that are newer than the ones in the existing archive. Newer files are added only if older files are already present in the archive.
`zip -u documents *`	Updates the existing archive (**documents.zip**) by adding only those files that are newer than the ones in the existing archive, or that are not yet listed in the existing archive.
`zip -g documents essays/*`	Appends all the files in the specified subdirectory (**essays/**) to the existing archive (**documents.zip**).
`zip -mT documents *`	Moves all the files in the working directory to the specified archive (**documents.zip**) and deletes the input files. However, do not perform the deletion if the archive fails to pass the integrity test (specified by **-T**).
`zip -r documents *`	Archives all the files in the specified directory and all of its associated directories.
`zip -R *`	Archives all the files in the working directory and all of its associated subdirectories.
`zip -R archive * -x *.doc`	Archives all the files in the working directory and all of its associated subdirectories, excluding those with the **.doc** suffix.
`find . -name "*.doc'	zip documents -@`	Finds all the files in the working directory (**.**) and all of its associated subdirectories that have the **.doc** suffix. Pipes the file list to **zip**, which accepts the file list from standard input (**-@**) and creates the specified archive (**documents.zip**).

zipinfo

zipinfo [option] *archive* [*filename*]

Displays information about the files stored in a **zip** archive. If you specify a filename, the utility shows information about the specified file. To specify the filename, you can use a shell pattern (see the "Shell Patterns" section in Chapter 4).

See also **zipnote**.

OPTIONS

Use This Option	To Do This
–1	List only the filenames.
–2	List the filenames, headers, trailers, and comments.
–h	List the header line only, which shows archive name, size in bytes, and the total number of files.
–l	List information in long format.
–M	Display all output using an internal pager program.
–m	List information in a format similar to **ls –l** (this is the default setting) but omit compression percentage.
–s	List information in a format similar to **ls –l**. This is the default setting.
–T	List the file dates and times in a sortable format.
–t	List totals only.
–v	List information in verbose, multipage format.
–z	Show the comments if any.

zipnote

zipnote [option] *archive*

Displays or enables you to edit the comments appended to filenames in a **zip** archive.

See also **zipinfo**.

OPTIONS

Use This Option	To Do This
–b *path name*	Write the temporary **zip** files to the specified path name
–h	Show available options
–v	Display the version number
–w	Create the comments for each file

This Command	Does the Following
`zipnote interior.zip> interior.tmp`	Writes the comments to a temporary file.
`joe interior.tmp`	Opens the comments for editing in the **joe** editor (see Chapter 11).
`zipnote-w interior.zip< interior.tmp`	Adds the edited comments to the archive.

zipsplit

zipsplit [option] [**–b** *path name*] *archive*

Divides a **zip** archive into segments small enough to be written to removable media, such as floppy disks, and outputs the files to the specified device name.

OPTIONS

Use This Option	To Do This
–b *device name*	Write the output files to the specified device name.
–h	Show available options.
–i	Make an index file.
–L	Show the program license.

OPTIONS *(CONT.)*

–n *size*	Make **zip** files no larger than the specified size in bytes. The default is 36000.

Use This Option	To Do This
–p	Pause between files so that the disks can be removed and inserted.
–r *n*	Leave *n* bytes blank on each of the output disks.
–s	Perform a sequential split.
–t	Show how many files will be required without actually splitting or outputting them.
–v	Display the version number.

---

znew

znew [option] *filename*

Recompresses the specified filename, which must be a compressed file created with the **compress** utility, using the patent-free **gzip** format.

OPTIONS

Use This Option	To Do This
–f	Overwrite existing output files
g	Use the slowest compression method for optimal compression
–K	Keep the original `.Z` file if it is smaller than the `.gz` file
–P	Use pipes for the conversion to reduce the amount of disk space used
–t	Test the new `.gz` files before deleting the originals
–v	Show information about each file being processed

CHAPTER 7

Managing Disk and Tape Drives

$\mathbf{T}$his chapter details the Linux knowledge you'll need to work with hard disks, floppy disks, CD-ROM drives, tape drives, and other block devices. *Block devices* are distinguished from other devices by the fact that they store data in units of more than one character, called *blocks*.

AT A GLANCE

How Do I	See This Entry	Example
Create partitions on a new hard drive that does not contain any data?	**cfdisk, fdisk**	`fdisk /dev/hdb`
Show the amount of disk space remaining for all mounted filesystems?	**df**	`df -h`
Find out how much space a directory consumes, including all of its associated subdirectories?	**du**	`du -h /home/suzanne/`
Eject an unmounted audio CD?	**eject**	`eject /dev/cdrom`
Format a high-density 3.5-inch floppy disk in drive fd0?	**fdformat**	`fdformat /dev/fd0H1440`
Repair a Linux filesystem that is mounted read only following detection of errors in the boot process?	**fsck, efs2ck**	`fsck -t efs2 -a`
Mount a Macintosh floppy disk?	**hmount**	`hmount /dev/fd0`
Create a Linux filesystem on a formatted floppy disk?	**mke2fs**	`mke2fs -c /dev/fd0`
Mount an MS-DOS floppy disk?	**mount**	`mount -t msdos /dev/fd0 /mnt/floppy`

AT A GLANCE *(CONT.)*

How Do I	See This Entry	Example
Mount a CD-ROM disk?	**mount**	`mount -t iso9660 /dev/cdrom /mnt/cdrom`
Rewind a tape drive?	**mt**	`mt /dev/tape rewind`
Create an emergency floppy boot disk?	**dd**	`dd if=/boot/vmlinuz of=/dev/fd0 bs=8192`
Write the contents of the filesystem buffers to the disk so that disk usage statistics are as accurate as possible?	**sync**	`sync`
Unmount a floppy disk so that it can be safely removed?	**umount**	`umount /dev/fd0`

Block Device Fundamentals

This section details the following information about block devices:

- Typical block devices
- Block device configuration files

Typical Block Devices

The block devices shown in the following table are typically available in the /dev directory. Some drivers install additional devices.

TYPICAL BLOCK DEVICES IN THE */DEV* DIRECTORY

Device	Description
/dev/cdrom	Symbolic link to the installed CD-ROM device.
/dev/fd*n*	Drive-independent driver for floppy drive *n* that automatically detects media format and capacity, where *n*=0 to 7 (fd0, fd1, etc.).

TYPICAL BLOCK DEVICES IN THE */DEV* DIRECTORY *(CONT.)*

Device	Description
/dev/fdnD1040	3.5-inch, double-density drive (360K).
/dev/fdnD1120	3.5-inch, double-density drive (360K).
/dev/fdnd360	5.25-inch, double-density drive (360K).
/dev/fdnD360	3.5-inch, double-density drive (360K).
/dev/fdnD720	3.5-inch, double-density drive (360K).
/dev/fdnD800	3.5-inch, double-density drive (360K).
/dev/fdnE2880	3.5-inch, extra-density drive (2880K).
/dev/fdnE3200	3.5-inch, extra-density drive (3200K).
/dev/fdnE3520	3.5-inch, extra-density drive (3520K).
/dev/fdnE3840	3.5-inch, extra-density drive (3840K).
/dev/fdnECompaQ	3.5-inch, extra-density drive (2880K).
/dev/fdnh1200	5.25-inch, high-density drive (1200K).
/dev/fdnh1440	5.25-inch, high-density drive (1440K).
/dev/fdnH1440	3.5-inch, high-density drive (1440K).
/dev/fdnh1476	5.25-inch, high-density drive (1476K).
/dev/fdnh1494	5.25-inch, high-density drive (1494K).
/dev/fdnh1600	5.25-inch, high-density drive (1600K).
/dev/fdnH1600	3.5-inch, high-density drive (1600K).
/dev/fdnH1680	3.5-inch, high-density drive (1680K).
/dev/fdnH1722	3.5-inch, high-density drive (1722K).
/dev/fdnH1760	3.5-inch, high-density drive (1760K).
/dev/fdnH1840	3.5-inch, high-density drive (1840K).
/dev/fdnH1920	3.5-inch, high-density drive (1920K).
/dev/fdnh360	5.25-inch, high-density drive (360K).
/dev/fdnH360	3.5-inch, high-density drive (360K).
/dev/fdnh410	5.25-inch, high-density drive (410K).
/dev/fdnh420	5.25-inch, high-density drive (420K).
/dev/fdnh720	5.25-inch, high-density drive (720K).
/dev/fdnH720	3.5-inch, high-density drive (720K).

TYPICAL BLOCK DEVICES IN THE */DEV* DIRECTORY *(CONT.)*

Device	Description
/dev/fdnH820	3.5-inch, high-density drive (820K).
/dev/fdnH830	3.5-inch, high-density drive (830K).
/dev/fdnh880	5.25-inch, high-density drive (880K).
/dev/floppy	Symbolic link to installed floppy drive.
/dev/ft*n*	Tape device *n* connected to floppy drive controller, where *n*=0 through 7.
/dev/hda	IDE hard drive, master drive on the primary controller.
/dev/hdb	IDE hard drive, slave drive on the primary controller.
/dev/hdc	IDE hard drive, master drive on the secondary controller.
/dev/hdd	IDE hard drive, slave drive on the secondary controller.
/dev/hdx*n*	Partition *n* on IDE hard drive hd*x* (/dev/hda1, /dev/hda2, /dev/hda3, etc.).
/dev/nrft*n*	Non-rewinding tape device *n* connected to floppy drive controller, where *n*=0 through 7.
/dev/nst*n*	Non-rewinding SCSI tape device *n*, where *n*=0 through 7.
/dev/null	Null device. Output directed to this device disappears.
/dev/scd*n*	SCSI CD-ROM drive, where *n*=0 through 7. Other devices may be available depending on the installed drivers.
/dev/sdx	SCSI drive *x* (/dev/sda, /dev/sdb, /dev/sdc, etc.).
/dev/sdx*n*	Partition *n* on SCSI drive sd*x* (/dev/sda1, /dev/sda2, /dev/sda3, etc.).
/dev/st*n*	SCSI tape device *n*, where *n*=0 through 7.
/dev/tape	Symbolic link to installed tape device.

Configuration Files

Two important configuration files, /etc/fstab and /etc/mtab, control block devices.

/etc/fstab

One of the most important configuration files on a Linux system, /etc/fstab lists the currently available block devices in a columnar list (see the "Fields in /etc/fstab" table). This file names the block device drivers, indicates the mount point, specifies the filesystem type (see the Filesystem Types table), and indicates the type of mount to be performed (see the Mount Options table). The following is an example of /etc/fstab:

/dev/hda8	/	ext2	defaults	1	1
/dev/hda5	/home	ext2	defaults	1	2
/dev/hda1	/home/bryan/	auto	defaults	0	0
/dev/hda7	/usr	ext2	defaults	1	2
/dev/hda9	/usr/local	ext2	defaults	1	2
/dev/hda6	swap	swap	defaults	0	0
/dev/fd0	/mnt/floppy	ext2	noauto,user	0	0
/dev/cdrom	/mnt/cdrom	iso9660	user,noexec,nodev,suid,rw	0	0
none	/proc	proc	defaults	0	0
none	/dev/pts	devpts	gid=5,mode=620	0	0

FIELDS IN /ETC/FSTAB

Use This Field	To Indicate This	Examples
fs_spec	Block special device or remote filesystem.	Hard disk: /dev/hda1 CD-ROM drive: /dev/cdrom Floppy drive: /dev/fd0 NFS mount (*hostname*:*directory*) lothlorien.mydomain.org: /home/suzanne Proc filesystem: proc
fs_file	Mount point for the specified filesystem.	Swap partitions: Specify none Root filesystem: / CD-ROM drive: /mnt/cdrom Floppy drive: /mnt/floppy

FIELDS IN */ETC/FSTAB (CONT.)*

Use This Field	To Indicate This	Examples
fs_vfstype	Filesystem type. For the available options, see the Filesystem Types table in this section.	Linux filesystem: ext2 MS-DOS filesystem: MSdOS Windows 95/98 filesystem: vfat
fs_mntops	Mount options in a comma-separated list. For the available options, see the Mount Options table in this section.	Hard disk: defaults Floppy drive: user,owner,exec, dev,sui0,rw,noauto CD-ROM drive: user, owner, exec, dev, suid, ro, noauto
fs_freq	Dump frequency. **0** No dumping. **1** Dumping enabled.	Hard disk: 1 CD-ROM drive: 0 Floppy drive: 0
fs_passno	Order of filesystem checks at boot time. **0** Do not check. **1** Check first. **2** Check later.	Root partition: 1 Other partitions: 2 CD-ROM drive: 0 Floppy drive: 0

FILESYSTEM TYPES

Use This Type	To Mount This Type of Filesystem
adfs	Acord Advanced Disc Filing System
affs	Amiga Fast File System
auto	User-mounted floppy disks (autodetection of filesystem)
ext2	Linux Extended File System 2 (efs2)
hpfs	OS/2 filesystem
iso9660	CD-ROM filesystem
msdos	MS-DOS disk or partition
ncpfs	Novell NetWare filesystem
nfs	Network File System

FILESYSTEM TYPES *(CONT.)*

Use This Type	To Mount This Type of Filesystem
ntfs	Windows NT disk or partition
proc	Proc filesystem for system devices
smbfs	Windows NT server filesystem
smbfs	Samba share
sysv	UNIX System V filesystem
umsdos	Linux on an MS-DOS partition
vfat	Windows 95/98 disk or partition

MOUNT OPTIONS

Use This Option	To Do This
async	Perform input and output options at different times.
atime	Update the access time for each access. This is the default.
auto	Enable the filesystem to be mounted by **mount –a**, a command commonly found in boot scripts.
defaults	Use the following default options: **async**, **auto**, **dev**, **exec**, **nouser**, **rw**, **suid**.
dev	Interpret character or block special devices.
exec	Enable execution of binary files.
noatime	Skip updating access times with each access. This option speeds up filesystem performance for news or mail servers.
noauto	Require the filesystem to be mounted manually. This option does not mount with **mount –a**.
nodev	Skip character or block special devices.
noexec	Prevent execution of binary files.
nosuid	Prevent the use of set user ID or set group ID permissions.
nouser	Prevent an ordinary user from mounting the filesystem.
remount	Attempt to remount an already-mounted filesystem.

MOUNT OPTIONS *(CONT.)*

Use This Option	To Do This
ro	Mount the filesystem as read only.
rw	Mount the filesystem as read and write.
suid	Enable the use of set user ID and set group ID permissions on the specified device.
sync	Perform input and output operations at the same time.
user	Allow an ordinary user to mount the filesystem.

/etc/mtab

Automatically updated by **mount** and related utilities, /etc/mtab (called the *mount table*) shows the currently mounted block devices on your system. The device name, filesystem type, and settings are shown. The following is an example of a portion of an /etc/mtab file:

```
/dev/hda8     /              ext2   rw   0 0
none          /proc          proc   rw   0 0
/dev/hda5     /home          ext2   rw   0 0
/dev/hda1     /home/bryan    ext2   rw   0 0
/dev/hda7     /usr           ext2   rw   0 0
/dev/hda9     /usr/local     ext2   rw   0 0
```

Alphabetical Command Reference

This section details commands for the following tasks:

- Analyzing and repairing a Linux ext2 filesystem (**badblocks, debugfs, e2fsck, fsck, tune2fs**)

- Creating an emergency boot floppy (**dd, rdev**)

- Displaying information on available disk space and disk usage (**df, du, dumpe2fs, sync**)

- Mounting and unmounting filesystems (**hmount, humount, mount, umount**)

- Preparing a new hard drive for use (**cfdisk, fdisk, mke2fs**)

- Working with floppy disks, CD-ROM, and tape drives (**autorun, eject, fdformat, hformat, mt, setfdprm**)

autorun

autorun [option] [*device*]

Automatically recognizes all available CD-ROM drives in the current system, mounts them when a disk is inserted, and optionally executes specified applications, such as an audio CD-ROM player. To use **autorun**, you must add the mount options **user** and **exec** to the CD-ROM drive's entry in /etc/fstab.

OPTIONS

Use This Option	To Do This
–a *command*	Run the specified command if the CD-ROM is changed.
–c *command*	Run the specified command if an audio CD-ROM is inserted.
–i *time*	Specify the time in milliseconds to wait between checks.
–l	Lock the mounted media so that it must be unmounted manually.
–m	Mount and unmount only. Do not execute commands.
–n *string*	Display the specified string if the CD-ROM changes.
–t *string*	Display the specified string if a CD-ROM is inserted.
–e *string*	Display the specified string if a CD-ROM is ejected.
–q	Hide all output.
–v	Display all messages.
–?, – –help	Display available options.
– –usage	Display a short usage message.
–V	Show the program version.

badblocks

badblocks [option] *device*

Scans the specified device for corrupted segments, also called *bad sectors*.

OPTIONS

Use This Option	To Do This
–b *size*	Specify the default block size. The default is 512.
–o *filename*	Write a list of bad blocks to the specified filename.
–s	Show the command's progress.
–v	Display messages.

EXAMPLE

This Command	Does the Following
badblocks –s /dev/sda1	Scans the specified device for bad sectors and displays a progress indicator.

cfdisk

cfdisk [option] [*device*]

Launches an interactive hard disk partition utility in text-only mode (does not require X). Requires root user status (see **su** in Chapter 1). Requires block sizes.

WARNING Do not run this utility on a disk that contains valuable data.

OPTIONS

Use This Option	To Do This
−a	Highlight the current partition with a cursor instead of reverse video
−c *n*	Specify the number (*n*) of cylinders
−h *n*	Specify the number (*n*) of heads
−s *n*	Specify the number (*n*) of sectors
−z	Do not read the current partition table
−P < **r** | **s** | **t** >	Specify the format: **r** Raw data **s** Sector order **t** Formatted raw data

COMMANDS

Use This Command	To Do This
up arrow (↑), **down arrow** (↓)	Move among partitions
b	Toggle the boot flag
d	Delete the partition
g	Specify a new disk geometry in cylinders, heads, or sectors
h	Display the available options
m	Use the maximum available space
n	Create a new partition
p	Display the partition table
q	Quit without saving the partition information
t	Specify a new filesystem type
u	Change the partition size units
W	Save the partition information

dd

dd [option]

Copy a file with the conversions specified by one or more options. Use **if** to specify the input file, and **of** to specify the output file. To specify block sizes with options that require them, you can use the abbreviations shown in the Block Sizes table in this section. Note that with the exception of – –**help** and – –**version**, the options do not require a leading hyphen. Also, note that the equals signs are mandatory. You can use this utility to create an emergency boot disk (see the examples for more information).

See also **rdev.**

OPTIONS

Use This Option	To Do This
bs=*n*	Force the input and output bit streams (see **ibs** and **obs**) to read or write *n* bytes at a time.
cbs=*n*	Convert *n* bytes at a time.
conv=*keywords*	Convert the file using the specified keywords expressed in a comma-separated list. See the Keywords table in this section.
count=*n*	Copy only *n* input blocks.
– –**help**	Show the available options.
ibs=*n*	Read *n* bytes at a time.
if=filename	Use the specified filename as the input file.
obs=*n*	Write *n* bytes at a time.
of=*filename*	Use the specified filename as the output file.
seek=*n*	Skip *n* blocks at the start of output. Use **obs** to specify the block size.
skip=*n*	Skip *n* blocks at the start of input. Use **ibs** to specify the block size.
– –**version**	Show the version number.

BLOCK SIZES

Use This Abbreviation	To Specify This Block Size
c	1 byte
w	2 bytes
b	512 bytes
kD	1,000 bytes
k	1,024 bytes
MD	1,000,000 bytes
M	1,048,576 bytes
GD	1,000,000,000 bytes
G	1,097,741,824 bytes

KEYWORDS

Use This Keyword	To Do This
ascii	Convert from EBCDIC to ASCII
block	Pad newline-terminated records with spaces up to the block size specified by **cbs**.
ebcdic	Convert from ASCII to alternated EBCDIC.
ibm	Convert from ASCII to alternated EBCDIC.
lcase	Convert uppercase characters to lowercase.
noerror	Continue processing even if an error is generated.
notrunc	Skip truncating the output file.
swab	Swab each pair of input bytes.
sync	Pad every input block to the block size specified by **ibs**.
ucase	Convert lowercase characters to uppercase characters.
unblock	Replace trailing spaces with newlines in records padded to the block size specified by **cbs**.

EXAMPLES

This Command	Does the Following
`dd if=/boot/vmlinuz of=/dev/fd0 bs=8192`	Creates an emergency boot disk.
`dd if=uppercase.txt of=lowercse.txt conv=lcase`	Change all the uppercase characters in `uppercase.txt` to lowercase and write the results to `lowercase.txt`.

---

debugfs

debugfs [[option] *device*]

Starts an interactive utility that can perform fine-grained examinations and repairs of an ext2 filesystem on the specified device. This utility requires superuser status (see **su** in Chapter 1) and should be used only by knowledgeable system administrators. See the Commands table in this section for commands that you can use in the program's interactive mode.

OPTIONS

Use This Option	To Do This
−w	Open the filesystem as read and write
−V	Display the version number

COMMANDS

Use This Command	To Do This
cat *filename*	Write the contents of the specified filename to the standard output.
cd *directory*	Switch to the specified directory.
chroot *directory*	Switch to the specified directory and make it the root for this utility.
close	Close the filesystem that is open.
clri *filename*	Clear this file's inode contents.

COMMANDS *(CONT.)*

Use This Command	To Do This
dump [**–p**] *filename1 filename2*	Write the contents of *filename1* to *filename2*.
expand_dir *directory*	Expand the specified directory.
find_free_block *goal*	Find the first free block from the specified goal.
find_free_inode [*directory* [*mode*]]	Find a free inode and allocate it. You can specify the directory and set the permissions mode.
freeb *block*	Mark the specified block as not allocated.
freei *filename*	Free the inode linked to the specified filename.
help	Display the available options.
icheck *block number*	Print a list of the inodes that use the specified block number.
initalize *device size*	Create an ext2 filesystem on the specified device using the specified size.
kill_file *filename*	De-allocate the inode linked to the specified filename.
In *filename target*	Link the specified filename to the specified target.
ls *directory*	List the files in the specified directory.
modify_inode *filename*	Modify the inode linked to the specified filename.
mkdir *directory*	Make the specified directory.
mknod *filename*	Create a device file.
ncheck *inode*	Show which file is linked to the specified inode.
open *device*	Open the filesystem on the specified device.

COMMANDS *(CONT.)*

Use This Command	To Do This
pwd	Show the current working directory.
quit	Quit this program.
rm *path name*	Unlink the specified path name.
rmdir *directory*	Remove the specified directory.
setb *block*	Mark the specified block as allocated.
seti *filename*	Mark the specified filename as in use.
show_super_stats	Display information about the superblock.
stat *filename*	Show inode information about the specified filename.
testb *block*	Determine whether the specified block is allocated.
testi *inode*	Determine whether the specified inode is allocated.
unlink *path name*	Remove the link to an inode specified by *path name*.
write *filename1 filename2*	Write *filename1* to *filename2*.

df

df [option] [*filename*]

Displays the amount of disk spaced used and remaining on all mounted filesystems. If you specify a filename, **df** reports information for the device that contains the specified file. On most systems, **df** displays block sizes in units of 1K (1,024 bytes) by default. Use the **–h** option to display block sizes in a human-readable form.

OPTIONS

Use This Option	To Do This
–a, – –all	Include all filesystems, including those containing no data.
– –block-size=*size*	Use the specified size instead of the default.
–h	Display sizes in a human-readable format, for example, 1.5K, 2M, or 3.5G.
–H	Display sizes in a human-readable format using powers of 10.
–i	List inode instead of block usage.
–k	Display block sizes in kilobytes (K). This option is the same as **– –block-size=1024**.
–l	Limit listing to the filesystems on this computer.
–m	Display block sizes in megabytes (M). This option is the same as **– –block-size=1048576**.
– –no-sync	Do not run **sync** before getting usage information.
–P, – –portability	Use the POSIX output format.
– –sync	Run **sync** before getting usage information.
–t *type*, **– –type=***type*	Limit the listing to filesystems of the specified type.
–T, – –print-type	Display the filesystem type.
–x *type*, **– –exclude-type=***type*	Skip the specified type of filesystem.
– –help	Display the available options.
– –version	Display the version number.

EXAMPLES

This Command	Does the Following
df –h	Uses human-readable block sizes (such as kilobytes, megabytes, or gigabytes) to display the amount of used and available disk space on all mounted filesystems. Also shows the percentage of space used and each device's current mount point.

EXAMPLES *(CONT.)*

This Command	Does the Following
df –h – –sync	Runs **sync** to write buffered data to the disk before determining disk usage. This example gives the most accurate results.

du

du [option] [*filename*]

When used without an argument, this command displays the amount of disk space used in the current directory. By default, block sizes are reported in units of 1K (1,024). You can change this by specifying options. If you specify a filename, **du** reports the amount of space used by the specified file. To find out how much space a directory uses, including all of its associated subdirectories, type a directory name instead of a filename. To find out how much free space remains on a device, see **df**.

OPTIONS

Use This Option	To Do This
–a, – –all	Show sizes for individual files.
–c, – –total	Print a grand total for all arguments after all have been processed.
–D, – –dereference-args	Do not include paths indicated by symbolic links.
– –h, – –human-readable	Display sizes in human-readable format, for example, 1.5K, 2M, or 3.5G.
–H, – –si	Display sizes in a human-readable format using powers of 10.
– –help	Display the available options.
–k, – –kilobytes	Display block sizes in kilobytes (K). This option is the same as **– –block-size=1024**.
–L, – –dereference	Do not include the sizes of files to which symbolic links point.

OPTIONS *(CONT.)*

Use This Option	To Do This
–m, – –megabyte	Display block sizes in megabytes (M). This option is the same as **– –block-size=1048576**.
– –max-depth=n	Display directory totals only if they are n or fewer levels below the current directory.
–S, – –separate-dirs	Do not include the size of subdirectories.
–s, – –summarize	Display only a total for each argument.
– –version	Display the version number.
–x, – –one-file-system	Skip directories on filesystems other than the current filesystem.
–X *filename*, **– –exclude-from=***filename*	Exclude files that match the specified filename. You can use a shell pattern (see Chapter 4).

EXAMPLES

This Command	Does the Following
du –h	Uses human-readable block sizes (such as kilobytes, megabytes, or gigabytes) to display the amount of disk space used in the current directory.
du –h autobiography.doc	Displays the amount of disk space used by the specified file (**autobiography.doc**).
du –h *.doc	Displays the amount of disk space used by all the **.doc** files in the current directory.
du –h /home/suzanne/	Displays the amount of disk space used by the **/home/suzanne** directory, including all of its associated subdirectories.

dumpe2fs

> **dumpe2fs** [option] *device*
>
> Displays superblock and block information for the specified device.

OPTIONS

Use This Option	To Do This
−b	Print a list of blocks that are marked as bad and are not used by the filesystem
−ob *superblock*	Use the specified superblock
−oB *block size*	Use the specified block size when examining the filesystem
−V	Display the version number

EXAMPLE

This Command	Does the Following
dumpe2fs −b /dev/hda8	Displays a list of blocks marked as bad on the specified device (/dev/hda8).

e2fsck

e2fsck [option] *device*

Performs an analysis of a Linux e2fs filesystem's integrity and optionally repairs errors that are encountered. See the Exit Codes table in this section for an explanation of the program's exiting message.

WARNING Never run **ef2sck** on a mounted filesystem. Unmount the filesystem first (see **umount**).

See also fsck.

OPTIONS

Use This Option	To Do This
−a	Repair the filesystem automatically. This option is the same as **−p**.
−b *superblock*	Use the specified superblock instead of the default.

OPTIONS *(CONT.)*

Use This Option	To Do This
–B *size*	Use the specified size instead of attempting to determine the block size automatically.
–c	Run the **badblocks** utility.
–C *filename*	Write completion information to the file specified by *filename*.
–f	Force checking even if the filesystem appears to be clean.
–F	Flush the filesystem's buffer caches before performing the check.
–l *filename*	Write a list of bad blocks to the file specified by *filename*.
–n	Open the filesystem as read only and answer no to all prompts.
–p	Repair the filesystem automatically.
–s	Byte-swap the specified filesystem so that it uses the standard little-endian byte order required for Intel-based systems. This option has no effect if the filesystem is already little-endian.
–S	Forces a byte swap to little-endian order, even if the filesystem already uses it.
–v	Display messages.
–V	Display the version number.
–y	Answer yes to all questions.

EXIT CODES

This Code	Indicates the Following
0	No errors.
1	Errors encountered but they were all corrected.
2	Errors encountered but they were all corrected. Reboot the system if the filesystem was mounted.
4	Errors encountered but left uncorrected.

EXIT CODES *(CONT.)*

This Code	Indicates the Following
8	Program error.
16	Usage or syntax error.
128	Shared library error.

EXAMPLE

This Command	Does the Following
e2fsck -p /dev/sda1	Automatically repair errors on the specified file-system (in this example, /dev/sda1).

eject

eject [option] *device*

Ejects the media in the specified device, which can be a CD-ROM drive, an SCSI device, a removable floppy device, or a tape drive. If the device is mounted, **eject** unmounts the device before ejecting it.

OPTIONS

Use This Option	To Do This
-h, - -help	Display available options.
-v, - -verbose	Display messages.
-d, - -default	Display the default device names.
-a *setting,* **- -auto** *setting*	Enable or disable the auto-eject mode supported by some devices. When the mode is enabled, the device automatically ejects when the filesystem is unmounted. Available settings are

       1 (on)   Enable auto-eject mode.
       0 (off)   Disable auto-eject mode.

OPTIONS *(CONT.)*

Use This Option	To Do This
–c *slot number,* **– –changerslot** *slot number*	Select a slot from an ATAPI/IDE CD-ROM changer.
–t, – –trayclose	Close the CD-ROM tray.
–r, – –cdrom	Eject a CD-ROM.
–s, – –scsi	Eject an SCSI device.
–f, – –floppy	Eject a removable floppy device.
–q, – –tape	Eject a tape drive.

EXAMPLES

This Command	Does the Following
`eject /dev/cdrom`	Ejects media from a CD-ROM drive.
`eject /dev/sda1`	Ejects a ZIP disk from the specified SCSI ZIP drive (`/dev/sda1`).
`eject -c0 /dev/cdrom`	Ejects the first disk from a multi-disk CD-ROM changer.

fdformat

fdformat [option] *device*

Formats the floppy disk contained in the specified device. See the Devices table for commonly used device names. See the "Typical Block Devices in the /dev Directory" table earlier in this chapter for a complete list.

DEVICES

Use This Device Name	To Format This Type of Disk
`/dev/fd0d360`	Double-density, 5.25-inch disk (360K) in drive fd0
`/dev/fd0D720`	Double-density, 3.5-inch disk (720K) in drive fd0

DEVICES *(CONT.)*

Use This Device Name	To Format This Type of Disk
/dev/fd0H1440	High-density, 3.5-inch disk (1440K) in drive fd0
/dev/fd0E2880	Extra-density, 3.5-inch disk (2880K) in drive fd0
/dev/fd1d360	Double-density, 5.25-inch disk (360K) in drive fd1
/dev/fd1D720	Double-density, 3.5-inch disk (720K) in drive fd1
/dev/fd1H1440	High-density, 3.5-inch disk (1440K) in drive fd1
/dev/fd1E2880	Extra-density, 3.5-inch disk (2880K) in drive fd1

OPTION

Use This Option	To Do This
−r	Skip format verification

EXAMPLES

This Command	Does the Following
fdformat /dev/fd0H1440	Formats a high-density, 3.5-inch floppy disk in drive fd0.

fdisk

fdisk [option] *device*

Launches a menu-driven program that partitions a hard disk.

WARNING Repartitioning a hard disk will destroy all the data it contains. Do not run this program unless you are installing a new hard disk drive.

OPTIONS

Use This Option	To Do This
–l *device*	List the current partition tables for the specified device
–u	When listing partitions, specify sizes in sectors instead of cylinders
–s *partition*	Display the size of the specified partition
–v	Display the version number

EXAMPLE

This Command	Does the Following
fdisk –l /dev/hda1	Lists the current partitions for the specified device (**/dev/hda1**).

---

fsck

fsck [option] [**–t** *type*] [**–a** | **–r**] *device*

Performs an analysis of the specified device and optionally repairs errors. This command is essentially a front end to other utilities (such as **e2fsck**) that perform the analysis and repairs on the specified type of filesystem.

WARNING   Never run **fsck** on a mounted filesystem. Unmount the filesystem first (see **umount**).

See also **e2fsck**.

OPTIONS

Use This Option	To Do This
–a	Repair the filesystem automatically. This option is the same as **–p**.

OPTIONS *(CONT.)*

Use This Option	To Do This
–A	Check all filesystems listed in **/etc/fstab** if possible.
–C	Display progress bars if possible.
–N	Show the actions that would be performed without actually executing them.
–r	Repair the filesystem interactively.
–R	Skip the root filesystem, which may be mounted as read and write.
–t *type*	Specify the type of filesystem. Available types are listed in **/proc/filesystems**.
–V	Display messages.

EXIT CODES

This Code	Indicates the Following
0	No errors
1	Errors encountered but they were all corrected.
2	Errors encountered but they were all corrected. Reboot the system if the filesystem was mounted.
4	Errors encountered but left uncorrected.
8	Program error.
16	Usage or syntax error.
128	Shared library error.

EXAMPLE

This Command	Does the Following
fsck –a /dev/sda1	Automatically repairs errors on the specified filesystem (/dev/sda1).

hformat

hformat [option] *device*

Creates a Macintosh Hierarchical File System (HFS) on the specified device (/dev/fd0 or /dev/fd1). You must first perform a low-level format using **fdformat**. This command is part of the HFS Utilities package (hfsutils), which is not distributed with most versions of Linux. To obtain a copy, visit the HFS Utilities home page at http://www.mars.org/home/rob/proj/hfs.

See also **hmount**.

OPTION

Use This Option	To Do This
–l *string*	Create a volume label using the specified string

hmount

hmount *device*

Mounts a Macintosh floppy disk in the specified device (/dev/fd0 or /dev/fd1). This command is part of the HFS Utilities package (hfsutils), which is not distributed with most versions of Linux. To obtain a copy, visit the HFS Utilities home page at http://www.mars.org/home/rob/proj/hfs.

See also **hformat, humount**.

humount

humount *device*

Unmounts a Macintosh floppy disk in the specified device (/dev/fd0 or /dev/fd1). This command is part of the HFS Utilities package (hfsutils), which is not distributed with most versions of Linux. To obtain a copy, visit the HFS Utilities home page at http://www.mars.org/home/rob/proj/hfs.

mke2fs

mke2fs [option] *device*

Creates a Linux e2fs filesystem on the specified device, such as a disk partition or a floppy disk.

WARNING This command erases all the data on the specified device.

OPTIONS

Use This Option	To Do This
–b *size*	Specify the size of blocks in bytes. The default is 512.
–c	Check the device for bad blocks before creating the filesystem.
–f *size*	Specify the size of fragments in bytes.
–i *size*	Specify the number of bytes used for each inode.
–N *n*	Manually set the number of inodes reserved for the filesystem.
–l *filename*	Read the list of bad blocks from the specified filename.
–m *n*	Set the percentage of blocks reserved for the superuser to the integer *n*. The default is 5.
–o *type*	Manually set the name of the creator operation system.
–q	Hide all messages.
–s *setting*	Set the sparse superblock flag, which saves space on large filesystems. Do not use on kernels earlier than version 2.2. Available settings are 0 (off) and 1 (on).

OPTIONS *(CONT.)*

Use This Option	To Do This
–F	Force **mke2fs** to run.
–L *string*, **– –volume-label** *string*	Set the filesystem's volume label using a string of no more than 16 characters.
–M, – –last-mounted-directory	Manually set the last mounted directory.
–r	Set the filesystem revision.
–R stride=*n*	Set the number (*n*, an integer) of blocks in a RAID stripe.
–T *type*	Set the intended usage type so that **mke2fs** can optimize the filesystem. The only available type is news.
–V	Display the version number.

EXAMPLES

This Command	Does the Following
mke2fs –c /dev/fd0	Checks the formatted floppy disk in drive fd0 for bad blocks and creates the Linux filesystem on the disk.

mlabel

> **mlabel** [option] *drive:string*
>
> Used on a mounted MS-DOS filesystem, sets the volume label of the specified drive (A or B) to the specified string.

OPTIONS

Use This Option	To Do This
–c	Clear the existing label without replacing it
–s	Show the existing label without replacing it

mount

mount [option] *device* | *directory*

Attaches the device to the specified directory, which will serve as the filesystem's mount point. The directory must exist for this command to succeed. Superuser status (see **su** in Chapter 1) is required to mount all devices except those for which the **user** option is specified in /etc/fstab.

See also **umount**.

OPTIONS

Use This Option	To Do This
−a	Mount all the filesystems listed in /etc/fstab, except those set to **noauto**.
−f	Run through the **mount** procedure and generate all relevant messages but do not actually mount the device.
−r	Mount the device as read only.
−w	Mount the device as read and write. This is the default.
−L *label*	Mount the device that has the specified label.
−t *type*	Mount the device with the specified type of filesystem (see the Filesystem Types table).
−h	Display the available options.
−v	Display the version number.

EXAMPLES

This Command	Does the Following
mount −a	Mounts all the devices listed in /etc/fstab.
mount −t iso9660 /dev/cdrom /mnt/cdrom	Mounts the disk in the CD-ROM drive to the specified mount point (/mnt/cdrom). To mount this device to the specified mount point, the directory /mnt/cdrom must exist.

EXAMPLES *(CONT.)*

This Command	Does the Following
mount -t msdos /dev/ fd0 /mnt/fd0	Mounts the MS-DOS floppy disk in drive fd0 to the specified mount point (/mnt/fd0). To mount this device to the specified mount point, the directory /mnt/fd0 must exist.
mount /dev/cdrom	Mounts the disk in the CD-ROM drive to the mount point given in /etc/fstab.
mount /dev/fd0	Mounts the disk in the floppy disk drive to the mount point given in /etc/fstab.

---

mt

mt [option] *operation*

Instructs the tape drive to carry out the specified operation. Operations that change device defaults require superuser status (see **su** in Chapter 1).

OPERATIONS

Use This Operation	To Do This
asf *n*	Position the tape at the beginning of the *n*th file.
bsfm *n*	Go back *n* files and position the tape on the first block of the next file.
bsf *n*	Go back *n* files and position the tape on the last block of the previous file.
bsr *n*	Go backward *n* records.
bss *n*	Go backward *n* setmarks. This operation is for SCSI tapes only.
compression	Enable data compression if the drive supports it.
datacompression *n*	Set the compression status specified by *n*.

OPERATIONS *(CONT.)*

Use This Operation	To Do This
defblksize *n*	Set the block size to *n* bytes. This operation is for SCSI drives only.
defcompression *compression*	Set the default compression specified by *compression*. This operation is for SCSI drives only.
defdensity *n*	Set the density specified by *n*. This operation is for SCSI drives only.
defdrvbugger *n*	Set the drive buffer code specified by *n*. This operation is for SCSI drives only.
densities	Display some common density codes.
drvbuffer *n*	Set the tape drive buffer to the value specified by *n*.
eod, **seod**	Go to end of valid data.
erase	Erase the tape.
fsfm *n*	Go forward *n* files and position the tape on the last block of the previous file.
fsf *n*	Go forward *n* files and position the tape on the first block of the next file.
fsr *n*	Go forward *n* records.
fss *n*	Go forward *n* setmarks. This operation is for SCSI tapes only.
load	Load the tape. This operation is for SCSI drives only.
lock	Lock the tape drive door. This operation is for SCSI drives only.
mkpartition [*size*]	When used without an argument, formats the tape with one partition. When you specify a size in megabytes, formats the tape with two partitions and makes the second partition the specified size.
offline, **rewoffl**	Rewind the tape and unload.
partseek *n partition*	Set the position to the *n*th block in the specified partition.

OPERATIONS *(CONT.)*

Use This Operation	To Do This
retension	Rewind the tape and retension.
rewind	Rewind the tape.
seek *n*	Go to the *n*th block. This operation is for SCSI tapes only.
setblk *n*	Set the block size of the drive to *n* bytes per record.
setdensity *n*	Set the tape density code to the number specified by *n*.
setpartition *n*	Switch to the partition specified by *n*.
status	Display status information.
stclearoptions *option*	Clear the specified option (see the Driver Options table in this section). This operation is for SCSI drives only.
stlongtimeout *n*	Set the long timeout to the number of seconds specified by *n*.
stopoptions *option*	Enable the specified option (see the Driver Options table in this section). This operation is for SCSI drives only.
stsetoptions *option*	Enable the specified option (see the Driver Options table in this section). This operation is for SCSI drives only.
sttimeout *n*	Set the device timeout to the number of seconds specified by *n*.
stwrthreshold *n*	Set the write threshold to *n* kilobytes. This operation is for SCSI drives only.
tell	Display the current block number.
unlock	Unlock the tape drive door. This operation is for SCSI drives only.
weof *n*	Write *n* end-of-file (EOF) marks at the current position.
wset *n*	Write *n* setmarks at the current position. This operation is for SCSI tapes only.

DRIVER OPTIONS

Use This Option	To Do This
async-writes	Enable asynchronous writes
auto-lock	Automatically lock the drive door
buffer-writes	Enable buffer writes
can-bsr	Specify that this drive can space backward, as well
can-partitions	Specify that the drive can handle partitioned tapes
debug	Turn debugging off
def-writes	Set block size and density for writes
fast-eod	Space directory to eod
no-blklimits	Specify that the drive does not support read block limits
read-ahead	Enable read-ahead
scsi2logical	Use SCSI-2 logical block addresses instead of device-dependent addresses
sysv	Enable System V semantics
two-fms	Write two filemarks when the file is closed

rdev

rdev [option] [*image*] [*value*]

When used without any options or arguments, displays information about the current Linux (ext2) filesystem. When used by a knowledgeable system administrator, this command can also be used to change the default RAM disk size and change other kernel parameters. After you use **rdev** to set the image to the root device of your Linux system (normally /**boot**/vmlinuz), you can use this command to specify the location of the root device. You can then use **cp** (discussed in Chapter 5) to create a boot floppy for emergency boot purposes.

See also **dd**.

EXAMPLES

This Command	Does the Following
rdev /boot/vmlinuz /dev/hda5	Sets the root device (**/boot/vmlinuz**) to the specified boot device (**/dev/hda5**).
dd if=/boot/vmlinuz of=/dev/fd0 bs=8192	Creates an emergency floppy boot disk.

setfdprm

setfdprm [option] *device* [*name*] [parameter]

Set the parameters for the specified device, which is an auto-detecting floppy drive device (**/dev/fd0** or **/dev/fd1**). You can specify the parameters manually by using options, or you can specify a name (such as 720/1440) that corresponds to a line in **/etc/fdprm**.

OPTIONS

Use This Option	To Do This
–c	Clear the current parameters.
–n	Disable format-configuring messages.
–p	Set the specified parameter (dev, size, sec, heads, tracks, stretch, gap, rate, spec1, or fmt_gap). See **/etc/fdprm** for these values. You can specify more than one parameter in a blank, space-separated list.
–y	Enable format-configuring messages.

sync

sync [option]

Flushes the filesystem buffers. After **sync** runs, disk usage statistics are accurate.

See also **df**, **du**.

tune2fs

tune2fs [option] *device*

Adjusts filesystem settings on a Linux e2fs filesystem.

WARNING This command should be used only by experienced system administrators. *Do not run this command on a mounted filesystem.*

See also **dumpe2fs, e2fsck.**

OPTIONS

Use This Option	To Do This
–c *n*	Specify the number of mounts permitted before a mandated filesystem check occurs.
–e *type*	Specify one of the following types of error-handling behavior: **continue** Continue normal operation. **remount-ro** Remount the filesystem as read only. **panic** Initiate a kernel panic.
–g *group*	Specify the group that can use reserved blocks. You can specify the group using a group name or numeric ID.
–i *interval*	Specify one of the following time intervals between mandated filesystem checks, where *n* is an integer: *n***d** Days. *n***m** Months. *n***w** Weeks. To disable forced checks at intervals, use **–i 0**.

OPTIONS *(CONT.)*

Use This Option	To Do This
–l	Display the contents of the filesystem's superblock.
–m *n*	Adjust the percentage of the device set aside for reserved blocks.
–r *n*	Specify the number of reserved blocks.
–s *setting*	Set the sparse superblock flag, which saves space on large filesystems. Do not use on kernels earlier than version 2.2. The available settings are 0 (off) and 1 (on).
–u *user,* **– –user** *user*	Specify the user who can use the reserved blocks. You can specify the user with a username or numeric ID.
–C *n,* **– –mount-count** *n*	Manually set the number of times the filesystem has been mounted.
–L *string,* **– –volume-label** *string*	Set the filesystem's volume label using a string of no more than 16 characters.
–M, – –last-mounted-directory	Manually set the last mounted directory.
–U *uuid*	Manually set the filesystem ID (*uuid*).

umount

umount [option] *device* | *directory*

Unmounts the filesystem specified by the device name or the directory that serves as the filesystem's mount point.

See also **mount.**

OPTIONS

Use This Option	To Do This
–a	Unmount all of the filesystems listed in `/etc/mstab`
–f	Force the unmount

OPTIONS *(CONT.)*

Use This Option	To Do This
–h	Display available options
–n	Unmount without altering /etc/mtab
–r	Try to remount as read only if unmounting fails
–t *type*	Unmount only on the specified filesystem type
–V	Display the version number

EXAMPLES

This Command	Does the Following
umount –t vfat /dev/hda3 /mnt/windoze	Unmounts the vfat filesystem contained on /dev/hda3 and mounted at /mnt/windoze.
umount /dev/cdrom	Unmounts the CD-ROM drive by specifying the device name.
umount /mnt/cdrom	Unmounts the CD-ROM drive by specifying the mount point.

CHAPTER 8

Working with Text Files

$\mathbf{T}$his chapter details the numerous commands you can use to perform operations on text files, including viewing their contents, searching for text in files, summarizing the contents of text files, performing a variety of processing operations on sorted files, checking spelling, formatting text files for printing, and sending files to the printer. This chapter also discusses *regular expressions*, which enable you to write highly specific search strings that are used in many of the utilities discussed in this chapter. You will also find reference documentation for **gawk**, the GNU version of the AWK text-processing language.

AT A GLANCE

How Do I	See This Entry	Example
View a file's contents on-screen and page through the output?	**cat**, **less**, **more**	cat example.txt | less
Quickly compare two files to see whether any differences exist between them?	**cmp**	cmp first-draft.txt second-draft.txt
Compare two sorted files and view the lines that are unique to each?	**comm**	comm file-1.txt file-2.txt | less
Compare two sorted files and view the differences between them with surrounding context?	**diff**	diff -i first-draft .txt second-draft.txt
Search all the files in the working directory for lines containing either of two words?	**egrep**	egrep "winner | loser" *
Convert a text file to PostScript?	**enscript**	enscript -p bug-form.ps bug-form.txt

AT A GLANCE *(CONT.)*

How Do I	See This Entry	Example
Search all the files in the working directory for lines containing a specified word and view the matching lines on-screen?	**grep, egrep, fgrep**	`grep "winner" *`
Search all the files in the working directory for lines containing a specific word and show just the filenames?	**grep, egrep, fgrep**	`grep -l "winner" *`
Search an entire directory tree for files containing a specified word and show just the filenames?	**grep, egrep, fgrep**	`grep -rl "winner" / home/suzanne`
View the first 10 lines of all the .txt files in the working directory?	**head**	`head *.txt | less`
Check the spelling of a text file?	**ispell**	`ispell magic.txt`
Quickly find a line in a sorted file that begins with a specified string?	**look**	`look 'Secret #47' secrets.txt`
View the status of the printing queue?	**lpq**	`lpq`
Print a file using the default print spooler?	**lpr**	`cat example.ps | lpr`
Stop printing all of a user's jobs?	**lprm**	`lprm -`
Number the lines in a text file?	**nl**	`nl magic.txt > magic-numbered.txt`
Convert a Portable Document Format (PDF) file to PostScript?	**pdf2ps**	`pdf2ps resume.pdf resume.ps`

AT A GLANCE *(CONT.)*

How Do I	See This Entry	Example
Prepare a text file for printing with headers and page numbers?	**pr**	`pr magic.txt > lpr`
Create a key-word-in-context (KWIC) concordance of a text file?	**ptx**	`ptx memory.txt > memory.ptx`
Sort the lines of a text file in dictionary order?	**sort**	`sort list.txt > sorted-list.txt`
Translate all the uppercase characters in a text file to lowercase?	**tr**	`cat uppercase.txt	tr '[A-Z]' '[a-z]'`
Remove duplicate lines from two sorted text files?	**uniq**	`uniq dupes.txt nodupes.txt`
View a compressed file on-screen?	**zcat**	`zcat bibliography.gz	less`

Using Regular Expressions

This section discusses the following:

- Basic character matching
- Bounding operators
- Repetition operators
- Bracket operators
- Expression concatenation
- Named character classes

Basic Character Matching

Special characters for basic character matching differ from their shell pattern counterparts (see the section "Shell Patterns" in Chapter 4). For example, the asterisk (*) stands for zero or more repetitions of the preceding character.

SPECIAL CHARACTERS FOR BASIC CHARACTER MATCHING

Special Character	Description	Example	Matches
.	Matches any single character.	essay1	essay1, essay2, essay3, ect.
*	Matches zero or more instances of the preceding character.	hmm*	hmm, hmmm, hmmmm
\	Disables the special meaning of the following character.	essay*	essay*
.*	Matches zero or more instances of any character. This is the equivalent of the shell **regexp ***.	essay.*	essay1, essay2, essay3, essay4

Bounding Operators

Bounding operators enable you to create regular expressions that are linked to the beginning or end of a line or a word. These special characters lose their meaning in bracketed expressions.

SPECIAL CHARACTERS FOR BOUNDING OPERATORS

Bounding Operator	Description	Example	Matches
^	Matches the beginning of a line.	^Dear	*Dear* only if it occurs at the beginning of a line

SPECIAL CHARACTERS FOR BOUNDING OPERATORS *(CONT.)*

Bounding Operator	Description	Example	Matches
\\<	Matches the beginning of a word (**ex** and **vi** only).	`\<location`	*location* but not *dislocation*
\\>	Matches the end of a word (**ex** and **vi** only).	`social\>`	*social* but not *socialism*
$	Matches the end of a line.	`water-front$`	*waterfront* only if it occurs at the end of a line

Repetition Operators

Repetition operators enable you to search for zero or more repetitions of a character or a matching expression. It is not necessary to escape the bracket characters with a backslash (\\{, \\}) when you are using **awk** and **grep**. The ? and + operators are available only with the utilities (**awk, grep –e,** and **egrep**) that recognize *extended regular expressions*, a superset of the regular expression standard.

SPECIAL CHARACTERS FOR REPETITION

Repetition Operator	Description	Example	Matches
?	The preceding item is optional and will be matched at most once (extended regular expressions only).	`do?r`	dor, door
+	The preceding item will be matched one or more times (extended regular expressions only).	`do+r`	door, dooor, dooor, etc.

SPECIAL CHARACTERS FOR REPETITION *(CONT.)*

Repetition Operator	Description	Example	Matches
\\{*n*\\}	The preceding item will be matched exactly *n* times.	do\\{1\\}r	door
\\{*n,*\\}	The preceding item will be matched *n* or more times.	do\\{1,\\}r	door, dooor, doooor
\\{*,n*\\}	The preceding item is optional and will be matched at most one time.	do\\{,1\\}	dor, door

Bracket Operators

Bracket operators enable you to specify alternative characters and character ranges for matching any one character.

SPECIAL CHARACTERS FOR BRACKET OPERATORS

Bracket Operator	Description	Example	Matches
[ ]	Matches any *one* of the enclosed characters	essay[123]	essay1, essay2, essay3
[^]	Matches anything *other* than the enclosed characters.	essay[^123]	essay4, essay5, essay6, etc.
[–]	Matches any character within the range of characters.	essay[1-5]	essay1, essay2, essay3, essay4, essay5, etc.

Expression Concatenation

In **egrep**, expressions can be combined as shown in the following table:

EXPRESSION CONCATENATION METHODS

Concatenation Operator	Description	Example	Matches
expr1 expr2	Matches one or more instances of either *expr* (expression).	`[12] [21]`	11, 12, 21, 22
*expr1	expr2*	Match either of the expressions.	`fish	fowl`	fish, fowl

Named Character Classes

Named character classes comprise a group of predefined bracket expressions. They enable you to specify common character classes more conveniently than their bracketed counterparts. For example, [:alpha:] is the equivalent of [A–Za–z].

CHARACTER CLASSES

Class	Description
[:alpha:]	a b c d e f g h i j k l m n o p q r s t u v w x y z, A B C D E F G H I J K L M N O P Q R S T U V W X Y Z
[:cntrl:]	Any of the following: BEL, BS, CR, FF, HT, NL, or VT
[:alnum:]	Any of the following: [:digit:], [:alpha:]

CHARACTER CLASSES *(CONT.)*

Class	Description
[:punct:]	Any one of the following: ! " #% & ' ( ) ; < = > ? [\ ] * + , – . / : ^ _ { | }
[:digit:]	Any one of the following: 0, 1, 2, 3, 4, 5, 6, 7, 8, 9
[:xdigit:]	Any one of the following: a, b, c, d, e, f, A, B, C, D, E, F, 0, 1, 2, 3, 4, 5, 6, 7, 8, 9
[:lower:]	Any one of the following: a, b, c, d, e, f, g, h, i, j, k, l, m, n, o, p, q, r, s, t, u, v, w, x, y, z
[:upper:]	Any one of the following: A, B, C, D, E, F, G, H, I, J, K, L, M, N, O, P, Q, R, S, T, U, V, W, X, Y, Z
[:space:]	Any one of the following: CR, FF, HT, NL, VT, SPACE
[:graph:]	Anything that is not a [:alphanum:] or a [:punct:]

Alphabetical Command Reference

This section details commands for the following tasks:

- Checking spelling (**ispell**)

- Comparing files (**cmp, diff, sdiff**)

- Creating and using string databases (**fortune, strfile, unstr**).

- Formatting file contents (**column, eqn, fmt, fold, grops, groff, nroff, pr, rev**)

- Operating on characters (**tr, expand, unexpand**)

- Operating on fields within a line (**cut, paste, join**)

- Operating on sorted files (**comm, ptx, sort, tsort, uniq**)

- Printing (**lpr, lpq**)

- Searching for text in files (**egrep, grep, fgrep, awk, gawk, zegrep, zgrep, zfgrep**)

- Summarizing file contents (**cksum, md5sum, sum**)

- Viewing and working with compressed files (**zcat, zcmp, zdiff, zmore**)

- Viewing portions of files (**head, split, tail**)

- Viewing the output of text files (**cat, head, less, more, nl, od, tac, tail**)

- Working with PostScript and Portable Document Format files (**enscript, pdf2ps, pdftotext**)

awk

See **gawk**.

cat

cat [option] [*filename*]

Displays the specified filename on the standard output. If you do not specify a filename, the command reads from the standard input. You can also use a dash (–) by itself to specify input from the standard input. You can specify more than one filename in a space-separated list or by using a shell pattern (see the section "Shell Patterns" in Chapter 4). If you redirect the output to a file, this command concatenates the input files (see the Examples table in this section).

TIP   To view a text file that takes up more than one screenful of display, pipe the output to **less**, for example, `cat README | less`.

OPTIONS

Use This Option	To Do This
–e	Display control and nonprinting characters, except linefeeds and tab, and display $ at the end of each line (same as **–vE**)
–E, – –show-ends	Display $ at the end of each line
– –help	Show available options
–n, – –number	Number all output lines, even blank ones
–s, – squeeze-lank	Show no more than one blank line
–t	Display control and nonprinting characters, except linefeeds (same as **–vT**)
–T, – –show-tabs	Display Tab characters as ^I
–v, – –show-nonprinting	Display control and nonprinting characters, except linefeeds and Tab
– –version	Show the version number
– –b, – –number-nonblank	Number the output lines unless they are blank

EXAMPLES

This Command	Does the Following
cat example.txt	Displays the specified file (example.txt). If the file is too long to view conveniently on one screen, use **less** or **more**, as in the following examples.
cat example.txt | less	Displays the specified file (example.txt) using the **less** utility.
cat example.txt | more	Displays the specified file (example.txt) using the **more** utility.
cat -s example.txt | less	Displays the specified file (example.txt) using the **less** utility and suppresses blank lines.
cat -n example.txt | less	Displays the specified file (example.txt) using the **less** utility and numbers the lines.
cat file1.txt file2.txt > file3.txt	Concatenates the two input files (file1.txt and file2.txt) and writes the output to a third file (file3.txt).

cksum

cksum [*filename*]

Performs a cyclic redundancy check (CRC) for the specified filename to determine whether the file has been altered or damaged. You can specify more than one filename in a space-separated list or by using a shell pattern (see the section "Shell Patterns" in Chapter 4). This command's output consists of an identifying code that uniquely identifies the file's contents; a change in even one of the file's characters will cause the code to differ.

EXAMPLES

This Command	Does the Following
cksum *.txt	Performs a CRC check on all the .txt files in the working directory; the output consists of the CRC code and the filenames in a columnar list.
cksum article.doc > article.crc	Writes the checksum of the specified file (article.doc) to a file (article.crc).

cmp

cmp [option] *filename1 filename2*

Quickly compares the two specified files (*filename1* and *filename2*) to determine whether any differences exist. If the files are identical, the program exits without displaying a message.

See also **diff**.

OPTIONS

Use This Option	To Do This
–l, – –verbose	Print the byte numbers of each difference and show the differing values (in octal notation)
–s, – –silent, – –quiet	Indicate nothing but generate the following exit codes: 0 (the files are identical) or 1 (the files differ)
–c, – –char	Print the differing bytes as characters

EXAMPLE

This Command	Does the Following
cmp first–draft.txt second–draft.txt	Displays the first encountered difference between the two files, if any.

column

column [option] [*filename*]

Formats the input text specified by *filename* into a five-column list, filling the rows first. You can change the number of columns by using the -c option, and you can fill the columns first by using the -x option. The default delimitation character is white space. The input file must be a sorted text file (see **sort**). By default, the utility writes to the standard output. Use output redirection to write to a file.

OPTIONS

Use This Option	To Do This
–c *n*	Output is formatted for a display *n* columns wide
–s *character*	Specify a character to be used to delimit columns for the **–t** option
–t	Create a table with columns delineated by white space or the character specified by the **–s** option
–x	Fill columns before filling rows

EXAMPLES

This Command	Does the Following
`column list.txt > list-table.txt`	Organizes the lines in `list.txt` into columns and writes the result to `list-table.txt`.
`columns -x list.txt > list-table.txt`	Same as above, except fills the columns before the rows.

comm

comm [option] *filename1 filename2*

Compares the lines that are common to *filename1* and *filename2*. The output shows three columns. In column 1, you see the lines unique to *filename1*. In column 2, you see the lines unique to *filename2*. In column 3, you see the lines that are common to both files.

See also **cmp, diff, diff3, uniq.**

OPTIONS

Use This Option	To Do This
–1	Omit column 1
–2	Omit column 2
–3	Omit column 3
– –help	Show the available options
– –version	Show the version number

EXAMPLE

This Command	Does the Following
comm file-1.txt file-2.txt | less	Shows the lines unique to file-1.txt and file-2.txt and the lines that are common to both files. Displays the results on-screen.

cut

cut [option] [*filename*]

Displays a range of characters from the specified filename. You can specify more than one filename in a space-separated list or by using a shell pattern (see the section "Shell Patterns" in Chapter 4). If you omit the filename, the utility takes input from the standard input.

OPTIONS

Use This Option	To Do This
–b *range*, **– –bytes=***range*	Output only the bytes specified by *range* (see the Ranges table in this section).
–c *range*, **– –characters=***range*	Output only the characters specified by *range* (see the Ranges table in this section).
–d, **– –delimiter=***character*	Use *character* instead of tab for the field delimiter.
–f *range*, **– –fields=***range*	Output only the fields specified by *range* (see the Ranges table in this section).
– –help	Display this help and exit.
– –output–delimiter=*string*	Use *string* as the output delimiter. The default is to use the input delimiter.
–s, **– –only-delimited**	Print only those lines that contain delimiters.
– –version	Show the version number.

RANGES

Range	Description
n	The *n*th byte, character, or field
–m	A range extending from the first to the *m*th byte, character, or field
n–	A range extending from the *n*th byte, character, or field to the end of line
n–m	A range extending from the *n*th to the *m*th byte, character, or field

diff

diff [option] *filename1 filename2*

Compares the two text files specified by *filename1* and *filename2*. By default, the output shows each change in context, with the *filename1* text preceded by a < and the *filename2* text preceded by a >. You can also compare directories. If you specify two directories instead of files, **diff** compares only those files with the same names.

See also **cmp**, **diff3**.

OPTIONS

Use This Option	To Do This
–p, **– –show-c-function**	Display the C programming function in which each change is located.
–t, **– –expand-tabs**	Expand tabs to spaces in the output file.
–e – –ed	Generates a script that can transform the first file into the second file using the **ed** editor.
–b, **– –ignore-space-change**	Ignore changes in the amount of white space.
–i, **– –ignore-case**	Ignore changes in case.
–B, **– –ignore-blank-lines**	Ignore changes that insert or delete blank lines.
–I *regexp*	Ignore changes that insert or delete *regexp* (regular expression).
–w, **– –ignore-all-space**	Ignore white space when comparing lines.
–N – –new-file	In a directory comparison, if a file is found in only one directory, treat it as present but empty in the other directory.

OPTIONS *(CONT.)*

Use This Option	To Do This
–X *filename*, **– –exclude-from=** *filename*	In a directory comparison, ignore the files and directories specified by the base names in the specified filename.
– –exclude=*shell regexp*	In a directory comparison, ignore the files and directories specified by *shell regexp* (see the section "Shell Patterns," in Chapter 4).
–F *regexp*, **– –show-function-line=** *regexp*	In context and unified format, show portions of the line preceding *regexp* (regular expression).
–T, **– –initial-tab**	In normal or context format, display a tab rather than a space before the text of a line.
–q, **– –brief**	Report only whether the files differ not the details of the differences.
–s, **– –report-identical-files**	Report when two files are the same.
–l, **– –paginate**	Route the output through **pr** to paginate it.
–v, **– –version**	Show the version number.
–H, **– –speed-large-files**	Speed the handling of large files with many scattered small changes.
–a, **– –text**	Treat all files as text and compare them line by line.
–C [*n*], **– –context** [**=** *n*]	Use the context output format, showing *n* lines (an integer) of context. The default is three lines.
–y, **– –side-by-side**	Use the side-by-side output format.
–L *string* **– –label=***string*	Use *string* instead of the filename in the context and unified format headers.

OPTIONS *(CONT.)*

Use This Option	To Do This
–U [*n*], – –**unified**[=*n*]	Use the unified output format (shows the old line and the new line in a block) with *n* lines of context. The default is three lines.
–x *regexp*	When comparing directories, ignore files and subdirectories whose base names match *regexp*.
–r, – –**recursive**	When comparing directories, recursively compare any subdirectories found.
–S, *filename*, – –**starting-file**=*filename*	When comparing directories, start with the specified filename.
–r, – –**recursive**	Compare a directory and all of its associated subdirectories.

EXAMPLE

This Command	Does the Following
`diff –i first–draft.txt second–draft.txt`	Compares the two specified files and shows the differences between them, ignoring all changes involving white space.

diff3

diff3 [option] *filename1 filename2 filename3*

Compare the three files specified by *filename1, filename2,* and *filename3* and show which files differ. A line of equals marks (=) indicates that all three files differ. A line of equals marks followed by the number 1, 2, or 3 indicates which of the three files differs from the other two. This utility can also find changes made in two newer files (*filename1* and *filename3*) from an original version of the two files (*filename2*). It can merge differences in one of the newer files to the other newer file. If all three files differ in the same place, the instance is called *overlapping*.

See also **cmp, comm, diff.**

OPTIONS

Use This Option	To Do This
–3	Create an **ed** script that incorporates all changes between *filename2* (the original file) and *filename3* into the *filename1,* but make changes only when they are non-overlapping
–A, – –show-all	Incorporate all changes, surrounding all conflicts with bracket lines
–a, – –text	Treat all files as text and compare them line by line
–e, – –ed	Create an **ed** script that incorporates all changes between *filename2* (the original file) and *filename3* into *filename1*
–E, – –show-overlap	Create an **ed** script that incorporates all changes between *filename2* (the original file) and *filename3* into *filename1* and show the overlap conflicts in brackets
–m – –merge	Directly incorporate all changes between *filename2* (the original file) and *filename3* into filename1, without making an **ed** script
–T, – –initial-tab	Display with a tab before each line
–v – –version	Show the version number
–X	Create an **ed** script to incorporate all overlap conflicts into *filename1* and show the overlap conflicts with brackets
–x, – –overlap-only	Create an **ed** script to incorporate all overlap conflicts into *filename1*

egrep

egrep [option] *regexp filename*

Search the specified filename for the *regexp* (a regular expression). Unlike **grep**, **egrep** supports the extended regular expression characters: +, ?, |, and ( ). You can specify more than one filename in a space-separated list or by using a shell pattern (see the section "Shell Patterns" in Chapter 4).

See also **fgrep**.

OPTIONS

Use This Option	To Do This
–A *n*, – –**after-context=***n*	Display *n* lines of trailing context after matching lines.
–b, – –**byte-offset**	Display the byte offset within the input file before each line of output.
–B *n*, – –**before-context=***n*	Display *n* lines of leading context before matching lines.
–c, – –**count**	Display a count of matching lines for each input file and hide normal output.
–C *n*, – –**context** *n*	Display *n* lines of output context. The default is two lines.
–d *action*, – –**directories=***action*	In directory searches, perform the specified action. Valid options are **read** (use this directory), **recurse** (same as **–r**), or **skip**.
–e *regexp*, – –**regexp=***regexp*	Use *regexp* (regular expression). This option is provided in case you need to perform a search that begins with a hyphen.
–F, – –**fixed-strings**	Force **grep** to behave like **fgrep** (searches using standard regular expressions).

OPTIONS *(CONT.)*

Use This Option	To Do This
–f *filename*, **– –file**=*filename*	Get the regular expressions from the specified filename, one per line.
–G – –basic-regexp	Force **egrep** to behave like **grep** (searches using basic regular expressions).
–h, **– –no-filename**	Hide the display of filenames during the search.
–i, **– –ignore-case**	Ignore case distinctions in both the *regexp* and the input files.
–l, **– –files-with-matches**	Show only the names of matching files but not the matching content. The search stops with the first match.
–L, **– –files-without-match**	Show only the names of files that do not match.
–n	Show *n* lines of leading and trailing content.
–n, **– –line-number**	Show line numbers.
–q, **– –quiet**, **– –silent**	Hide messages.
–r, **– –recursive**	Search all the files in the directory and all of its associated subdirectories.
–s, **– –no-messages**	Suppress error messages about nonexistent or unreadable files.
–v, **– –revert-match**	Show non-matching instead of matching lines.
–V, **– –version**	Show the version number.
–w, **– –word-regexp**	Match whole words only.
–x, **– –line-regexp**	Match the whole line only.

EXAMPLES

This Command	Does the Following
`egrep " (money | cash) " *.txt`	Search all the `.txt` files in the working directory for those that contain the word *money* or *cash*.

EXAMPLES *(CONT.)*

This Command	Does the Following
egrep "9+50" *.txt	Search all the .txt files in the working directory for those that contain 9950, 99950, 999950, etc.
egrep -r " ([Ss]uzanne | [Ll]ydia)" .	Search the working directory (.) and all associated subdirectories for files containing *Suzanne*, *suzanne*, *Lydia*, or *lydia*.

enscript

enscript [option] [*filename*]

Converts the text file specified by *filename* into PostScript. The output can be directed to the printer or to a file. You can specify more than one filename in a space-separated list or by using a shell pattern (see the section "Shell Patterns" in Chapter 4).

OPTIONS

UseThis Option	To DoThis
–*n*	Print *n* copies of each page.
–1, **–2**, **– –columns=***n*	Use 1, 2, or *n* columns on each page.
–A *n*, **– –file-align=***n*	Align input files to the page count specified by *n*.
–a *pages*, **– –pages=***pages*	Specify which pages are printed using one of the following settings for *pages*: **begin-end** Print all pages. **–end** Print from 0 to end. ***n*** Print page *n*. **odd** Print odd pages. **even** Print even pages.
–B, **– –no-header**	Omit page headers.

OPTIONS *(CONT.)*

Use This Option	To Do This
–b *string,* **– –header=***string*	Use *string* as a page header. The default page header is constructed from the file's name and last modification time.
–c, **– –truncate-lines**	Omit lines that will not fit on the page rather than wrapping them. Wrapping is the default.
–C [*n*], **– –line-numbers** [= *n*]	Show line numbers. Optionally, start printing line numbers at line *n*.
– –color[=*color*]	Set the pretty-printing color model to *color*.
–D key[:*value*], **– –setpagedevice=key**[:*value*]	Pass a page device definition to the generated PostScript output.
– –download-font=*font*	Include the font description file (`.pfa` or `.pfb` file) of *font* in the output.
–d *printer*	Spool output to *printer*.
–e[*character*], **– –escapes**[=*character*]	Enable escape interpretation for *character*.
–E [*lang*], **– –pretty-print** [= *lang*]	Print source code attractively. You can optionally specify the programming language (*lang*).
–f *font,* **– –font=***font*	Use the specified font for body text.
–F *font,* **– –header-font=***font*	Use the specified font for header text.
– –filter-stdin=*name*	Specify how **stdin** is shown to the input filter.
–G	Print fancy page header.
–g, **– –print-anyway**	Print file even if it contains binary data.
–h, **– –no-job-header**	Suppress printing of the job header page.

OPTIONS *(CONT.)*

Use This Option	To Do This
–H[*n*], **– –highlight-bars**[**=***n*]	Print highlight bars with a height of two lines (the default) or *n* lines.
– –h-column-height=*points*	Set the horizontal column height to the number of points.
– –help	Display the available options.
– –help-pretty-print	Describe all supported pretty-print languages and file formats.
– –highlight-bar-gray=*level*	Specify the gray level used to print highlight bars.
–I *filter*, **– –filter=***filter*	Read all input files through the input filter.
–i *n*, **– –indent=***n*	Indent every line *n* characters.
–j, **– –borders**	Print borders around columns.
–J *string*	Use *string* as a title.
–K, **– –no-page-prefeed**	Disable page prefeed, which is the default.
–k, **– –page-prefeed**	Enable page prefeed.
–l, **– –lineprinter**	Emulate a line printer. This option is a shortcut for the **– –lines-per-page=66** and **– –no-header** options.
– –list-media	List the names of all known output media.
– –list-options	List all options and their current values.
–L *n*, **– –lines-per-page=***n*	Print only *n* lines per each page.
–m, **– –mail**	Send mail notification to the user when the print job is complete.
– –margins=*points:points:points:points*	Set the left, right, top, and bottom margins to the specified number of points.

OPTIONS *(CONT.)*

Use This Option	To Do This
– –**mark-wrapped-lines**[=*style*]	Mark wrapped lines in specified style. Valid values for *style* are the following: **none**　No marking. This is the default. **plus**　Print a plus (+) character to the end of each wrapped line. **box**　Print a black box to the end of each wrapped line. **arrow**　Print a small arrow at the end of each wrapped line.
–**M** *name*, – –**media=***name*	Select the output media name. The default is *Letter*.
–**N** *character*, – –**newline=***character*	Select the newline character. For *character*, use one of the following: **n**　Linux newline character. **r**　Mac newline character.
–**n** *n*, – –**copies=***n*	Print *n* copies of each page.
– –**non-printable-format=***format*	Specify the format for non-printable characters. Valid values for *format* are the following: **caret**　Caret notation. **octal**　Octal notation. This is the default. **questionmark**　Replace non-printable characters with a question mark (?). **space**　Replace non-printable characters with a space.
– –**nup-xpad=***points*	Set the page x-padding to the number of points. The default is 10.
– –**nup-ypad=***points*	Set the page y-padding to the number of points. The default is 10.
–**O**, – –**missing-characters**	Print a listing of unprintable character codes.

OPTIONS *(CONT.)*

Use This Option	To Do This
–o *filename*	Print and also save the output to the specified filename.
– –page-label-format=format	Set the page label format to the specified format. Valid values for *format* are the following: **short** Print the current page number. **long** Print the current filename and page number.
–p *filename*, **– –output=**filename	Direct output to the file specified by *filename.*
–P *printer*, **– –printer=**printer	Print using the specified printer.
– –printer-options=options	Pass extra options to the printer command.
– –ps-level=level	Set the PostScript language level (1 or 2).
–q, **– –quiet**, **– –silent**	Suppress messages.
–r, **– –landscape**	Print in landscape mode.
–R, **– –portrait**	Print in portrait mode. This is the default.
– –rotate-even-pages	Rotate each even-numbered page 180 degrees.
–S key[:*value*], **– –statusdict= key**[:*value*]	Pass a statusdict definition to the generated PostScript output.
– –slice=n	Print vertical slice *n.*
–s *n*, **– –baselineskip=**n	Specify the baseline skip in *n* Post-Script points.
–T *n*, **– –tabsize=**n	Set tab width to *n.* The default is 8.
– –toc	Print the table of contents.
–t *string*, **– –title=**string	Set the banner page's job title to *string.*

OPTIONS *(CONT.)*

Use This Option	To Do This
–u[*string*], **– –underlay**[=*string*]	Print *string* under every page. You can change the text's properties with the following options: **– –ul-angle**, **– –ul-font**, **– –ul-gray**, **– –ul-position**, and **– –ul-style**.
– –ul-angle=*angle*	Set the underlay text's angle.
– –ul-font=*name*	Select the font for the underlay text.
– –ul-gray=*value*	Print the underlay text with a gray value ranging from 0 to 1.
– –ul-position=*position_spec*	Set the underlay text's starting position according to *position_spec*.
– –ul-style=*style*	Set the underlay text's style to *style*. Valid values for *style* are the following: **outline** Print outline underlay texts. This is the default. **filled** Print filled underlay texts.
–U *n*, **– –nup**=*n*	Print *n* logical pages on each output page.
–v, **– –verbose**[=*level*]	Show messages.
–V, **– –version**	Display the version number.
–W [*format*], **– –language**[=*format*]	Generate output in the specified format. Valid values for *format* are the following: **PostScript** PostScript output. **html** HTML output. **overstrike** Overstrike output. **rtf** Rich Text Format output.
– –word-wrap	Wrap long lines.

OPTIONS *(CONT.)*

Use This Option	To Do This
–X *encoding*, **– –encoding**=*encoding*	Use character encoding. Valid values for *encoding* are the following: **88591, latin1** ISO-8859-1 (ISO Latin1). **88592, latin2** ISO-8859-2 (ISO Latin2). **88593, latin3** ISO-8859-3 (ISO Latin3). **88594, latin4** ISO-8859-4 (ISO Latin4). **88595, cyrillic** ISO-8859-5 (ISO Cyrillic). **88597, greek** ISO-8859-7 (ISO Greek). **ascii** 7-bit ascii. **asciifise, asciifi, asciise** 7-bit ascii with some scandinavian (fi, se) extensions. **asciidkno, asciidk, asciino** 7-bit ascii with some scandinavian (dk, no) extensions. **ibmpc, pc, dos** IBM PC charset. **mac** Mac charset. **vms** VMS multinational charset. **hp8** HP Roman-8 charset. **koi8** Adobe Standard Cyrillic Font KOI8 charset. **ps, PS** PostScript font's default encoding. **pslatin1, ISOLatin1Encoding** PostScript interpreter's ISO Latin 1 Encoding.
–z, – –no-formfeed	Turn off form feed character interpretation.
–Z, – –pass-through	Pass through all PostScript and PCL files without any modifications.

EXAMPLE

This Command	Does the Following
`enscript -p bug-form.ps bug-form.txt`	Converts input file (`bugform.txt`) to PostScript and writes to the output file (`bug-form.ps`).

eqn

eqn [option] [*filename*]

Compiles descriptions of equations in the **troff** input filename into commands recognized by **troff**. You can specify more than one filename in a space-separated list or by using a shell pattern (see the section "Shell Patterns" in Chapter 4). Although the GNU version of **eqn** closely resembles the Unix version, its output files require the GNU version of **troff**. The utility's default configuration file is /usr/lib/groff/tmac/eqnrc.

OPTIONS

Use This Option	To Do This
–C	Recognize .EQ and .EN even when followed by a character other than space or newline.
–N	Prohibit the use of newlines within delimiters.
–v	Display the version number.
–r	Reduce by one size.
–m *points*	Set the minimum point size to *points*.
–T *device*	Route output to *device*. The default is ps.
–M *directory*	Search the specified directory for **eqnrc** before searching the default directories.
–R	Run without consulting the configuration file.
–f *font*	Use the specified font.
–p *points*	Format subscripts and superscripts using a size that is the specified number of points smaller than the surrounding text.

expand

expand [option] *filename*

Converts the tabs in the specified filename to spaces and writes to the standard output. To write to a file, use output redirection. You can specify more than one filename in a space-separated list or by using a shell pattern (see the section "Shell Patterns" in Chapter 4). If you specify the filename with a hyphen (–), the utility accepts input from the standard input.

OPTIONS

Use This Option	To Do This
–i, – –initial	Omit conversion of tabs after anything other than white space
–t, – –tabs=*n*	Use number (*n*) of spaces for the default tab width
–t, – –tabs=*list*	Set tab positions to the positions specified in the comma-separated list
– –help	Show the available options
– –version	Show the version number

fgrep

fgrep [option] *string-list filename*

Search the specified filename for lines that match one or more strings listed in *string-list,* which is typed in a newline-separated list. You can specify more than one filename in a space-separated list or by using a shell pattern (see the section "Shell Patterns" in Chapter 4).

See also **egrep, grep.**

OPTIONS

Use This Option	To Do This
–A *n*, **– –after-context=***n*	Display *n* lines of trailing context after matching lines.
–b, **– –byte-offset**	Display the byte offset in the input file before each line of output.
–B *n*, **– –before-context=***n*	Display *n* lines of leading context before matching lines.
–C *n*, **– –context** *n*	Display *n* lines of output context. The default is 2.
–c, **– –count**	Display a count of matching lines for each input file and hide normal output.
–d *action*, **– –directories=***action*	In directory searches, perform the specified action. Valid options are **read** (use this directory), **recurse** (same as **–r**), or **skip**.
–e *regexp*, **– –regexp=***regexp*	Use *regexp* (regular expression). This option is provided in case you need to perform a search that begins with a hyphen.
–f *filename*, **– –file=***filename*	Get the regular expressions from the specified filename, one per line.
–h, **– –no-filename**	Hide the display of filenames during the search.
–i, **– –ignore-case**	Ignore case distinctions in both the *regexp* and the input files.
–l, **– –files-with-matches**	Show only the names of matching files but not the matching content. The search stops with the first match.
–L, **– –files-without-match**	Show only the names of files that do not match. The search stops with the first match.
–*n*	Show *n* lines of leading and trailing content.
–n, **– –line-number**	Show line numbers.

OPTIONS *(CONT.)*

Use This Option	To Do This
–q, – –quiet, – –silent	Hide messages.
–r, – –recursive	Search all the files in the directory and all of its associated subdirectories.
–s, – –no-messages	Suppress error messages about nonexistent or unreadable files.
–v, – –revert-match	Show non-matching instead of matching lines.
–V, – –version	Show the version number.
–w, – –word-regexp	Match whole words only.
–x, – –line-regexp	Match the whole line only.
–G, – –basic-regexp	Force **fgrep** to behave like **grep** (searches using standard regular expressions).
–E, – –extended– –regexp	Force **fgrep** to behave like **egrep** (searches using extended regular expressions).

fmt

fmt [option] *filename*

Reformats each line in the specified filename so that the lines are filled to the specified width and writes to the standard output. You can specify more than one filename in a space-separated list or by using a shell pattern (see the section "Shell Patterns" in Chapter 4). If you specify the filename with a dash (–), this utility accepts input from the standard input.

OPTIONS

Use This Option	To Do This
–c, – –crown-margin	Preserve indentations.
–p, – –prefix=*string*	Combine lines that begin with *string*.

OPTIONS *(CONT.)*

Use This Option	To Do This
–s, – –split-only	Wrap lengthy lines without refilling.
–t, – –tagged-paragraph	Indent the first line differently from the second line.
–u, – –uniform-spacing	Place one space between words and two spaces between sentences.
–w *n*, **– –width=***n*	Specify the maximum line length in *n* columns. The default is 75 columns.
– –help	Show the available options.
– –version	Show the version number.

EXAMPLE

This Command	Does the Following
`fmt –w 65 notes.txt >` `notes–formatted.txt`	Formats the specified input file (`notes.txt`) so that the lines take up no more than 65 spaces. Writes the output to `notes. formatted.txt`.

---

fold

fold [option] [*filename*]

Wrap the lines in the specified filename to the width specified by the –w option. You can specify more than one filename in a space-separated list or by using a shell pattern (see the section "Shell Patterns" in Chapter 4).

OPTIONS

Use This Option	To Do This
–b, – –bytes	Set the width in bytes rather than columns
–s, – –spaces	Create the break at spaces

OPTIONS *(CONT.)*

Use This Option	To Do This
–w *n*, **– –width=***n*	Set the width to *n* columns
– –help	Show the available options
– –version	Show the version number

EXAMPLE

This Command	Does the Following
`fold –w 45 example.txt >` `example-narrow.txt`	Reformats the specified input file (`example.txt`) with a line length of 45 columns and writes the result to `example-narrow.txt`.

---

fortune

fortune [option]

Displays quotations, aphorisms, poems, jokes, and witticisms from a series of text databases on a variety of subjects (including kids, literature, love, magic, pets, Star Trek, and many more).

See also **strfile**.

OPTIONS

Use This Option	To Do This
–e	Consider all fortune files to be of equal size.
–f	Print a list of available fortune files.
–l	Show long fortunes only.
–m *regexp*	Print all fortunes that contain a match for the *regexp* (a basic regular expression).
–n *length*	Set the longest length in characters for short fortunes. The default is 160 characters.

OPTIONS *(CONT.)*

Use This Option	To Do This
–s	Print short fortunes only.
–i	Ignore case for **–m** searches.
–w	Wait before terminating.

EXAMPLES

This Command	Does the Following
fortune	Prints a random fortune.
fortune –m lonely	Finds all the fortunes that match the string "lonely".

gawk

gawk [option] **–f** *program file* [– –] *filename*

gawk [option] [– –] *'statement' filename*

Launches the GNU version of the program interpreter for the AWK programming language. Note that this entry is not intended to teach the fundamentals of AWK programming; it is intended for reference purposes only.

Gawk uses the program file specified by **–f** *program file* or a statement typed at the command line and enclosed in single quotation marks. It then performs pattern scanning and processing on the specified filename. You can specify more than one filename in a space-separated list or by using a shell pattern (see the section "Shell Patterns" in Chapter 4). AWK enables you to write programs that search the input filename for lines matching a pattern and then performs an action on the line. The basic syntax of an AWK program is a one-line statement, such as the following:

```
pattern { action }
```

In this statement, `pattern` specifies the text to match (see the Patterns table in this section), while `action` is one of the available actions described in Actions table in this section. When **gawk** reads a text file, it regards each line of text as a record. The built-in variable **RS** specifies how the record should be broken into sequentially numbered fields ($1, $2, $3, etc.). The built-in variable $0 refers to the whole record.

OPTIONS

Use This Option	To Do This
–F *string*, **– –field-separator** *string*	Use *string* for the input field separator. You can also use a regular expression.
–v *variable=value*	Create *variable* and assign the indicated value.
–f *filename* **– –file** *filename*	Read the AWK program source from *filename* instead of from the first command line argument.
–mf *n* **–mr** *n*	Set the **mf** or **mr** memory flags to *n*.
–W traditional, –W compat – –traditional, – –compat	Run in IUNIX-AWK compatibility mode.
–W copyleft, –W copyright, – –copyleft, – –copyright	Display the program license.
–W help, –W usage, – –help, – –usage	Show the available options.
–W lint, – –lint	Provide warnings about constructs that are not portable to other AWK versions.
–W lint-old, – –lint-old	Provide warnings about constructs that are not portable to the original Unix version of AWK.
–W posix, – –posix	Enable POSIX compatibility mode.
–W re-interval, – –re-interval	Enable the use of interval expressions in regular expression matching.
–W source *program text*, **– –source** *program text*	Use *program text* as the AWK program source code.
–W version, – –version	Show the version number.
– –	Signal the end of options.

PATTERNS

Pattern Type and Example	Description
Regular expression: `/[Aa]bout/`	An extended regular expression. Note that ^ and $ can be used to anchor the beginning and end of records, respectively. The example specifies a search for *About* or *about*.
Relational expression: `$2 > 11219`	An expression that compares one string or numeric value to another. See the Operators table in this section for a list of valid operator symbols. The example specifies a search in which Field 2 contains a value greater than 11,219.
Quoted string: `"Sea Foam"`	A string to match exactly. The example specifies a search for *Sea Foam*.
Concatenated expressions: `$3 ~"sloop" && $4 > 80000`	Two or more expressions linked by logical operators. You can use || (OR), && (AND), or ! (NOT). The example specifies a search for a record in which Field 3 contains sloop, and Field 4 is greater than 80,000.

ACTIONS

Use This Action	To Do This
atan2(y,x)	Return the arc tangent of y/x in radians.
break	Exit from a **for** or **while** loop.
close(filename**)**	Close the specified filename or a pipe.
continue	Begin the next iteration of a loop (see **for** and **while** in this table).
cos(x)	Return the cosine of x.
delete(array[element]**)**	Delete the specified array or, optionally, one element in it.
do command **while(**condition**)**	Perform the specified command while the specified condition remains true.

ACTIONS *(CONT.)*

Use This Action	To Do This
exit	Skip remaining instructions and stop reading the input.
exp(*x*)	Return the natural exponent of *x*.
fflush(*filename*)	Write output to the specified filename.
for(*lower; upper* [; *increment*]) *command*	When the variable *i* lies in the range specified by *lower* and *upper,* perform the specified command. Use relational expressions to specify *lower* and *upper,* as in this example: i>15; i<29. You can also specify an increment. Use **++** to increase the value of the variable or **– –** to decrease the value, as in i++.
for(*item* **in** *array*) *command*	For each item in *array,* perform the specified command.
gensub(*regexp, substitute string, action* [, *string*])	Search the target string, or the entire record if *string* is omitted, for *regexp* (regular expression). If *action* is a string beginning with *g* or *G*, replace the string with *substitute string*; otherwise, the substitution is made only in output and only one substitution is made (see **gsub** in this table). For *action*, you can also specify a number indicating which match to replace.
getline *variable* [*<filename*]	Set the indicated *variable* to the next input record. If you specify a *filename*, this action uses the next input record in the file.
gsub(*regexp, substitute-string* [, *string*])	Search for the specified string, or the entire record if *string* is omitted, for all the matches of *regexp* (regular expression) and replace them with the specified substitute string. Compare with **sub** in this table.

ACTIONS *(CONT.)*

Use This Action	To Do This
if (*condition*) *command1* [**else** *command2*]	Perform a conditional execution: if *condition* is true, perform *command1*. You can optionally specify a command to perform (*command2*) if the condition is not met. Use a relational expression (see the Operators table in this section) to specify the condition.
index(*substring, string*)	Return the position of *substring* within *string,* or 0 if the string is not present.
int(*x*)	Truncate *x* to an integer. For example, **int**(3.9) yields 3.
length([*string*])	Return the length of *string* or the length of $0 (the entire record) if *string* is omitted.
log(*x*)	Return the natural logarithm of *x*.
match(*string, regexp*)	Return the position in *string* where *regexp* starts and sets the values of RSTART and RLENGTH.
next	Stop processing the current input record and go to the next one.
nextfile	Stop processing the current input file and go to the next one.
print [*expression*] [**>** *filename*]	Print the current record if *expression* is not specified. Use output redirection to send the output to the specified filename. For *expression*, you can use one or more of the following: quoted text to display on-screen; a comma-separated list of fields to display, such as $1, $2, etc. (The fields will be shown in the order indicated, and they will be separated by the character specified by the OFS variable. By default, this is a space.); a variable name.

ACTIONS *(CONT.)*

Use This Action	To Do This
printf [*format* [*expression*]] [**>** *filename*]	Generate formatted output using the conventions of the C programming language's printf statement.
rand()	Return a random number between 0 and 1.
sin(*x***)**	Returns the sine of *x*, which is in radians.
split(*string, array* [, *regexp*]**)**	Split the specified string into the specified array at the location of *regexp*, a regular expression, and return the number of fields. If you omit *regexp*, **gawk** uses the current value of FS. By default, this value is a space.
sprintf(fmt, expr-list)	Generate formatted output using the conventions of the C programming language's printf statement but do not print the resulting string; instead, it is returned as an exit value.
sqrt(*x***)**	Return the square root of *x*.
srand([*string*]**)**	Use *string* as the new seed for the random number generator. If no string is specified, the time of day is used.
strftime([*format* [, *time*]]**)**	Format the time according to the specifications in *format*. These specifications use the conventions of the C programming language's strftime statement.
sub(*regexp, substitute string* [, *string*]**)**	Search for the specified string (or the entire record, if *string* is omitted) for the first match of *regexp* (regular expression) and replace it with the specified substitute string. Compare to **gsub** in this table.
substr(*string, i* [, *n*]**)**	Return the substring of the specified string that begins at character position *i* and ends at position *n*. If you omit *n*, the end position is defined as the end of the string.

ACTIONS *(CONT.)*

Use This Action	To Do This
systime()	Return the current time of day as the number of seconds since the Dawn of Time, as defined in Unix (Midnight UTC, January 1, 1970).
tolower(*string***)**	Return a copy of the specified string using all lowercase letters.
toupper(*string***)**	Return a copy of the specified string using all uppercase letters.

OPERATORS

Operator	Description
$*n*	Field *n*. $0 refers to the whole record.
++ – –	Increment or decrement.
^	Exponentiation.
+ – !	Unary plus, unary minus, and logical negation.
* / %	Multiplication, division, and modulus.
+ –	Addition and subtraction.
space	String concatenation.
<	Relational operators.
>	
<=	
>=	
!=	
==	
~ !~	Regular expression match, negated match.
in	Array membership.
&&	Logical AND.
‖	Logical OR.
?:	The C conditional expression.

OPERATORS *(CONT.)*

Operator	Description
=	Assignment operators.
+=	
- =	
*=	
/=	
%=	
^=	

BUILT-IN VARIABLES

Variable	Description
ARGC	The number of command line arguments.
ARGIND	The index in ARGV of the current file being processed.
ARGV	Array of command line arguments.
CONVFMT	The conversion format for numbers.
ENVIRON	An array containing the current environmental variables.
ERRNO	The last error.
FIELDWIDTHS	A white-space-separated list of field widths.
FILENAME	The name of the current input file.
FNR	The input record number in the current input file.
FS	The input field separator. By default, this is a space.
IGNORECASE	The case sensitivity setting.
NF	The number of fields in the current input record.
NR	The total number of input records seen so far.
OFMT	The output format for numbers, %.6g by default.
OFS	The output field separator, a space by default.
ORS	The output record separator, a newline by default.
RS	The input record separator, a newline by default.
RT	The record terminator.
RSTART	The index of the first character matched by match().
RLENGTH	The length of the string matched by match().
SUBSEP	The character used to separate multiple subscripts in array elements, \034 by default.

EXAMPLES

This Command	Does the Following
gawk '/Rich/ { print $0 }' *.txt	Searches all the files in the working directory that have the .txt extension for lines containing *Rich* and displays the lines on-screen.
gawk '/Rich/ { print $0 } /Laura/ { print $0 } /Lydia/ { print $0 }' *.txt	Searches all the files in the working directory that have the .txt extension for lines containing a *Rich*, *Laura*, or *Lydia*. Displays the lines on-screen. Each AWK statement must be typed on its own line, followed by a newline (Enter).
gawk '$1 ~ /Astronomy/ { print $0 }' dissertation.doc	Searches **dissertation.doc** for all lines that begin with *Astronomy* and displays the lines on-screen.
gawk '$4 ~ /B/ { print "Students receiving a B were: " $1, $2 }' grades.txt	Search **grades.txt** for lines in which the fourth field ($4) contains *B* and prints the first two fields ($1 and $2) with the message, "Students receiving a B were . . . ."
gawk '$1 ~ /Zapf/ { print "File: "FILENAME " Line: " FNR " " $0 }' *.txt	Finds all lines in all the text (*.txt) files of the working directory that begin with *Zapf* and prints them in a format that looks like this: File: fonts.txt Line: 443 Zapf Dingbats

---

grep

grep [option] *regexp* [*filename*]

Searches *filename* for lines that match the *regexp* (a regular expression). There are three versions of the program: **grep –G** (uses basic regular expressions; this is the default), **grep –E** (uses extended regular expressions; similar to **egrep**), and **grep –F** (uses fixed strings instead of a regular expression; similar to **fgrep**). Default output consists of the name of the file containing a match followed by a colon and the text of the line containing the match.

OPTIONS

Use This Option	To Do This
–A *n*, **– –after-context=***n*	Display *n* lines of trailing context after matching lines.
–b, **– –byte-offset**	Display the byte offset in the input file before each line of output.
–B *n*, **– –before-context=***n*	Display *n* lines of leading context before matching lines.
–C, **– –context"**[=*n*]**"**	Display *n* lines of output context. The default is 2.
–c, **– –count**	Display a count of matching lines for each input file and hide normal output.
–d *action*, **– –directories=***action*	In directory searches, perform a specified action. Valid options for *action* are the following: **read** (use this directory), **recurse** (same as **–r**), or **skip**.
–E, **– –extended-regexp**	Search using extended regular expressions.
–e *regexp*, **– –regexp=***regexp*	Use *regexp* (regular expression). This option is provided in case you need to perform a search that begins with a hyphen.
–F, **– –fixed-strings**	Match strings not regular expressions.
–f *filename*, **– –file=***filename*	Get the regular expressions from *filename*, one per line.
–h, **– –no-filename**	Hide the display of filenames during the search.
–i, **– –ignore-case**	Ignore case distinctions in both the *regexp* and in the input files.
–l, **– –files-with-matches**	Show only the names of matching files but not the matching content. The search stops with the first match.

OPTIONS *(CONT.)*

Use This Option	To Do This
–L, – –files-without-match	Show only the names of files that do not match. The search stops with the first match.
–n	Show *n* lines of leading and trailing content.
–n, – –line-number	Show line numbers.
–q, – –quiet, – –silent	Hide messages.
–r, – –recursive	Search all the files in the directory and all of its associated subdirectories.
–s, – –no-messages	Suppress error messages about nonexistent or unreadable files.
–v, – –revert-match	Show non-matching instead of matching lines.
–V, – –version	Show the version number.
–w, – –word-regexp	Match whole words only.
–x, – –line-regexp	Match the whole line only.

EXAMPLES

This Command	Does the Following
grep hello *	Searches all the files in the working directory for those containing lines that contain *hello*. Shows the names of the files containing the word and the text of the line in which the word occurs.
grep –l [Cc]ash *	Searches all the files in the working directory for those containing the words *Cash* or *cash*. Displays the names of the files containing either of these words but does not display the context.

groff

groff [option] *filename*

Runs the **troff** program and a postprocessor to generate output. **groff** uses the PostScript device by default.

OPTIONS

Use This Option	To Do This
–a	Generate ASCII output.
–e	Preprocess with **eqn**.
–h	Print a help message.
–l	Send output to the printer.
–L *arg*	Pass *arg* to the printer.
–N	Prohibit newlines with **eqn** delimiters.
–p	Preprocess with pic.
–P *arg*	Pass *arg* to the printer.
–R	Preprocess with refer.
–s	Preprocess with soelim.
–S	Safer mode.
–t	Preprocess with tbl.
–T *dev*	Prepare output for device *dev.* The default device is ps.
–v	Print out the version number of programs run by **groff**.
–V	Print to stdout instead of to the printing device.
–X	Preview with a viewer utility (requires X).
–z	Suppress **troff** output.
–Z	Skip postprocessing.

gs

gs [option] [*filename*]

Launches an interactive utility that reads the specified filename and executes the file as a PostScript program. Subsequently, the utility remains available to read commands from the standard input.

Depending on the instructions in *filename,* **gs** may open a primitive viewer. If you are using X, GNOME, or KDE, view files using a more capable viewer, such as ghostview. Type **quit** and press Enter to exit the command interpreter.

OPTIONS

Use This Option	To Do This
–	Accept input from the standard input
–dDISKFONTS	Load character outlines from disk when they are first encountered
–Dname=*string*	Define *string* as a name in the system dictionary
–Dname, –dname	Define a name in the system dictionary with value=null
–dNOPAUSE	Disable the prompt and pause at the end of each page
–dNOPLATFONTS	Disable the use of system fonts
–dSAFER	Disable features that could rewrite, rename, or delete files
–dWRITESYSTEMDICT	Leaves the system dictionary writable
– –filename *filename*	Execute *filename* and exit to the shell
–g *value1***x***value2*	Set the width to *value1* and the height to *value2*
–l*directory*	Add *directory* to the search path for library files
–q	Hide messages
–r *value1***x***value2*	Set the X resolution to *value1* and the Y resolution to *value2*
–sDEVICE=*device*	Use the specified output device
–Sname=*string*	Define *string* as a value in the system dictionary
–sOutputFile=*filename*	Write the output to *filename*
–r*resolution*	Use the resolution specified in pixels per inch
–dBATCH	Exit after processing the last file

EXAMPLE

This Command	Does the Following
gs bug–form.ps	Displays the file (**bug–form.ps**) in the default Ghostscript viewer. Press Enter to page through the document. Type **quit** and press Enter to exit the viewer.

head

head [option] *filename*

Displays the first 10 lines of *filename* to the standard output. You can specify more than one filename in a space-separated list or by using a shell pattern (see the section "Shell Patterns" in Chapter 4). When more than one file is displayed, the output of each is preceded by the file's name.

OPTIONS

Use This Option	To Do This
–c *bytes*, **– –bytes=***bytes*	Print the first number of specified bytes in the file.
– –help	Show available options.
–n *n*, **– –lines=***n*	Print *n* lines. The default is 10.
–q, **– –quiet**, **– –silent**	Do not show the filenames.
–v, **– –verbose**	Always print filenames.
– –version	Show version numbers.

EXAMPLES

This Command	Does the Following
head *.txt | less	Displays the first 10 lines of all the .txt files in the working directory.

ispell

ispell [option] *filename*

Launches an interactive utility that checks the spelling of *filename*. You can specify more than one filename in a space-separated list or by using a shell pattern (see the section "Shell Patterns" in Chapter 4). In the interactive mode, you can use the commands listed in the Commands table in this section.

OPTIONS

Use This Option	To Do This
–b	Create a backup file.
–B *n*	Mark run-together words as errors.
–C	Skip run-together words.
–d *filename*	Use an alternate dictionary.
–L *n*	Show *n* lines of context.
–m	Create root/affix combinations that are not in the dictionary.
–M	Show the mini menu.
–n	Use an **nroff/troff** input file.
–N	Suppress the mini menu.
–P	Skip generation of root/affix combinations.
–p *filename*	Use the personal dictionary.
–S	Sort the list of guesses by probable correctness.
–t	Use a TeX or LaTeX input file.
–T *type*	Assume a given formatter type for all files.
–w *characters*	Specify additional characters that can be part of a word.
–W *n*	Specify the length of words (in *n* characters) that are always legal.
–x	Skip the backup file.

COMMANDS

Use This Option	To Do This
R	Replace the misspelled word completely
!	Escape to the shell
Ctrl + L	Redraw the screen
Ctrl + Z	Suspend **ispell**
?	Show available commands
n	Replace with the *n*th suggested words
A	Accept the word for the rest of this **ispell** session
I	Accept the word, capitalized as it is in the file, and update the private dictionary
L	Look up words in system dictionary (controlled by the WORDS compilation option)
Q	Exit immediately and leave the file unchanged
Space	Accept the word this time only
U	Accept the word and add an uncapitalized version to the private dictionary
X	Write the rest of this file, ignoring misspellings, and start the next file

EXAMPLE

This Command	Does the Following
`ispell magic.txt`	Checks the spelling of the specified file (`magic.txt`).

---

join

join [option] *filename1 filename2*

Joins lines in the specified files that have the same text in their join fields. The default join field is the first field. Fields are delimited by white space by default.

OPTIONS

Use This Option	To Do This
–i, – –ignore-case	Ignore case differences when comparing the two files
–t *separator*	Use the specified separator to identify field boundaries
–1 *n*	Join on field *n* of *filename1*
–2 *n*	Join on field *n* of *filename2*

less

less [option] [*filename*]

Displays the specified filename on-screen and enables you to page through it easily. You can specify more than one filename in a space-separated list or by using a shell pattern (see the section "Shell Patterns" in Chapter 4). If you omit the filename, the utility accepts input from the standard input; **less** is often used this way as the destination for a pipe (see the Examples table in this section). In the interactive mode, you can use the commands listed in the Commands table in this section.

See also **more**.

OPTIONS

Use This Option	To Do This
–?, – –help	Display available options.
– –	Mark the end of the options. Items after **– –** are interpreted as filenames.
+*command*	Start **less** with *command* (see the Commands table in this section).
–~, – –tilde	Suppress the use of tildes to display blank lines at the end of files.
– –window=*n*	Changes the default scrolling window size to *n* lines.

OPTIONS *(CONT.)*

Use This Option	To Do This
−a, − −**search-skip-screen**	Begin searches after the screen's last line.
−b*n*, − −**buffers=***n*	Use *n* number of buffers.
−B, − −**auto-buffers**	Disable automatic memory buffers.
−"*character*, − −**quotes=***character*	Use *character* for filename quoting.
−c, − −**clear-screen**	Repaint the screen from the top down.
−C, − −**CLEAR-SCREEN**	Clear the screen and then repaint the screen from the top down.
−e, − −**quit-at-eof**	Quit after encountering the end of the file twice.
−E, − −**QUIT-AT-EOF**	Quit after encountering the end of the file.
−f, − −**force**	Open directories and device files.
−g, − −**hilite-search**	Highlight the next matching string encountered by a search rather than all matching strings.
−G, − −**HILITE-SEARCH**	Suppress string highlighting in searches.
−h *n*, − —**max-back-scroll=***n*	Scroll back no more than *n* lines.
−i, − −**ignore-case**	Ignore case in searches.
−I, − −**IGN, E-CASE**	Ignore case in searches even when the search expression contains uppercase letters.
−j *n*, − −**jump-target=***n*	Jump to line number *n*. The first line of the screen is line 1.
−k *filename*, − −**lesskey-file=***filename*	Use *filename* as a lesskey file.
−m, − −**long-prompt**	Use more informative prompts.
−M, − −**LONG-PROMPT**	Use the most informative prompts.
−n, − −**line-numbers**	Suppress the line numbers.
−N, − −**LINE-NUMBERS**	Display the line numbers.

OPTIONS *(CONT.)*

Use This Option	To Do This
–o *filename*, **– –log-file=***filename*	Write a log to *filename.*
–O *filename*, **– –LOG-FILE=***filename*	Write a log to *filename* and over-write an existing file without confirmation.
–p *pattern*, **– –pattern=***pattern*	Display the file starting at *pattern.*
–P*prompt string*, **– –prompt=***prompt string*	Use the specified string for *prompt.* For *prompt,* choose from the following: **s** The short prompt. This is the default. 　**m** The medium prompt. 　**M** The long prompt. 　**h** The help prompt. 　**=** The **=** command prompt. In addition to the string, you can use the special escape sequences detailed in the Prompt Expansion table in this section.
–q, **– –quiet**, **– –silent**	Silence the terminal bell in most cases.
–Q, **– –QUIET**, **– –SILENT**	Silence the terminal bell in all cases.
–r, **– –raw-control-chars**	Display raw control characters.
–S, **– –chop-long-lines**	Truncate lengthy lines rather than folding them.
–s, **– –squeeze-blank-lines**	Combine consecutive blank lines into a single blank line.
–t *tag*, **– –tag=***tag*	Open the file containing *tag.*
–T tagsfile, **– –tag–file=tagsfile**	Specifies a tags file to be used instead of «tags".
–u, **– –underline-special**	Display backspaces and carriage returns as control characters.
–U, **– –UNDERLINE-SPECIAL**	Display backspaces, tabs, and carriage returns as control characters.

OPTIONS *(CONT.)*

Use This Option	To Do This
–V, – –version	Displays the version number of **less**.
–w, – –hilite-unread	Highlight the first new line after scrolling.
–W, – –HILITE-UNREAD	Highlight the first new line after any forward movement.
–x *n*, **– –tabs=***n*	Set tab stops every *n* spaces. The default is 8.
–X, – –no-init	Omits the termcap initialization and deinitialization strings.
–y *n*, **– –max-f=***n*, **w-scroll=***n*	Scroll forward no more than *n* lines.

COMMANDS

Use This Command	To Do This
– –	Enable *option* (see the Options table in this section) using the long option form.
– –!	Reverse the setting of *option* using the long option form.
__*option*	Display the current option setting (see the Options table in this section); specify the option using the long option form.
_*option*	Display the current option setting (see the Options table in this section). Specify the option using the short option form (one letter).
+*command*	Execute *command* each time a new file is opened.
– –+*option*	Reset *option* to the default (see the Options table in this section). Specify the option using the short option form (one letter).
–+*option*	Reset *option* to the default (see the Options table in this section); specify the option using the short option form (one letter).

COMMANDS *(CONT.)*

Use This Command	To Do This
=, Ctrl + G, :f	Show information about the file.
`, Ctrl + XX	Go to mark.
| *<mark> shell command*	To the shell command, pipe the portion of the file from the first line on the current screen to the mark. Use ^ to indicate the beginning of the file, or $ to indicate the end of the file. Press Enter to send the current screen.
/regexp	Search forward for the next occurrence of the *regexp* (a regular expression). You can modify the search by entering the following at the beginning of *regexp*: **^N** or **!** Search for lines that do not match the pattern. **^E** or ***** Search multiple files. **^F** or **@** Begin the search at the first line of the first file in the command line list. **^K** Highlight matches but do not move to the position. **^R** Ignore regular expression metacharacters. Certain characters are special as in the **/** command. **^N** or **!** Search for lines that do not match the pattern. **^E** or ***** Search multiple files. That is, if the search reaches the beginning of the current file without finding a match, the search continues in the previous file in the command line list. **^F** or **@** Begin the search at the last line of the last file in command line list, regardless of what is currently displayed on the screen or the settings of the **–a** or **–j** options. **^K** Same as in forward searches. **^R** Same as in forward searches. **Esc +/pattern** Same as «/*". **Esc +?pattern** Same as «?*".

COMMANDS *(CONT.)*

Use This Command	To Do This
:d	Remove the current file from the list of files.
:e, Ctrl + XV, E	Examine a new file.
:n	Examine the next file.
:p	Examine the previous file.
:x	Examine the first file in the command line list.
?*regexp*	Search backward for the next occurrence of the *regexp* (a regular expression). You can modify the search by entering the following at the beginning of *regexp*: **^N or !** Search for lines that do not match the pattern. **^E or *** Search multiple files. **^F or @** Begin the search at the first line of the first file in the command line list. **^K** Highlight matches but do not move to the position. **^R** Ignore regular expression metacharacters.
(	Find the closing parenthesis when the opening parenthesis appears on the first line.
)	Find the opening parenthesis when the closing parenthesis appears on the last line.
[	Find the closing bracket when the opening bracket appears on the first line.
]	Find the opening bracket when the closing bracket appears on the last line.
{	Find the closing brace when the opening brace appears on the first line.
}	Find the opening brace when the closing brace appears on the last line.
b, Ctrl + B, Esc +v	Scroll backward one window.
d, Ctrl + D	Scroll forward one half window.
Enter, Ctrl + N, e, Ctrl + E, j, Ctrl + J, down arrow ($\downarrow$)	Scroll forward one line.

COMMANDS *(CONT.)*

Use This Command	To Do This
Esc +(, Left arrow (←)	Scroll left eight characters.
Esc +), Right arrow (→)	Scroll right eight characters.
Esc +Ctrl + B	Prompt for two paired characters. When the second is positioned on the bottom line, search backward for the next instance of the first character.
Esc +Ctrl + F	Prompt for two paired characters. When the first is positioned on the top line, search forward for the next instance of the second character.
Esc +n	Repeat the previous search, going forward in the file list.
Esc +N	Repeat the previous search, going backward in the file list.
Esc +s	Scroll forward one screen.
Esc +u	Undo search highlighting.
F	Scroll forward and keep trying to read when the end of file is reached.
g, <, Esc + <	Go to the first line in the file.
G, >, Esc + >	Go to the last line in the file.
h, H	Show the available commands.
m*mark*	Marks the current position with *mark*, a lowercase letter.
–n	Set the default number of lines to scroll to *n*. This affects the behavior of all scrolling commands that normally scroll one window full.
n	Repeat the previous search.
N	Repeat the previous search but in the opposite direction.
–!option	Reverse the setting of *option* using the short option form (one letter).
–option	Enable *option* (see the Options table in this section) using the short option form (one letter).

COMMANDS *(CONT.)*

Use This Command	To Do This
p, %	Go to a position *n* percent into the file.
q, Q, :q, :Q, ZZ	Quit.
R	Repaint the screen.
r, Ctrl + R, Ctrl + L	Repaint the screen.
s *filename*	Save piped input to *filename*.
! *shell command*	Run the specified shell command. You can use the following symbols for expansions: **%** The name of the current file. **#** The name of the previous file. **!!** Repeats the last shell command.
SPACE, Ctrl + V, f, Ctrl + F	Scroll forward one window.
u, Ctrl + U	Scroll backward one-half window.
v	Edit the current file.
V	Show the version number.
y, Ctrl + Y, Ctrl + P, k, Ctrl + K, up arrow (↑)	Scroll backward one line.

PROMPT EXPANSION

Use This Option	To Do This
%b< **t** | **m** | **b** | **B** | **j** >	Display the byte offset in the current input file at one of the following lines: **t** The top line. **m** The middle line. **b** The bottom line. **B** The next line after the bottom line. **j** The target line as specified by **–j**.
%B	Display the size of the current input file.
%D	Display the number of pages in the input file or, equivalently, the page number of the last line in the input file.

PROMPT EXPANSION *(CONT.)*

Use This Option	To Do This
%d< **t** | **m** | **b** | **B** | **j** >	Display the page number of one of the following lines in the input file: **t** Top line. **m** Middle line. **b** Bottom line. **B** The next line after the bottom line. **j** The target line (as specified by **–j**).
%E	Display the name of the editor.
%f	Display the name of the current input file.
%i	Display the index of the current file in the list of input files.
%L	Display the line number of the last line in the input file.
%l< **t** | **m** | **b** | **B** | **j** >	Display the line number of one of the following lines in the input file: **t** The top line. **m** The middle line. **b** The bottom line. **B** The next line after the bottom line. **j** The target line as specified by **–j**.
%m	Display the total number of input files.
%p< **t** | **m** | **b** | **B** | **j** >	Display the percent into the current input file at one of the following lines: **t** The top line. **m** The middle line. **b** The bottom line. **B** The next line after the bottom line. **j** The target line as specified by **–j**.
%s	Display the size of the current input file. This is the same as **%B**.
%t	Remove trailing spaces.
%x	Display the name of the next input file in the list.

EXAMPLES

This Command	Does the Following
less magic.txt	Displays the specified file (`magic.txt`) in the **less** paging utility.
sort magic.txt | less	Sorts the lines of the specified file (`magic.txt`) and displays the output on-screen.
pr magic.txt | less	Formats the specified file (`magic.txt`) for printing and views the output on-screen.

look

look [option] *string* [*filename*]

Displays lines in *filename* that begin with *string*. The file must be sorted. If you do not specify a filename, the utility uses the default **ispell** dictionary.

OPTIONS

Use This Option	To Do This
–a	Use the alternate dictionary
–d	Search alphanumeric characters only
–f	Ignore case
–t *character*	Stop searching the string at *character*

EXAMPLES

This Command	Does the Following
look mus	Displays all the words in the default **ispell** dictionary that begin with *mus*.
look 'Secret #47' secrets.txt	Displays the line in `secrets.txt` that begins with *Secret #47*.

lpq

lpq [option] [*job#*] [*user*]

Reports the status of the printing queue. You can optionally specify the job number (with *job#*) and the user name.

See also **lpr**.

OPTIONS

Use This Option	To Do This
-P *printer*	Use *printer* rather than the default
-l	List printer queue information

EXAMPLE

This Command	Does the Following
lpq	Shows the status of the current print queue, including the job numbers of waiting jobs if there are any.

lpr

lpr [option] *filename*

Prints *filename*. Uses a print spooling daemon to store the files temporarily until the facilities become available.

OPTIONS

Use This Option	To Do This
-#*n*	Print *n* copies
-C *string*	Print the specified string as the job classification on the burst page
-h	Suppress the printing of the burst page

OPTIONS *(CONT.)*

Use This Option	To Do This
–i [*n*]	Indent by *n* columns
–J *string*	Use *string* as the job name on the burst page
–l	Allow printing of control characters
–m	Send mail upon completion
–P *device*	Use *device* for output
–p	Use **pr** to format the files
–r	Remove the file when printing is complete
–s	Create copies in the temporary directory using symbolic links
–T *string*	Use *string* as the title for **pr** output
–U *user*	Print the specified username on the burst page
–w*n*	Set the page width to *n*

EXAMPLES

This Command	Does the Following
cat example.ps | lpr	Reads the specified file (example.ps) and sends the output to the default print spool.
pr database.txt | lpr	Formats the specified file (database.txt) with page numbers and headers and sends the output to the default print spool.

lprm

lprm [option] [–] *job#* [*user*]

Removes *job#* from the printer queue. To determine the job number, use **lpq –l**.

See also **lpr.**

OPTIONS

Use This Option	To Do This
–P *printer*	Use the specified printer queue rather than the default
–	Remove all of the user's print jobs

md5sum

md5sum [option] [*filename*]

Displays or checks an MD5 checksum on the specified *filename*. When used without an argument, this utility reads from the standard input.

OPTIONS

Use This Option	To Do This
–b, – –binary	Read the file in binary mode.
–c, – –check	Check MD5 sums against the list given in *filename*.
–t, – –text	Read files in text mode. This is the default.
– –help	Display available options.
– –version	Show the version number.

more

more [option] [*filename*]

Displays *filename* on-screen and enables you to page through it easily. You can specify more than one filename in a space-separated list or by using a shell pattern (see the section "Shell Patterns" in Chapter 4). In the interactive mode, you can use the commands listed in the Commands table in this section.

See also **less**.

OPTIONS

Use This Option	To Do This
–n	Use a screen size of n lines
+/	Specify a search string
+*n*	Start at line number n
–c	Paint screen from the top rather than scrolling
–d	When an illegal key is pressed, prompt the user with the message "[Press space to continue, 'q' to quit.]" and "[Press 'h' for instructions.]"
–f	Count actual (unfolded) lines rather than screen lines
–l	Prevent pauses after encountering a form feed character (^l)
–p	Clear the whole screen and display the text instead of scrolling
–s	Squeeze multiple blank lines into one
–u	Suppress underlining

COMMANDS

Use This Command	To Do This
h, ?	Display a summary of these commands. If you forget all the other commands, remember this one.
!<cmd>, :!<cmd>	Execute <cmd> in a subshell.
=	Display the current line number.
Ctrl+L	Redraw the screen.
`	Go to the place where the previous search started.
.	Repeat the previous command.
[*n*] **/***regexp*	Search for the nth occurrence of *regexp,* a regular expression. The default occurrence is 1.
:f	Display the current filename and line number.
[*n*] **:n**	Go to nth next file. The default setting for n is 1.
[*n*] **:p**	Go to nth previous file. The default setting for n is 1.

COMMANDS *(CONT.)*

Use This Command	To Do This
[*n*] **b**, [*n*] **Ctrl + B**	Go back *n* screenfuls of text. The default setting for *n* is 1.
[*n*] **d**, [*n*] **Ctrl +D**	Scroll *n* lines. The default is the current scroll size, which is initially 11. If you specify a different scroll size, it becomes the new current scroll size.
[*n*] **f**	Skip forward *n* screenfuls of text. The default setting for *n* is 1.
[*n*] **n**	Search for the *n*th occurrence of the last regular expression you searched for. The default setting for *n* is 1.
q, **Q**	Exit.
[*n*] **Enter**	Display the next *n* lines of text. Defaults to 1. The argument becomes the new default.
[*n*] **s**	Skip forward *n* lines of text. Defaults to 1.
[*n*] **Spacebar**	Display the next *n* lines of text. Defaults to the current screen size.
v	Start up /usr/bin/vi at the current line.
[*n*] **z**	Display the next *n* lines of text. Defaults to the current screen size. The argument becomes the new default.

EXAMPLES

This Command	Does the Following
more magic.txt	Displays the specified file (magic.txt) in the **less** paging utility.
sort magic.txt | more	Sorts the lines of the specified file (magic.txt) and displays the output on-screen.
pr magic.txt | more	Formats the specified file (magic.txt) for printing and views the output on-screen.

nl

nl [option] [*filename*]

Numbers the lines of *filename*. You can specify more than one filename in a space-separated list or by using a shell pattern (see the section "Shell Patterns" in Chapter 4). By default, the utility writes to standard output. Use output redirection to save the output to a file. If you do not specify a *filename*, the utility accepts input from the standard input.

OPTIONS

Use This Option	To Do This
–b *style*, **– –body-numbering=***style*	Use *style* for numbering body lines. (See the Styles table in this section.)
–d *style*, **– –section-delimiter=***charchar*	Use *charchar* (two characters) for separating logical pages.
–f *style*, **– –footer-numbering=***style*	Use *style* for numbering footer lines. (See the Styles table in this section.)
–h *style*, **– –header-numbering=***style*	Use *style* for numbering header lines. (See the Styles table in this section.)
– –help	Display the available options.
–i *n*, **– –page-increment=***n*	Use the line number increment specified by *n*.
–l *n*, **– –join-blank-lines=***n*	Count *n* empty lines as one.
–n *format*, **– –number-format=***format*	Insert line numbers according to the specified format.
–p, **– –no-renumber**	Do not reset line numbers at logical pages.
–s, **– –number-separator=***string*	Use *string* as a number separator.
–v, **– –first-page=***n*	Use *n* as the first line number for each logical page.
– –version	Show the version number.
–w, **– –number-width=***n*	Use *n* columns for line numbers.

STYLES

Use This Style	To Do This
a	Number all lines
t	Number only non-empty lines
p_regexp_	Number only the lines that contain a match for _regexp_
n	Number no lines

FORMATS

Use This Option	To Create This Format
ln	Left justified, no leading zeros
rn	Right justified, no leading zeros
rz	Right justified, leading zeros

EXAMPLES

This Command	Does the Following
`nl magic.txt > magic-numbered.txt`	Numbers the lines of `magic.txt` and writes the output to `magic.numbered.txt`.
`nl -bp magic magic.txt | less`	Numbers only the lines containing the specified regular expression (`magic`), and shows the output on-screen.

---

nroff

See **groff**.

---

od

od [option] [_filename_]

Writes _filename_ to the standard output in octal and other formats. When no filename is specified, the utility accepts input from the standard input.

OPTIONS

Use This Option	To Do This
–A *radix*, **– –address-radix=***radix*	Use *radix* as the file offset. For *radix*, you can use d for decimal, o for octal, x for hexadecimal, or n for none.
– –help	Show the available options.
–j *n*, **– –skip-bytes=***n*	Skip *n* bytes at the start of each file.
–N *n*, **– –read-bytes=***n*	Do not process more than *n* bytes per file.
–s [*n*], **– –strings**[**=***n*]	Output strings of *n* graphics characters.
–t *type*, **– –format=***type*	Use the specified type of output format (see the Output Types table in this section).
– –traditional	Accept arguments in pre-POSIX form.
–v, **– –output-duplicates**	Suppress use of asterisks to mark line suppression.
– –version	Output version information and exit.
–w *n*, **– –width**[**=***n*]	Write *n* bytes per output line.

OUTPUT TYPES

Name	Description
a	Named character
c	ASCII character or backslash Escape
d[*n*]	Signed decimal with *n* bytes per integer
f[*n*]	Floating point with *n* bytes per integer
o[*n*]	Octal with *n* bytes per integer
u[*n*]	Unsigned decimal with *n* bytes per integer
x[*n*]	Hexadecimal with *n* bytes per integer

paste

paste [option] [*filename1 filename2*]

Merge the corresponding lines of *filename1* and *filename2* into tab-separated columns. You can merge more than two files, if you wish. If no filename is specified, the utility accepts input from the standard input.

OPTIONS

Use This Option	To Do This
–d *list*, **– –delimiters=**list	Use the characters in *list* instead of tabs
–s, **– –serial**	Paste one line at a time
– –help	Show available options
– –version	Show the version number

EXAMPLE

This Command	Does the Following
paste first.txt second.txt > combined.txt	Combines the two files (first.txt and second.txt) into one file (combined .txt) and writes the output to disk.

pdf2ps

pdf2ps *filename output file*

Converts a Portable Document File (*filename*) to PostScript (*output file*).

EXAMPLES

This Command	Does the Following
pdf2ps resume.pdf resume.ps	Translates the PDF file (resume.pdf) into a PostScript file (resume.ps) and writes the result to disk.

pdftotext

pdftotext [option] [*filename* [*output file*]]

Converts a Portable Document File (*filename*) to plain text. Unless you specify an output file, writes to the standard input.

EXAMPLES

This Command	Does the Following
pdf2text resume.pdf resume.txt	Translates the PDF file (resume.pdf) into a text file (resume.txt) and writes the result to disk.

pr

pr [option] [*filename*]

Prepares text files for printing by formatting them with pagination and columns. You can specify more than one filename in a space-separated list or by using a shell pattern (see the section "Shell Patterns" in Chapter 4).

OPTIONS

Use This Option	To Do This
– –**pages=***first*[:*last*]	Start printing at the first page and, optionally, stop at the last page.
–**a**, – –**across**	Print columns across rather than down.
–**c**, – –**show-control-chars**	Show control characters.
–*n*, – –**columns=***n*	Use *n* columns per page.
–**d**, – –**double-space**	Double space the output.

OPTIONS *(CONT.)*

Use This Option	To Do This
–e[*character*[***n***]], **– –expand-tabs** [=*character*[*n*]]	Expand the width of *character* to the default tab width (8 spaces) or *n* spaces.
–F, –f, **– –form-feed**	Use form feeds instead of newlines to separate pages.
– –help	Show the available options.
–h *string*, **– –header=***string*	Use *string* as a centered header instead of the filename.
–i[*character*[*n*]], **– –output-tabs** [=*character*[*n*]]	Replace spaces with *character* to the default tab width (8 spaces) or *n* spaces.
–J, **– –join-lines**	Merge full lines.
–l *n*, **– –length=***n*	Set the page length to *n* lines.
–m, **– –merge**	Print all files in parallel.
–n[*character*[*n*]], **– –number-lines** [=***character***[*n*]]	Number the lines. Optionally, use *character* instead of a tab and use *n* spaces instead of the default of eight spaces.
–N *n*, **– –first-line-number=***n*	Start counting with *n*.
–o *n*, **– –indent=***n*	Offset each line with *n* spaces.
–r, **– –no-file-warnings**	Omit warning when a file cannot be opened.
–s[*character*], **– –separator** [=*character*]	Separate columns using *character*.
–S[*string*], **– –sep-string**[=*string*]	Separate columns using *string*.
–t, **– –omit-header**	Omit page headers and trailers.
–T, **– –omit-pagination**	Omit page headers and trailers.
–v, **– –show-nonprinting**	Show nonprinting characters.
– –version	Show the version number.
–W *n*, **– –page-width=***n*	Set page width to *n* characters.
–w *n* **– –width=***n*	Set page width to *n* characters for multiple column output only.

EXAMPLES

This Command	Does the Following
pr magic.txt > lpr	Prepares the specified file (magic.txt) for printing and sends the output to the default print spool.
pr -2 magic.txt > lpr	Prepares the specified file (magic.txt) for printing with two-column text and sends the output to the default print spool.

ptx

ptx [option] [*filename*]

Reads the input filename and produces a *permuted index* (a list of keywords shown in their context, also called key-word-in-context [KWIC]). Unless you use the –G option, you can specify more than one filename by using a shell pattern (see the section "Shell Patterns" in Chapter 4).

OPTIONS

Use This Option	To Do This
–A, – –auto-reference	Show the filename and line number at the beginning of each line
–b *filename*, – –break-file=*filename*	Obtain word-break characters from *filename*
–C, – –copyright	Show the program license
–F, – –flag-truncation=*string*	Use *string* to flag line truncations
–f, – –ignore-case	Combine upper and lowercase for sorting
–g *n*, – –gap-size=*n*	Use *n* spaces between columns in the output
–G, – –traditional	Disable GNU extensions
– –help	Show available options

OPTIONS *(CONT.)*

Use This Option	To Do This
–i *filename*, **– –ignore-file=***filename*	Read the Ignore Word list from *filename*
–M *string*, **– –macro-name=***string*	Use *string* as the macro name to use instead of *xx*
–O *roff*, **– –format=***roff*	Generate output as *roff* directives
–o *filename*, **– –only-file=***filename*	Read the Only Word list from the specified filename
–r, **– –references**	Use the first field of each line for the reference
–R, **– –right-side-refs**	Place the references on the right
–S *regexp*, **– –sentence-regexp=***regexp*	Search for the *regexp* to determine the ends of lines or sentences
–T, **– –format=tex**	Generate output as TeX directives
–w *n* **– –width** *n*	Use *n* columns for output
– –version	Show the version number
–W, **– –word-regexp=***regexp*	Use *regexp* to match the keywords

EXAMPLES

This Command	Does the Following
`ptx memory.txt >memory.ptx`	Creates a permuted index (keyword in context) to the specified file (`memory.txt`) and writes the output to `memory.ptx`.
`ptx –A *.txt >memory.ptx`	Creates a permuted index (keyword in context) to all of the `.txt` files in the working directory. Each line begins with the name of the file and the line number on which the keyword appears. Writes the output to `memory.ptx`.

rev

rev [*filename*]

Reverse the order in which characters appear on each line of the specified filename. You can specify more than one filename in a space-separated list or by using a shell pattern (see the section "Shell Patterns" in Chapter 4).

See also **tac.**

sdiff

sdiff [option] *filename-1 filename-2*

Launches an interactive utility that enables you to compare two sorted files (*filename-1* and *filename-2*). See **sort** for information on sorting files. The program shows the differences between the two files in two side-by-side columns. To compare non-sorted text files, use **diff.**

See also **cmp, comm, diff, diff3.**

OPTIONS

Use This Option	To Do This
–a	Treat all files as text and compare them line by line
–B, – –ignore-blank-lines	Ignore changes that insert or delete blank lines
–b, – –ignore-space-change	Ignore changes involving white space
–H, – –speed-large-files	Speed the processing of files with numerous small, scattered changes
–i, – –ignore–case	Ignore changes in case
–I *regexp*, **– –ignore-matching-lines**=*regexp*	Ignore changes that insert or delete lines matching *regexp* (regular expression)

OPTIONS *(CONT.)*

Use This Option	To Do This
–l, – –left-column	Display only the left column of two common lines
–o *filename* **– –output=**_filename_	Specify the output filename
–s, – –suppress-common-lines	Omit the display of lines common to both files
–t, – –expand-tabs	Use spaces instead of tabs in the output
–v – –version	Show the version number
–W, – –ignore-all-space	Ignore horizontal white space when comparing lines
–w *n* **– –width=**_n_	Use an output width of *n* columns

EXAMPLES

This Command	Does the Following
`sdiff -o drafts-compared.txt draft-1.txt draft-2.txt`	Compares the two specified files (`draft-1.txt` and `draft-2.txt`) and writes the results to `drafts-compared.txt`.
`sdiff -s -o drafts-compared .txt draft-1.txt draft-2.txt`	Same as the previous example, except suppresses common lines in the output.

sort

sort [option] [*filename*]

Sorts the specified filename line by line in character order. You can specify more than one filename in a space-separated list or by using a shell pattern (see the section "Shell Patterns" in Chapter 4). The utility merges the lines of the specified files into the sorted output. Use the – –o option or output redirection (see the Examples table in this section) to save the results.

OPTIONS

Use This Option	To Do This
–b	Ignore leading blanks in sort fields or keys.
–c	Check to see whether the file is already sorted; if not, you'll see a message providing an example of the type of disorder found in the file.
–d	Use only alphanumeric characters in keys.
–f	Convert lowercase to uppercase characters in keys.
–g	Compare according to general numerical value.
– –help	Show the available options.
–i	Use the characters between ASCII 40 and 176 for keys.
–k *pos1*[**,** *pos2*]	Start a key at *pos1* and end it at *pos2*.
–m	Merge but do not sort sorted files.
–o *filename*	Write the output to *filename*.
–r	Reverse the result of comparisons.
–s	Restabilize sort by disabling last resort comparison.
–T *directory*	Use *directory* for temporary files.
–t *character*	Use *character* for white space transition.
–u	With **–c**, check for strict ordering. With **–m**, output the first of an equal sequence only.
– –version	Show the version number.
–z	End lines for compatibility with **find** (see Chapter 4).

EXAMPLES

This Command	Does the Following
`sort file1.txt > file1.sort`	Sorts the lines of the specified file (`file1.txt`) and writes the results to `file1.sort`.
`sort *.txt > allfiles.sort`	Sorts the lines of all the `*.txt` files in the working directory and writes the results to `allfiles.sort`.

split

split [option] [*filename* [*prefix*]]

Split *filename* into pieces. The default prefix is *x*. Specify a prefix to change this setting. If you omit the filename, this utility reads from the standard input.

OPTIONS

Use This Option	To Do This
–b *n*, **– –bytes=**n	Write *n* bytes to each output file
–C *n*, **– –line-bytes=**n	Write no more than *n* bytes of lines to each output file
– –help	Show the available options
–l *n*, **– –lines=**n	Write *n* lines per output file
–n	Write *n* lines per output file
– –verbose	Show all messages
– –version	Show the version number

strfile

strfile [option] [*input filename* [*output filename*]]

This command is installed with the console games packages. It stores character-based data in a random-access file so that the stored data can be accessed quickly. The input filename contains groups of lines separated by a percent sign (%). The output filename contains a data structure that enables quick access to the groups of lines. This is the data storage format used by **fortune**.

See also **unstr.**

OPTIONS

Use This Option	To Do This
–c *character*	Change the delimiting character from the percent sign to the specified character
–i	Ignore case when sorting the strings
–o	Sort the strings in alphabetical order
–r	Randomize access to the strings
–s	Hide program messages
–x	Use ROT-13 encryption

EXAMPLES

This Command	Does the Following
`strfile my-quotes.txt` `my-quotes.dat`	Transforms the file `my-quotes.txt` (a file in which quotations are delimited by % marks) into a **fortune**-accessible database (`my-quotes.dat`).

sum

> **sum** [option] [*filename*]

Prints checksum and blocks counts for each filename. You can specify more than one filename in a space-separated list or by using a shell pattern (see the section "Shell Patterns" in Chapter 4). The utility prints the name of each file before the text. If you omit the filename, the utility accepts input from the standard input.

OPTIONS

Use This Option	To Do This
–r	Use BSD sum algorithm with 1K blocks
– –help	Show the available options
–s, **– –sysv**	Use System V sum algorithm with 512 bytes blocks
– –version	Show the version number

EXAMPLE

This Command	Does the Following
sum *.txt	Displays the checksum and blocks the count for all the .txt files in the working directory.

tac

tac [option] [*filename*]

Display *filename* in reverse line order, starting from the last line (the opposite of **cat**).

See also **rev**.

OPTIONS

Use This Option	To Do This
–b, – –before	Attach the separator before instead of after
– –help	Show the available options
–r, – –regex	Interpret the separator as a regular expression
–s, – –separator=*string*	Use *string* as the separator instead of newline
– –version	Show the version number

tail

tail [option] [*filename*]

Print the last ten lines of each file to the standard output. You can specify more than one filename in a space-separated list or by using a shell pattern (see the section "Shell Patterns" in Chapter 4). The utility prints the name of each file before the text. If you omit the filename, the utility accepts input from the standard input.

OPTIONS

Use This Option	To Do This
– –retry	Keep trying to open the file.
–c, – –bytes=_n_	Output the last _n_ bytes.
–f, – –follow[**={name|descriptor}**]	Output appended data as the file grows. **–f**, **– –follow**, and **– –follow= descriptor** are equivalent.
– –help	Show the available options.
–_n_, **– –lines=**_n_	Output the last _n_ lines instead of the last 10 lines.
– –pid=_pid_	Terminate after **pid** terminates.
–q, – –quiet, – –silent	Suppress the display of filenames.
–s, – –sleep-interval=_n_	Sleep _n_ seconds after iterations.
–v, – –verbose	Always show filenames.
– –version	Show the version number.

EXAMPLE

This Command	Does the Following
`tail *.txt`	Prints the last 10 lines of all the `.txt` files in the working directory. Indicates the filename before the output for each file.

tr

tr [option] _expression1_ [_expression2_]

Accept text from the standard input, find the characters matching _expression1_ and translate them according to _expression2_. Form the expressions with bracket statements or character classes. You can also use the special characters listed here (see the Special Characters table in this section).

OPTIONS

Use This Option	To Do This
–c, – –complement	Complement *expression1*
–d, – –delete	Delete the characters defined by *expression1*
–s, – –squeeze-repeats	Replace any sequences of two or more characters defined by *expression1* with one character
– –help	Show the available options
– –version	Show the version number

SPECIAL CHARACTERS

Character	Description
\a	Bell
\b	Backspace
\f	Form feed
\n	Newline
\r	Carriage return
\t	Tab
\v	Vertical tab
\nnn	Character with octal value *nnn*
\\	Literal backslash
char1-char2	Range of characters from octal char1 to octal char2

EXAMPLES

This Command	Does the Following
cat uppercase.txt | tr '[A-Z]' '[a-z]' or cat uppercase.txt | tr '[:upper:]' '[:lower:]'	Converts uppercase characters from the file (**uppercase.txt**) to lowercase.
cat tabs.txt | tr –d tr '\t' > notabs.txt	Removes the tabs from **tabs.txt** and writes the output to **notabs.txt**.

troff

See **groff**.

unexpand

unexpand [option] [*filename*]

Convert spaces in the specified filename to tabs, writing to standard output (compare **expand**). You can specify more than one filename in a space-separated list or by using a shell pattern (see the section "Shell Patterns" in Chapter 4). The utility prints the name of each file before the text. If you omit the filename, the utility accepts input from the standard input.

OPTIONS

Use This Option	To Do This
–a, – –all	Convert all white space not just the initial white space
– –help	Show the available options
–t *list*, **– –tabs**=*list*	Use a comma-separated list of tab positions
–t *n*, **– –tabs**=*n*	Set the default tab width to *n* spaces
– –version	Show the version number

uniq

uniq [option] [*input file* [*output file*]]

Removes duplicate lines from a sorted input file and writes to the output file.

See also **sort**.

OPTIONS

Use This Option	To Do This
–c, – –count	Prefix lines by the number of occurrences
–d, – –repeated	Print the duplicate lines but no unique lines
–n **–f** *n*, **– –skip–fields=**n	Skip the first *n* fields
– –help	Show the available options
–i, – –ignore-case	Ignore case
–n	Skip the first *n* lines
+n, **–s, – –skip-chars=**n	Skip the first *n* characters
–u, – –unique	Print only the unique lines but not duplicate ones
– –version	Show the version number
–w *n* **– –check-chars=**n	Compare only the first *n* characters per line

EXAMPLE

This Command	Does the Following
`uniq dupes.txt nodupes.txt`	Removes the duplicate lines from `dupes.txt` (a sorted file) and writes to `nodupes.txt`.

---

unstr

unstr [option] [*datafile*] [*output-file*]

Reverses the work of **strfile** by printing out the stored strings in the data file to the output file.

See also **fortune**.

zcat

zcat *filename*

Displays *filename* (a **gzip** compressed file) on-screen without decompressing the file. For more information on **gzip**, see Chapter 6.

See also **zmore**.

EXAMPLE

This Command	Does the Following
`zcat bibliography.gz	less`	Displays the compressed file (`bibliography.gz`) on-screen and pipes the output to **less**.

zcmp

zcmp [option] *filename1* [*filename2*]

Compares *filename1* and *filename2* where both files are compressed files created with **gzip** (see Chapter 6). For available options, see **cmp**.

zdiff

zdiff [option] *filename1* [*filename2*]

Compare *filename1* and *filename2* where both files are compressed files created with **gzip** (see Chapter 6). For available options, see **diff**.

zegrep

zegrep [option] *regexp filename*

Search the specified filename for the *regexp*, an extended regular expression, where *filename* is a compressed file created with **gzip** (see Chapter 6). You can specify more than one filename in a space-separated list or by using a shell pattern (see the section "Shell Patterns" in Chapter 4). For available options, see **egrep**.

zfgrep

zfgrep [option] *string filename*

Search the specified filename, where *filename* is a compressed file created with **gzip** (see Chapter 6), for the specified string, a list of one or more search terms separated by newlines. You can specify more than one filename in a space-separated list or by using a shell pattern (see the section "Shell Patterns" in Chapter 4). For available options, see **fgrep**.

zgrep

zgrep [option] *regexp filename*

Search the specified filename for *regexp*, a basic regular expression, where *filename* is a compressed file created with **gzip** (see Chapter 6). You can specify more than one filename in a space-separated list or by using a shell pattern (see the section "Shell Patterns" in Chapter 4). For available options, see **grep**.

zmore

zmore *filename*

Displays *filename* (a compressed file created with **gzip** or **compress**) without decompressing the file. (For more information on **gzip** and **compress**, see Chapter 6.) You can specify more than one filename in a space-separated list or by using a shell pattern (see the section "Shell Patterns" in Chapter 4). If you omit the filename, the utility accepts input from the standard input.

OPTIONS

Use This Option	To Do This
=	Display the current line number.
.	Repeat the previous command.
:q, :Q, q, Q	Quit.
[*n*] **/***regexp*	Search for the *n*th occurrence of *regexp* (a regular expression). By default, *n* is 1, so the search finds the next occurrence.
[*n*] **Ctrl + D**, [*n*]**d**	Display *n* more lines. 11 is the default.
!*command*	Run the specified shell command.
n	Display *n* more lines. Press the spacebar after typing the number.
*n***f**	Skip *n* screenfuls and print a screenful of lines.
*n***n**	Search for the *n*th occurrence of the last regular expression entered.
*n***s**	Skip *n* lines and print a screenful of lines.
s	Skip to the next file.

CHAPTER 9

Working with Sound and Graphic Files

This chapter covers utilities that enable you to process sound and graphic files. These utilities can make disk-based recordings of CD-ROM audio tracks, play MP3 and MIDI audio files, translate virtually any type of computer graphic file into another graphic format, and much more.

TIP   Some of the commands discussed in this chapter are not installed by default with most Linux distributions. See the Introduction for information on obtaining these commands by downloading them from the Internet.

AT A GLANCE

How Do I	See This Entry	Example
Convert a graphic file from one format to another?	**convert**	convert jpeg image1.bmp image1.jpg
Create a thumbnail index of all the graphic files in the working directory?	**convert**	convert 'vid:*.jpg' catalog.jpg
Create a printed jewel case label for a CD-ROM that I've just burned?	**cdlabelgen**	cdlabelgen -c 'My Favorites'-s '2000' -i 'Blues%Jazz%Rock%Alternative Rock%Techno%Industrial' -e images/mp3.eps > cover.ps
Play an audio CD-ROM?	**cdp**	cdp
Make WAV recordings of all the audio tracks on an audio CD-ROM?	**cdparanoia**	cdparanoia -B "1-"

How Do I	See This Entry	Example
Create a composite image of two or more graphic files using special effects?	**combine**	`combine -compose bumpmap image1.jpg image2.jpg com-bined.jpg`
View detailed information about a graphic file?	**identify**	`identify -verbose image1.jpg`

Sound and Graphics Files

This section details the following:

- Sound file types
- Graphic file types

Sound File Types

The following table lists the sound file types that you are likely to encounter on a Linux system, organized by suffix (extension).

COMMON SOUND FILE FORMATS

Extension	Description
`.aiff`	Apple/Silicon Graphics AIFF sound
`.au`	Sun/NeXT AU sound
`.cdr`	RAW, unsigned samples of CD-ROM audio
`.cvs`	Continuously Variable Slope modulation, used for speech compression
`.voc`	Sound Blaster VOC sound
`.wav`	Microsoft WAV sound
`.mp3`	MP3 compressed digital audio
`.mid, .midi`	MIDI sound

Graphic File Types

The following table lists the graphic file formats that you are likely to encounter on a Linux system, organized by suffix (extension).

COMMON GRAPHIC FILE FORMATS

Extension	Description
.bmp, .dib	Microsoft Windows bitmap image file
.cgm	Computer Graphics Metafile
.eps	Adobe Encapsulated PostScript file
.gif	CompuServe graphics interchange format
.hpgl	Hewlett Packard plotter file
.ico	Microsoft Windows icon
.jpg, .jpeg, .jfif	Joint Photographic Experts Group JFIF format
.pbm	Portable bitmap format file
.pcd	Kodak Photo CD-ROM file
.pcx	PC Paintbrush file
.pgm	Portable graymap format (gray scale)
.pict	Apple Macintosh QuickDraw/PICT file
.png	Portable Network Graphics
.pnm	Portable anymap
.tga	Truevision Targa image file
.tiff	Tagged Image File Format
.xbm	X Windows system bitmap
.xpm	X Windows system pixmap file
.xwd	X Windows system window dump file

Alphabetical Command Reference

This section details commands for the following tasks:

- Playing, recording, and manipulating sound files (**aumix, mikmod, mpg123, play, playmidi, rec, sox**).

- Playing audio CD-ROMs (**cdp**).

- Converting and processing graphic files (**combine, convert, identify, mogrify, montage**).

- Recording CD-ROM audio tracks to WAV files (**cdda2wav, cdparanoia**).

- Creating labels for CD-ROM jewel boxes (**cdlabelgen**).

aumix

aumix [option]

If typed without an argument, this command launches an interactive, text-based program that controls the various settings of the audio device. See the Commands table in this section for commands you can use in the interactive mode.

OPTIONS

Use This Option	To Do This
–b[**+**	**–**] [*n*]	Set the bass gain. Specify one of the following: **+** to increment by one level, **–** to decrement by one level, *n* to set the specific level (10–100).
–C *filename*	Specify a filename containing a color scheme.
–c[**+**	**–**] [*n*]	Set the CD-ROM gain. Specify one of the following: **+** to increment by one level, **–** to decrement by one level, *n* to set the specific level.
–d *device*	Use the specified device instead of the default.
–f *filename*	Save settings to the specified filename.
–i [**+**	**–**] [*n*]	Set the line-in gain. Specify one of the following: **+** to increment by one level, **–** to decrement by one level, *n* to set the specific level (10–100).
–l [**+**	**–**] [*n*]	Set the line gain. Specify one of the following: **+** to increment by one level, **–** to decrement by one level, *n* to set the specific level (10–100).

OPTIONS *(CONT.)*

Use This Option	To Do This
–L	Load settings from $HOME/.aumixrc, or /etc/aumixrc if the former is inaccessible.
–m [**+** | **–**] [*n*]	Set the microphone level. Specify one of the following: **+** to increment by one level, **–** to decrement by one level, *n* to set the specific level (10–100).
–o [**+** | **–**] [*n*]	Set the line-out level. Specify one of the following: **+** to increment by one level, **–** to decrement by one level, *n* to set the specific level (10–100).
–p [**+** | **–**] [*n*]	Set the PC speaker level. Specify one of the following: **+** to increment by one level, **–** to decrement by one level, *n* to set the specific level (10–100).
–q	Query all devices and print their settings.
–s [**+** | **–**] [*n*]	Set the synthesizer level. Specify one of the following: **+** to increment by one level, **–** to decrement by one level, *n* to set the specific level (10–100).
–S [**+** | **–**] [*n*]	Save settings to $HOME/.aumixrc.
–t [**+** | **–**] [*n*]	Set the treble level. Specify one of the following: **+** to increment by one level, **–** to decrement by one level, *n* to set the specific level (10–100).
–v*n*	Set the main volume to the desired percentage (*n*).
–w[**+** | **–**] [*n*]	Set the PCM level. Specify one of the following: **+** to increment by one level, **–** to decrement by one level, *n* to set the specific level (10–100).
–x [**+** | **–**] [*n*]	Set the imix level. Specify one of the following: **+** to increment by one level, **–** to decrement by one level, *n* to set the specific level (10–100).

COMMANDS

Use This Command	To Do This
+, **right arrow** (→)	Increase level of the selected channel by 3%.
–, **left arrow** (←)	Decrease the level of the selected channel by 3%.
[	Set the level of the selected channel to 0%.

COMMANDS *(CONT.)*

Use This Command	To Do This
]	Set the level of the selected channel to 100%.
1	Set the level of the selected channel to 10%.
2	Set the level of the selected channel to 20%.
3	Set the level of the selected channel to 30%.
4	Set the level of the selected channel to 40%.
5	Set the level of the selected channel to 50%.
6	Set the level of the selected channel to 60%.
7	Set the level of the selected channel to 70%.
8	Set the level of the selected channel to 80%.
9	Set the level of the selected channel to 90%.
Q, q	End the program.
K, k	Show a description of the functions of keys and return to the Level/Balance screen.
L, l	Load settings from $HOME/.aumixrc, or from /etc/aumixrc if $HOME/.aumixrc is not available.
M, m	Mute or unmute.
O, o	Mute all channels but the current one. Use **U** or **u** to return to the main screen.
PgDn, down arrow (↓)	Select the next control down.
PgUp, up arrow (↑)	Select the next control up.
S, s	Save settings to the rc file.
U, u	Undo any muting.
Tab, Enter, <, >, comma and period (,.)	Toggle between level and balance controls.

EXAMPLE

This Command	Does the Following
aumix	Starts the volume control utility in the interactive mode.

cdda2wav

cdda2wav [option] [*filename*]

Reads audio tracks from audio CD-ROMs and writes the data to WAV files. If you do not specify a filename, the utility writes to audio.wav in the working directory. By default, the program samples the CD-ROM audio in stereo, using a sampling rate of 44,100 cycles per second.

TIP Works if downloaded from RPM.

See also **cdparanoia.**

OPTIONS

Use This Option	To Do This
–D *device* – *–device*	Use the specified device (such as /dev/cdrom). For SCSI drives, use the generic_scsi interface (see **–I**) and indicate the SCSI bus number, ID, and LUN. Use the following syntax: –D0, 4 ,0 (bus 0, ID 4, LUN 0).
–A *auxdevice,* – *–auxdevice auxdevice*	Use *auxdevice* as the CD-ROM drive for cooked ioctl usage.
–a *divider,* – *–divider divider*	Set the rate to 44100Hz / *divider.*
–B, – *–bulk*	Copy each track into a separate file.
–b *bits,* – *–bits-per-sample bits*	Set the number of bits to sample per channel (8, 12, or 16).
–c *channels,* – *–channels channels*	Specify the number of channels to use, as follows: **1** Mono recording. **2** Stereo recording. **s** Stereo recording with both channels swapped.

OPTIONS *(CONT.)*

Use This Option	To Do This
–C *endianess*, **– –cdrom-endianess** *endianess*	Sets the endianess (bit order) of the CD-ROM device to little (LSB), big (MSB), or guess.
–d *duration* **– –duration**	Set the recording duration in seconds. Use 0 for the whole track.
–e, **– –echo**	Copy audio data to the sound device while recording.
–E *endianess*, **– –output-endianess** *endianess*	Set the endianess (bit order) of the output device to little (LSB) or big (MSB).
–F, **– –find-extremes**	Find extreme amplitudes in samples.
–G, **– –find-mono**	Determine whether input samples are in mono.
–H, **– –no-infofile**	Skip writing the info and cddb files.
–i *index*, **– –index** *index*	Start at the specified index.
–I *interface*, **– –interface** *interface*	Set the interface for CD-ROM access to generic_scsi or cooked_ioctl. For SCSI CD-ROM drives on Linux, use the generic_scsi interface.
–J, **– –info-only**	Provide information about the disk without actually writing any information.
–l *n*, **– –buffers-in-ring** *n*	Uses a ring buffer with *n* buffers total.
–m, **– –mono**	Record in mono.
–M *n* **– –md5** *n*	Calculate MD-5 checksum for *n* bytes from the beginning of the track.
–n *n*, **– –sectors-per-request** *n*	Read *n* sectors per request.
–O *type* **– –output-format** *type*	Specify the output type (WAV, SUN, CDR, or RAW).
–o *n* **– –offset** *n*	Start *n* offset sectors behind the start track.

OPTIONS *(CONT.)*

Use This Option	To Do This
-p, *percentage* – **-set-pitch** *percentage*	Change the pitch by the specified percentage.
-P *n*, – **-set-overlap** *n*	Set the number (*n*) of overlap sectors for jitter correction.
-q, – **-quiet**	Hide messages.
-R, – **-dump-rates**	Show the possible dump rates.
-r *n*, – **-rate** *n*	Set the sample rate to *n* samples per second.
-s, – **-stereo**	Record in stereo.
-S *n*, – **-speed-select** *n*	Set the CD-ROM to speed *n*.
-T, – **-deemphasize**	Undo the effect of pre-emphasis in the input samples.
-t *start track*[*+end track*], – **-track** *start track*[*+end track*]	Specify the start track and, optionally, the end track.
-v *n*, – **-verbose-level** *n*	Set the level of verbosity from 0 (messages hidden) to 63 (maximum).
-V, – **-verbose-SCSI**	Enable SCSI command logging to the console.
-w, – **-wait**	Wait for signal before recording.
-x, – **-max**	Set maximum CD-ROM quality.

EXAMPLE

This Command	Does the Following
`cdda2wav -I generic_scsi -D0,4,0 -t1+5`	Reads tracks 1 through 5 on the specified SCSI CD-ROM drive (bus 0, ID 4, LUN 0) and writes WAV files to the working directory.

cdlabelgen

cdlabelgen–c [**title**] **–s** [**subtitle**] [option]

Creates PostScript files for printing frontcards and traycards for CD-ROM jewel cases. This utility requires Perl version 5.003 or higher.

OPTIONS

Use This Option	To Do This
–c *string*	Set the category for the CD-ROM with the specified string.
–b	Suppress printing of the plaque on the traycard to leave room for more than 192 and up to 256 items.
–t *template*	Specify the template to use.
–D	Suppress printing of dates.
–d [*string*]	Set the date to today's date or use the specified string.
–e *filename*	Use the specified filename (an .eps file) to print on the cover.
–E *filename*	Use the specified filename (an .eps file) to print on the traycard.
–f *filename*	Use *filename* as the source of the item names.
–h	Show the available options.
–i *list*	Print the list of items on the CD's traycard. The list should consist of items separated by percentage (%) delimiters.
–o *filename*	Print to the specified filename.
–S *n*	Scale the cover graphic file to the ratio *n*.
–s *string*	Specify the CD-ROM's subcategory.
–T *n*	Scale the traycard graphic file to the ratio *n*.
–w	Enable word-wrapping of the items that print on the traycard.

EXAMPLE

This Command	Does the Following
cdlabelgen −c 'My Favorites' −s '2000' −i 'Blues%Jazz%Rock%Alternative Rock%Techno%Industrial' −e images/ mp3.eps > cover.ps	Creates a file, called cover.ps, containing the specified output of **cdlabelgen**.

cdp

cdp [option] [**play** *track*]

Launches an interactive, text-mode player for audio CD-ROMs. To use this utility, you must configure your CD-ROM device to be accessible by means of /dev/cdrom. If necessary, change to /dev and create a symbolic link to your actual CD-ROM device (see **ln −s** in Chapter 5). To use the utility, press the NumLock key and control the audio CD-ROM using the numeric keypad commands (see the Commands table in this section). You can start playing immediately by adding **play** followed by a track number (an integer). The utility begins playing from the specified track.

OPTIONS

Use This Option	To Do This
−h	Show the available options
−I	Wait for initialization before starting
−n	Suppress autoplay mode

COMMANDS

Use This Command	To Do This
9	Play.
0	Exit without stopping playback.
1	Go back within the current track.

COMMANDS *(CONT.)*

Use This Command	To Do This
2	Quit and stop playing.
3	Go forward within the current track.
4	Go to the previous track.
5	Play again.
6	Go to the next track.
7	Stop playing.
8	Pause or resume playing.
c	Edit the CD-ROM name. Press Enter to restore the menu.
Enter	Edit the name of the current track.
Right arrow (→)	Go to the next item.
Left arrow (←)	Go to the previous item.
Up arrow (↑)	Pause.
Down arrow (↓)	Exit.

EXAMPLES

This Command	Does the Following
cdp	Opens the interactive CD-ROM audio player.
cdp play 5	Opens the interactive CD-ROM audio player and starts playing on Track 5.

cdparanoia

cdparanoia [option] *span* [*filename*]

Reads audio tracks from audio CD-ROMs and writes the data to WAV, AIFF, AIFF-C, or RAW format files. If you do not specify a filename, the utility writes automatically-named files in the working directory. By default, the program samples the CD-ROM audio in stereo, using a sampling rate of 44,100 cycles per second. For *span*, specify the tracks using the form *begin [hh:mm:ss:sectors]–end[hh:mm:ss:sectors]*, where *begin* and *end* are track numbers, and *hh:mm:ss:sectors* corresponds to track timings (*hh:mm:*ss) and sectors. To record the entire disk, specify a *span* of **1–** (1 followed by a hyphen).

See also **cdda2wav.**

OPTIONS

Use This Option	To Do This
–a, – –output-aifc	Output data in uncompressed Apple AIFF-C format
–B, – –batch	Split the output of multiple tracks at track boundaries
–C – –force-cdrom-big-endian	Treat the CD-ROM drive as a big-endian device
–c – –force-cdrom-little-endian	Treat the CD-ROM drive as a little-endian device
–d *device* **– –force-cdrom-device** *device*	Read from the specified device rather than from the first drive encountered
–e, – –stderr-progress	Force output of progress information to **stderr**
–f, – –output-aiff	Output data in Apple AIFF format
–g *device*, **– –force-generic-device** *device*	Use with **–d** to specify the device
–h – –help	Show the available options
–n – –force-default-sectors *n*	Force the interface backend to do atomic reads of *n* sectors per read
–p, – –output-raw	Output headerless data as RAW, 16-bit PCM data with interleaved samples in host-byte order
–Q, – –query	Detect the CD-ROM drive and report information
–q, – –quiet	Hide program messages

OPTIONS *(CONT.)*

Use This Option	To Do This
–R – –output-raw-big-endian	Output headerless data as RAW, 16-bit PCM data with interleaved samples in MSB first byte order
–r, – –output-raw-little-endian	Output headerless data as RAW, 16-bit PCM data with interleaved samples in LSB first byte order
–S *n* **– –force-read-speed** *n*	Use speed *n* for reading the CD-ROM drive
–s – –search-for-drive	Force a search for a CD-ROM drive
–v, – –verbose	Show all messages
–V – –version	Show the version number
–W, – –disable-scratch-repair	Disable scratch compensation
–w, – –output-wav	Output data in WAV format
–X, – –disable-scratch-detection	Disable scratch compensation during verification
–Y, – –disable-extra-paranoia	Disables intraread data verification
–Z, – –disable-paranoia	Disable data verification and correction features

EXAMPLES

This Command	Does the Following
`cdparanoia -B "1-"`	Makes WAV files from the entire CD-ROM audio disk starting from Track 1. Places each track in its own disk file.
`cdparanoia -B "-4"`	Makes WAV files of Tracks 1 through 4 (–4 indicates that the utility should start at the beginning of the CD-ROM). Places each track in its own disk file.
`cdparanoia -B "5-8"`	Makes WAV files of Tracks 5 through 8. Places each track in its own disk file.

combine

combine [option] *source image1 source image2* [*mask*]
combined image

Combines two or more graphics files (specified by *source image1*, *source image2*) into a composite image (*combined image*). You can specify a wide variety of combination types and add special effects. Use the **–compose** options to specify the combination effect. To create a composite image with two or more graphics in separate tiles, see **montage**. This utility is part of the ImageMagick package and can be downloaded at `http://www.imagemagick.org`.

See also **convert, identify, mogrify.**

OPTIONS

Use This Option	To Do This
–blend *percentage*	Blend the two images by the specified percentage.
–colors *n*	Use *n* colors in the image.
–colorspace *type*	Specify the type of colorspace. Valid values are GRAY, OHTA, RGB, Transparent, XYZ, YCbCr, YIQ, YPbPr, YUV, or CMYK. The default is RGB.
–comment "*string***"**	Annotate the image with the specified string. Be sure to surround the string with double quotes.
–compose *type*	Specify the type of combination. Valid values are **add** The sum of the image data plus overflow wrapping. **atop** *Source image 2* obscures *source image 1*, but the composite image is trimmed to *source image 1*'s size. **bumpmap** *Source image 1* shaded by the same image. **difference** The result of *source image 2* minus *source image 1*. **in** *Source image 2* obscures *source image 1*. **minus** *Source image 2* minus *source image 1*.

OPTIONS *(CONT.)*

Use This Option	To Do This
–compose *type*	**out** *Source image 2* with the shape of *source image 1* cut out. **over** The union of the two images. **plus** The sum of the image data. **replace** *Source image 1* replaced by *source image 2.* **subtract** *Source image 2* minus *source image 1* with underflow wrapping. **xor** Shows only the image data that is outside the overlap region. Overlap areas are blank.
–compress *type*	Set the type of compression. The options are None, BZip, Fax, Group4, JPEG, LZW, RunlengthEncoded, or Zip.
–density *width* **x** *height*	Set the vertical and horizontal resolution in pixels.
–displace *horizontal scale* **x** *vertical scale*	Shift image pixels as defined by a displacement map.
–dispose *type*	Use the specified type of GIF disposal. The options are **0** No disposal. **1** Do not dispose between frames. **2** Overwrite frame with background color. **3** Overwrite with previous frame.
–dither	Apply Floyd/Steinberg error diffusion to the image.
–font *font*	Set the font for normal text.
–geometry *width* **x** *height* [**%** | **!**]	Set the width and height of the image in pixels. Append a percentage sign to adjust the width and height by percentage. Append an exclamation point to force the exact size.
–gravity *type*	Set the direction to which the image gravitates. The options are NorthWest, North, NorthEast, West, Center, East, SouthWest, South, SouthEast.
–interlace *type*	Set the type of interlacing scheme. The options are None, Line, Plane, or Partition.

OPTIONS *(CONT.)*

Use This Option	To Do This
–**label** "*string*"	Use the string as a label. Be sure to surround the string with double quotes.
–**matte**	Store the matte channel information if the image has one.
–**monochrome**	Transform the image to black and white.
–**negate**	Replace every pixel with its complementary color.
–**page** *width* **x** *height* [**%** | **!**]	Set the width and height of the image canvas in pixels. Append a percentage sign to adjust the width and height by percentage. Append an exclamation point to force the exact size. For PostScript pages, the available widths and heights correspond to page sizes, as follows:

Page Size	Width	Height
11x17	792	1224
A0	2380	3368
A1	1684	2380
A2	1190	1684
A3	842	1190
A4	595	842
A4Small	595	842
A5	421	595
A6	297	421
A7	210	297
A8	148	210
A9	105	148
A10	74	105
ArchA	648	864
ArchB	864	1296
ArchC	1296	1728
ArchD	1728	2592
ArchE	2592	3456
B0	2836	4008
B1	2004	2836
B2	1418	2004
B3	1002	1418
B4	709	1002
B5	501	709

OPTIONS *(CONT.)*

Use This Option	To Do This		
	Page Size	**Width**	**Height**
	C0	2600	3677
	C1	1837	2600
	C2	1298	1837
	C3	918	1298
	C4	649	918
	C5	459	649
	C6	323	459
	Flsa	612	936
	Flse	612	936
	HalfLetter	396	612
	Ledger	1224	792
	Legal	612	1008
	Letter	612	792
	LetterSmall	612	792
–quality *value*	Set the JPEG, MIFF, or PNG compression level.		
–size *width* **x** *height* [**%** | **!**]	Set the width and height of RAW images with unknown dimensions. Append a percentage sign to adjust the width and height by percentage. Append an exclamation point to force the exact size.		
–stegano	Hide a watermark in the image.		
–stereo	Combine two images to create a stereo anaglyph.		
–tile	Repeat a composite operation across the image.		
–treedepth 0 | 1	Set a tree depth of 0 or 1. You must also use the **–colors** option.		
–verbose	Display all messages.		

EXAMPLE

This Command	Does the Following
`combine -compose bumpmap image1.jpg image2.jpg combined.jpg`	Combine the specified input files (`image1.jpg` and `image2.jpg`) into a composite image (`combined.jpg`) in which `image1.jpg` transparently shades `image2.jpg`.

convert

convert [option] *input file output file*

Converts the specified input file (a graphic file) into the specified output file. This utility automatically recognizes a wide variety of image formats. To specify the format of the converted file, append a recognized suffix to the output filename (such as .jpg or .bmp). This utility is part of the ImageMagick package, which is downloadable from http://www.imagemagick.org.

See also **combine, identify, montage.**

OPTIONS

Use This Option	To Do This
despeckle	Reduce speckles in the image.
–dispose *type*	Use the specified type of GIF disposal. The options are
	0 No disposal.
	1 Do not dispose between frames.
	2 Overwrite frame with background color.
	3 Overwrite with previous frame.
–dither	Apply Floyd/Steinberg error diffusion to the image.
–draw *string*	Annotate an image with one or more graphic primitives. The primitives include the following: circle, color, ellipse, fillCircle, fillEllipse, fillPolygon, fillRectangle, image, line, matte, point, polygon, rectangle, and text.
–edge *factor*	Detect edges in an image using the specified enhancement factor (a percentage).
–enhance	Enhance a noisy image.
–equalize	Perform histogram equalization.

OPTIONS *(CONT.)*

Use This Option	To Do This
–filter *type*	Use the specified filter type when resizing the image with **–geometry**. The following filters are available: Bessel, Blackman, Box, Catrom, Cubic, Gaussian, Hamming, Hanning, Hermite, Lanczos (the default), Mitchell, Point, Quadratic, Sinc, Triangle.
–flip	Create a mirror image by reversing scan lines vertically.
–flop	Create a mirror image by reversing scan lines horizontally.
–font *font*	Set the font for normal text.
–frame *width* **x** *height* **+** *outer-bevel width* **+** *inner-bevel width*	Use an ornamental border with the specified width, height, outer-bevel width, and inner-bevel width.
–fuzz *distance*	Combine colors in the specified distance.
–gamma *n*	Use the specified level (*n*) of gamma correction, where *n* is a level from 0.8 to 2.3.
–geometry *width* **x** *height* [**%** | **!**]	Create the image with the specified maximum width and height while maintaining the original image's aspect ratio. Append **%** (a percentage sign) to adjust the width and height by a percentage. To force the dimensions you specify, append **!** (an exclamation point).
–gravity *type*	Set the direction to which the image gravitates. The options are NorthWest, North, NorthEast, West, Center, East, SouthWest, South, SouthEast.
–implode *factor*	Implode image pixels about the center by the specified factor. The options are implosion (0–99.9%) or explosion (–99.9–0%).
–interlace *type*	Set the type of interlacing scheme. The options are None, Line, Plane, or Partition.

OPTIONS *(CONT.)*

Use This Option	To Do This
–label "*string*"	Use the specified string as a label. Be sure to surround the string with double quotation marks.
–layer *type*	Set the type of layer. The options are Red, Green, Blue, or Matte.
–linewidth *n*	Set the width of a line to *n* pixels.
–loop *n*	Repeat the GIF animation *n* times. Specify 0 to loop forever.
–map *filename*	Obtain the color set from the specified filename.
–matte	Store the matte channel information if the image has one.
–modulate *brightness, saturation, hue*	Vary the brightness, saturation, and hue by specifying percentage increases or decreases. Omit the percentage sign.
–monochrome	Transform the image to black and white.
–morph *image sequence*	Morph the image sequence.
–negate	Replace every pixel with its complementary color.
–noise *type*	Add or reduce noise using the specified filter type. The options are Uniform, Gaussian, Multiplicative, Impulse, Laplacian, and Poisson.
–normalize	Transform the image and enhance the contrast by spanning the full range of color values.
–opaque *color*	Use the specified color for the pen (see **–pen**).
–page *width* **x** *height* [**%** | **!**]	Set the width and height in pixels of the image canvas. Append a percentage sign to adjust the width and height by percentage. Append an exclamation point to force the exact size. For PostScript pages, the available widths and heights correspond to page sizes as follows:

Page Size	Width	Height
11x17	792	1224
A0	2380	3368
A1	1684	2380
A2	1190	1684

OPTIONS *(CONT.)*

Use This Option	To Do This		
	Page Size	Width	Height
	A3	842	1190
	A4	595	842
	A4Small	595	842
	A5	421	595
	A6	297	421
	A7	210	297
	A8	148	210
	A9	105	148
	A10	74	105
	ArchA	648	864
	ArchB	864	1296
	ArchC	1296	1728
	ArchD	1728	2592
	ArchE	2592	3456
	B0	2836	4008
	B1	2004	2836
	B2	1418	2004
	B3	1002	1418
	B4	709	1002
	B5	501	709
	C0	2600	3677
	C1	1837	2600
	C2	1298	1837
	C3	918	1298
	C4	649	918
	C5	459	649
	C6	323	459
	Flsa	612	936
	Flse	612	936
	HalfLetter	396	612
	Ledger	1224	792
	Legal	612	1008
	Letter	612	792
	LetterSmall	612	792
–paint *radius*	Simulate an oil painting using the specified radius of circular brushstrokes.		

OPTIONS *(CONT.)*

Use This Option	To Do This
–pen *color*	Set the color of the font or opaque color.
–pointsize *point*	Use the specified point size for the PostScript font.
–preview *type*	Use the following image preview type: Add Noise, Blur, Brightness, CharcoalDrawing, Despeckle, Dull, EdgeDetect, Gamma, Grayscale, Hue, Implode, JPEG (the default), OilPaint, Quantize, Raise, ReduceNoise, Roll, Rotate, Saturation, Segment, Shade, Sharpen, Shear, Solarize, Spiff, Spread, Swirl, Threshold, and Wave.
–profile *string*	Add ICC color or IPTC newswire information profile to an image by means of the specified string.
–quality *value*	Set the JPEG, MIFF, or PNG compression level.
–raise *width* **x** *height*	Create a 3D effect with the specified width and height.
–region *width* **x** *height*	Apply options to the region of the image specified by width and height.
–roll *x offset y offset*	Roll an image vertically by the specified x offset and y offset.
–rotate *degrees* **< | >**	Rotate the image left (<) or right (>) by the specified number of degrees.
–sample *width* **x** *height* [**%** | **!**]	Scale the image with pixel sampling to the specified maximum width and height while preserving the original image's aspect ratio. Append **%** (a percentage sign) to adjust the width and height by a percentage. Append **!** (an exclamation point) to force the dimensions that you specify.
–scene *n*	Specify image scene number *n*.
–seed *value*	Use the specified value for the pseudo-random number generator.

OPTIONS *(CONT.)*

Use This Option	To Do This
–segment *cluster threshold* **x** *smoothing threshold*	Segment an image using the specified cluster threshold and smoothing threshold.
–shade *azimuth* **x** *elevation*	Shade the image using a distant light source at the specified azimuth and elevation.
–sharpen *factor*	Sharpen an image by the specified factor (0.0 – 99.9%).
–shear *x degrees* **x** *y degrees*	Shear the image along the x or y axis by the specified shear angle.
–solarize *factor*	Negate all pixels above the threshold level specified by the factor (0–99.9%).
–spread *n*	Displace image pixels by *n* pixels.
–swirl *degrees*	Swirl image pixels about the center by the specified number of degrees.
–texture *filename*	Use the texture found in the specified filename for the image background.
–threshold value	Create a bi-level image in which only the pixels exceeding the specified value are displayed.
–transparency *color*	Make the specified color transparent.
–treedepth 0 | 1	Set a tree depth of 0 or 1.
–units *type*	Specify the type of image resolution. The options are Undefined, PixelsPerInch, or PixelsPerCentimeter.
–verbose	Display all messages.
–view *string*	Use the FlashPix viewing parameters specified by string.
–wave *amplitude wavelength*	Alter an image along a sine wave with the specified amplitude and wavelength.

EXAMPLE

This Command	Does the Following
`convert mypicture.gif mypicture.jpg`	Converts the specified input file (`mypicture.gif`) into a JPEG graphic.

identify

identify *filename*

Determines the format and characteristics of the graphic file specified by *filename* and checks to see whether the image is incomplete or corrupt. You can specify more than one filename using shell patterns (see the section "Shell Patterns" in Chapter 4). Use with the **–verbose** option to see a wealth of information about each graphic file. This utility is part of the ImageMagick package, which can be downloaded at http://www.imagemagick.org.

See also **combine, convert, mogrify, montage.**

OPTIONS

Use This Option	To Do This
–ping	Determine image characteristics efficiently
–verbose	Show detailed information about the image

EXAMPLE

This Command	Does the Following
identify –verbose image1.jpg	Displays information about the specified graphics file (image1.jpg).

mikmod

mikmod [option] [*module* | *playlist*]

Launches an interactive text-based utility that plays a variety of SoundTracker and SoundTracker-derived module formats. Also handles playlists. Supported module formats include IT, XM, MOD, MTM, S3M, STM, ULT, FAR, MED, DSM, AMF, IMG, and 669. See the Commands table in this section for commands that you can use in the interactive mode.

OPTIONS

Use This Option	To Do This
–a, – –panning	Process panning effects. This is the default.
–c, – –curious	Look for hidden patterns in the module.
–d *n*, **– –driver** *n*	Use the specified device driver for output. The default is 0.
–f *frequency*, **– –frequency** *frequency*	Set mixing frequency in hertz.
–F, – –fadeout	Fade out the volume during the last pattern of each module.
–h, – –help	Display available options.
–hq, – –hqmixer	Use the high quality software mixer.
–i	Show the version number.
–i– –interpolate	Use interpolated mixing.
–l, – –loops	Enable in-module backward loops.
– –nocurious	Disable looking for hidden patterns in module. This is the default.
– –nofadeout	Disable fading the volume during the last pattern of each module. This is the default.
– –nohqmixer	Skip using the high-quality mixer. This is the default.
– –nointerpolate	Skip interpolated mixing. This is the default.
– –noloops	Disable in-module reverse looping. This is the default.
– –nopanning	Skip processing panning effects.
– –noprotracker	Disable ProTracker extended speed effects.
– –noprotracker	Disable Protracker extended speed effect.
– –norc	Skip using the .mikmodrc configuration file, which is stored by default in the user's home directory. The file is used by default and is updated to store your configuration settings when you exit this utility.
– –norealtime	Skip rescheduling MikMod to gain real-time priority. This is the default.
– –norenice	Skip re-nicing to –20. This is the default.
– –nosurround	Skip using surround mixing. This is the default.

COMMANDS

Use This Command	To Do This
H, **F1**	Display on-screen help
+, **Right arrow** ($\rightarrow$)	Skip to next pattern
>	Increase the volume
–, **Left arrow** ($\leftarrow$)	Restart the current pattern or skip to the previous pattern
:, ;	Toggle interpolation mixing
(	Play the module faster
)	Play the module slower
{	Use a slower tempo
}	Use a faster tempo
<	Decrease the volume
C, **F6**	Display the configuration panel
Ctrl+L	Refresh the screen
0–9	Set the volume from 10% (digit 1) to 100% (digit 0)
End	Go to the end of the panel
Home	Go to the top of the panel
I, **F3**	Display the instruments panel
L, **F5**	Display the playlist panel
M, **F4**	Display the song message panel if it is present in the module
N	Switch to the next module in the playlist
P	Switch to the previous module in the playlist
PgUp, **PgDn**	Scroll the panel faster
Q	Exit MikMod
R	Restart the current module
S, **F2**	Display samples panel
space	Toggle pause
U	Toggle surround mixing
Up, **Down**	Scroll the panel

EXAMPLE

This Command	Does the Following
mikmod	Starts the module player in the interactive mode.

---

mogrify

mogrify [option] *filename*

Transforms the graphics file specified by *filename* and overwrites the original file. Use **convert** to transform the input file into a new output file without overwriting the original input file. This utility is part of the ImageMagick package, which can be downloaded at http://www.imagemagick.org.

See also **combine, identify, montage.**

OPTIONS

Use This Option	To Do This
–antialias	Remove pixel aliasing.
–blur *factor*	Blur an image by the specified factor (0.0–99.9%).
–border *width* **x** *height*	Surround the image with a border of the specified width and height.
–bordercolor *color*	Set the border color.
–box *color*	Set the color of the annotation bounding box.
–charcoal *factor*	Simulate a charcoal drawing with the specified factor (0.0–99.9%)
–colorize *percentage*	Colorize the image using the pen color and the specified factor (0.0–99.9%).
–colorspace *type*	Set the type of colorspace. The options are as follows: CMYK, GRAY, OHTA, RGB, Transparent, XYZ, YCbCr, YIQ, YPbPr, and YUV.
–colors *n*	Specify the preferred number (*n*) of colors in the image.

OPTIONS *(CONT.)*

Use This Option	To Do This
–comment *string*	Annotate an image using the specified string. You can use the following expansion symbols:
	%b File size.
	%d Directory.
	%e Filename extension.
	%f Filename.
	%h Height.
	%m Magick.
	%p Page number.
	%s Scene number.
	%t Top of filename.
	%w Width.
	%x X resolution.
	%y Y resolution.
	\n Newline.
	\r Carriage return.
–compress *type*	Set the type of image compression. The options are as follows: BZip, Fax, Group4, JPEG, LZW, RunlengthEncoded, None, and Zip.
–contrast, +contrast	Enhance (**–contrast**) or reduce (**+contrast**) the image contrast.
–crop *width* **x** *height*	Crop the image at the specified width and height.
–cycle *n*	Displace the image color map by the specified amount (*n*).
–density *width* **x** *height*	Set the vertical and horizontal resolution of the image to the specified width and height in pixels.
–depth *value*	Set the color depth of the image (8 or 16).
–despeckle	Reduce speckles in the image.
–dispose *type*	Use the specified type of GIF disposal. The options are as follows:
	0 No disposal.
	1 Do not dispose between frames.
	2 Overwrite the frame with the background color.
	3 Overwrite with the previous frame.

OPTIONS *(CONT.)*

Use This Option	To Do This
–dither	Apply Floyd/Steinberg error diffusion to the image.
–draw *string*	Annotate an image with one or more graphic primitives. The primitives include the following: circle, color, ellipse, fillCircle, fillEllipse, fillPolygon, fillRectangle, image, line, matte, point, polygon, rectangle, and text.
–edge *factor*	Detect edges within an image using the specified enhancement factor (a percentage).
–emboss	Emboss the image.
–enhance	Enhance a noisy image.
–equalize	Perform histogram equalization.
–filter *type*	Use the specified filter type when resizing the image with **–geometry**. The following filters are available: Bessel, Blackman, Box, Catrom, Cubic, Gaussian, Hamming, Hanning, Hermite, Lanczos (the default), Mitchell, Point, Quadratic, Sinc, and Triangle.
–flip	Create a mirror image by reversing scan lines vertically.
–flop	Create a mirror image by reversing scan lines horizontally.
–font *font*	Set the font for normal text.
–format *type*	Set the image format to the specified type using one of the following: **AVS**　AVS X image file. **BIE**　Joint Bilevel Image experts Group file interchange format. **BMP**　Microsoft Windows bitmap image file. **BMP24**　Microsoft Windows 24-bit bitmap image file. **CGM**　Computer Graphics Metafile. **CMYK**　RAW cyan, magenta, yellow, and black bytes.

OPTIONS *(CONT.)*

Use This Option	To Do This
	DCX ZSoft IBM PC multipage Paintbrush file.
	DIB Microsoft Windows bitmap image file.
	DICOM Medical image file.
	EPDF Encapsulated Portable Document Format.
	EPI Adobe Encapsulated PostScript Interchange format.
	EPS Adobe Encapsulated PostScript file.
	EPS2 Adobe Level II Encapsulated PostScript file.
	EPSF Adobe Encapsulated PostScript file.
	EPSI Adobe Encapsulated PostScript Interchange format.
	EPT Adobe Encapsulated PostScript Interchange format with TIFF preview.
	FAX Group 3.
	FIG TransFig image format.
	FITS Flexible Image Transport System.
	FPX FlashPix Format.
	GIF CompuServe graphics interchange format. 8-bit color.
	GIF87 CompuServe graphics interchange format. 8-bit color (version 87a).
	GRAY RAW gray bytes.
	GRADATION Gradual passing from one shade to another. Specify the desired shading with the filename (for example, gradation:red blue).
	GRANITE Granite texture.
	HDF Hierarchical data format.
	HISTOGRAM Histogram data format.
	HPGL HP GL plotter language.
	HTML Hypertext Markup Language a with client-side image map.
	JBIG Joint Bilevel Image Experts Group file interchange format.

OPTIONS *(CONT.)*

Use This Option   **To Do This**

JPEG   Joint Photographic Experts Group JFIF format, compressed 24-bit color.

ICO   Microsoft icon.

LABEL   Text image.

MAP   Color map intensities and indices.

MIFF   Magick image file format.

MNG   Multiple image Network Graphics.

MONO   Bilevel bitmap in least significant byte (LSB) first order.

MPEG   Motion Picture Experts Group file interchange format.

MTV   MTV raytracing data format.

M2V   Motion Picture Experts Group file interchange format (version 2).

NETSCAPE   Netscape 216 color cube.

NULL   Null image.

PBM   Portable bitmap format (black and white).

PCD   Photo CD-ROM. The maximum resolution written is 512×768 pixels.

PCDS   Photo CD-ROM. Decode with the sRGB color table.

PCL   Page Control Language.

PCX   ZSoft IBM PC Paintbrush file.

PDF   Portable Document Format.

PGM   Portable graymap format (gray scale).

PICT   Apple Macintosh QuickDraw/PICT file.

PIX   Alias/Wavefront RLE image format.

PLASMA   Plasma fractal image. Specify the base color as the filename (for example, plasma:gray). Use fractal to initialize to a random value (for example, plasma:fractal).

PNG   Portable Network Graphics.

PNM   Portable anymap.

PPM   Portable pixmap format (color).

PS   Adobe PostScript file.

PSD   Adobe Photoshop bitmap file.

OPTIONS *(CONT.)*

Use This Option	To Do This
PS2	Adobe Level II PostScript file.
RAD	Radiance image file.
RGB	RAW red, green, and blue bytes.
RGBA	RAW red, green, blue, and matte bytes.
RLA	Alias/Wavefront image file, read only.
RLE	Utah Run length-encoded image file, read only.
SGI	Irix RGB image file.
SHTML	Hypertext Markup Language with a client-side image map.
SUN	SUN Rasterfile.
TEXT	RAW text file, read only.
TGA	Truevision Targa image file.
TIFF	Tagged Image File Format.
TIFF24	24-bit Tagged Image File Format.
TILE	Tile image with a texture.
TIM	PSX TIM file.
TTF	TrueType font file.
UIL	X Motif UIL table.
UYVY	Interleaved YUV.
VICAR	Read only.
VID	Visual Image Directory.
VIFF	Khoros Visualization image file.
WIN	Select image from or display image to your computer screen.
X	Select image from or display image to your X server screen.
XC	Constant image of X server color. Specify the image color as the filename (e.g. xc:yellow).
XBM	X Windows system bitmap, black and white only.
XPM	X Windows system pixmap file (color).
XWD	X Windows system window dump file (color).
YUV	CCIR 601 4:1:1 file.

OPTIONS *(CONT.)*

Use This Option	To Do This
–frame *width* **x** *height* **+** *outer bevel width* **+** *inner bevel width*	Use an ornamental border with the specified width, height, outer bevel width, and inner bevel width.
–fuzz *distance*	Combine colors within the specified distance.
–gamma *n*	Use the specified level (*n*) of gamma correction, where *n* is a level from 0.8 to 2.3.
–geometry *width* **x** *height* [**%** | **!**]	Create the image with the specified maximum width and height while maintaining the original image's aspect ratio. Append **%** (a percentage sign) to adjust the width and height by a percentage. To force the dimensions you specify, append **!** (an exclamation point).
–gravity *type*	Set the direction to which the image gravitates: NorthWest, North, NorthEast, West, Center, East, SouthWest, South, SouthEast.
–implode *factor*	Implode image pixels about the center by the specified factor. The options are implosion (0–99.9%) or explosion (–99.9–0%).
–interlace *type*	Set the type of interlacing scheme. The options are None, Line, Plane, or Partition.
–label *string*	Use the string as a label.
–layer *type*	Set the type of layer. The options are Red, Green, Blue, or Matte.
–linewidth *n*	Set the width of a line to *n* pixels.
–loop *n*	Repeat the GIF animation *n* times. Specify 0 to loop forever.
–map *filename*	Obtain the color set from the specified filename.
–matte	Store the matte channel information if the image has one.
–modulate *brightness, saturation, hue*	Vary the brightness, saturation, and hue by specifying percentage increases or decreases. Omit the percentage sign.
–monochrome	Transform the image to black and white.

OPTIONS *(CONT.)*

Use This Option	To Do This
–negate	Replace every pixel with its complementary color.
–noise *type*	Add or reduce noise using the specified filter type. The options are Uniform, Gaussian, Multiplicative, Impulse, Laplacian, Poisson.
–normalize	Transform image and enhance contrast by spanning the full range of color values.
–opaque *color*	Use the specified color for the pen (see **–pen**).
–page *width* **x** *height* [**%** | **!**]	Set the width and height in pixels of the image canvas. Append **%** (a percentage sign) to adjust the width and height by a percentage. Append **!** (an exclamation point) to force the exact size. The choices for a Postscript page are

Page Size	Width	Height
11x17	792	1224
A0	2380	3368
A1	1684	2380
A2	1190	1684
A3	842	1190
A4	595	842
A4Small	595	842
A5	421	595
A6	297	421
A7	210	297
A8	148	210
A9	105	148
A10	74	105
ArchA	648	864
ArchB	864	1296
ArchC	1296	1728
ArchD	1728	2592
ArchE	2592	3456
B0	2836	4008
B1	2004	2836
B2	1418	2004
B3	1002	1418
B4	709	1002

OPTIONS *(CONT.)*

Use This Option	To Do This

Page Size	Width	Height
B5	501	709
C0	2600	3677
C1	1837	2600
C2	1298	1837
C3	918	1298
C4	649	918
C5	459	649
C6	323	459
Flsa	612	936
Flse	612	936
HalfLetter	396	612
Ledger	1224	792
Legal	612	1008
Letter	612	792
LetterSmall	612	792

Use This Option	To Do This
–paint *radius*	Simulate an oil painting using the specified radius of circular brushstrokes.
–pen *color*	Set the color of the font or opaque color.
–pointsize *point*	Use the specified point size for the PostScript font.
–quality *n*	Set the JPEG, MIFF, or PNG compression level. For JPEG graphics, qualities range from 0 (worst) to 100 (best). The default is 75.
–raise *width* **x** *height*	Create a 3D effect with the specified width and height.
–region *width* **x** *height* [**+** | **–** *x offset*] [**+** | **–** *y offset*]	Apply options to the region of the image specified by width and height.
–roll *x offset y offset*	Roll an image vertically by the specified x offset and y offset.
–rotate *degrees* **<** | **>**	Rotate the image left (<) or right (>) by the specified number of degrees.
–sample *width* **x** *height* [**%** | **!**]	Scale the image with pixel sampling to the specified maximum width and height, while preserving the original image's aspect ratio. Append **%** (a percentage sign) to adjust the width and height by a percentage. To force the dimensions you specify, append **!** (an exclamation point).

OPTIONS *(CONT.)*

Use This Option	To Do This
–scene *n*	Specify the image scene number *n*.
–seed *value*	Use the specified value for the pseudo-random number generator.
–segment *cluster threshold* **x** *smoothing threshold*	Segment an image using the specified cluster threshold and smoothing threshold.
–shade *azimuth* **x** *elevation*	Shade the image using a distant light source at the specified azimuth and elevation.
–sharpen *factor*	Sharpen an image by the specified factor (0.0–99.9%).
–shear *x degrees* **x** *y degrees*	Shear the image along the x or y axis by the specified shear angle.
–solarize *factor*	Negate all pixels above the threshold level specified by the factor (0–99.9%).
–spread *n*	Displace image pixels by *n* pixels.
–swirl *degrees*	Swirl image pixels about the center by the specified number of degrees.
–texture *filename*	Use the texture found in the specified filename for the image background.
–threshold *n*	Create a bi-level image in which only the pixels exceeding the specified value are displayed.
–transparency *color*	Make the specified color transparent.
–treedepth *n*	Sets a tree depth of 0 or 1 for the optimal tree depth for the color reduction algorithm. This is the default. Specify an integer from 2 to 8 to try more computationally intensive tree depth renderings. This option requires the **–colors** or **–monochrome** option.
–units *type*	Specify the type of image resolution. The options are Undefined, PixelsPerInch, or PixelsPerCentimeter.
–verbose	Display all messages.

OPTIONS *(CONT.)*

Use This Option	To Do This
–view *string*	Use the FlashPix viewing parameters specified by *string*.
–wave *amplitude wavelength*	Alter an image along a sine wave with the specified amplitude and wavelength.

EXAMPLES

This Command	Does the Following
mogrify –format jpeg image1.bmp image1.jpg	Converts image1.bmp to image1.jpg.
mogrify 'vid:*.jpg' catalog.jpg	Creates a visual directory of all the .jpg files in the working directory and writes the output to catalog.jpg.

---

montage

montage [option] *input filenames output file*

Transforms two or more input filenames into a composite image in which the source images are shown in separate tiles (compare **combine**). This utility is part of the ImageMagick package, which can be downloaded at http://www.imagemagick.org.

See also **convert, identify, mogrify.**

OPTIONS

Use This Option	To Do This
–adjoin	Join images into a single multi-image file.
–blur *factor*	Blur an image by the specified factor (0.0–99.9%).
–colorspace *type*	Set the type of colorspace. The options are CMYK, GRAY, OHTA, RGB, Transparent, XYZ, YCbCr, YIQ, YPbPr, and YUV.

OPTIONS *(CONT.)*

Use This Option	To Do This
–colors *n*	Set the preferred color depth to *n* (8 or 16).
–comment *string*	Annotate an image using the specified string. You can use the following expansion symbols:

    %b File size.
    %d Directory.
    %e Filename extension.
    %f Filename.
    %h Height.
    %m Magick.
    %p Page number.
    %s Scene number.
    %t Top of filename.
    %w Width.
    %x X resolution.
    %y Y resolution
    \n Newline.
    \r Carriage return.

Use This Option	To Do This
–compress *type*	Set the type of image compression. The options are BZip, Fax, Group4, JPEG, LZW, RunlengthEncoded, None, Zip.
–contrast, +contrast	Enhance (**–contrast**) or reduce (**+contrast**) the image contrast.
–crop *width* **x** *height*	Crop the image at the specified width and height.
–cycle *n*	Displace the image color map by the specified amount (*n*).
–density <*width*>**x**<*height*>	Set the vertical and horizontal resolution in pixels of the image.
–density *width* **x** *height*	Set the vertical and horizontal resolution of the image to the specified width and height in pixels.
–depth *value*	Set the color depth of the image (8 or 16).
–despeckle	Reduce speckles in the image.

OPTIONS *(CONT.)*

Use This Option	To Do This
–dispose *type*	Use the specified type of GIF disposal. The options are **0** No disposal. **1** Do not dispose between frames. **2** Overwrite the frame with the background color. **3** Overwrite with the previous frame.
–draw *string*	Annotate an image with one or more graphic primitives. The primitives include the following: circle, color, ellipse, fillCircle, fillEllipse, fillPolygon, fillRectangle, image, line, matte, point, polygon, rectangle, and text.
–font *font*	Set the font for normal text.
–frame *width* **x** *height* **+** *outer bevel width* **+** *inner bevel width*	Use an ornamental border with the specified width, height, outer-bevel width, and inner-bevel width.
–gamma *n*	Use the specified level (*n*) of gamma correction, where *n* is a level from 0.8 to 2.3.
–geometry *width* **x** *height* [**%** | **!**] [**+** | **–** *x offset*] [**+** | **–** *y offset*]	Create the image with the specified maximum width and height while maintaining the original image's aspect ratio. Append **%** (a percentage sign) to adjust the width and height by a percentage. To force the dimensions you specify, append **!** (an exclamation point).
–gravity *type*	Set the direction to which the image gravitates. The options are NorthWest, North, NorthEast, West, Center, East, SouthWest, South, and SouthEast.
–interlace *type*	Set the type of interlacing scheme. The options are None, Line, Plane, or Partition.
–label *string*	Use the string as a label.
–matte	Store the matte channel information if the image has one.

OPTIONS *(CONT.)*

Use This Option	To Do This
–mode *type*	Set the type of montage. The options are Frame, Unframe (the default), or Concatenate.
–monochrome	Transform the image to black and white.
–page *width* **x** *height* [**%** | **!**]	Set the width and height in pixels of the image canvas. Append a percentage sign to adjust the width and height by percentage. Append an exclamation point to force the exact size. The choices for a Postscript page are

Page Size	Width	Height
11x17	792	1224
A0	2380	3368
A1	1684	2380
A2	1190	1684
A3	842	1190
A4	595	842
A4Small	595	842
A5	421	595
A6	297	421
A7	210	297
A8	148	210
A9	105	148
A10	74	105
ArchA	648	864
ArchB	864	1296
ArchC	1296	1728
ArchD	1728	2592
ArchE	2592	3456
B0	2836	4008
B1	2004	2836
B2	1418	2004
B3	1002	1418
B4	709	1002
B5	501	709
C0	2600	3677
C1	1837	2600

OPTIONS *(CONT.)*

Use This Option	To Do This
	Page Size Width Height

Page Size	Width	Height
C2	1298	1837
C3	918	1298
C4	649	918
C5	459	649
C6	323	459
Flsa	612	936
Flse	612	936
HalfLetter	396	612
Ledger	1224	792
Legal	612	1008
Letter	612	792
LetterSmall	612	792

Use This Option	To Do This
–pen *color*	Set the color of the font or opaque color.
–pointsize *point*	Use the specified point size (*point*) for the PostScript font.
–quality value	Set the JPEG, MIFF, or PNG compression level.
–rotate *degrees* < | >	Rotate the image left (<) or right (>) by the specified number of degrees.
–scene *n*	Specify image scene number *n*.
–shadow	Add a shadow beneath a tile to simulate depth.
–sharpen *factor*	Sharpen an image by the specified factor (0.0–99.9%).
–size *width* **x** *height*	Set the width and height of the image when these cannot be obtained automatically.
–texture *filename*	Use the texture found in the specified filename for the image background.
–tile *width* **x** *height*	Set the width and height of tiles in the composite image.
–transparency *color*	Make the specified color transparent.
–treedepth 0 | 1	Set a tree depth of 0 or 1.
–verbose	Display all messages.

EXAMPLE

This Command	Does the Following
`montage image1.jpg image2.jpg`	Creates a montage that includes `image1.jpg` and `image2.jpg`.

mpg123

mpg123 [option] *filename | URL*

Plays the MP3 audio file specified by *filename* or *URL* (a Web address) on the default audio device. For *filename,* you can specify a list of files separated by spaces, a shell pattern (see the section "Shell Patterns" in Chapter 4), or a URL. To stop playing the current file and skip to the next one, press Ctrl + C. To stop playing and quit, press Ctrl + C twice, rapidly. To play WAV, AU, and other sampled sounds, see **play**. To play MIDI sounds, see **playmidi**.

OPTIONS

Use This Option	To Do This
–t, – –test	Test mode (no audio output).
–@ *filename,* **– –list** *filename*	Obtain the input from the specified filename, which can be a filename, a shell pattern (see the section "Shell Patterns" in Chapter 4), or a URL.
–0, – –single0, –1, – –single1	Play the left channel (0) or right channel (1) only. Works only for MPEG streams.
–2, – –2to1, –4, – –4to1	Reduce the sampling rate by the specified factor.
– –8bit	Force 8-bit output.
–a *device,* **– –audiodevice** *device*	Specify the audio device to use.
–b *n,* **– –buffer size** *n*	Use an audio output buffer of size *n* kilobytes (K).
–c, – –check	Check for filter range violations.

OPTIONS *(CONT.)*

Use This Option	To Do This
–d *n*, **– –doublespeed** *n*	Play every *n*th frame, skipping the others.
–f *factor*, **– –scale** *factor*	Change the scale factor. The default is 32768.
–g *gain*, **– –gain** *gain*	Set the output volume to the specified gain.
–h *n*, **– –halfspeed** *n*	Play each frame *n* times.
–k *n*, **– –skip** *n*	Skip the first *n* frames.
–m, **– –singlemix**	Mix both channels. Works only for MPEG streams.
–n *n*, **– –frames** *n*	Decode only *n* frames. By default, the complete stream is decoded.
–o h, **– –headphones**	Direct audio output to the headphone connector.
–o l, **– –lineout**	Direct audio output to the line-out connector.
–o s, **– –speaker**	Direct audio output to the speaker.
–p *URL* | **none**, **– –proxy** *URL* | **none**	Use the specified URL as a proxy for HTTP requests.
–q, **– –quiet**	Suppress messages.
– –reopen	Reopen the audio device after every song.
–r *rate*, **– –rate** *rate*	Set the sample to the specified rate.
–s, **– –stdout**	Write to the standard output instead of the audio device.
– –stereo	Force stereo output.
–u *password*, **– –auth** *password*	Use the specified password for HTTP authentication.
–v, **– –verbose**	Show more program messages.
–y, **– –resync**	Continue decoding if an error occurs.
–z, **– –shuffle**	Play tracks randomly.

EXAMPLES

This Command	Does the Following
mpg123 *mp3	Plays all the MP3 files in the working directory.
mpg123 - -auth mypassword http://www.sounds.org/ sample.mp3	Plays the specified MP3 file (sample.mp3) available from the Internet at http:// www.sounds.org and supplies the specified password (mypassword).

play

play [option] *filename* [*effect*]

Plays the audio file specified by *filename*. Normally, the utility auto-detects the sound file type and other file parameters, so you won't need to use the options unless the utility fails to detect the file type correctly. You can also use one of the effects specified in the Effects table in the "**sox**" section. This utility is a front end to the **sox** utility. To play MIDI sounds, see **playmidi**. To play MP3s, see **mpg123**.

OPTIONS

Use This Option	To Do This
–c *n*, **– –channels=***n*	Define the number (*n*) of channels of the file.
–d *device*, **– –device=***device*	Specify a device other than the default output device.
–f *format*, **– –format=***format*	Specify bit format of sample. Available options are **a** ADPCM. **A** Alaw (logarithmic). **g** GSM. **s** signed linear (2's complement). **U** Ulaw (logarithmic). **u** Unsigned linear.

OPTIONS *(CONT.)*

Use This Option	To Do This
–h, **– –help**	Show available options.
–r *rate*, **– –rate=***rate*	Use the specified sample rate to decode the audio data.
–s size, **– –size=size**	Use the specified size to describe the size of the sample. Available options are
	b Bytes.
	d 64-bit double floats.
	D 80-bit IEEE floats.
	f 32-bit float.
	l 32-bit word.
	w 16-bit words.
–t *type*, **– –type=***type*	Specify the type of audio file format to use, as follows:
	8svx Amiga musical instrument description format.
	aiff Apple/Silicon Graphics AIFF sound.
	au Sun/NeXT AU sound.
	auto Autodetection of sound file type (default).
	cdr RAW, unsigned samples of CD-ROM audio.
	cvs Continuously Variable Slope modulation used for speech compression.
	dat Text data file containing a textual representation of the sample data.
	gsm Global Standard for Mobil (GSM) telecommunications file used for speech compression.
	hcom Macintosh compressed audio files.
	maud Amiga sound file.
	ossdsp OSS device driver.
	sb Signed byte RAW sound file.
	sf IRCAM sound files used by CSound and MixView applications.

OPTIONS *(CONT.)*

Use This Option	To Do This
–t *type*, – –**type**=*type*	**smp** Turtle Beach SampleVision sound. **sunau** Sun/NeXT AU sound file. **txw** Yamaha TX-16W sampler. **ub** Unsigned byte RAW sound file. **ul** Ulaw RAW sound file. **uw** Unsigned word sound file. **vms** Compressed speech file. **voc** Sound Blaster VOC sound. **wav** Microsoft WAV sound.
–**v** *volume*, – –**volume**=**volume**	Change the audio output to the specified volume (less than 1.0 decreases, more than 1.0 increases).
– –**version**	Show version of play/rec.
–**x**, – –**xinu**	Reverse the byte order of the sample.

EXAMPLES

This Command	Does the Following
play mysound.wav	Plays the specified sound file (mysound.wav).
play mysound.wav echo 40 12	Plays the specified sound file (mysound.wav) with an echo effect (40-millisecond delay and 12-millisecond delay).

---

playmidi

playmidi [option] [*filename*]

Plays the MIDI file specified by *filename*. Available options enable you to play or suppress specified MIDI channels (see the MIDI Channels table in this section). To play WAV, AU, and other wave-table sounds, see **play**. To play MP3s, see **mpg123**.

NOTE Version 2.3 of **playmidi** is current at the time of this writing and is not compatible with the Awe 32 SoundBlaster driver.

OPTIONS

Use This Option	To Do This
–8	Use 8-bit patches for the Gravis Ultrasound sound card
–c n	Specify the MIDI channels (using n, a hexidecimal number) to play
–C n	Set the initial chorus level to n (0–127)
–d	Silence the tracks defined as percussion tracks (see –m)
–E n	Specify the MIDI channels (using n, a hexidecimal number) to output to the external MIDI device
–f	Send output to the FM synthesizer, which is required for sound cards that lack wave-table synthesis.
–F n	Specify the MIDI channels (using n, a hexidecimal number) to output to the FM synthesis device
–g	Use a Gravis UltraSound sound card
–G n	Specify the MIDI channels (using n, a hexidecimal number) to output to the Gravis UltraSound sound card
–l	Show a list of available MIDI channels
–i n	Specify the MIDI channels (using n, a hexadecimal number) to ignore
–m n	Define the specified MIDI channels (using n, a hexadecimal number) as percussion tracks
–P n	Remap percussion channels to play on the channel specified by n (a hexadecimal number)
–r	Show playback graphics
–R n	Set the reverb level to the value specified by n (0–127)
–t n	Change the tempo by the float factor specified by n
–Vn,velocity	Set the velocity for all notes in channel n
–x n	Suppress the channel specified by n

MIDI CHANNELS

Channel	Hexadecimal	General MIDI Instrument	PlayMIDI Instrument Name
1	001	Acoustic Grand Piano	acpiano
2	002	Bright Acoustic Piano	britepno
3	003	Electric Grand Piano	synpiano
4	004	Honky-tonk Piano	honky
5	005	Electric Piano 1	epiano1
6	006	Electric Piano 2	epiano2
7	007	Harpsichord	hrpschrd
8	008	Clavi	clavinet
9	009	Celesta	eleste
10	00A	Glockenspiel	glocken
11	00B	Music Box	musicbox
12	00C	Vibraphone	vibes
13	00D	Marimba	marimba
14	00E	Xylophone	xylophon
15	00F	Tubular Bells	tubebell
16	010	Dulcimer	santur
17	011	Drawbar Organ	homeorg
18	012	Percussive Organ	percorg
19	013	Rock Organ	rockorg
20	014	Church Organ	church
21	015	Reed Organ	reedorg
22	016	Accordion	accordn
23	017	Harmonica	harmonca
24	018	Tango Accordion	concrtna
25	019	Acoustic Guitar (nylon)	nyguitar
26	01A	Acoustic Guitar (steel)	acguitar
27	01B	Electric Guitar (jazz)	jazzgtr
28	01C	Electric Guitar (clean)	cleangtr

MIDI CHANNELS *(CONT.)*

Channel	Hexadecimal	General MIDI Instrument	PlayMIDI Instrument Name
29	01D	Electric Guitar (muted)	mutegtr
30	01E	Overdriven Guitar	odguitar
31	01F	Distortion Guitar	distgtr
32	020	Guitar harmonics	gtrharm
33	021	Acoustic Bass	acbass
34	022	Electric Bass (finger)	fngrbass
35	023	Electric Bass (pick)	pickbass
36	024	Fretless Bass 1	fretless
37	025	Slap Bass 1	slapbas1
38	026	Slap Bass 2	slapbas2
39	027	Synth Bass 1	synbass1
40	028	Synth Bass 2	synbass2
41	029	Violin	violin
42	02A	Viola1	viola
43	02B	Cello1	cello
44	02C	Contrabass1	contraba
45	02D	Tremolo Strings	marcato
46	02E	Pizzicato Strings	pizzcato
47	02F	Orchestral Harp	harp
48	030	Timpani1	timpani
49	031	String Ensemble	marcato
50	032	String Ensemble	slowstr
51	033	SynthStrings	synstr1
52	034	SynthStrings	synstr2
53	035	Choir Aahs	choir
54	036	Voice Oohs	doo
55	037	Synth Voice	voices
56	038	Orchestra Hit	orchhit

MIDI CHANNELS *(CONT.)*

Channel	Hexadecimal	General MIDI Instrument	PlayMIDI Instrument Name
57	039	Trumpet	trumpet
58	03A	Trombone	trombone
59	03B	Tuba1	tuba
60	03C	Muted Trumpet	mutetrum
61	03D	French Horn	frenchrn
62	03E	Brass Section	hitbrass
63	03F	SynthBrass	synbras1
64	040	SynthBrass	synbras2
65	041	Soprano Sax	sprnosax
66	042	Alto Sax	altosax
67	043	Tenor Sax	tenorsax
68	044	Baritone Sax	barisax
69	045	Oboe	oboe
70	046	English Horn	englhorn
71	047	Bassoon	bassoon
72	048	Clarinet	clarinet
73	049	Piccolo	piccolo
74	04A	Flute	flute
75	04B	Recorder	recorder
76	04C	Pan Flute	woodflut
77	04D	Blown Bottle	bottle
78	04E	Shakuhachi	shakazul
79	04F	Whistle	whistle
80	050	Ocarina	ocarina
81	051	Lead 1 (square)	sqrwave
82	052	Lead 2 (sawtooth)	sawwave
83	053	Lead 3 (calliope)	calliope
84	054	Lead 4 (chiff)	chiflead

MIDI CHANNELS *(CONT.)*

Channel	Hexadecimal	General MIDI Instrument	PlayMIDI Instrument Name
85	055	Lead 5 (charang)	charang
86	056	Lead 6 (voice)	voxlead
87	057	Lead 7 (fifths)	lead5th
88	058	Lead 8 (bass + lead)	basslead
89	059	Pad 1 (new age)	fantasia
90	05A	Pad 2 (warm)	warmpad
91	05B	Pad 3 (polysynth)	polysyn
92	05C	Pad 4 (choir)	ghostie
93	05D	Pad 5 (bowed)	bowglass
94	05E	Pad 6 (metallic)	metalpad
95	05F	Pad 7 (halo)	halopad
96	060	Pad 8 (sweep)	sweeper
97	061	FX 1 (rain)	aurora
98	062	FX 2 (soundtrack)	soundtrk
99	063	FX 3 (crystal)	crystal
100	064	FX 4 (atmosphere)	atmosphr
101	065	FX 5 (brightness)	freshair
102	066	FX 6 (goblins)	unicorn
103	067	FX 7 (echoes)	sweeper
104	068	FX 8 (sci-fi)	startrek
105	069	Sitar	sita
106	06A	Banjo	banjo
107	06B	Shamisen	shamisen
108	06C	Koto	koto
109	06D	Kalimba	kalimba
110	06E	Bag pipe	bagpipes
111	06F	Fiddle	fiddle
112	070	Shanai	shannai

MIDI CHANNELS *(CONT.)*

Channel	Hexadecimal	General MIDI Instrument	PlayMIDI Instrument Name
113	071	Tinkle Bell	carillon
114	072	Agogo	agogo
115	073	Steel Drums	steeldrm
116	074	Woodblock	woodblk
117	075	Taiko Drum	taiko
118	076	Melodic Tom	toms
119	077	Synth Drum	syntom
120	078	Reverse Cymbal	revcym
121	079	Guitar Fret Noise	fx-fret
122	07A	Breath Noise	fx-blow
123	07B	Seashore	seashore
124	07C	Bird Tweet	jungle
125	07D	Telephone Ring	telephon
126	07E	Helicopter	helicptr
127	07F	Applause	applause
128	080	Gunshot	ringwhsl

EXAMPLE

This Command	Does the Following
`playmidi sample.midi`	Plays the specified MIDI file.

---

rec

rec [option] *filename* [*effect*]

Records the microphone input to the audio file specified by *filename*. Specify the sound type with the – –**type** option. You can also use one of the effects specified in the Effects table in the **"sox"** section. This utility is a front end to the **sox** utility.

OPTIONS

Use This Option	To Do This
–c *n*, **– –channels=***n*	Define the number (*n*) of channels of the file.
–d *device*, **– –device=***device*	Specify a device other than the default input device.
–f *format*, **– –format=***format*	Specify the bit format of the sample. The available options are **a** ADPCM. **A** Alaw (logarithmic). **g** GSM. **s** Signed linear (2's complement). **U** Ulaw (logarithmic). **u** Unsigned linear.
–h, **– –help**	Show the available options.
–r *rate*, **– –rate=***rate*	Use the specified sample rate to decode the audio data.
–s size, **– –size=***size*	Use the specified size to describe the size of the sample. The available options are **b** Bytes. **d** 64-bit double floats. **D** 80-bit IEEE floats. **f** 32-bit float. **l** 32-bit word. **w** 16-bit words.
–t *type*, **– –type=***type*	Specify the type of audio file format to use. The options are as follows: **8svx** Amiga musical instrument description format. **aiff** Apple/Silicon Graphics AIFF sound. **au** Sun/NeXT AU sound. **auto** Autodetection of sound file type. This is the default. **cdr** RAW, unsigned samples of CD-ROM audio. **cvs** Continuously Variable Slope modulation; used for speech compression. **dat** Text data file containing a textual representation of the sample data.

OPTIONS *(CONT.)*

Use This Option	To Do This
	gsm Global Standard for Mobil (GSM) telecommunications file used for speech compression.
	hcom Macintosh compressed audio files.
	maud Amiga sound file.
	ossdsp OSS device driver
	sb Signed byte RAW sound file.
	sf IRCAM sound files used by CSound and MixView applications.
	smp Turtle Beach SampleVision sound.
	sunau Sun/NeXT AU sound file.
	txw Yamaha TX–16W sampler.
	ub Unsigned byte RAW sound file.
	ul Ulaw RAW sound file.
	uw Unsigned word sound file.
	vms Compressed speech file.
	voc Sound Blaster VOC sound.
	wav Microsoft WAV sound.
–v *volume*, **– –volume=***volume*	Change the audio output to the specified volume (less than 1.0 decreases, more than 1.0 increases).
– –version	Show version of play/rec.
–x, **– –xinu**	Reverse the byte order of the sample.

EXAMPLE

This Command	Does the Following
`rec – –format gsm mygreeting.gsm`	Records the microphone input to the specified file (`mygreeting.gsm`) using the GSM sound format.

SOX

sox [option] *input file output file* [*effect*]

Translates sampled sounds from the input format specified by *input file* to another format, stored in *output file,* with the optional effect. This command is most often used in shell scripts or as a filter between two other commands. To play sampled sounds, use **play.** To play MP3s, use **mpg123.** To play MIDI files, use **playmidi.**

OPTIONS

Use This Option	To Do This
–a	Set the data format type to ADPCM.
–A	Set the data format type to Alaw (logarithmic).
–b	Use bytes to describe the size of the sample.
–c *n,* **– –channels=***n*	Define the number (*n*) of channels of the file.
–d	Use 64-bit, double-floating point notation to describe the size of the sample.
–D	Use 80-bit, IEEE-floating point notation to describe the size of the sample.
–f	Use 32-bit floating point notation to describe the size of the sample.
–f *format,* **– –format=***format*	Specify the bit format of the sample. The available options are **a** ADPCM. **A** Alaw (logarithmic). **g** GSM. **s** Signed linear (2's complement). **U** Ulaw (logarithmic). **u** Unsigned linear.
–g	Set the data format type to GSM.
–h, **– –help**	Show the available options.
–l	Use 32-bit words to describe the size of the sample.
–p	Run in preview mode.

OPTIONS *(CONT.)*

Use This Option	To Do This
–r *rate*, **– –rate=***rate*	Use the specified sample rate to decode the audio data.
–s	Set the data format type to signed linear (2's complement).
–t *type*	Specifies the type of audio file format to use. The options are

    8svx Amiga musical instrument description format.

    aiff Apple/Silicon Graphics AIFF sound.

    au Sun/NeXT AU sound.

    auto Autodetection of sound file type. This is the default.

    cdr RAW, unsigned samples of CD-ROM audio.

    cvs Continuously Variable Slope modulation; used for speech compression.

    dat Text data file containing a textual representation of the sample data.

    gsm Global Standard for Mobil (GSM) telecommunications file used for speech compression.

    hcom Macintosh compressed audio files.

    maud Amiga sound file.

    ossdsp OSS device driver.

    sb Signed byte RAW sound file.

    sf IRCAM sound files used by CSound and MixView applications.

    smp Turtle Beach SampleVision sound.

    sunau Sun/NeXT AU sound file.

    txw Yamaha TX-16W sampler.

    ub Unsigned byte RAW sound file.

    ul Ulaw RAW sound file.

    uw Unsigned word sound file.

    vms Compressed speech file.

    voc Sound Blaster VOC sound.

    wav Microsoft WAV sound.

–u	Set the data format type to unsigned linear.

OPTIONS *(CONT.)*

Use This Option	To Do This
–U	Set the data format type to Ulaw (logarithmic).
–V	Print detailed program messages.
–w	Use 16-bit words to describe the size of the sample.
–x, – –xinu	Reverse the byte order of the sample.

EFFECTS

Use This Effect	To Do This
avg [**l** | **r**]	Average the channels or optionally duplicate the left channel (**l**) or the right channel (**r**).
band [–*n*] **center** [**width**]	Apply a band-pass filter. Optionally specify a noise factor (*n*) and the width of the slope of the drop.
deemph	Attenuate the treble using a treble attenuation shelving filter.
echo *delay decay*	Add **echo** to the sound sample with the specified delay and decay (both in milliseconds).
flanger *delay decay speed*	Add a flanger to a sound sample with the specified delay, decay, and speed in milliseconds.
highp *center*	Apply a high-pass filter with the specified center frequency.
lowp *center*	Apply a low-pass filter with the specified center frequency.
mask	Add a masking noise to the signal.
phaser *delay decay speed*	Add a phaser to a sound sample with the specified delay, decay, and speed (in milliseconds).
reverb *delay*	Add reverberation to a sound sample with the specified delay.

EFFECTS *(CONT.)*

Use This Effect	To Do This
reverse	Detect possible Satanic subliminal messages in the sound message by playing it in reverse.
split	Transform mono input into simulated stereo.
vibro *speed depth*	Add a Fender Vibro-Champ effect to the sound with the specified speed and depth.

CHAPTER 10

Working with Fonts

$\mathbf{T}$his chapter details utilities that facilitate the use of fonts in the X Window System environment. It will discuss utilities that install new fonts from binary distributions and convert TrueType fonts into PostScript fonts that the X server can display. It will also cover the basic utilities needed to install new fonts and make them available to the X server.

AT A GLANCE

How Do I	See This Entry	Example
Convert a Binary Distribution Format (BNF) font so that the X server can use it?	**bdtopcf**	bdftopcf -o myfont .pcf myfont.bdf
Make new fonts available to the X server?	**mkfontdir, ttmkfdir**	mkfontdir -e > fonts.dir
Convert a Type 1 PFB font to a Type 1 PFA font?	**t1ascii**	t1ascii myfont.pfa myfont.pfb
Convert a Type 1 PFA font to a Type 2 PFB font?	**t1binary**	t1binary myfont .pfb myfont.pfa
Convert a TrueType font to a Type 1 font so that I can use it without running a TrueType font server?	**ttf2pt1**	ttf2pt1 -A myfont .ttf, ttf2pt1 -e myfont .ttf
Make TrueType fonts available to the font server?	**ttmkfdir**	ttmkfdir -o fonts .scale
View and search a list of fonts currently available to the X server?	**xlsfonts**	xlsfonts
Add a new font directory to the X server path?	**chkfontpath, xset**	xset fp+ '/usr/ fonts/newfonts'

Font Essentials

This section covers the following:

- Font names in the X environment

- Font aliases

- Types of fonts found on Linux systems

- Font encodings

- Bitmapped fonts typically provided with Linux distributions

- Scalable fonts typically provided with Linux distributions

Font Names

To be recognized by the X font server, a font must be fully described by a valid font name, as defined by the X Logical Font Description (XLFD) standard. An XLFD-conformant name looks like the following:

```
-b&h-lucida-medium-r-normal-sans-20-140-100-100-p-114-
iso8859-1
```

This name consists of a fixed number of fields, delimited by hyphens, that describe the following types of information (from left to right):

Foundry   The firm or organization that designed the font.

Family   The name of the family of fonts to which the current font belongs, such as Helvetica or Times Roman.

Weight   The darkness of the font. Settings include light, medium, bold, demibold, and extra bold.

Slant   The vertical orientation of the font. Settings include -r (roman, with vertical orientation), -o (oblique, which is slanted like italic, except that the slant tilts to the left), and -i (italic).

Set Width   The relative width of the characters. Settings include *extra condensed* (very narrow), *condensed* (narrow), *normal* (normal width), *expanded* (wide), and *ultra expanded* (very wide).

Additional Style   Some fonts contain additional information in this field, such as *sans* (sans-serif font) or *serif* (serif font). This field is infrequently used.

Pixel Size   The size of a font character in pixels.

Point Size   The height of the font's tallest characters from the baseline, measured in printer's points (72 per inch). For scalable fonts, the size is generally indicated with a 0. For bit-mapped fonts, the size is indicated in points multiplied by 10. For example, a size of 140 indicates 14 points.

X Axis Resolution   The font's horizontal resolution in pixels.

Y Axis Resolution   The font's vertical resolution in pixels.

Spacing   The type of spacing used by the font. Options include -c (*character cell,* a spacing method used for terminal displays), -m (*monospace,* in which all the characters in the font are exactly the same width), and -p (*proportional,* in which characters such as *m* and *w* are wider than characters such as *l* or *i*).

Average Width   The average width of a character in the font in pixels.

Character Set Registry and Encoding   The method used to encode the font in order to accommodate foreign languages (see the section "Font Encodings"). This portion of the font name consists of two sections, the registry (such as iso-8859) and the language encoding (an integer such as 1).

Font Aliases

Because XLFD-conformant font names are tedious to type, you can create font aliases. To do so, create a file named `fonts.alias` and put it in the same directory that contains the fonts. Each line of this file should contain an alias followed by the XLFD name, as in the following example:

```
lucidasans-bolditalic-8 -b&h-lucida-bold-i-normal-sans-
11-80-100-100-p-69-iso8859-1
```

In this example, `lucidasans-bolditalic-8` is an alias for *–b&h–lucida–bold–i–normal–sans–11–80–100–100–p–69–iso8859–1.* Once you have defined the alias, you can use the alias instead of typing the full font name.

Types of Fonts

Linux distributions typically include a variety of font types, which fall into two general categories:

bit-mapped fonts   A single font file contains a representation of the font in one font size.

scalable fonts   A single font file contains the information needed to represent the font at any size up to 127 points.

In addition to this basic distinction, the X Window System works optimally with *character cell fonts,* also called *terminal fonts,* in which the width of each character has been adjusted to fit a standard on-screen character cell.

Fonts are also distinguished by the format used to store them on disk. The following table describes the types of fonts found on most Linux systems.

COMMON LINUX FONTS

Font Type	Description
Portable Compiled Font (PCF)	The standard format for bit-mapped fonts on X systems. Typically provided at two resolutions (75x75dpi and 100x100dpi). PCF fonts are typically compressed with **gzip** (see Chapter 6). XFree86 can decompress `pcf.gz` files on the fly.
Speedo (SPD)	A bitstream format for scalable fonts.
Type 1 ASCII (hexadecimal) font (PFA)	An ASCII-encoded version of a Type 1 (PostScript) font. The X server can display this type of font when it is made available to the X server with a corresponding AFM file with the same base name.

COMMON LINUX FONTS *(CONT.)*

Font Type	Description
Type 1 binary font (PFB)	A binary version of a Type 1 (PostScript) font designed for downloading to Post-Script printers. Requires a paired AFM file with the same base name.
Type 1 font metrics (AFM)	A font metrics file for scalable Type 1 (Post-Script) fonts. These files specify character widths and other information needed to represent the fonts with precision. To use Type 1 fonts, your system must have an AFM file and a corresponding PFA or PFB file with the same base name in the same directory.
Bitmap Distribution Format (BDF)	A format for distributing bitmapped fonts. These fonts must be converted to PCF fonts before they are used.

Font Encodings

Most of the fonts provided with Linux distributions conform to the International Organization for Standards (ISO) specifications for 8-bit character sets. However, some of the fonts use proprietary encoding schemes, such as those devised by Apple Computer, Microsoft Corporation, DEC, and Hewlett-Packard. A transition is underway to *Unicode*, a universal character set capable of representing the characters of most human languages.

COMMON ENCODINGS

Encoding	Description
GB2312-80	Chinese
HP-ROMAN8	Hewlett-Packard Roman character set
ISO-10646	Universal Character Set (Unicode)
ISO-646	ASCII

COMMON ENCODINGS *(CONT.)*

Encoding	Description
ISO-8859-1	ISO Latin1 (Western European)
ISO-8859-10	ISO Nordic (Icelandic, Nordic, Baltic)
ISO-8859-11	ISO Thai
ISO-8859-13	Baltic Rim
ISO-8859-14	Celtic
ISO-8859-15	Updated Latin-1 character set with Euro symbol
ISO-8859-2	ISO Latin2 (Eastern European)
ISO-8859-3	ISO Latin3 (Southern European)
ISO-8859-4	ISO Latin4 (Northern European)
ISO-8859-5	ISO Cyrillic (Russian)
ISO-8859-6	ISO Arabic (Latin representation)
ISO-8859-7	ISO Greek
ISO-8859-8	ISO Hebrew (Latin representation)
ISO-8859-9	ISO Turkish
JIS-X201	Japanese (Katakana)
JIS-X208	Japanese
KSC5601.1987	Korean
MACINTOSH	Macintosh character set
MICROSOFT-CP1250	Microsoft Windows character set (Eastern European languages)
MICROSOFT-CP1251	Microsoft Windows character set (Cyrillic)
MICROSOFT-CP1252	Microsoft Windows character set (Western European languages)
MICROSOFT-CP1253	Microsoft Windows character set (Greek)
MICROSOFT-CP1254	Microsoft Windows character set (Turkish)
MICROSOFT-CP1255	Microsoft Windows character set (Hebrew)
MICROSOFT-CP1256	Microsoft Windows character set (Arabic)
MICROSOFT-CP1257	Microsoft Windows character set (Baltic)
UTF-7	Unicode version of ASCII
UTF-8	Unicode version of ISO-8859-1 (Latin-1)

Bitmapped Fonts

This section lists the bitmapped fonts that are typically provided with Linux distributions, organized into the following sections:

- 75dpi monospace fonts (bitmapped)

- 100dpi monospace fonts (bitmapped)

- 75dpi character cell fonts (bitmapped)

- 100dpi character cell fonts (bitmapped)

- 75dpi and 100dpi proportionally-spaced fonts (bitmapped)

75DPI MONOSPACE FONTS (BITMAPPED)

Foundry	Font Family	Weight	Slant	Set Width	Point Size	Charset
adobe	courier	bold	oblique	normal	8, 10, 12, 14, 18, 24,	iso8859-1
adobe	courier	bold	roman	normal	8, 10, 12, 14, 18, 24	iso8859-1
adobe	courier	medium	oblique	normal	8, 10, 12, 14, 18, 24	iso8859-1
adobe	courier	medium	roman	normal	8, 10, 12, 14, 18, 24	iso8859-1
b&h	lucida typewriter	bold	roman	normal	8, 10, 12, 14, 18, 19, 24	iso8859-1
b&h	lucida typewriter	medium	roman	normal	8, 10, 12, 14, 18, 19, 24	iso8859-1

100DPI MONOSPACE FONTS (BITMAPPED)

Foundry	Family	Weight	Slant	Set Width	Additional Style	Point Sizes	Charset
adobe	courier	bold	oblique	normal		8, 10, 12, 14, 18, 24	iso8859-1
adobe	courier	bold	roman	normal		8, 10, 12, 14, 18, 24	iso8859-1
adobe	courier	medium	oblique	normal		8, 10, 12, 14, 18, 24	iso8859-1
adobe	courier	medium	roman	normal		8, 10, 12, 14, 18, 24	iso8859-1
b&h	lucida typewriter	bold	roman	normal	sans	8, 10, 12, 14, 18, 19, 24	iso8859-1
b&h	lucida typewriter	medium	roman	normal	sans	8, 10, 12, 14, 18, 19, 24	iso8859-1

75DPI CHARACTER CELL FONTS (BITMAPPED)

Foundry	Family	Weight	Slant	Set Width	Point Sizes	Charset
misc	fixed	medium	roman	semicondensed	11	iso646.1991-1
misc	fixed	medium	roman	semicondensed	11, 12	iso8859-1
jis	fixed	medium	roman	normal	11, 15, 17, 23	jisx0208.1983-0
misc	fixed	medium	roman	semicondensed	12	iso8859-8
misc	fixed	medium	roman	normal	12	iso8859-8
misc	fixed	medium	roman	normal	12	iso8859-15
misc	fixed	bold	roman	normal	12	iso8859-15
misc	fixed	medium	roman	normal	13	jisx0208.1983-0

75DPI CHARACTER CELL FONTS (BITMAPPED) *(CONT.)*

Foundry	Family	Weight	Slant	Set Width	Point Sizes	Charset
misc	fixed	medium	roman	normal	13	jisx0201.1976-0
dec	terminal	medium	roman	normal	14	iso8859-1
dec	terminal	bold	roman	normal	14	iso8859-1
dec	terminal	medium	roman	normal	14	dec-dectech
dec	terminal	bold	roman	normal	14	dec-dectech
sony	fixed	medium	roman	normal	15, 23	jisx0201.1976-0
sony	fixed	medium	roman	normal	15, 23	iso8859-1
isas	song ti	medium	roman	normal	16	gb2312.1980-0
isas	fangsong ti	medium	roman	normal	16	gb2312.1980-0
misc	nil	medium	roman	normal	2	misc-fontspecific
isas	song ti	medium	roman	normal	24	gb2312.1980-0
schumacher	clean	medium	roman	normal	6, 8, 10, 12, 13, 14, 15, 15	iso8859-1
schumacher	clean	medium	roman	normal	6, 8, 10, 12, 14, 15, 16	iso646.1991-irv
misc	fixed	medium	roman	normal	7, 8, 9, 10, 12, 13, 14, 20	iso8859-1
misc	fixed	bold	roman	semicondensed	7, 8, 9, 10, 12, 13, 14, 20	iso8859-1
schumacher	clean	bold	roman	normal	8, 10, 12, 13, 14, 15, 16	iso646.1991-irv
schumacher	clean	medium	italic	normal	8, 12	iso646.1991-irv
misc	fixed	medium	roman	normal	8, 9	iso646.1991-irv

100DPI CHARACTER CELL FONTS (BITMAPPED)

Foundry	Family	Weight	Slant	Set Width	Point Sizes	Charset
bitstream	terminal	bold	roman	normal	14	dec-dectech
bitstream	terminal	medium	roman	normal	14	dec-dectech
bitstream	terminal	medium	roman	normal	14	iso8859-1
daewoo	gothic	medium	roman	normal	12	ksc5601.1987-0
daewoo	mincho	medium	roman	normal	12, 17	ksc5601.1987-0
misc	fixed	bold	roman	normal	10, 12	iso8859-1
misc	fixed	bold	roman	semicondensed	10	iso8859-1
misc	fixed	medium	roman	normal	5, 6, 7, 8, 9, 10, 11, 12, 14	iso8859-1
misc	fixed	medium	roman	semicondensed	10	iso8859-8
sony	fixed	medium	roman	normal	12, 17	iso8859-1
sony	fixed	medium	roman	normal	12, 17	jisx0201.1976-0

75DPI AND 100DPI PROPORTIONALLY SPACED FONTS (BITMAPPED)

Foundry	Font Family	Weight	Slant	Set Width	Additional Style	Point Sizes	Charset
adobe	helvetica	bold	oblique	normal		8, 10, 12, 14, 18	iso8859-1
adobe	helvetica	bold	roman	normal		8, 10, 12, 14, 18	iso8859-1
adobe	helvetica	medium	oblique	normal		8, 10, 12, 14, 18	iso8859-1
adobe	helvetica	medium	roman	normal		8, 10, 12, 14, 18	iso8859-1
adobe	new century schoolbook	bold	roman	normal		8, 10, 12, 14, 18, 24	iso8859-1

75DPI AND 100DPI PROPORTIONALLY SPACED FONTS (BITMAPPED) *(CONT.)*

Foundry	Font Family	Weight	Slant	Set Width	Additional Style	Point Sizes	Charset
adobe	new century schoolbook	bold	italic	normal		8, 10, 12, 14, 18, 24	iso8859-1
adobe	new century schoolbook	bold	roman	normal		8, 10, 12, 14, 18, 24	iso8859-1
adobe	new century schoolbook	bold	italic	normal		8, 10, 12, 14, 18, 24	iso8859-1
adobe	new century schoolbook	medium	roman	normal		8, 10, 12, 14, 18, 24	iso8859-1
adobe	new century schoolbook	medium	italic	normal		8, 10, 12, 14, 18, 24	iso8859-1
adobe	new century schoolbook	medium	roman	normal		8, 10, 12, 14, 18, 24	iso8859-1
adobe	new century schoolbook	medium	italic	normal		8, 10, 12, 14, 18, 24	iso8859-1
adobe	times	bold	italic	normal		08, 10, 12, 14, 18	iso8859-1
adobe	times	bold	roman	normal		8, 10, 12, 14, 18	iso8859-1
adobe	times	medium	italic	normal		8, 10, 12, 14, 18	iso8859-1
adobe	times	medium	roman	normal		8, 10, 12, 14, 18	iso8859-1

75DPI AND 100DPI PROPORTIONALLY SPACED FONTS (BITMAPPED) *(CONT.)*

Foundry	Font Family	Weight	Slant	Set Width	Additional Style	Point Sizes	Charset
adobe	utopia	regular	italic	normal		8, 10, 12, 14, 18	iso8859-1
adobe	utopia	regular	roman	normal		8, 10, 12, 14, 18	iso8859-1
b&h	lucida	bold	italic	normal	sans	8, 10, 12, 14, 18	iso8859-1
b&h	lucida	bold	roman	normal	sans	8, 10, 12, 14, 18	iso8859-1
b&h	lucida	medium	italic	normal	sans	8, 10, 12, 14, 18	iso8859-1
b&h	lucida	medium	roman	normal	sans	8, 10, 12, 14, 18	iso8859-1
b&h	lucidabright	demibold	italic	normal		8, 10, 12, 14, 18	iso8859-1
b&h	lucidabright	demibold	roman	normal		8, 10, 12, 14, 18	iso8859-1
b&h	lucidabright	medium	italic	normal		8, 10, 12, 14, 18	iso8859-1
b&h	lucidabright	medium	roman	normal		8, 10, 12, 14, 18	iso8859-1
bitstream	charter	medium	italic	normal		8, 10, 12, 14, 18, 24	iso8859-1
bitstream	charter	medium	roman	normal		8, 10, 12, 14, 18, 24	iso8859-1

Scalable Fonts

This section lists the bitmapped fonts that are typically provided with Linux distributions, organized into the following sections:

- 75dpi monospace fonts (scalable)

- 100dpi monospace fonts (scalable)

- 75dpi character cell fonts (scalable)

- 100dpi character cell fonts (scalable)

- 75dpi and 100dpi proportionally spaced fonts (scalable)

75DPI MONOSPACE FONTS (SCALABLE)

Foundry	Family	Weight	Slant	Set Width	Charset
adobe	courier	bold	oblique	normal	iso8859-1
adobe	courier	medium	oblique	normal	iso8859-1
adobe	courier	bold	roman	normal	iso8859-1
adobe	courier	medium	roman	normal	iso8859-1
b&h	lucida typewriter	bold	roman	normal	iso8859-1

100DPI MONOSPACE FONTS (SCALABLE)

Foundry	Font Family	Weight	Slant	Set Width	Charset
adobe	courier	bold	oblique	normal	iso8859-1
adobe	courier	bold	r	normal	iso8859-1
adobe	courier	medium	r	normal	iso8859-1
adobe	courier	medium	oblique	normal	iso8859-1

75DPI CHARACTER CELL FONTS (SCALABLE)

Foundry	Family	Weight	Slant	Set Width	Charset
dec	terminal	bold	roman	normal	dec-dectech
dec	terminal	bold	roman	normal	iso8859-1
dec	terminal	medium	roman	normal	dec-dectech
dec	terminal	medium	roman	normal	iso8859-1
isas	fangsong ti	medium	roman	normal	gb2312.1980-0
isas	song ti	medium	roman	normal	gb2312.1980-0
jis	fixed	medium	roman	normal	jisx0208.1983-0
misc	fixed	bold	roman	normal	iso8859-1
misc	fixed	bold	roman	semicondensed	iso8859-1
misc	fixed	bold	roman	normal	iso8859-15
misc	fixed	medium	roman	normal	iso646.1991-0
misc	fixed	medium	roman	semicondensed	iso646.1991-0
misc	fixed	medium	roman	normal	iso8859-1
misc	fixed	medium	roman	semicondensed	iso8859-1
misc	fixed	medium	roman	normal	iso8859-15
misc	fixed	medium	roman	normal	iso8859-8
misc	fixed	medium	roman	semicondensed	iso8859-8
misc	fixed	medium	roman	normal	jisx0201.1976-0
misc	fixed	medium	roman	normal	jisx0208.1983-0
misc	nil	medium	roman	normal	misc-fontspecific
schumacher	clean	bold	roman	normal	iso646.1991-irv
schumacher	clean	medium	italic	normal	iso646.1991-irv
schumacher	clean	medium	roman	normal	iso646.1991-irv

100DPI CHARACTER CELL FONTS (SCALABLE)

Foundry	Family	Weight	Slant	Set Width	Charset
bitstream	terminal	bold	roman	normal	iso8859-1
bitstream	terminal	bold	roman	normal	iso8859-1
bitstream	terminal	bold	roman	normal	dec-dectech
bitstream	terminal	medium	roman	normal	iso8859-1
bitstream	terminal	medium	roman	normal	dec-dectech
daewoo	gothic	medium	roman	normal	ksc5601.1987-0
daewoo	mincho	medium	roman	normal	ksc5601.1987-0
sony	fixed	medium	roman	normal	iso8859-0
sony	fixed	medium	roman	normal	jisx0201.1976-0

75DPI AND 100DPI PROPORTIONALLY SPACED (SCALABLE)

Foundry	Family	Weight	Slant	Set Width	Additional Style	Charset
adobe	helvetica	bold	oblique	normal		iso8859-1
adobe	helvetica	bold	roman	normal		iso8859-1
adobe	helvetica	medium	oblique	normal		iso8859-1
adobe	helvetica	medium	roman	normal		iso8859-1
adobe	new century schoolbook	bold	italic	normal		iso8859-1
adobe	new century schoolbook	bold	roman	normal		iso8859-1
adobe	new century schoolbook	bold	italic	normal		iso8859-1
adobe	new century schoolbook	bold	roman	normal		iso8859-1
adobe	new century schoolbook	medium	roman	normal		iso8859-1
adobe	new century schoolbook	medium	italic	normal		iso8859-1
adobe	new century schoolbook	medium	roman	normal		iso8859-1

75DPI AND 100DPI PROPORTIONALLY SPACED (SCALABLE) *(CONT.)*

adobe	new century schoolbook	medium	italic	normal		iso8859-1
adobe	symbol	medium	roman	normal		adobe-font-specific
adobe	times	bold	roman	normal		iso8859-1
adobe	times	medium	italic	normal		iso8859-1
adobe	utopia	regular	italic	normal		iso8859-1
adobe	utopia	regular	roman	normal		iso8859-1
b&h	lucida	bold	italic	normal	sans	iso8859-1
b&h	lucida	bold	roman	normal	sans	iso8859-1
b&h	lucida	medium	italic	normal	sans	iso8859-1
b&h	lucida	medium	roman	normal	sans	iso8859-1
b&h	lucidabright	demibold	italic	normal		iso8859-1
b&h	lucidabright	demibold	roman	normal		iso8859-1
b&h	lucidabright	medium	italic	normal		iso8859-1
b&h	lucidabright	medium	roman	normal		iso8859-1
bitstream	charter	medium	italic	normal		iso8859-1
bitstream	charter	medium	roman	normal		iso8859-1

Font Configuration Files

In order to make fonts available to the X server, a directory must contain, minimally, a `fonts.dir` file created with **mkfontdir**. For scalable fonts, the directory must also contain `fonts.scale`. This file is referenced by **mkfontdir**, so it must be created before the `fonts.dir` file. If the fonts contain an encoding that the X server does not recognize by default, you must create the `fonts.dir` file with **mkfontdir –e**, which creates the `fonts.encoding` file. You can also create a `fonts.alias` file so that you can refer to the fonts using a shorter name.

You must also configure the X server by indicating the location of the directories containing fonts. With XFree86, this information is contained in the XF86Config file (in the `/etc` directory on most systems) in the form of a comma-separated list of path names located at the FontPath instruction. You can add path names to this list using the **xset** command. On systems running font servers (such as xfs), such as Red Hat Linux 6.0 and later, this information is made available in the font server's configuration file, such as `/etc/X11/fs/config`. The following table lists the configuration files commonly found on Linux systems.

CONFIGURATION FILES IN FONT DIRECTORIES

Filename	Description
`encodings.dir`	Lists available character encodings. Created by **mkfontdir** with the **-e** option. This file is needed if any of the fonts in the directory use encodings that are not recognized by the X server by default.
`fonts.alias`	Lists aliases for lengthy font names.
`fonts.dir`	Lists available fonts in the directory. Created by **mkfontdir**.
`fonts.scale`	Lists scalable fonts in the directory. Created manually or with **type1inst**. The contents are automatically added to `fonts.dir` by **mkfontdir**.
`Fontmap`	Lists available fonts in the current directory. Required by Ghostscript.

Alphabetical Command Reference

This section details commands for the following tasks:

- Converting fonts from one format to another (**bdftopcf, t1ascii, t1binary, t1unmac, t1asm, t1disasm, ttf2pt1**)

- Installing fonts and creating the necessary configuration files, such as `fonts.dir` and `fonts.scale`, in font directories (**mkfontdir, ttmkfdir, type1inst, xset, chkfontpath**)

- Viewing information about fonts (**xlsfonts**)

bdftopcf

bdftopcf [option] **-o** *pcf file bdf file*

Converts the specified BDF file (a Binary Distribution Format font file) to a PCF file (a bitmapped font in Portable Compiled Format that the X server can use).

OPTIONS

Use This Option	To Do This
-i	Inhibit the normal computation of ink metrics
-l	Set the font bit order to LSB (least significant bit) first
-L	Set the font byte order to LSB first
-m	Set the font bit order to MSB (most significant bit) first
-M	Set the font byte order to MSB first
-o *filename*	Write to the specified filename
-p*n*	Set the font glyph padding to a multiple of *n* bytes, where *n* is 1, 2, 4, or 8
-t	Convert fonts into character cell fonts, also called terminal fonts, when possible
-un	Set the font scan line unit

chkfontpath

chkfontpath [option]

On Red Hat version 6.0 systems and later, as well as Red-Hat-derived systems, this utility adds, removes, or lists the directories containing fonts accessible to the xfs font server.

See also **xset**.

OPTIONS

Use This Option	To Do This
--**add** *directory*	Add the specified directory to the font path
--**help**	Display available options
--**list** *directory*	List the directories available to the X font server
--**remove** *directory*	Remove the specified directory from the font path

---

mkfontdir

mkfontdir [option]

Creates a fonts.dir file in the working directory (including the fonts .scale file, if it exists) that lists the valid Type 1 bitmap fonts available in this directory. Automatically included in the fonts.dir file are fonts listed in the fonts.scale file in the same directory, if this file exists.

See also **type1inst, ttmkfdir.**

OPTIONS

Use This Option	To Do This
--	End options
-**e** *directory*	Specify a directory containing encoding files
-**p**	Specify a prefix that is prepended to the encoding file's path names when they are written to the encodings.dir file
-**r**	Keep non-absolute encoding directories in their relative form when writing the encodings.dir file

EXAMPLES

This Command	Does the Following
mkfontdir	Creates the fonts.dir file listing the Type 1 bitmap files in the working directory.

EXAMPLES *(CONT.)*

This Command	Does the Following
mkfontdir -e /usr/share/enscript	Creates the encodings.dir file that lists all the font encodings found in the specified directory (/usr/share/enscript).

---

t1ascii

t1ascii [*input* [*output*]]

Converts Type 1 PFB font specified by *input* to a font file (*output*) in PFA (ASCII) format. This utility is part of the Type 1 Utilities package, available from http://www.lcdf.org/~edditwo/type/.

See also **t1binary.**

OPTIONS

Use This Option	To Do This
– –line–length=*n*, –l num *n*	Set the maximum length of encrypted lines in the output to *n*

---

t1asm

t1asm [*input* [*output*]]

Converts the specified input file (a Type 1 font program in human-readable form) to an output file in PFA (hexadecimal) or PFB (binary) format. This utility is part of the Type 1 Utilities package, available from http://www.lcdf.org/~edditwo/type/.

See also **t1disasm.**

OPTIONS

Use This Option	To Do This
− −block-*n*=num, **−l num** *n,*	Set the maximum output block length to *n* (PFB files only).
− −line-length=*n*, **−l** *n,*	Set the maximum length of encrypted lines in the output to *n* (PFA files only).
− −pfa, **−a**	Output in PFA (ASCII) format.
− −pfb, **−b**	Output in PFB (binary) format. This is the default.

t1binary

t1binary [option] [*input.pfa* [*output.pfb*]]

Converts the Type 1 PFA (ASCII) font specified by *input.pfa* to a font file (*output.pfb*) in PFB (binary) format. This utility is part of the Type 1 Utilities package, which is available at http://www.1cdf .org/~edditwo/type/.

See also **t1ascii**.

OPTIONS

Use This Option	To Do This
− −block-length=*n*, **−l** *n*	Set the maximum length of sections in PFB output to *n*. The default is to output sections as large as possible.

EXAMPLE

This Command	Does the Following
t1binary myfont.pfa myfont.pfb	Converts myfont.pfa (ASCII format) to myfont.pfb (binary format).

t1disasm

t1disasm [*input* [*output*]]

Converts the specified input file (a Type 1 font file in PFA or PFB format) to an output file containing a human-readable font program. This utility is part of the Type 1 Utilities package, which is available at http://www.lcdf.org/~eddietwo/type/.

See also **t1asm**.

t1unmac

t1unmac *macintosh font* [*output*]

Converts the Macintosh font (a Macintosh Type 1 font file in any of the following formats: MacBinary I or II, AppleSingle, BinHex, AppleDouble, or a raw resource fork). The utility creates an output file in PFA (hexadecimal) or PFB (binary) format. The default output is PFB. This utility is part of the Type 1 Utilities package, which is available at http://www.lcdf.org/~eddietwo/type/.

OPTIONS

Use This Option	To Do This
–a, – –pfa, –a	Output in PFA (ASCII) format.
– –appledouble	Indicate that the input is an AppleDouble file.
– –applesingle	Indicate that the input is an AppleSingle file.
–b, – –pfb	Output in PFB (binary) format.
– –binhex	Indicate that the input is a BinHex file.
–macbinary	Indicate that the input is a MacBinary file. This is the default.
–r, – –raw, –r	Indicate that the input is a raw resource fork.

ttf2pt1

ttf2pt1 [option] *truetype font type1 font*

Converts the specified TrueType font into a Type 1 font file (PFA or PFB format). To obtain **ttf2pt1,** visit `http://www.netspace.net.au/~mheath/ttf2pt1`.

OPTIONS

Use This Option	To Do This
–A	Create a font metrics (AFM) file.
–b	Create a PFB file.
–e	Create a PFA file.
–f	Skip trying to guess the ForceBold parameter.
–h	Disable the autogeneration of hints.
–l *language*	Extract the characters for the specified language. You can use the following options: latin1, latin2, latin4, latin5, bulgarian, and russian.
–o	Disable outline code optimization.
–r	Disable outline direction reversal.
–s	Disable outline smoothing.
–t	Disable auto-scaling.
–v *n*	Rescale the font to the specified size (*n*) of an upper-case letter.
–w	Attempt to correct the glyph widths.

EXAMPLE

This Command	Does the Following
`ttf2pt1 myfont.ttf myfont.pfa`	Converts the specified TrueType font (`myfont.ttf`) into a Type 1 font (`myfont.pfa`).

ttmkfdir

ttmkfdir [option] –o fonts.scale

Creates a `fonts.scale` file listing available TrueType fonts in the working directory. The TrueType font filenames must not contain uppercase letters. Run **mkfontdir** after using this utility. XFree86 cannot work with TrueType fonts directly. To use TrueType fonts on your system, you must install and run a TrueType font server. If you do not wish to install a TrueType-compatible font server, you can use TrueType fonts by converting them to Type 1 (PostScript) fonts.

See also **ttf2pt1**.

OPTIONS

Use This Option	To Do This
–c	Use less strict completeness tests for encoding tables.
–d *directory*	Scan the specified directory for TrueType files, or the working directory if *directory* is not specified.
–f *name*	Use the specified foundry name for unknown font vendors. The default is misc.
–m *n*	Specify the maximum number (n) of missing characters per encoding. The default is 5.
–o *filename*	Write output to the specified filename. Use `fonts.scale.`
–p	Use panose information.

EXAMPLE

This Command	Does the Following
`ttmkfdir –o fonts.scale`	Creates the `fonts.scale` file containing information about the TrueType fonts in the working directory.

type1inst

type1inst [option]

When run in a directory containing scalable Type 1 fonts, creates the fonts.scale file that the X server needs in order to work with the fonts. This utility also generates the fonts.dir file. You can obtain a copy of **type1inst** from the utility's official distribution site, located at http://metalab.unc.edu/pub/Linux/X11/utils.

See also **mkfontdir, ttmkfdir.**

OPTIONS

Use This Option	To Do This
–nogs	Skip creating the fontmap file
–nolog	Skip creating the log file
–nox	Skip creating the fonts.scale file
–q, silent, –quiet	Hide program messages
–samples	Create samples of the Type 1 fonts in the working directory
–v, –version	Show the current version

EXAMPLE

This Command	Does the Following
typelinst	Creates a fonts.scale file listing all the scalable Type 1 fonts in the working directory.

xlsfonts

xlsfonts [option] [**–fn** *pattern*]

Lists the fonts currently available to the X server that match the specified pattern. By default, the utility lists all the available fonts if you do not specify a pattern. You can use wildcards; * matches any character, while ? matches one character. Be sure to quote these characters.

OPTIONS

Use This Option	To Do This
–1	Use a single column.
–C	Use multiple columns.
–fn *pattern*	Match the specified pattern. You can use shell wildcards in your search.
–l	Show font attributes.
–ll	Show font attributes and properties.
–lll	Show font attributes, properties, and character metrics.
–m	Show the minimum and maximum bounds of each font.
–n *n*	Use *n* columns to display the font information.
–u	Skip sorting the output.
–w *n*	Use an output width of *n* columns. The default is 79.

EXAMPLES

This Command	Does the Following
xlsfonts | less	Lists all the fonts currently available to the X server.
xlsfonts –fn *utopia* | less	Shows only those fonts that match the specified string (**utopia**).

xset

xset [option]

Sets various characteristics of the X display, including fonts. To use this command, you must log in as the root user or switch to superuser status (see **su** in Chapter 1).

See also **chkfontpath.**

TIP On Red Hat 6.0 and later systems, fonts are controlled by a font server called xfs; to control font characteristics, you use a Red Hat utility called **chkfontpath**. The **xset** utility will not work on Red Hat and Red-Hat-derived systems.

OPTIONS

Use This Option	To Do This
+fp *list*, **fp+** *list*	Prepend (**+fp**) or append (**fp+**) fonts to the current font list. *List* must be a comma-separated list of valid X font names.
fp=*path list*	Provide a path list indicating all the directories, in a comma-separated list, where the X server can find fonts.
fp default	Restore the font path to the server's default settings.
–fp, **fp–**	Remove fonts from the beginning (**–fp**) or the end (**fp–**) of the current font list. *List* must be a comma-separated list of valid X font names.
fp rehash	Reset the font path to its current value, causing the server to reread the font databases in the current font path. This is generally only used when adding new fonts to a font directory, after running **mkfontdir** to recreate the font database.
q	Show the current settings.

EXAMPLE

This Command	Does the Following
`xset fp+ '/usr/fonts/newfonts'`	Adds the specified path name (**/usr/fonts/newfonts**) to the XConfig file.

CHAPTER 11

Using Text Editors

This chapter provides a reference guide to the most widely used features of the text editors likely to be found on a Linux system, ranging from simple, easy-to-use editors such as **joe** and **pica** to highly complex editors such as **emacs** and **vi**, which are designed for use by programmers. Although Linux systems are typically configured to use **emacs** or **vi** as the default editor, you may prefer to edit simple text files (such as configuration files) with a more user-friendly, simpler editor such as **joe** (see the section "Specifying the Default Editor" in this chapter).

Note that some of the text editors discussed in this chapter offer many options for advanced uses, including scripting and programming, that are not listed. Included are the commands intended for text-editing applications. For more information on these advanced commands, consult the program's documentation.

TIP Some of the keyboard shortcuts described in this chapter require the user to hold down the Ctrl key while two additional keys are pressed. To indicate this type of shortcut, a comma is used to link two Ctrl key shortcuts. For example, Ctrl + k, Ctrl + e means "hold down the Ctrl key and continue holding it down while you press k followed by e." Certain other commands require you to enter a Ctrl key shortcut, release the Ctrl key, and type a second key. To indicate this type of shortcut, a comma is used to link a Ctrl key shortcut with a second key. For example, Ctrl + h, b means "hold down the Ctrl key, *release the Ctrl key,* type the first letter (in this case *h*), and type the second letter (b)." The keyboard shortcuts discussed in this chapter are, in general, case sensitive; Ctrl + L differs from Ctrl + l.

AT A GLANCE

How Do I

Check spelling?

Example

emacs: `Alt + $`
joe: `Ctrl + [, n`
pico: `Ctrl + t[`

AT A GLANCE *(CONT.)*

How Do I	Example
Close the window in which the cursor is positioned?	emacs: `Ctrl + x, 0` joe: `Ctrl + k, i` vi: `Ctrl + w, q`
Create a new file?	emacs: `Ctrl +x, Ctrl + f` joe: `Ctrl + k, e` vi: `:x`
Delete a line?	emacs: `Ctrl + k` joe: `Ctrl + j` pico: `Ctrl + k` vi: `dd`
Mark a block of text?	emacs: `Ctrl + spacebar` joe: `Ctrl + k, b` pico: `Ctrl + ^`
Move to the beginning of the file?	emacs: **Home** pico: `Ctrl + w, Ctrl + y or 1G (1, shift G)]`
Move to the end of the file?	emacs: **End** pico: `Ctrl + w, Ctrl +v`
Open a file?	emacs: `Ctrl + K, Ctrl + v` joe: `Ctrl + k, e` pico: `Ctrl + r` vi: `:e`
Quit the editor?	emacs: `Ctrl + x, Ctrl + c` joe: `Ctrl + k, x` pico: `Ctrl + x` vi: `:x or :q!`
Reformat the text after an editing change?	emacs: `Alt + q` joe: `Ctrl + r` pico: `Ctrl + j`
Save a file?	emacs: `Ctrl + x, Ctrl + s` joe: `Ctrl +k, d` pico: `Ctrl + o` vi: `:w`

AT A GLANCE *(CONT.)*

How Do I	Example
Scroll down?	emacs: `PgDn` joe: `PgDn` pico: `Ctrl +n` vi: `PgDn` or `j` or `down arrow`
Scroll up?	emacs: `PgUp` joe: `PgUp` pico: `Ctrl + p` vi: `PgUp` or `k` or `up arrow`
Search for text?	emacs: `Ctrl + s` joe: `Ctrl + k, f` pico: `Ctrl +w` vi: `/pattern`
See the program's keyboard shortcuts on-screen?	emacs: `F1` joe: `Ctrl + k, h` pico: `Ctrl + g` vi: `F1`
Split the screen into two windows?	emacs: `Ctrl + x, 3` joe: `Ctrl + k, o` vi: `:sp`
Undo an editing change?	emacs: `Ctrl + _` joe: `Ctrl + _` vi: `u`

Specifying the Default Editor

To determine the default editor currently in use, type **echo $EDITOR** and press Enter; you'll see the path name to the default editor, if any. Should you wish to change the default editor, do the following:

1. In your home directory, use a text editor to open the file named `.bash_profile`.

2. Add the following lines:

```
EDITOR=pathname
export EDITOR
```

In this syntax, `pathname` is the path name to the editor you want to use. For example, to use Joe as the default editor, type the following:

```
EDITOR=/usr/bin/joe
```

assuming that Joe is located at `/usr/bin/joe`. To determine where Joe is located, type **whereis joe** and press Enter.

TIP To make your default editor change effective, log out of your current session and log in again.

Alphabetical Command Reference

This section discusses the following types of editors:

- Full-featured editors for programmers (**emacs, vi**)

- Easy-to-use editors for making changes to text files (**joe, pico**)

- Stream-oriented editors for automatic text file processing (**sed**)

---

emacs

emacs [option] [*filename*]

In an X terminal window, this command launches the GNU Emacs text editor. At the console, it launches the text-mode version of the same utility. Both utilities use the same command shortcuts, which are described in this section (for a quick overview, see the section "Emacs Essentials"). Optionally, you can open one or more files by specifying a filename or by using a space-separated list of filenames.

GNU Emacs v. 20.3.1 is documented here. For more information and downloads, visit http://www.gnu.org. If you've never used Emacs before, be sure to begin with the well-crafted tutorial. To start it, press Ctrl + h, t.

Emacs is a huge, complex program with many optional modules that serve specialized purposes. Accordingly, this section covers only the fundamentals of Emacs. Not covered are commands used for *abbrevs* (user-defined codes that can be expanded into lengthier strings), accumulating text, ASCII pictures, binary file editing, calendars, diaries, directory editing, e-mail, formatting (with Postscript, Tex, and troff), frames (running the same Emacs session in multiple windows), indentation (used for writing programs), modes other than the fundamental (default) mode, rectangles, and Usenet. Note that Emacs is available in an X Window System version, which is distributed with most versions of Linux and enables you to use menu commands for most (but not all) of the keyboard commands discussed in this section.

TIP   If you run Emacs in text-only mode by launching the program at the console or with the **–nw** option, you may find that the Backspace or Delete keys are mapped to Emac's Help function. To fix this problem, create or modify a file named .emacs in your home directory. To this file, add the following lines:

```
(keyboard-translate ?\C-h ?\C-?)
(keyboard-translate ?\C-\\ ?\C-h}
```

After you make this change, you'll need to press Ctrl + \ (backslash) instead of Ctrl + h to access the various Help commands.

OPTIONS

Use This Option	To Do This
+*n*	Position the cursor at line *n* after opening the file
–bd *color*	Set the border to the specified color
–bg *color*	Set the background to the specified color
–b *n*	Set the border width to the specified number (*n*) of pixels

OPTIONS *(CONT.)*

Use This Option	To Do This
–cr *color*	Set the text cursor to the specified color
–d *display name*	Create the Emacs window on the specified display name
–fg *color*	Set the foreground to the specified color
–font *font name*	Use the specified font name as the default font
–geometry *geometry*	Create the window with the specified geometry
–i	Use a special icon when the Emacs window is minimized
–ib *n*	Set the inside border width to the specified number (*n*) of pixels
–ms *color*	Set the mouse cursor to the specified color
–name *name*	Create the window with the specified name
–nw	Run Emacs in text mode in the X terminal window
–q	Skip loading an initialization file
–r	Display the window in reverse video
–t *filename*	Use the specified filename as the terminal device instead of the standard terminal (**tty**)
–u *user*	Use the specified user's initialization file

Emacs Essentials

Emacs commands are mapped to the Ctrl and Meta keys. On Intel-based Linux systems, the Meta key is mapped to the Alt key, so the following tables show all Meta-mapped keyboard shortcuts with the Alt key listed instead of Meta. If you are using Linux on a computer that lacks an Alt key, you can press Esc instead. For example, you can press Esc, q to fill the current paragraph instead of Alt + q.

You can use a mouse with Emacs. For information on basic mouse maneuvers, see the table "Using a Mouse with Emacs" in this section.

USING A MOUSE WITH EMACS

Do This	To Do the Following
Click the left button.	Move the cursor to the pointer's location
Click the middle mouse button.	Paste text at the cursor's location
Click the right button or hold down the Shift key and click the middle button.	Copy the marked text into the cut buffer
Hold down the Ctrl key and click the middle or right buttons.	Cut the marked text into the cut buffer (kill the marked text)
Hold down the Shift key, and click the right mouse button.	Paste text at the cursor's location

Emacs Commands

The following tables detail keyboard shortcuts for the following actions:

- Getting help
- Using buffers
- Scrolling
- Moving the cursor
- Managing files
- Managing windows
- Inserting text
- Filling text
- Emphasizing text
- Transposing text
- Checking spelling
- Deleting text
- Marking text

- Changing case

- Copying text

- Killing text

- Undoing editing changes

- Searching for text

- Replacing text

TIP   Remember, there's a difference between Ctrl + h, Ctrl + h, and Ctrl + h, h. In the former, you hold down the Ctrl key and press h twice. In the latter, you press Ctrl + h, release the Ctrl key and type h. Do not type the comma.

GETTING HELP

Use This Keyboard Shortcut	To Do This
Ctrl + h, q	Close the Help window
Ctrl + h, Ctrl + h	Display options available while viewing the Help screen
Ctrl + h, ?	Display options available while viewing the Help screen
Ctrl + x, =	Display the current cursor position
Ctrl + h, w	Display the current key binding for a command name that you specify
Ctrl + h, F	Display the Emacs FAQ
Ctrl + z	Iconify the current frame
F1	Open the Help window
Ctrl + h, i	Open the GNU information utility
Ctrl + h, b	Show the current key bindings
Ctrl + h, c	Show help for the following command
Ctrl + h, Ctrl + k	Show the information help page for Emacs
Ctrl + h, Ctrl + f	Show the information help page for a command

GETTING HELP *(CONT.)*

Use This Keyboard Shortcut	To Do This
Ctrl + h, a	Show a list of commands that match a regular expression that you specify
Ctrl + h, k	Show the documentation for a key that you specify
Ctrl + h, n	View Emacs news
Ctrl + h, h	View the *hello file,* which shows scripts in various languages
Ctrl + h, l	View the last 100 characters that you typed

USING BUFFERS

Use This Keyboard Shortcut	To Do This
Ctrl + x, k	Kill the current buffer
Ctrl + x, 4, 0	Kill the current buffer and window
Ctrl + x, Ctrl + b	List the current buffers
Ctrl + h, m	Show the mode for the current buffer
Ctrl + x, b	Switch to a buffer you specify or type a new buffer name to create a buffer
Ctrl + x, Ctrl + q	Toggle the read-only status of the buffer

SCROLLING

Use This Keyboard Shortcut	To Do This
PgUp *or* Alt + V	Scroll up one window
PgDn *or* Ctrl + V	Scroll down one window
Alt + v, *n*	Scroll up by the number (*n*) of lines that you specify
Ctrl + v, *n*	Scroll down by the number (*n*) of lines that you specify

MOVING THE CURSOR

Use This Keyboard Shortcut	To Do This
Ctrl + b *or* left arrow	Move back one character
Ctrl + f *or* right arrow	Move forward one character
Ctrl + left arrow *or* Alt +left arrow	Move back one word
Ctrl + right arrow *or* Alt + right	Move forward one word
Ctrl + a	Move to the beginning of the line
Ctrl + e	Move to the end of the line
Ctrl + p *or* up arrow	Move up one line
Ctrl + n *or* down arrow	Move down one line
Alt + a	Move to the beginning of the sentence
Alt + e	Move to the end of the sentence
Ctrl + up arrow	Move up one paragraph
Ctrl + down arrow	Move down one paragraph
Ctrl + x, [	Move up one page
Ctrl + x,]	Move down one page
Home *or* Alt + <	Move to the beginning of the buffer
End *or* Alt + >	Move to the end of the current buffer

MANAGING FILES

Use This Keyboard Shortcut	To Do This
Ctrl + x, i	Insert a file that you specify at the cursor's location
Ctrl + x, Ctrl + d	List the directory that you specify
Ctrl + x, Ctrl + v	Open a file other than the one last opened
Ctrl + x, Ctrl + r	Open a file that you specify by name and display it as read only
Ctrl + x, Ctrl + f	Open a file that you specify by name
Ctrl + x, Ctrl + c	Save all open buffers and quit Emacs
Ctrl + x, s	Save only those buffers that contain unsaved changes

MANAGING FILES *(CONT.)*

Use This Keyboard Shortcut	To Do This
Ctrl + x, Ctrl + s	Save the current buffer to the filename associated with it
Ctrl + x, Ctrl + w	Save the current buffer to a filename that you specify

MANAGING WINDOWS

Use This Keyboard Shortcut	To Do This
Ctrl + x, +	Balance the space allocated to all the open windows
Ctrl + x, 0	Close the current window
Ctrl + x, ^	Enlarge the current window
Ctrl + x, }	Enlarge the current window horizontally
Ctrl + x, 1	Kill all other windows
Ctrl + x, o	Make the other window active
Ctrl + x, {	Reduce the window size horizontally
Esc Ctrl + l	Reposition the current window
Esc Ctrl + v	Scroll the other window
Ctrl + x, 3	Split the window horizontally
Ctrl + x, 2	Split the window vertically

INSERTING TEXT

Use This Keyboard Shortcut	To Do This
Insert	Toggle the insert and overwrite modes
Ctrl + Alt + /	Show completions for the current word by searching all the words in the current buffer
Alt + /	Insert the nearest completion for the current word
Esc (	Insert a pair of parentheses

INSERTING TEXT *(CONT.)*

Use This Keyboard Shortcut — To Do This

Use This Keyboard Shortcut	To Do This
Esc ;	Insert an indented comment
Alt + Tab	Complete the current word from words found in the spelling dictionary
Tab	Indent one tab stop
Esc Ctrl + \	Indent the marked region

FILLING TEXT

Use This Keyboard Shortcut	To Do This
Alt + x, auto-fill-mode	Fill text automatically
Alt + q	Fill the current paragraph
Ctrl + x, f	Set the fill column
Alt + x, fill-region	Fill each paragraph in the region
Alt + s	Center a line
Alt + j, l	Format the selected region flush left (enriched mode only)
Alt + j, r	Format the selected region flush right (enriched mode only)
Alt + j, f	Format the selected region with full justification (enriched mode only)
Alt + j, c	Center the selected region (enriched mode only)
Alt + j, u	Cancel justification for the selected region (enriched mode only)

EMPHASIZING TEXT

Use This Keyboard Shortcut	To Do This
Alt + g, i	Set the font style to bold
Alt + g, b	Set the font style to bold
Alt + g, l	Set the font style to bold italic

EMPHASIZING TEXT *(CONT.)*

Use This Keyboard Shortcut	To Do This
Alt + g, d	Set the font style to the default font
Alt + g, u	Set the font style to underline
Alt + g	Show the font style menu
Alt + g, o	Use a font style that you specify

TRANSPOSING TEXT

Use This Keyboard Shortcut	To Do This
Ctrl + t	Transpose characters
Ctrl + x, Ctrl + t	Transpose lines
Alt + t	Transpose words

CHECKING SPELLING

Use This Keyboard Shortcut	To Do This
Alt + x flyspell-mode	Highlight misspelled words on-screen on the fly
Alt + $	Check the spelling of the selected word

DELETING TEXT

Use This Keyboard Shortcut	To Do This
Ctrl + d	Delete the next character
Delete *or* Backspace	Delete the previous character
Alt + d	Delete the next word
Alt + Delete *or* Ctrl + Delete	Delete the previous word
Ctrl + x, Ctrl + o	Delete all the blank lines in the buffer

MARKING TEXT

Use This Keyboard Shortcut	To Do This
Ctrl + spacebar	Mark the beginning or end of a region
Esc h	Mark the current paragraph
Esc @	Mark the next word
Ctrl + x, h	Mark the entire buffer
Ctrl + x, Ctrl + p	Mark the entire page
Alt + x, transient-mark-mode	Toggle region highlighting on and off
ESC =	Count the number of lines within the marked region

CHANGING CASE

Use This Keyboard Shortcut	To Do This
Alt + u	Change the next word to uppercase
Alt + l	Change the next word to lowercase

COPYING TEXT

Use This Keyboard Shortcut	To Do This
Alt + W	Copy the marked region

KILLING TEXT

Use This Keyboard Shortcut	To Do This
Ctrl + k	Kill from the cursor's position to the end of the sentence
Ctrl + k, Ctrl + k	Kill from the cursor's position to the end of the sentence, delete the newline character, and close up the blank space
Alt + k	Kill from the cursor's position to the end of the current sentence
Ctrl + w	Kill the selected region

UNDOING EDITING CHANGES

Use This keyboard Shortcut	To Do This
Ctrl + _or_ Ctrl + x, u	Undo the previous editing change

YANKING TEXT

Use This Keyboard Shortcut	To Do This
Ctrl + y	Restore the most recently killed text
Alt + y	Restore the previously killed text
Ctrl + insert	Save the _kill ring_, a list of text blocks that have been killed

SEARCHING FOR TEXT

Use This Keyboard Shortcut	To Do This
Esc Ctrl + s	Search down for the regular expression that you specify
Ctrl + s, Enter, _string_, Enter	Search down for the string that you specify
Esc Ctrl + r	Search up for the regular expression that you specify
Ctrl + r, Enter, _string_, Enter	Search up for the string that you specify
Ctrl + s	Start searching down for characters matching those that you type
Ctrl –r	Start searching up for character matching those that you type

SEARCHING AND REPLACING TEXT

Use This Keyboard Shortcut	To Do This
Esc %	Search and replace the text that you specify, with confirmation
Esc Ctrl + %	Search using a regular expression and replace with confirmation

SEARCHING AND REPLACING TEXT *(CONT.)*

Use This Keyboard Shortcut	To Do This
Alt + x, replace-string, *string1*, Enter, *string2*, Enter	Search for *string1* and replace with *string2*, without confirmation
Alt + x, replace-string, *regexp1*, Enter, *regexp2*, Enter	Search for *regexp1* and replace with *regexp2* without confirmation

Emacs Keyboard Shortcuts

The following table lists all the Emacs keyboard shortcuts discussed in this section. For a list of all the current Emacs key bindings, open Emacs, and press Ctrl + h, b.

SELECTED KEYBOARD SHORTCUTS

Use This Keyboard Shortcut	To Do This
Alt + $	Check the spelling of the selected word
Alt + /	Insert the nearest completion for the current word
Alt + a	Move to the beginning of the sentence
Alt + d	Delete the next word
Alt + Delete *or* Ctrl + Delete	Delete the previous word
Alt + e	Move to the end of the sentence
Alt + g	Show the font style menu
Alt + g, b	Set the font style to bold
Alt + g, d	Set the font style to the default font
Alt + g, i	Set the font style to bold
Alt + g, l	Set the font style to bold italic
Alt + g, o	Use a font style that you specify
Alt + g, u	Set the font style to underline
Alt + j, c	Center the selected region (enriched mode only)

SELECTED KEYBOARD SHORTCUTS *(CONT.)*

Use This Keyboard Shortcut	To Do This
Alt + j, f	Format the selected region with full justi-fication (enriched mode only)
Alt + j, l	Format the selected region flush left (enriched mode only)
Alt + j, r	Format the selected region flush right (enriched mode only)
Alt + j, u	Cancel justification for the selected region (enriched mode only)
Alt + k	Kill from the cursor's position to the end of the current sentence
Alt + l	Change the next word to lowercase
Alt + q	Fill the current paragraph
Alt + s	Center a line
Alt + t	Transpose words
Alt + Tab	Complete the current word from words found in the spelling dictionary
Alt + u	Change the next word to uppercase
Alt + v, *n*	Scroll up by the number (*n*) of lines that you specify
Alt + W	Copy the marked region
Alt + x, auto-fill-mode	Fill text automatically
Alt + x, fill-region	Fill each paragraph in the region
Alt + x, replace-string, *regexp1*, Enter, *regexp2*, Enter	Search for *regexp1* and replace with *regexp2,* without confirmation
Alt + x, replace-string, *string1*, Enter, *string2*, Enter	Search for *string1* and replace with *string2,* without confirmation
Alt + x, transient-mark-mode	Toggle region highlighting on and off
Alt + x flyspell-mode	Highlight misspelled words on-screen on the fly
Alt + y	Restore previously killed text
Ctrl + a	Move to the beginning of the line

SELECTED KEYBOARD SHORTCUTS *(CONT.)*

Use This Keyboard Shortcut	To Do This
Ctrl + Alt + /	Show completions for the current word by searching all the words in the current buffer
Ctrl + b, *or* left arrow	Move back one character
Ctrl + d	Delete the next character
Ctrl + down arrow	Move down one paragraph
Ctrl + e	Move to the end of the line
Ctrl + f *or* right arrow	Move forward one character
Ctrl + h, ?	Display options available while viewing the Help screen
Ctrl + h, a	Show a list of commands that match a regular expression that you specify
Ctrl + h, b	Show the current key bindings
Ctrl + h, c	Show help for the following command
Ctrl + h, Ctrl + f	Show the information help page for a command
Ctrl + h, Ctrl + h	Display options available while viewing the Help screen
Ctrl + h, Ctrl + k	Show the information help page for Emacs
Ctrl + h, F	Display the Emacs FAQ
Ctrl + h, h	View the hello file, which shows scripts in various languages
Ctrl + h, i	Open the GNU information utility
Ctrl + h, k	Show the documentation for a key that you specify
Ctrl + h, l	View the last 100 characters that you typed
Ctrl + h, m	Show the mode for the current buffer
Ctrl + h, n	View Emacs news
Ctrl + h, q	Close the Help window

SELECTED KEYBOARD SHORTCUTS *(CONT.)*

Use This Keyboard Shortcut	To Do This
Ctrl + h, w	Display the current key binding for a command name that you specify
Ctrl + insert	Save the kill ring, a list of text blocks that have been killed
Ctrl + k	Kill from the cursor's position to the end of the sentence
Ctrl + k, Ctrl + k	Kill from the cursor's position to the end of the sentence, delete the newline character, and close up the blank space
Ctrl + left arrow *or* Alt +left arrow	Move back one word
Ctrl + n *or* down arrow	Move down one line
Ctrl + p *or* up arrow	Move up one line
Ctrl + r, Enter, *string*, Enter	Search up for the string that you specify
Ctrl + right *or* Alt + right	Move forward one word
Ctrl + s	Start searching down for characters matching those that you type
Ctrl + s, Enter, *string*, Enter	Search down for the string that you specify
Ctrl + spacebar	Mark the beginning or end of a region
Ctrl + t	Transpose characters
Ctrl + up arrow	Move up one paragraph
Ctrl + v, *n*	Scroll down by the number (*n*) of lines that you specify
Ctrl + w	Kill the selected region
Ctrl + x +	Balance the space allocated to all the open windows
Ctrl + x =	Display the current cursor position
Ctrl + x, ^	Enlarge the current window
Ctrl + x, [	Move up one page
Ctrl + x,]	Move down one page
Ctrl + x, {	Reduce window size horizontally

SELECTED KEYBOARD SHORTCUTS *(CONT.)*

Use This Keyboard Shortcut	To Do This
Ctrl + x, }	Enlarge the current window horizontally
Ctrl + x, 0	Close the current window
Ctrl + x, 1	Kill all other windows
Ctrl + x, 2	Split the window vertically
Ctrl + x, 3	Split the window horizontally
Ctrl + x, 4, 0	Kill the current buffer and window
Ctrl + x, b	Switch to a buffer that you specify or type a new buffer name to create a buffer
Ctrl + x, Ctrl + b	List the current buffers
Ctrl + x, Ctrl + d	List the directory that you specify
Ctrl + x, Ctrl + f	Open a file that you specify by name
Ctrl + x, Ctrl + o	Delete all the blank lines in the buffer
Ctrl + x, Ctrl + p	Mark the entire page
Ctrl + x, Ctrl + q	Toggle the read-only status of the buffer
Ctrl + x, Ctrl + r	Open a file that you specify by name and display it in read-only format
Ctrl + x, Ctrl + t	Transpose lines
Ctrl + x, Ctrl + w	Save the current buffer to a filename that you specify
Ctrl + x, f	Set the fill column
Ctrl + x, h	Mark the entire buffer
Ctrl + x, i	Insert a file that you specify at the cursor's location
Ctrl + x, k	Kill the current buffer
Ctrl + x, o	Make the other window active
Ctrl + x, s	Save only those buffers that contain unsaved changes
Ctrl + x Ctrl + c	Save all open buffers and quit Emacs
Ctrl + x Ctrl + s	Save the current buffer to the filename associated with it

SELECTED KEYBOARD SHORTCUTS *(CONT.)*

Use This Keyboard Shortcut	To Do This
Ctrl + x Ctrl + v	Open a file other than the one last opened
Ctrl + y	Restore the most recently killed text
Ctrl + z	Iconify the current frame
Ctrl -r	Start searching up for characters matching those that you type
Delete *or* Backspace	Delete the previous character
End or Alt + >	Move to the end of the current buffer
Esc %	Search and replace the text that you specify, with confirmation
ESC =	Count the number of lines within the marked region
Esc @	Mark the next word
Esc ;	Insert an indented comment
Esc (	Insert a pair of parentheses
Esc Ctrl + %	Search using a regular expression and replace with confirmation
Esc Ctrl + \	Indent the marked region
Esc Ctrl + l	Reposition the current window
Esc Ctrl + r	Search up for the regular expression that you specify
Esc Ctrl + s	Search down for the regular expression that you specify
Esc Ctrl + v	Scroll the other window
Esc h	Mark the current paragraph
F1	Open the Help window
Home *or* Alt + <	Move to the beginning of the buffer
Insert	Toggle the Insert key and overwrite modes
PgDn *or* Ctrl + V	Scroll down one window
PgUp *or* Alt + V	Scroll up one window
Tab	Indent one tab stop

joe

joe [option] [file option][*filename*]

Launches an easy-to-use, text-based editor that enables you to edit text on-screen directly, without having to switch from a command to an edit mode. You can optionally specify a filename to load with the program. The file options (see the table File Options in this section) must precede the filename. For keyboard shortcuts that you can use once the program has started, see the tables in the "joe Commands" section. The most commonly used features of version 2.8 are documented here. The program's download site is `ftp://ftp.std.com/src/editors`.

OPTIONS

Use This Option	To Do This
–asis	Display characters with codes above 128
–backpath *directory*	Store backup files in the specified directory
–beep	Sound the bell on errors
–columns *nnn*	Set the number of screen columns
–csmode	Repeat the previous search by default
–exask	Verify filename before writing
–force	Insert a line feed at the end of the file if necessary
–help	Start the editor with the Help window displayed
–keepup	Update column and line information immediately rather than delaying one second
–lightoff	Hide block highlighting after block commands are given
–lines *n*	Show *n* lines on-screen
–marking	Highlight the text between the first mark and the cursor
–mid	Scroll right to bring lengthy lines into view
–nobackups	Prevent backup files
–nonotice	Prevent the display of the copyright notice

OPTIONS *(CONT.)*

Use This Option	To Do This
–nosta	Hide the status line
–pg *n*	Retain *n* previously viewed lines after scrolling

FILE OPTIONS

Use This Option	To Do This
+*n*	Display the file starting with line *n*
–autoindent	Duplicate indentations on the next line after pressing Enter
–crlf	Use DOS-style line feeds
–linums	Show the line numbers
–lmargin *n*	Set the left margin at *n* columns
–overwrite	Use the overwrite mode
–rdonly	Open the file in read-only format
–rmargin *n*	Set the right margin at *n* columns
–tab *n*	Set the tab width at *n* columns
–wordwrap	Use word-wrapping for lengthy lines

joe Commands

The following tables detail keyboard shortcuts for the following actions:

- Getting help
- Choosing program modes
- Reformatting and refreshing
- Quitting and suspending
- Scrolling
- Moving the cursor
- Managing files

- Checking spelling
- Deleting text
- Marking text
- Copying and moving text
- Undoing and redoing editing changes
- Searching for text
- Replacing text

GETTING HELP

Use This Keyboard Shortcut	To Do This
Ctrl + k, h	Open or close the Help window

CHOOSING PROGRAM MODES

Use This Keyboard Shortcut	To Do This
Ctrl + t, t	Toggle between overtype and indent modes
Ctrl + t, w	Toggle word-wrapping on and off
Ctrl + t, i	Toggle auto-indent on and off

REFORMATTING AND REFRESHING

Use This Keyboard Shortcut	To Do This
Ctrl + r	Refresh the screen
Ctrl + k, j	Reformat the text

QUITTING AND SUSPENDING

Use This Keyboard shortcut	To Do This
Ctrl + k, x	Quit the program and optionally save any unsaved edits

QUITTING AND SUSPENDING *(CONT.)*

Use This Keyboard shortcut

To Do This

Ctrl + k, z   Suspend the editor (type **fg** and press Enter to return to **joe**)

SCROLLING

Use This Keyboard Shortcut	To Do This
PgUp *or* Ctrl + u	Scroll up one window
PgDn *or* Ctrl + v	Scroll down one window

MOVING THE CURSOR

Use This Keyboard Shortcut	To Do This
Ctrl + b, *or* left arrow	Move back one character
Ctrl + z	Move back one word
Ctrl + n *or* down arrow	Move down one line
Ctrl + f *or* right arrow	Move forward one character
Ctrl + x	Move forward one word
Ctrl + k, l	Move to a line number that you specify
Ctrl + k, u	Move to the beginning of the file
Ctrl + a	Move to the beginning of the line
Ctrl + k, v	Move to the end of the current file
Ctrl + e	Move to the end of the line
Ctrl + p *or* up arrow	Move up one line

MANAGING FILES

Use This Keyboard Shortcut	To Do This
Ctrl + k, e	Open a file
Ctrl + k, r	Insert a file at the cursor's location
Ctrl + k, d	Save a file

MANAGING WINDOWS

Use This Keyboard Shortcut	To Do This
Ctrl + k, i	Close the current window
Ctrl + k, g	Enlarge the current window
Ctrl + k, n	Move to the bottom window
Ctrl + k, p	Move to the top window
Ctrl + k, i	Show only the window in which the cursor is positioned
Ctrl + k, t	Shrink the current window
Ctrl + k, o	Split the screen into two windows

CHECKING SPELLING

Use This Keyboard Shortcut	To Do This
Ctrl + [, n	Check the spelling of the entire file
Ctrl + [, l	Check the spelling of the selected word

DELETING TEXT

Use This Keyboard Shortcut	To Do This
Ctrl + d	Delete the next character
Delete *or* Backspace	Delete the previous character
Ctrl + w	Delete the next word
Ctrl + o	Delete the previous word
Ctrl + j	Delete the line
Ctrl + k, y	Delete a marked block

MARKING TEXT

Use This Keyboard Shortcut	To Do This
Ctrl + k, b	Mark the beginning of a block
Ctrl + k, k	Mark the end of a block

COPYING AND MOVING TEXT

Use This Keyboard Shortcut	To Do This
Ctrl + k, c	Copy the marked region
Ctrl + k, m	Move the marked region
Ctrl + k, w	Save the marked region to a file
Ctrl + k, / (to return from the shell, press Ctrl + C)	Filter the marked text through a Linux command

UNDOING AND REDOING EDITING CHANGES

Use This Keyboard Shortcut	To Do This
Ctrl + _	Undo the previous editing change
Ctrl + ^	Redo the previous editing change

SEARCHING AND REPLACING

Use This Keyboard Shortcut	To Do This
Ctrl k, f *string*	Search down for the string that you specify
Ctrl k, f *string*, b	Search up for the string that you specify
Ctrl k, f *string*, i	Perform a case-insensitive search for the string that you specify
Ctrl k, f *string*, *n*	Search for the *n*th occurrence of the string that you specify
Ctrl k, f *string*, r, Enter, *replacement*	Replace the specified string with the replacement that you specify
Ctrl + l	Find the next occurrence of the search string

joe Keyboard Shortcuts

This section details joe's keyboard shortcuts, sorted in alphabetical order.

KEYBOARD SHORTCUTS

Use This Keyboard Shortcut	To Do This
Ctrl + _	Undo the previous editing change.
Ctrl + ^	Redo the previous editing change.
Ctrl + [, l	Check the spelling of the selected word.
Ctrl + [, n	Check the spelling of the entire file.
Ctrl + a	Move to the beginning of the line.
Ctrl + b, *or* left arrow	Move back one character.
Ctrl + d	Delete the next character.
Ctrl + e	Move to the end of the line.
Ctrl + f *or* right arrow	Move forward one character.
Ctrl + j	Delete the line.
Ctrl + k, /	Filter the marked text through a Linux command.
Ctrl + k, b	Mark the beginning of a block.
Ctrl + k, c	Copy the marked region.
Ctrl + k, d	Save a file.
Ctrl + k, e	Open a file.
Ctrl + k, g	Enlarge the current window.
Ctrl + k, h	Open or close the Help window.
Ctrl + k, i	Close the current window.
Ctrl + k, i	Show only the window in which the cursor is positioned.
Ctrl + k, j	Reformat the text.
Ctrl + k, k	Mark the end of a block.
Ctrl + k, l	Move to a line number that you specify.
Ctrl + k, m	Move the marked region.
Ctrl + k, n	Move to the bottom window.
Ctrl + k, o	Split the screen into two windows.
Ctrl + k, p	Move to the top window.
Ctrl + k, r	Insert a file at the cursor's location.

KEYBOARD SHORTCUTS *(CONT.)*

Use This Keyboard Shortcut	To Do This
Ctrl + k, t	Shrink the current window.
Ctrl + k, u	Move to the beginning of the file.
Ctrl + k, v	Move to the end of the current file.
Ctrl + k, w	Save the marked region to a file.
Ctrl + k, x	Quit the program and optionally save any unsaved edits.
Ctrl + k, y	Delete a marked block.
Ctrl + k, z	Suspend the editor. Type **fg** and press Enter to return to **joe**.
Ctrl + l	Find the next occurrence of the search string.
Ctrl + n *or* down arrow	Move down one line.
Ctrl + o	Delete the previous word.
Ctrl + p *or* up arrow	Move up one line.
Ctrl + r	Refresh the screen.
Ctrl + t, i	Toggle auto-indent on and off.
Ctrl + t, t	Toggle between overtype and indent modes.
Ctrl + t, w	Toggle word-wrapping on and off.
Ctrl + w	Delete the next word.
Ctrl + x	Move forward one word.
Ctrl + z	Move back one word.
Ctrl k, f *string*	Search down for the string that you specify.
Ctrl k, f *string*, b	Search up for the string that you specify.
Ctrl k, f *string*, i	Perform a case-insensitive search for the string that you specify.
Ctrl k, f *string*, n	Search for the *n*th occurrence of the string that you specify.
Ctrl k, f *string*, r, Enter, *replacement*	Replace the specified string with the replacement that you specify.
Delete *or* Backspace	Delete the previous character.

KEYBOARD SHORTCUTS *(CONT.)*

Use This Keyboard Shortcut	To Do This
PgDn *or* Ctrl + v	Move down one window.
PgUp *or* Ctrl + u	Move up one window.

---

pico

pico [option] [*filename*]

Launches a simple, easy-to-use text editor based on the Pine e-mail program's message composer. This utility is a good choice for editing configuration and other simple text files. For commands that you can use while editing, see the tables in the "Pico Commands" section. For more information, visit the Pine home page at http://www.washington.edu/pine. The most commonly used features of version 3.5 are documented here.

OPTIONS

Use This Option	To Do This
+*n*	Start at line *n*
–b	Enable the Replace option while searching
–d	Rebind the Delete key so that it deletes the current character
–e	Enable filename completion
–f	Enable function key commands
–h	Display available options
–m	Enable mouse functionality (X version only)
–o *directory*	Specify the default directory
–r*n*	Set the right margin to *n* columns from the left
–s *spell-checker*	Specify an alternate spell-checker to use when spell checking
–v	View the file in read-only format
–w	Disable word-wrapping
–x	Disable the Key menu at the bottom of the screen

pico Commands

The following tables detail keyboard shortcuts for the following commands:

- Getting help
- Reformatting and refreshing
- Quitting the program
- Scrolling
- Moving the cursor
- Managing files
- Checking spelling
- Deleting text
- Marking text
- Copying and moving text
- Searching for text

TIP To use the function key commands discussed in this section, start **pico** with the **–f** option.

GETTING HELP

Use This Keyboard Shortcut	To Do This
Ctrl + g *or* F1	Open the Help window
Ctrl + x	Close the Help window

REFORMATTING

Use This Keyboard Shortcut	To Do This
Ctrl + j *or* F4	Reformat the text

QUITTING THE PROGRAM

Use This Keyboard Shortcut	To Do This
Ctrl + x *or* F2	Quit the program and optionally save any unsaved edits

SCROLLING

Use This Keyboard Shortcut	To Do This
Ctrl + y *or* F7 *or* PgUp	Scroll up one window
Ctrl + v *or* F8 *or* PgDn	Scroll down one window
Ctrl + w, Ctrl + y	Scroll to the first line of the file
Ctrl + w, Ctrl + v	Scroll to the last line of the file

MOVING THE CURSOR

Use This Keyboard Shortcut	To Do This
Ctrl + b, *or* left arrow	Move back one character
Ctrl + n *or* down arrow	Move down one line
Ctrl + f *or* right arrow	Move forward one character
Ctrl + k, l	Move to a line number that you specify
Ctrl + a	Move to the beginning of the line
Ctrl + e	Move to the end of the line
Ctrl + p *or* up arrow	Move up one line

MANAGING FILES

Use This Keyboard Shortcut	To Do This
Ctrl + r *or* F5	Insert a file at the cursor's location
Ctrl + o *or* F3	Save a file

CHECKING SPELLING

Use This Keyboard Shortcut	To Do This
Ctrl + t *or* F12	Check the spelling of the entire file

DELETING TEXT

Use This Keyboard Shortcut	To Do This
Ctrl + d	Delete the next character
Delete *or* Backspace	Delete the previous character
Ctrl + k	Delete the line
Ctrl + k	Delete a marked block

MARKING TEXT

Use This Keyboard Shortcut	To Do This
Ctrl + ^	Mark the beginning of a block

COPYING AND MOVING TEXT

Use This Keyboard Shortcut	To Do This
Ctrl + u *or* F10	Insert a cut block at the cursor's location
Ctrl + k, w	Save the marked region to a file

SEARCHING FOR TEXT

Use This Keyboard Shortcut	To Do This
F6 *or* Ctrl + w *string*	Search down for the string that you specify

pico Command Reference

This section details **pico**'s keyboard shortcuts, sorted in alphabetical order.

PICO KEYBOARD SHORTCUTS

Use This Keyboard Shortcut	To Do This
Backspace	Delete the previous character
Ctrl + ^	Mark the beginning of a block
Ctrl + a	Move to the beginning of the line
Ctrl + b	Move back one character
Ctrl + d	Delete the next character
Ctrl + e	Move to the end of the line
Ctrl + f	Move forward one character
Ctrl + g	Open the Help window
Ctrl + j	Reformat the text
Ctrl + k	Delete the line or the marked block
Ctrl + k, l	Move to a line number that you specify
Ctrl + k, w	Save the marked region to a file
Ctrl + n	Move down one line
Ctrl + o	Save a file
Ctrl + p *or* up arrow	Move up one line
Ctrl + r	Insert a file at the cursor's location
Ctrl + t	Check the spelling of the entire file
Ctrl + u	Insert a cut block at the cursor's location
Ctrl + v	Scroll down one window
Ctrl + w, Ctrl + v	Scroll to the last line of the file
Ctrl + w, Ctrl + y	Scroll to the first line of the file
Ctrl + x	Quit the program and optionally save any unsaved edits
Ctrl + x	Closed the Help window
Ctrl + y	Scroll up one window

PICO KEYBOARD SHORTCUTS *(CONT.)*

Use This Keyboard Shortcut	To Do This
Ctrl w *string*	Search down for the string that you specify
Delete *or* Backspace	Delete the previous character
down arrow	Move down one line
F1	Open the Help window
F10	Insert a cut block at the cursor's location
F12	Check the spelling of the entire file
F2	Quit the program and optionally save any unsaved edits
F3	Save a file
F4	Reformat the text
F5	Insert a file at the cursor's location
F6 *string*	Search down for the string that you specify
F7	Scroll up one window
F8	Scroll down one window
F9	Delete the line or the marked block
left arrow	Move back one character
PgDn	Scroll down one window
PgUp	Scroll up one window
right arrow	Move forward one character
up arrow	Move up one line

sed

sed [option] ['*command*'] *filename*

Starts a non-interactive editor that performs the specified command on the file specified by *filename*. You can list two or more files in a space-separated list. Alternatively, you can use the commands listed in a file specified by the –f option. For information on **sed** commands, see the table Commands in this section. Version 3.02 is documented here.

TIP The reference information presented here is not intended to teach the fundamentals or use of **sed**, nor is it intended to be comprehensive. Summarized here is information that will prove useful to users who have learned the fundamentals of **sed** and need reminders concerning commonly used options and commands.

OPTIONS

Use This Option	To Do This
–V, – –version	Display the version number.
–e *script– –***expression=script**	Use the commands in the specified script. Be sure to enclose the script name in quotation marks.
–f *filename, – –***file=***filename* **FILE'**	Use the commands in the specified file.
–h, – –help	Show the available options.
–n, – –quiet, – –silent	Hide most messages.

sed Commands

sed commands use the following syntax:

```
[ address ][ ! ] command [ argument ]
```

You can specify from zero to two addresses. An address can be a line number, a regular expression enclosed in forward slash marks, or $ for the last line. The command applies only to the address that you specify. If you omit the address, the command applies to all the lines. If you specify two addresses separated by a comma, **sed** interprets this as a range, and the command applies to all the lines from the first to the second address. If you include an exclamation point (!), the command applies to all lines except the ones that match the address. Braces are used to nest one address within another or to apply more than one command to the same address. The closing brace should be on its own line without any other spaces. The opening brace must end the line without any trailing spaces.

The following tables cover using the **sed** command to

- Insert text
- Delete text
- Replace text
- Copy, cut, and move text
- Print matching lines
- Control execution

INSERTING TEXT

Use This Command	To Do This
a *text*	Append the specified text after a line. Accepts one address only.
c *text*	Replace the block with the specified text.
i *text*	Insert the specified text before the line. Accepts one address only.
r *filename*	Insert the contents of the specified filename after the line. Accepts one address only.

DELETING TEXT

Use This Option	To Do This
d	Delete the line
D	Delete up to the next newline character

REPLACING TEXT

Use This Option	To Do This
s/*pattern*/*replacement*/[option]	In matching lines, search for the specified pattern and replace it with *replacement*. You can use the following options:
	n Replace the *n*th occurrence of the pattern on each matching line. The default is 1.
	g Replace all instances of the pattern on each matching line.
	p Print the line if a successful replacement is performed.
	w *filename* Write the line to the specified filename if a replacement is performed.
y/*character1*/*character2*	In matching lines, search for *character1* and replace it with *character2*.

COPYING, CUTTING, AND MOVING TEXT

Use This Option	To Do This
h	Copy the matching line to the buffer, erasing the buffer's contents
H	Append the matching line to the buffer
g	Delete the matching line and insert the buffer's contents
G	Append the buffer's contents below the matching line
x	Copy the matching line to the buffer

PRINTING MATCHING LINES

Use This Option	To Do This
p	Print the matching lines. Use the **–n** option to eliminate duplicates.
P	Print the multiple lines matched by an **N** command.
=	Print the line numbers of matching lines. Accepts one address only.

CONTROLLING EXECUTION

Use This Option	To Do This
b	When a match is encountered, branch to the line in the script marked by *label*. Note that *label* must be preceded by a colon.
n	When a match is encountered, skip this line and go to the next line.
q	Quit when the first match is encountered. This option accepts one address only.
t *label*	Determine whether replacements have been made on the matching line; if so, branch to the line in the command script marked by *label*. Note that *label* must be preceded by a colon.

EXAMPLES

This Command	Does the Following
`sed -n '10p' test.txt`	Displays line 10 of the input file (`test.txt`).
`sed -n '10p' test.txt > test-out.txt`	Displays line 10 of the input file (`test.txt`) and writes the output to the specified file (`testout.txt`). Be sure to place a space on either side of the greater-than sign (>).
`sed -n '10,20p' test.txt`	Displays lines 10 through 20 of the input file `test.txt`.
`sed -n '/essay/ p' test.txt`	Displays all the lines that contain *essay* in the input file `test.txt`.
`sed -n '/[Ee]ssay/p' test.txt`	Displays all the lines that match the regular expression (`/[Ee]ssay/`) in the input file `test.txt`.
`sed -n 's/essay/dissertation/ p' test.txt`	Finds all the lines in the input file `test.txt` that contain *essay*, changes the first instance of this word to *dissertation*, and displays the replacements.

vi

vi [option] [*filename*]

On most Linux systems, this command launches VIM (VI Improved), an extended version of the classic Unix text editor called vi. If you specify a filename, VIM opens the file in the current buffer. You can specify more than one filename in a space-separated list. By default, the program starts in the command mode, from which you cannot edit the text directly. To make changes to the file, you must do one of the following: enter the insert mode (see the section "Using the Insert Mode") or use editing commands within the command mode (see the section "Using the Command Mode").

Version 5.4 of VIM is documented here. For upgrades, documentation, and a FAQ, see http://www.vim.org.

TIP Like Emacs, VIM is a huge, complex program with many commands designed for specialized purposes. Accordingly, this section covers only the fundamental VIM commands for basic editing operations. To view all the available VIM commands, type **:help**.

OPTIONS

Use This Option	To Do This
+*n*	Position the cursor on line *n*.
+/*pattern*	Position the cursor at the first instance of the specified pattern.
–b	Edit the file in binary mode.
–C	Start VIM in **vi** compatibility mode.
–g	Start VIM in the GUI mode, if this was enabled when the program was compiled.
–m	Prevent modifications to files.
–n	Operate without creating a swap file. This makes recovery impossible in case of a system failure during editing.

OPTIONS *(CONT.)*

Use This Option	To Do This
–o [*n*]	Open one window for each of the specified filenames, or open *n* windows if *n* is included.
–R	Display files in read-only mode.

vi Essentials

This section details keyboard shortcuts to do the following:

- Get help
- Scroll and move the cursor
- Work with files
- Work with windows
- Work with buffers

GETTING HELP

Use This Keyboard Shortcut	To Do This
:help *or* F1	Get help with **vi** commands
Ctrl +]	Go to a tagged subject
Ctrl + t	Go back after jumping to a tagged subject

SCROLLING

Use This Keyboard Shortcut	To Do This
Ctrl + e *or* down arrow	Move down one line
Left arrow *or* h	Move left one character
b	Move left one word
Right arrow *or* l	Move right one character
w	Move right one word
Home	Move to the beginning of the line

SCROLLING *(CONT.)*

Use This Keyboard Shortcut	To Do This
End	Move to the end of the line
Ctrl + y *or* up arrow *or* k	Move up one line
z *or* Ctrl + L	Redraw the screen with the current line at the top of the window
Ctrl + f	Scroll down one page
Ctrl + d *or* PgDn	Scroll down one window
Ctrl + u *or* PgUp	Scroll up one-half window
Ctrl + b	Scroll up one page

WORKING WITH FILES

Use This Keyboard Shortcut	To Do This
:w >> *filename*	Append to the specified filename
:qall	Close all buffers and exit **vi**
:q	Close the current buffer and exit **vi** if no other buffers exist
:e *filename*:	Open the specified filename
:x	Save the current file only if changes have been made and exit
:wq	Save the current file and exit
:x *filename*	Save the current file to the specified filename only if changes have been made and exit
:w	Save to the current file
:w *filename*	Save to the specified filename
:n	Edit the next file when two or more files are open

WORKING WITH WINDOWS

Use This Keyboard Shortcut	To Do This
:sp	Split the screen into two windows
Ctrl + w, q	Close the current window
Ctrl + w, k	Move to window above
Ctrl + w, j	Move to window below
Ctrl + w, =	Make all windows equal height
Ctrl + w, -	Decrease the current window height
Ctrl + w, +	Increase the current window height

WORKING WITH BUFFERS

Use This Keyboard Shortcut	To Do This
:buffers	Show all buffers
:bunload *buffer*	Remove the specified buffer from the memory
:buffer *buffer*	Go to the specified buffer
:bnext	Go to the next buffer
:bprevious	Go to the previous buffer

Using the Insert Mode

To insert text in the current document, you can use one of the commands that switch to the insert mode (see the table "Starting the Insert Mode"). You can then use deletion commands that are available only while you are in this mode (see the table "Deleting Text in Insert Mode").

STARTING THE INSERT MODE

Use This Keyboard Shortcut	To Do This
a	Append text after the cursor
A	Append text at the end of the current line

STARTING THE INSERT MODE *(CONT.)*

Use This Keyboard Shortcut	To Do This
i	Insert text before the cursor
I	Insert text at the beginning of the line
o	Open a line below current line
O	Open a line above the current line
R	Begin overwriting the text at the cursor
s	Substitute a character
S	Substitute a line
Esc	Exit insert mode

DELETING TEXT IN INSERT MODE

Use This Keyboard Shortcut	To Do This
Backspace	Delete the previous character
Delete	Delete the current character

Using the Command Mode

The following tables detail commands that you can use to edit text in the command mode, including the following actions:

- Changing text
- Copying (yanking) and deleting text to buffers (registers)
- Pasting (putting) text
- Undoing editing changes
- Repeating editing changes
- Deleting text
- Searching for text

CHANGING TEXT

Use This Command	To Do This
cw	Change the current word
cc	Change the current line
p	Insert the last deleted text before the cursor
P	Insert the last deleted text after the cursor
r*character*	Replace the current character with *character*
R*string*	Replace the string beginning at the cursor
s	Substitute the current character
S	Substitute the entire line
~	Change the case of the selected character

COPYING (YANKING) AND DELETING TEXT TO BUFFERS (REGISTERS)

Use This Command	To Do This
"*register name*	Create a register named *register name* (use one character only) to store the next delete or yank (copy) operation
Y	Copy the current line into the current register
:reg *register name*	Show the contents of the specified register
:reg	Show the contents of all registers
"*register name***Y**	Delete the current line into *register name*

PASTING (PUTTING) TEXT

Use This Command	To Do This
p	Insert the contents of the current register after the cursor
P	Insert the contents of the current register before the cursor
"*register name***p**	Insert the contents of the specified register name after the cursor

UNDOING EDITING CHANGES

Use This Command	To Do This
u	Undo the last change
U	Restore the current line

REPEATING EDITING CHANGES

Use This Command	To Do This
	Repeat the lasts change

DELETING TEXT

Use This Command	To Do This
dd	Delete the current line
D	Delete the remainder of the line
dw	Delete the current word
D}	Delete up to the next paragraph
d^	Delete back to the beginning of the line
d/*string*	Delete up to the next occurrence of the specified string
df*pattern*	Delete up to and including the specified pattern on the current line
dt*pattern*	Delete up to but not including the specified pattern on the current line
dL	Delete up to the last line on the screen
dG	Delete to the end of the file
x	Delete the current character
X	Delete the previous character

SEARCHING FOR TEXT

Use This Command	To Do This
I string	Search forward for the specified string
? string	Search backward for the specified string
I	Repeat the forward search
?	Repeat the backward search

vi Keyboard Shortcuts

This section lists the keyboard shortcuts to the **vi** commands discussed in this section, sorted alphabetically.

VI KEYBOARD SHORTCUTS

Use This Keyboard Shortcut	To Do This
~	Change the case of the selected character.
.	Repeat the last change.
/	Repeat the forward search.
/string	Search forward for the specified string.
:bnext	Go to the next buffer.
:bprevious	Go to the previous buffer.
:buffer *buffer*	Go to the specified buffer.
:buffers	Show all buffers.
:bunload *buffer*	Remove the specified buffer from the memory.
:e *filename or* :r *filename*	Open the specified filename.
:help *or* F1	Get help with **vi** commands.
:n	When two or more files are open, edit the next file.
:q	Close the current buffer and exit **vi** if no other buffers exist.
:qall	Close all buffers and exit **vi**.
:reg	Show the contents of all registers.

VI KEYBOARD SHORTCUTS *(CONT.)*

Use This Keyboard Shortcut	To Do This
:reg *register name*	Show the contents of the specified register.
:w	Save to the current file.
:w >> *filename*	Append to the specified filename.
:w *filename*	Save to the specified *filename*.
:wq	Save the current file and exit.
:x	Save the current file if changes have been made and exit.
:x *filename*	Save the current file to the specified filename if changes have been made and exit.
?	Repeat the backward search.
?*string*	Search backward for the specified string.
a	Append text after the cursor.
A	Append text to the end of the current line.
Backspace	Delete the previous character.
cc	Change the current line.
Ctrl +]	Go to a tagged subject.
Ctrl + b	Scroll up one page.
Ctrl + d *or* PgDn	Scroll down one window.
Ctrl + e *or* down arrow *or* j	Move down one line.
Ctrl + f	Scroll down one page.
Ctrl + t	Go back after jumping to a tagged subject.
Ctrl + u *or* dd	Delete the current line.
Ctrl + u *or* PgUp	Scroll up one-half window.
Ctrl + w *or* :sp	Split the screen into two windows.
Ctrl + w	Delete the previous word.
Ctrl + w, −	Decrease the current window height.
Ctrl + w, +	Increase the current window height.
Ctrl + w, =	Make all windows equal height.
Ctrl + w, j	Move to the window below.
Ctrl + w, k	Move to the window above.

VI KEYBOARD SHORTCUTS *(CONT.)*

Use This Keyboard Shortcut	To Do This
Ctrl + w, q	Close the current window.
Ctrl + y *or* up arrow *or* k	Move up one line.
cw	Change the current word.
D	Delete the remainder of the line.
d^	Delete back to the beginning of the line.
d/*string*	Delete up to the next occurrence of the specified string.
D}	Delete up to the next paragraph.
dd	Delete the current line.
Delete	Delete the current character.
df*pattern*	Delete up to and including the specified pattern on the current line.
dG	Delete to the end of the file.
dL	Delete up to the last line on the screen.
dt*pattern*	Delete up to but not including the specified pattern on the current line.
dw	Delete the current word.
End	Move to the end of the line.
Esc	Exit insert mode.
Home	Move to the beginning of the line.
i	Insert text before the cursor.
I	Insert text at the beginning of the line.
Left arrow *or* h	Move left one character.
o	Open a line below the current line.
O	Open a line above the current line.
p	Insert the contents of the current register after the cursor.
P	Insert the contents of the current register before the cursor.
R	Begin overwriting the text at the cursor.

VI KEYBOARD SHORTCUTS *(CONT.)*

Use This Keyboard Shortcut	To Do This
r*character*	Replace the current character with *character*.
"*register name*	Create a register name (*register name*) to store the next delete or yank (copy) operation. Use one character only for *register name*.
"*register name*p	Insert the contents of the specified register name after the cursor.
"*register name*Y	Delete current line into *register name*.
Right arrow	Move right one character.
R*string*	Replace the string beginning at the cursor.
s	Substitute the current character.
S	Substitute the entire line.
B *or* b	Move left one word.
W *or* w	Move right one word.
u	Undo the last change.
U	Restore the current line.
x	Delete the current character.
X	Delete the previous character.
Y	Copy the current line into the current register.
z *or* Ctrl + L	Redraw the screen with the current line at the top of the window.

CHAPTER 12

Configuring and Managing Your System

This chapter details the essentials of Linux system configuration, including boot processes, system initialization (init) processes, XFree86, printers, automated processes, and system logs. It also documents the commands used to schedule processes, manage users, load and unload kernel modules, establish and configure disk quotas, compile software from source code, install software from RPM packages, and more. Intended for intermediate to advanced readers, this chapter discusses procedures and utilities that, in general, require root user status and extensive background knowledge to use successfully. However, certain utilities (such as **crontab**, **make**, **mkpasswd**, **passwd**, and **rpm**) can be used safely by Linux beginners.

AT A GLANCE

How Do I	See This Entry	Example
Add a new user?	**useradd**	useradd -p k49dxGt ernie
Check the password database to make sure it contains no errors?	**grpck**, **pwck**	grpck pwck
Compile software from source code?	**make**	./configure make make install
Create the quota files (`quota.user` and `quota.group`) on filesystems for which quotas have been enabled?	**quotacheck**	quotacheck -av
Delete a user and remove the user's home directory and files?	**userdel**	userdel -r ernie
Edit quotas for an individual or group user?	**edquota**	edquota suzanne
Generate high-quality passwords for user and group accounts?	**mkpasswd**, **pwgen**	pwgen -6

AT A GLANCE *(CONT.)*

How Do I	See This Entry	Example
Install a Red Hat RPM package?	**rpm**	rpm -ivh newprogram-1.0.rpm
Load a module and specify the arguments (module parameters) that are required to install it correctly?	**insmod**, **modprobe**	insmode aha152x='0x340,12,7,5' modprobe aha152x
Remove a module from the kernel?	**rmmod**	rmmod aha152x
Remove an unwanted RPM package?	**rpm**	rpm -e unwanted
Schedule processes to run at a certain time or time interval?	"Scheduling Automated Processes with **cron**," **crontab**	crontab -e
Search the Internet for a package containing a word or part of a word?	**rpmfind**	rpmfind --apropos mail
Turn user quotas on?	**quotaon**	quotaon /home
Upgrade a Red Hat RPM package?	**rpm**	rpm -Uvh newprogram-2.0.rpm
View the current user's disk usage quotas?	**quota**	quota suzanne
View the system messages that fly by when my system starts?	**dmesg**	dmesg | less

System Configuration Fundamentals

This section details the following system configuration procedures:

- Configuring boot processes with LILO
- Configuring init processes

- Configuring XFree86

- Configuring printers

- Scheduling automated processes with **cron**

- Rotating system logs

- Enabling disk-usage quotas

Configuring Boot Processes with LILO

The installation utilities included with most Linux distributions install the LILO (Linux Loader) utility by default. LILO enables Linux to boot automatically from a hard drive. The less convenient alternative is to boot from a floppy. LILO enables you to choose a variety of boot configuration options, including the capability to boot more than one version of the Linux kernel or more than one operating system. LILO version 21 is documented here. Note that some Linux distributions customize LILO to some extent, or significantly. The version of LILO found on Red Hat and Red Hat-derived distributions is discussed here.

Master Boot Record and the Boot Loader

When a PC boots, the first loaded program is BIOS (Basic Input-Output System), which is loaded from the computer's read-only memory (ROM). Among this program's functions is to search for and load the *boot loader,* a small program that initiates loading the rest of the operating system. Since the Linux filesystem has not yet been loaded, the boot loader is generally located on the first sector of the hard drive's active partition. This sector is called the *master boot record* (MBR). The MBR also contains the partition table. When the BIOS detects and loads the boot loader, you will see the LILO prompt (LILO boot:) on-screen. By default, LILO will boot Linux after a pre-determined number of seconds if you do not select an option. To see the available options, press Tab. To select an option other than the default, type the option's name and press Enter.

WARNING   Don't install another operating system, such as Microsoft Windows, *after* you have installed Linux. Most operating systems will overwrite the master boot record without asking for confirmation. As a result, you will not be able to start Linux. You can overcome this problem by using a *rescue disk*, a floppy disk that most Linux installation utilities automatically create when you install Linux on your system. See your Linux distribution's documentation for details on making a rescue disk if you skipped this step during installation.

LILO uses a configuration file, /etc/lilo.conf, to enable you to specify boot options. You can make changes to /etc/lilo.conf to determine how LILO operates. You can make changes to this file by editing it directly, or by using a system administration utility such as **Linuxconf**. After you make changes to /etc/lilo.conf, run the LILO executable, /sbin/lilo, to rewrite the boot loader; **Linuxconf** does this automatically.

TIP   If Linux fails to start properly, restart your system. At the LILO prompt, type **linux single** and press Enter. This command starts the single-user mode. In this mode, the boot process loads a minimal set of drivers and utilities. If the problem concerns a disk error that **fsck** could not repair in its automatic mode, which runs automatically when you boot your system, you can run the utility in its manual mode, enabling it to solve problems that cannot be addressed in the automatic mode. If you modified a configuration file just before rebooting, the problem probably stems from an error in this file. In the single mode, you can run a text editor and fix the mistake. When you've solved the problem, type **exit** and press Enter to reboot your system.

The LILO Configuration File

The LILO configuration file, /etc/lilo.conf, begins with a *Global section*, which contains options that affect all the boot alternatives. Following the Global section is at least one *Per-image section*, which defines a specific boot procedure to be used for two or more *boot images* (versions of the Linux kernel that are designed to be loaded by LILO). If more than one Per-image section is present, you can choose which one you want to use by default. You do so by typing a label at the LILO prompt. If you have configured your system to run Microsoft Windows 98 as well as Linux, press Tab at the LILO prompt to see what to type to start Windows.

The Global section contains options that govern all the Per-image sections. This section must begin with a boot entry that specifies the location of the master boot record (MBR). The following illustrates a Global section in /etc/lilo.conf:

```
## Global section
boot=/dev/hda
map=/boot/map
install=/boot/boot.b
prompt
timeout=50
default=linux
```

This example is supplied for illustration only; the various commands must correspond to the partitions, directories, and boot images present on your system. The following table, Global Options, explains the entries that you can place in this section.

GLOBAL OPTIONS

Use This Entry	To Do This
backup=*filename*	Copy the original boot sector to the specified backup filename.
boot=*device*	Specify the name of the device that contains the boot sector.
compact	Attempt to merge sector read requests, which can shorten load time when booting from a floppy.
default=*name*	Use the specified image name as the default boot image.

GLOBAL OPTIONS *(CONT.)*

Use This Entry	To Do This
delay=*time*	Set the delay time (in seconds) before booting from the first image.
force-backup=*filename*	Copy the original boot sector to the specified backup filename. Overwrites the old backup copy.
ignore-table	Ignore corrupt partition tables.
install=*filename*	Install the specified filename as the new boot sector.
linear	Generate linear sector addresses instead of sector/head/cylinder addresses.
lock	Enable automatic recording of boot command lines as the defaults for the following boots.
map=*filename*	Specify the location of the map file.
message=*filename*	Specify a filename containing a message that is displayed before the boot prompt.
nowarn	Disable warnings about possible future dangers.
optional	Apply the per-image option optional to all images.
password=*password*	Apply the per-image option password to all images.
prompt	Forces manual initiation of the boot process unless timeout is set.
restricted	Apply the per-image option restricted to all images.
serial=*port*[,*bps*[*parity*[*bits*]]]	Enable control from a serial line. You must specify the serial port, and you can optionally specify the bits per second (bps), parity (**n** for no parity, **e** for even parity, or **o** for odd parity), and the number of bits per character (7 or 8).

Use This Entry	To Do This
timeout=*seconds*	Specify a timeout for keyboard input. If no input is received, the boot process begins using the default settings.
verbose=*level*	Control the amount of progress reporting with a level from 1 (low reporting) to 5 (high reporting).

Per-Image Options

Each Per-image section defines a specific boot procedure that can be initiated by typing its label (see **label** in the following table).

The following illustrates a Per-image section for booting Linux:

```
image=/boot/vmlinuz-2.2.12-20
label=linux
initrd=/boot/initrd-2.2.12-20.img
read-only
root=/dev/hda1
```

A Linux Per-image section must begin with an image entry. This entry specifies where the Linux boot image can be found.

This Per-image section illustrates a Windows 98 boot alternative:

```
other=/dev/hda1
label=windows
loader=/boot/chain.b
table=/dev/hda
```

A Windows, DOS, or OS/2 section must begin with another entry that specifies where the alternative operating system can be found.

The options for Linux and other operating systems differ. The following tables explain the options available for each.

PER-IMAGE OPTIONS FOR LINUX

Use This Entry	To Do This
alias=*name*	Specify a second name for this image.
append=*string*	Pass the specified string to the kernel.
image=*path name*	Specify the path name to the file or device containing a boot image of the Linux kernel. If you are configuring a device, you must also specify the range.
label=*name*	Display this name to identify the image.
literal=*string*	Pass the specified string to the kernel and remove all other options.
lock	Enable automatic recording of boot commands as the default for the next boot.
optional	Omit the image if it is not available at map creation time.
password=*password*	Require entry of the specified password to boot the image.
ramdisk=*size*	Specify the size of the optional RAM disk.
range=*start end*	Specify the start and end sectors of the image; required only if the image option points to a device rather than a filename.
read-only	Mount the filesystem in read-only mode.
read-write	Mount the filesystem in read-write mode.
restricted	Require a password only if boot parameters are specified on the command line.
root=*device*	Mount the specified device as root.
vga=*mode*	Select the VGA mode to be used during booting. Available options are **normal** Select normal 80x25 text mode. **extended** Select 80x50 text mode. **ask** Ask for user input at boot time.

PER-IMAGE OPTIONS FOR OPERATING SYSTEMS OTHER THAN LINUX

Use This Entry	To Do This
alias=*name*	Specify a second name for this image.
label=*name*	Display this name to identify the image.
loader=*loader*	Specify the loader to be used.
lock	Enable automatic recording of boot commands as the default for the next boot.
optional	Omit the image if it is not available at map creation time.
other=*path name*	Specify the path name to an alternative operating system.
password=*password*	Require entry of the specified password to boot the image.
restricted	Require a password only if boot parameters are specified on the command line.
table=*device*	Specify the device that contains the partition table.

Configuring Init Processes

After the boot process begins, a script called init starts automatically. This script begins by reading the default startup configuration file, called /etc/inittab. An important configuration option in this file concerns the default run level. A *run level* is an overall configuration that determines whether the Linux system is connected to the network and whether the X Window System starts automatically. When the default run level has been determined, init turns the system over to a system utility called *getty*. This utility opens up terminal connections and displays the login prompt. Then getty turns the system over to yet another utility, called *login*, which accepts the user's login name and password. In addition to getty and login, init launches the X server, as long as the default run level is the one that starts X automatically.

Typically, Linux distributions come with pre-configured init, getty, and login utilities, so you needn't worry about them. Most Linux installation utilities enable you to select the default run level. However, you may wish to change the default run level later, so it's wise to learn how your Linux distribution defines the various run levels, as explained in the next section.

Understanding Run Levels

In the file /etc/inittab, you will find a section containing a line such as the following:

```
id:5:initdefault:
```

This statement specifies the default run level setting by means of a number (5 in this example). The following table, Run Levels, explains what these numbers stand for. For example, if you replace 5 with 3, Linux will start in console mode. Run levels 0, 1, 2, 3, and 6 are reasonably well standardized among Linux distributions. However, some distributions use 4 to start X automatically, while others use 5. Consult your Linux system's documentation, or the comments in /etc/inittab, to determine which run level starts X in the distribution that you are using.

WARNING   Do not make any changes to /etc/inittab other than changing the run level number! If you do, your system may not start. Also, be aware that you shouldn't choose run level 0 or 6 as the default run level: You don't want your system to halt or reboot the minute you start it.

RUN LEVELS

Run Level	Description
0	Halts the system.
1	Single user mode (useful for troubleshooting).
2	Multi-user system (console mode) without Network Filesystem (NFS) support.
3	Full multi-user console mode (text-only).
4	Starts X Window System automatically or unused.
5	Starts X Window System automatically or unused.
6	Reboots.

Configuring XFree86

XFree86 is the default implementation of the X Window System on most Intel-based Linux distributions. Most users should configure XFree86 using configuration utilities, such as **XF86Setup** (see Chapter 1). On Red Hat and Red Hat-derived systems, a utility named **Xconfigurator** is available (see Chapter 1). These utilities considerably ease the difficulty of configuring XFree86 by probing for your system's video hardware and writing the configuration file, XF86Config. However, it is often necessary to modify this configuration file by hand in order to get the desired performance. Accordingly, this system presents the information necessary to modify XF86Config. The still-widely-distributed version 3.3.6 is documented here; see "XF86 Version 4," later in this section, for information on new features and changes. For the latest information on XFree86, including updated versions, visit http://www.xfree86.org.

XF86Config: The Overall Structure

The XFree86 configuration file, XF86Config, is located variously, depending on the distribution you are using. In Red Hat systems, you'll find the file in the /etc/X11 directory, organized into the following sections:

Files   Specifies the default paths for fonts and X program modules.

Module   Specifies the modules (if any) to be loaded when the X server starts.

ServerFlags   Specifies certain server options.

Keyboard   Defines the default keyboard configuration for your system.

Pointer   Defines the default mouse configuration for your system.

Monitor   Defines the default monitor configuration for your system.

Device   Defines the video adapter configuration for your system.

Screen   Specifies one or more video display modes that are possible with the video adapter that you are using.

Xinput   Defines certain input devices, such as joysticks and graphics tablets. This section is optional.

Each section begins with a Section statement and ends with an End-Section statement. These statements serve to delineate one section from another. Within each section, you can use the listed entries. Many of them enable you to specify a value or name (such as Load "xf86Jstk.so"); be sure to enclose strings (alphanumeric expressions) in quotation marks.

The Files Section

The Files section specifies the default paths for fonts, X system colors, and X program modules. The following illustrates the appearance of this section:

```
Section "Files"
    RgbPath     "/usr/X11R6/lib/X11/rgb"
    FontPath    "/usr/X11R6/lib/X11/fonts/local/,
        /usr/X11R6/lib/X11/fonts/misc/,
        /usr/X11R6/lib/X11/fonts/75dpi/:unscaled,
        /usr/X11R6/lib/X11/fonts/100dpi/:unscaled,
        /usr/X11R6/lib/X11/fonts/Type1/,
        /usr/X11R6/lib/X11/fonts/Speedo/,
        /usr/X11R6/lib/X11/fonts/75dpi/,
        /usr/X11R6/lib/X11/fonts/100dpi/"
    ModulePath      "/usr/X11R6/lib/modules"
EndSection
```

The next table shows the options you can use in the Files section.

FILES SECTION ENTRIES

Use This Entry	To Do This
FontPath *path names*	Specify the path names of available system fonts in a comma-separated list. Note: Red Hat 6.x and derived systems (including Mandrake 6.x and 7.x) provide font support by means of the xfs font server. The list of font path names should be listed in the Catalogue section of the xfs configuration file (`/etc/X11/fs/config`).

FILES SECTION ENTRIES

ModulePath *path name*   Specify the path name to search for program modules that handle extended input devices.

RGBPath *path name*   Specify the path name for the RGB color database.

The Module Section

This section specifies the modules (if any) to be loaded when the X server starts. The following is an example of a Module section:

```
Section "Module"
    Load "xf86Jstk.so"
EndSection
```

This section loads the joystick driver. To use this driver, you must also specify the driver's characteristics in the Xinput section.

MODULE SECTION ENTRIES

Use This Entry   **To Do This**

Load *module*   Instructs the server to load the specified module. The module's location must be specified by the ModulePath option (see the section "The Files Section"). Supported modules include two-button joysticks; Elographics and Microtouch touchscreens; Wacom styluses; cursors; erasers; Summasketch, AceCad, and CalComp Drawing-Board graphics tablets; Switch virtual devices; and SGI button boxes.

The ServerFlags Section

The *ServerFlags section* enables you to specify certain server options. The following is an example of this section:

```
Section "ServerFlags"
    DontZoom
EndSection
```

SERVERFLAGS SECTION ENTRIES

Use This Entry	To Do This
AllowMouseOpenFail	Instruct the server to start even if the mouse cannot be opened or initialized.
AllowNonLocalMod-InDev	Enable users from other hosts to modify keyboard and mouse settings. By default, such modifications are not allowed.
AllowNonLocalXvidtune	Enable an xvidtune client to connect from another host. By default, such connections are not allowed.
DisableModInDev	Disable dynamic modification of input device settings.
DisableVidMode	Prevent xvidtune from changing video modes, which could damage certain monitors.
DontZap	Prevent use of the Ctrl + Alt + Backspace sequence to terminate the server.
DontZoom	Prevent the use of the Ctrl + Alt + Keypad Plus and Ctrl + Alt + Keypad + Minus sequences.
NoTrapSignals	Instruct the server to exit when an error is encountered without attempting to trace the source of the error. This option is useful only for debugging purposes.

The Keyboard Section

This section defines the keyboard for your system. The following is an example of the Keyboard section:

```
Section "Keyboard"
    Protocol "Standard"
    AutoRepeat 500 5
    XkbKeycodes    "xfree86"
    XkbTypes       "default"
    XkbCompat      "default"
    XkbSymbols     "us(pc101)"
    XkbGeometry    "pc"
    XkbRules       "xfree86"
    XkbModel       "pc101"
    XkbLayout      "us"
EndSection
```

KEYBOARD SECTION ENTRIES

Use This Entry	To Do This
AltGr *key*	Map the right Alt key to one of the following keys: Compose, ModeShift, ModeLock, ScrollLock, or Control. By default, the key is mapped to Meta. Note that AltGR is a synonym for RightAlt.
AutoRepeat *delay rate*	Set the keyboard autorepeat delay rate in milliseconds. Note that this option doesn't work with all otherwise supported hardware.
LeftAlt *key*	Map the left Alt key to one of the following: Compose, ModeShift, ModeLock, ScrollLock, or Control. By default, the key is mapped to Meta.
Protocol *kbd-protocol*	Specify the kbd-protocol (either Standard or Xqueue) used for the event driver queue driver on SVR3 or SVR4.
RightAlt *key*	Map the right Alt key to one of the following keys: Compose, ModeShift, ModeLock, ScrollLock, or Control. By default, the key is mapped to Meta. Note that RightAlt is a synonym for AltGr.
RightCtl *key*	Map the right Ctrl key to one of the following keys: Meta, Compose, ModeShift, ModeLock, ScrollLock, and Control. By default, the key is mapped to Control.
ScrollLock *key*	Map the ScrollLock key to one of the following keys: Meta, Compose, ModeShift, ModeLock, ScrollLock, or Control. By default, the key is mapped to Compose.
ServerNumLock	Enable applications to make use of the numeric keypad.
VTInit *command*	Run the specified shell command after the terminal has been opened.

KEYBOARD SECTION ENTRIES *(CONT.)*

Use This Entry	To Do This
VTSysReq	Enable System V virtual terminal switch sequences on non-System V systems (including Linux) that support virtual terminal switching.
XkbDisable	Switch off the XKEYBOARD extensions.
XkbdKeycodes *keycode*	Specify the keycode map for the specified keyboard model (see **XkbModel** in this table). The default is XFree86. To view the available options, see `/usr/lib/X11/xkd/keycodes`.
XkbdSymbol *symbols*	Specify the symbols entered by symbol keys on the specified keyboard layout. To view the available options, see `/usr/lib/X11/xkd/symbols`.
XkbGeometry *geometry*	Specify the geometry of the keyboard model you are using. For a list of available geometries, consult your keyboard's geometry file in `/usr/lib/X11/xbd/geometry`.
XkbLayout *layout*	Specify the keyboard layout. Available options include the following:

be   Belgian.
bg   Bulgarian.
br   Brazilian.
ca   Canadian.
cs   Czechoslovakian.
de   German.
de_CH   Swiss German.
dk   Danish.
en_US   U.S. English w/ISO9995-3.
es   Spanish.
fi Finnish.
fr French.
fr_CH   Swiss French.
gb   United Kingdom.
hu   Hungarian.
it Italian.
jp Japanese.
nec/jp   PC-98xx Series.
no   Norwegian.

KEYBOARD SECTION ENTRIES *(CONT.)*

Use This Entry	To Do This
	pl Polish.
	pt Portugese.
	ru Russian.
	se Swedish.
	th Thai.
	us U.S. English.
	us_intl U.S. English with deadkeys.
XkbModel *model*	Specify the keyboard model. The default is pc101. Options include the following:
	abnt2 Brazilian ABNT2.
	dell101 Dell 101-key PC.
	everex Everex STEPnote.
	flexpro Keytronic FlexPro.
	jp106 Japanese 106-key.
	microsoft Microsoft Natural.
	omnikey101 OmniKey 101.
	pc101 Generic 101-key PC.
	pc102 Generic 102-key (Intl) PC.
	pc104 Generic 104-key PC.
	pc105 Generic 105-key (Intl) PC.
	pc98 PC-98xx Series.
	winbook Winbook Model XP5.
XkbOptions *option*	Specify one of the following keyboard mapping options:
	grp:switch The right Alt key engages the shift lock while pressed.
	grp:toggle The right Alt key changes the shift lock.
	grp:shift_toggle Both Shift keys together change the shift lock.
	grp:ctrl_shift_ toggle Control+Shiftchanges the shift lock.
	grp:ctrl_alt_toggle Alt + Control changes the shift lock.
	ctrl:nocaps Makes CapsLock an additional Ctrl key.
	ctrl:swapcaps Swap the functions of Ctrl and Caps Lock.

KEYBOARD SECTION ENTRIES *(CONT.)*

Use This Entry	To Do This
XkbRules *rule*	Specify the rule set employed to link a specific keyboard model, keycode set, and geometry. The default is XFree86. Alternatively, you can specify the XkbModel, XkbKeycodes, and Xkb-Geometry independently. For a list of available rules, see **xbd/rules** in the X11 directory.
XkbType *type*	Specify the keyboard type. For a list of available types, see `/usr/lib/X11/xbd/types./`.
XkbVariant *variant*	Specify the keyboard variant. The only available variant is nodeadkeys.
XLeds *led*	Makes the keyboard LED lights available for clients.

The Pointer Section

This section defines the mouse attached to your system. The following is an example of the Pointer section:

```
Section "Pointer"
    Protocol "PS/2"
    Device   "/dev/mouse"
    Emulate3Buttons
    Emulate3Timeout     50
EndSection
```

POINTER SECTION ENTRIES

Use This Entry	To Do This
BaudRate *rate*	Set the baud rate of a serial mouse.
Buttons *n*	Specify the number (*n*) of buttons actually present on the mouse.
ChordMiddle	Enable the use of mice that send left and right events together when the middle button is pressed, such as Logitech Mouseman.

POINTER SECTION ENTRIES *(CONT.)*

Use This Entry	To Do This
ClearDTR	Enable the use of the MouseSystems protocol.
ClearRTS	Enable the use of the MouseSystems protocol.
Device *device*	Specify the device that the server should open for pointer input, such as /dev/tty00 or /dev/mouse.
Emulate3Buttons	Enable a two-button mouse to emulate a three-button mouse. To use the third button, press both buttons simultaneously.
Emulate3Timeout *timeout*	Set the time (in milliseconds) that the server waits before deciding if two buttons were pressed simultaneously when three-button emulation is enabled. The default timeout is 50ms.
Port *device*	Same as the **Device** entry in this table.
Protocol *type*	Indicate the protocol type. The available options include Auto, BusMouse, GlidePoint, Glide-PointPS/2, IntelliMouse, IMPS/2, MMHitTab, MMSeries, Mouseman, MouseManPlusPS/2, MouseSystems, NetMousePS/2, NetScrollPS/2, OSMouse, PS/2, SysMouse, ThinkingMouse, ThinkingMousePS/2,and Xqueue.
Resolution *count*	Set the resolution of the device in counts per inch.
SampleRate *rate*	Set the number of motion and button events that the mouse sends per second.
ZAxisMapping *button1 button2*	Map the output of a wheel mouse to the specified mouse button, such as 1, 2, or 3. To emulate a mouse button press with negative movement, specify button1. To specify a mouse button press with positive movement, specify button2.
ZAxisMapping *X*	Map the output of a wheel mouse to the x (vertical) axis.
ZAxisMapping *Y*	Map the output of a wheel mouse to the y (horizontal) axis.

The Monitor Section

This section defines the monitor attached to your system. Version 3.3.6 of XFree86 can work with only one video card at a time; however, you can define more than one monitor in this section. Each monitor definition must begin with an Identifier entry. For each defined monitor, you can define one or more video modes, each specifying a screen resolution (such as 1024×768).

You can define modes in two different ways. The first type of mode definition begins with a Mode statement and ends with an End Mode statement, as illustrated here:

```
Section "Monitor"
    Identifier "Generic Monitor"
        VendorName "Unknown"
        ModelName "Unknown"
        HorizSync 30-64
        VertRefresh  50-100
        Mode "640x480"
                DotClock     25.175
                HTimings     640 664 760 800
                VTimings     480 491 493 525
        EndMode
        Mode "1024x768i"
                DotClock     45
                HTimings     1024 1048 1208 1264
                VTimings     768 776 784 817
                Flags        "Interlace"
                EndMode
    EndSection
```

The second type of mode definition employs a one-line ModeLine statement, as shown here:

```
Section "Monitor"
    Identifier "Generic Monitor"
        VendorName "Unknown"
        ModelName "Unknown"
        HorizSync 30-64
        VertRefresh  50-100
```

```
          ModeLine "640x480" 25.175 640 664 760 800 480 491
          493 525
          ModeLine "1024x768i" 45 1024 1048 1208 1264 768
          776 784 817 Interlace
EndSection
```

WARNING You can damage certain monitors by entering synchronization rates that are higher than the monitor's capacity. Never guess synchronization rates! Consult the monitor's documentation to determine the correct synchronization values to enter.

MONITOR SECTION ENTRIES

Use This Entry	To Do This
DotClock *rate*	Specify a dot clock (pixel) rate, if this is not stated by a ModeLine entry.
Flags *option*	Specify a monitor option, unless stated by a ModeLine entry. Available options include **Interlace**, **DoubleScan**, **+HSync**, **–HSync**, **+VSync**, **–VSync**, and **Composite**.
HorizSync *rate*	Specify the monitor's horizontal synch rate in a comma-separated list of discrete values or ranges of values.
HTimings *hdisp hysyncstart hsyncend htotal*	Specify the horizontal timings (horizontal displacement, horizontal synch start, horizontal synch end, and horizontal total) if these are not specified by a ModeLine entry.
Identifier *string*	Specify a string to identify this monitor in other entries.
Modeline *name mode description*	Specify the video mode in a single-line format, consisting of a name and the following mode description entries in a space-separated list: pixel clock rate, horizontal timings (hdisp, hysyncstart, hsyncend, htotal), vertical timings (vdisp, vsynchstart, vsyncend, vtotal), and optional settings. Note: For supported monitors, you will find correct ModeLine statements for all supported resolutions in the file **doc/Monitors**, located in the X11 directory on your system.

MONITOR SECTION ENTRIES *(CONT.)*

Use This Entry	To Do This
ModelName *name*	Specify the monitor's model name. This line is optional.
Mode *name*	Specify the name of the mode if this is not done with a **Modeline** entry. The section terminates with an EndMode entry.
VendorName *name*	Specify the name of the monitor's manufacturer.
VertRefresh *rate*	Specify the vertical refresh rate in a comma-separated list of discrete values or ranges of values.
VTimings *vdisp vsynchstart vsyncend vtotal*	Specify the vertical timings (vertical displacement, vertical sync start, vertical sync end, and vertical total) if these are not specified by a **Modeline** entry.

The Devices Section

The *Devices section* specifies the characteristics of the video card attached to your system. Although it is possible to install more than one video card at a time (two located on the PCI bus or one on the PCI bus and another in the AGP slot), XFree86 version 3.*x* cannot work with more than one video card at a time. Reportedly, version 4.0 will be able to work with two video cards and, consequently, with dual monitors.

In general, it's best to define a device using one of the X configuration utilities (such as XF86Setup or Xconfigurator, discussed in Chapter 1). These utilities can probe the video card to determine its characteristics. They can also determine which of the several available X servers should be installed. (For a list of all currently supported video card/server combinations, see http://www.xfree86.org/cardlist.html.) After using one of these utilities, you may wish to "tweak" this section by enabling server-specific options. See http://www.xfree86.org/3.3.6/index .html for specific information on the available options for the server you're using.

The following illustrates a Device section, which must begin with an Identifier entry:

```
Section "Device"
    Identifier  "MagicGraph NM2160"
    VendorName  "Unknown"
    BoardName   "Unknown"
    VideoRam 2048
    Chipset "NM2160"
    IOBase  0xfea00000
    MemBase 0xfd000000
    DacSpeed    90
    Option  "intern_disp"
EndSection
```

DEVICES SECTION ENTRIES

Use This Entry	To Do This
BIOSBase *address*	Specify the base address of the video BIOs if it is other than the default of 0xC0000.
BoardName *name*	Specify the name of the graphics adapter. For a list of supported graphics devices, see **/usr/lib/X11/Cards** in the X11 directory.
Chipset *chipset*	Specify the chipset used by the graphics adapter if this is not determined by the server's probe.
COPBase *address*	Specify the base address of the coprocessor, which is needed for some servers. Consult the server's documentation.
DACBase *address*	Specify the base address of the DAC, which is needed for some servers. Consult the server's documentation.
Instance *n*	Indicate whether the video circuitry is indicated on the motherboard, which is needed for some servers. Consult the server's documentation.
IOBase *address*	Specify the base address of the video I/O, which is needed for some servers. Consult the server's documentation.

DEVICES SECTION ENTRIES *(CONT.)*

Use This Entry	To Do This
Option *string*	This optional entry allows the user to select certain options provided by the drivers. Multiple-option entries may be given. The supported values for option string are given in the appropriate X server manual pages or in the chipset-specific README files.
POSBase *address*	Specify the base address of the POS, which is needed for some servers. Consult the server's documentation.
VendorName *vendor*	This optional entry specifies the graphics device's manufacturer.
VGABase *address*	Specify the base address of VGA memory, which is needed for some servers. Consult the server's documentation.
VideoRam *n*	Specify the amount (in K) of video RAM installed on the adapter, which is needed for some servers. Consult the server's documentation.

The Screen Section

The *Screen section* brings together the specifications previously entered in the Monitor and Device sections. It defines one or more Display subsections, which specifies the video modes that will be available when you use your system.

Here is an example of the Screen section:

```
Section "Screen"
    Driver  "accel"
    Device  "MagicGraph NM2160"
    Monitor "LCD Panel 1024x768"
    Subsection "Display"
        Depth   16
        Modes   "800 x 600"
        ViewPort 0 0
        Virtual 1024 786
```

```
        EndSubsection
        Subsection "Display"
            Depth    16
            Modes    "1024x768"
            ViewPort0 0
        EndSubsection
    EndSection
```

TIP f you define more than one Display subsection, you can switch among video modes by pressing Ctrl + Alt + keypad plus, or Ctrl + Alt + keypad minus.

SCREEN SECTION ENTRIES

Use This Entry	To Do This
Driver *name*	Begin a Screen section and specify the driver, which must be unique to each section. Available options include Accel, Mono, SVGA, VGA2, and VGA16.
BlankTime *time*	Set the inactivity time (in minutes) for screen-saver blanking. The default is 10 minutes.
DefaultColorDepth *depth*	Specify the color depth. Available options are 8, 16, 24, and 32.
Depth *depth*	Specify the default color depth (8, 16, 24, or 32) when more than one Display subsection is present.
Device *description*	Specify the graphics device description.
Monitor *name*	Specify the monitor name, which must match the name in the Monitor section.
OffTime *timeout*	Set the inactivity timeout (in minutes) for the DPMS mode. The default is 40.
Option *string*	Specify a string to enable an option made available by specific servers. Consult the server's documentation for details.

SCREEN SECTION ENTRIES *(CONT.)*

Use This Entry	To Do This
StandbyTime *timeout*	Set the inactivity timeout (in minutes) for the standby phase of DPMS mode. The default is 20.
SuspendTime *timeout*	Set the inactivity timeout (in minutes) for the suspend phase of DPMS mode. The default is 30 minutes.
ViewPort *x y*	Sets the x and y coordinates (in pixels) of the upper-left corner of the initial display. It is used only when the virtual screen resolution is different from the resolution of the initial video mode.
Virtual *x y*	Specify a virtual screen resolution that is larger than the physical display. *x* and *y* must be multiples of 8 or 16 for most color X servers, and 32 for monochrome servers.
Visual *type*	Specify the root visual type. Available options include StaticGray, GrayScale, StaticColor, PseudoColor, TrueColor, and DirectColor.

Xinput Section

The *Xinput section* is optional. It enables you to define certain input devices, such as joysticks and graphics tablets. The following Xinput example illustrates a joystick definition:

```
Section "Xinput"
    SubSection "Joystick"
        Port "/dev/joy0"
        DeviceName "Joystick"
        TimeOut 10
        MinimumXPosition 100
        MaximumXPosition 1300
        MinimumYPosition 100
        MaximumYPosition 1100
        CenterX 700
        CenterY 600
        Delta 20
    EndSubSection
EndSection
```

To use the devices defined in this section, you must tell the X server to load the appropriate module. You can do so by means of an entry in the Modules section, which was discussed earlier.

The following table discusses the entries you can use to define a joystick subsection.

JOYSTICK SUBSECTION OPTIONS

Use This Entry	To Do This
AlwaysCore	Enable core pointer sharing
CenterX *value*	Set the X center when the joystick is idle
CenterY *value*	Set the Y center when the joystick is idle
Delta *value*	Set the maximum value
DeviceName *name*	Specify the name of the device
MaximumXPosition *value*	Set the maximum X value
MaximumYPosition *value*	Set the maximum Y value
MinimumXPosition *value*	Set the minimum X value
MinimumYPosition *value*	Set the minimum Y value
Port *path*	Specify the path to the device driver
TimeOut *timeout*	Set the time (in milliseconds) between two polls of the device driver

XFree86 Version 4

The latest version of XFree 86, version 4, is now becoming available in Linux distributions and was released just as this book was going to press; future editions will fully document the version 4 configuration file. This section highlights the most important changes from version 3.3:

Single Binary   Previous versions of XFree86 used several separate binaries designed for the various classes of video drivers and displays. In version 4, there is one XFree86 binary; it is designed to work with loadable modules so that the binary itself does not have to be uninstalled (and a different one installed subsequently) when you change video drivers.

Option Flags   Version 4 makes much more extensive use of option flags, in which you specify certain options in a subsection by typing the word Option followed by a name, surrounded in quotes. Some options also enable you to specify numeric values; again, these must be typed in quotes.

Module Section   In this section, do not specify module names with the .so extension. Be sure to load the extmod module (Load "extmod"), which is not loaded by default but contains essential code. TrueType support is enabled with Load "freetype".

Keyboard, Pointer, and Xinput Sections   These sections have been grouped together in the InputDevice section. The configuration file can contain one or more InputDevice sections, each of which defines a given input device, such as a keyboard or mouse, by means of option flags.

Specifying Color Depth at Startup   The old –**bpp** option has been replaced by –**depth** n, where n is the desired color depth (8, 15, 16, or 24).

The Monitor, Device, and Screen sections are unchanged, with a few minor exceptions. For more information on version 4 of XFree86, see the program's home page at http://www.xf86.org.

Configuring Printers

Chances are that you configured your printer when you installed your Linux distribution. Most distributions now include utilities that walk you through the process interactively. If you upgrade to a new printer, you will need to change the printer settings. To do so, it's best to use the printer configuration utility supplied with your distribution. An example is **printtool**, the utility supplied with Red Hat's Control Panel utilities. You should attempt to configure a printer manually only if your distribution lacks a printer configuration utility.

The Printing Daemon

Linux distributions use varying methods to support printers but, by far, the most common is the Berkeley Software Distribution (BSD)-derived print spooling daemon called **lpd**. Started by a script that runs automatically every time your system is booted, **lpd** begins by scanning a file called /etc/printcap. This file contains printer definitions, which must be entered in accordance with strict rules of syntax. Subsequently, **lpd** waits for requests for print services. When such requests are made, **lpd** writes the file temporarily to /var/spool and begins feeding the data to the printer. If **lpd** receives additional printing requests before the first job is finished, the daemon creates a *print queue*, a list of files waiting to be printed.

The Printer Configuration File

Printer definitions are stored in /etc/printcap. Although you can edit this file manually, you should not do so if it was created by a printer configuration utility. Should you need to make changes to your printer configuration, run the utility again. **Linuxconf**, a system administration utility discussed in this chapter, includes a printer configuration utility. You should edit this file directly only if you want to take advantage of a special printer feature that your printer configuration utility does not support.

Entries in /etc/printcap must conform to the following rules:

- Each printer definition must be entered on one line only. To make the file more readable, you can break a line with a backslash (\). Make sure you don't enter a space or Tab character after the backslash.

- The first field contains the printer's name.

- Additional fields are separated by colons and begin with a printcap variable (see the table Printcap Variables in this section).

- Some variables are Boolean and are assigned if they are present in the file. Others are assignment variables and require an equals sign, for example, sd=/var/spool/lpd/lp. Still others are numeric variables and require the numeric operator (#), as in this example: mx#0.

- The printer named lp is the default printer.

The following is an example of a valid entry for the default printer lp. A network-accessible LaserJet printer is described.

```
lp:\
:sd=/var/spool/lpd/lp:\
:mx#0:\
:sh:\
:rm=192.168.100.3:\
:rp=raw:\
:if=/var/spool/lpd/lp/filter:
```

PRINTCAP VARIABLES

Use This Variable	To Do This
af=*filename*	Specify the filename of the accounting file.
br#rate	Specify the data transfer rate for a serial printer.
fc#n	Specify the clear flag bits (*n*) for a serial printer.
ff=string	Assign the form feed string to use with the printer if other than the default (\f).
fo	Send a form feed before printing the file. This is a Boolean variable.
fs#n	Specify the set flag bits (*n*) for a serial printer.
if=*filename*	Specify the filename of an input filter that is started every time a file is printed (*see also* **of**).
lf=*filename*	Specify the filename of the log file for error messages.
lo=*filename*	Specify the filename of the lock file.
lp=*device*	Specify the device to use as a local printer.
mx#n	Set the maximum file size in blocks. Specify **mx#0** for unlimited size.
of=*filename*	Specify the filename of a filter to be applied only at the beginning of a print queue (*see also* **if**).
pc#cost	Specify the cost per page in hundredths of a cent (500 = five U.S. cents). The default is 200.
pl#lines	Specify the number of lines per page. The default is 66.
pw#width	Specify the minimum page width in characters. The default is 132.

PRINTCAP VARIABLES *(CONT.)*

Use This Variable	To Do This
px#*width*	Specify the page width in pixels.
py#*length*	Specify the page length in pixels.
rg=*group*	Restrict access to this printer to members of the specified user group.
rm=*host*	Specify the address of the host used for remote printing. Use this option for a LaserJet network adapter.
rp=*name*	Specify the name of the remote printer or printer queue that is accessed with the **rm** command. For PostScript printing with LaserJets, use `rp=raw`.
rs	Restrict remote users to those with accounts on this machine. This is a Boolean variable.
rw	Enable two-way communication with the printer. This is a Boolean variable.
sb	Print a short banner page. This is a Boolean variable.
sc	Prevent printing of multiple copies. This is a Boolean variable.
sd=*directory*	Specify the print-spooling directory.
sf	Suppress the form feed sent to the printer at the end of the print run. This is a Boolean variable.
sh	Prevent printing of the burst page header. This is a Boolean variable.
st=*filename*	Specify the status filename.
tr=*string*	Specify the string to print when the queue is finished.

Scheduling Automated Processes with *cron*

The **cron** daemon, installed by default on most Linux distributions, "wakes up" every minute to see whether the system administrator or user has scheduled any jobs for the daemon to run. If so, the daemon runs the requested job (a shell command or script).

The system administrator (root user) can schedule jobs by placing a one-line instruction in `/etc/crontab`. This instruction consists of a statement containing six fields (see the table "Fields in Crontab Files" in this section), separated by a space, such as the following:

```
0 23 * * * tar -uf backup.tar /home/suzanne
```

This command runs the specified **tar** command at 11 P.M. every evening. In addition to the permitted values listed in the "Fields in Crontab Files" table you can also use an asterisk for fields for which no value is set, a range specified with a hyphen (such as mon-fri), or a comma-separated list of values (such as 5,7,9).

If your Linux distribution uses the Vixie **cron** system, the /etc/ crontab file may contain commands such as the following:

```
59 * * * *   root   run-parts /etc/cron.hourly
* 22 * * *   root   run-parts /etc/cron.daily
* 23 * * sun     root  run-parts /etc/cron.weekly
* 20 * 2 *   root run-parts /etc/cron.monthly
```

These commands tell **cron** to run the run-parts script, located by default in /usr/bin. This script looks in the specified configuration file (such as /etc/cron.hourly) for commands to run at a given interval, such as daily or hourly.

Users can set up their own **crontab** file, located in their home directory, by running the **crontab** utility.

FIELDS IN CRONTAB FILES

Field	Description
1	Minute (0 to 59)
2	Hour (0 to 23)
3	Day of month (1 to 31)
4	Month (1 to 12 or the first three letters of the month's name)
5	Day (0 to 6, with 0 referring to Sunday, or the first three letters of the day's name)
6	Command to execute at the specified time

EXAMPLES

This Command	Does The Following
`59 * * * * rm /home/suzanne /core`	Erases core dump files from the specified directory every hour (at the 59-minute mark).
`0 23 * * * tar -uf backup.tar / home/suzanne/documents/*.sdw`	Updates a backup archive every evening at exactly 11 P.M.
`0 23 * * mon-fri tar -uf backup.tar /home/suzanne/documents/*.sdw`	Updates a backup archive at 11 P.M. each day of the week, except Saturdays and Sundays.

Rotating System Logs

Your Linux system generates a variety of system logs, which record the messages generated by the kernel and various system utilities. One such log is `/var/log/messages`. Some of these files can grow quite large over time, rendering them difficult to read. If left to grow unchecked, `/var/log/messages` can grow to many thousands of lines. The **logrotate** command, discussed in this chapter, keeps these files small by copying all the new messages added since the last rotation to a backup file and then removing this data from the file. This operation is called truncating the file.

A configuration file, generally called `/etc/logrotate.conf`, enables you to specify how to rotate the system log files. The file begins with *global commands* (commands that apply to all system log files). A subsequent section contains commands for specific log files. In both sections, you can use the commands listed in the **Logrotate** Command Options table in this section. Any line beginning with a hash mark (#) is ignored. The following illustrates a typical Global Command section in `/etc/logrotate.conf`:

```
#Global commands
#Rotate log files daily
daily
#Keep 5 days' worth of backlogs
```

```
#Compress the backlogs
compress
#Don't bug me if some log files are missing
missingok
```

This global section tells **logrotate** to rotate the log files daily, to keep five days' worth of backlogs before deleting them, to compress the backlogs, and to omit error messages if one or more logs is missing.

Sections for specific log files begin with the log file's name. Commands must be enclosed within curly braces, as in the following example:

```
/var/log/messages {
    nocompress
    rotate 7
}
```

LOGROTATE COMMAND OPTIONS

Use This Command	To Do This
compress	Compress old log files with **gzip**
copytruncate	Truncate the log file if it cannot be closed
create *mode owner group*	Create the log file with the specified mode (a numerical permission mode such as one specified with **chmod** (see Chapter 5), **owner**, and **group**
daily	Rotate the log files daily
delaycompress	Postpone compression of the previous log file until the next **logrotate** cycle
errors address	Mail errors to the specified e-mail address
extension suffix	Create log files with the specified extension after rotation
ifempty	Rotate the log file even if it is empty
include *filename*	Include the specified filename in the rotated log.
mail *address*	Mail a log to the specified e-mail address when it is rotated out of existence
mailfirst	Mail the file that has just been rotated rather than the one that is about to expire

LOGROTATE COMMAND OPTIONS *(CONT.)*

Use This Command	To Do This
maillast	Mail the file that is about to expire rather than the one that has just been rotated
missingok	Continue rotating logs, even if a log file is missing
monthly	Rotate log files monthly
nocompress	Store old log files without compression
nocopytruncate	Skip truncating the log file after copying occurs
nocreate	Omit creation of new log files
weekly	Rotate log files weekly
nodelaycompress	Compress rotated logs immediately instead of waiting until the next log cycle
nomail	Skip mailing the logs
nomissingok	Display an error message if a log is missing
noolddir	Create rotated logs in the same directory as the original logs
notifempty	Skip the log if it is empty
olddir *directory*	Write rotated logs to the specified directory
rotate *n*	Rotate log files *n* times before removing them
size *n*	Rotate logs when they exceed *n* bytes

Enabling Disk Quotas

If you are administering a system that is used by more than one person, you may wish to consider establishing disk quotas. In brief, a *disk quota* places a limit on the number of blocks (1K in size, by default) of disk space that a user may consume. There are two types of limits, a soft limit and a hard limit. When the user reaches the soft limit, a warning message is generated, and the user is given a grace period to reduce file usage. When the user reaches the hard limit, no additional data can be written. Since users could lose data if they exceed the hard limit, you may wish to leave the hard limit undefined.

Users will still receive a warning when they exceed the soft limit, and most will take steps to reduce their disk usage.

To enable disk quotas, you must modify /etc/fstab by adding one or both of the following mount options to the fourth column in this file:

usrquota   This option enables user quotas.

grpquota   This option enables group quotas.

The following is an example of /etc/fstab with user quotas enabled in one of the filesystems:

```
/dev/hda8 /       ext2    defaults            1 1
/dev/hda5 /home   ext2    defaults,usrquota   1 2
```

After adding the quota options to /etc/fstab, run **quotacheck** to generate the quota.user and quota.group files, which must be positioned at the top-level directory of each of the quota-enabled filesystems. To establish and set quotas for specific users and groups, use **edquota**. You can then turn quotas on with the **quotaon** command. To turn quotas off, use **quotaoff**.

Alphabetical Command Reference

This section details commands for the following tasks:

- Scheduling processes (**crontab**)

- Managing kernel modules (**depmod, insmod, modprobe, rmmod**)

- Launching the print spooling daemon (**lpd**)

- Choosing run levels (**runlevel**)

- Viewing and managing system logs (**dmesg, klogd, logrotate, tmpwatch**)

- Establishing and managing disk usage quotas (**edquota, quota, quotacheck, quotaoff, quotaon, repquota**)

- Managing user and group accounts (**adduser, groupadd, groupdel, groupmod, useradd, userdel, usermod**)

- Managing passwords (**grpck, mkpasswd, passwd, pwck, pwgen**)

- Compiling and installing software (**install, ldconfig, ldd, make, rpm, rpmfind**)

adduser

See **useradd**.

crontab

crontab [option]

Launches the default text editor with which you can create or edit the user's **cron** settings. See the section "Configuring Automated Processes with cron," for the syntax to use when typing **cron** statements.

TIP   Don't try to edit a user's **crontab** file directly; it will have no effect. The **crontab** utility does more than enable you to configure the user's **crontab** file. It also modifies the system so that the commands listed in the user's **crontab** file will be executed.

OPTIONS

Use This Option	To Do This
–e	Edit the current user's **crontab** settings.
–l	List the current user's **crontab** settings.
–r	Delete the current user's **crontab** settings.

depmod

depmod [option] [module]

Creates a dependency file (modules.dep) that is installed in the default modules directory /lib/modules/kernel version, where *kernel version* is the name of the currently installed Linux kernel. Constructed by scanning all available modules, this file indicates which modules depend on other modules in order to function. Once the dependency file has been created, you can use **modprobe** to load a module. If the module requires one or more additional modules in order to function, they are loaded automatically. This utility is normally run by an initialization script.

See also **modprobe**.

OPTIONS

Use This Option	To Do This
–a, – –all	Check all available modules
–e	Display unresolved dependencies
–m *filename*, **– –system-map** *filename*	Use the dependency information in the specified filename
–s, – –system-log	Output errors to the system log instead of the terminal.
–v, – –verbose	Show all messages
–V, – –version	Show the version number

dmesg

dmesg [option]

Show the system messages generated by the kernel. These include the messages displayed on-screen when you started your Linux system, as well as additional messages that may have been generated since then.

TIP Use **dmesg** with **less** (type **dmesg | less**) so that the messages do not fly by so quickly that you cannot read them.

OPTIONS

Use This Option	To Do This
–c	Clear the buffer contents.
–s *n*	Choose the buffer size to view (in bytes). The default is 8196.
–n *level*	Set the logging level.

---

edquota

edquota [option] *name*

Launches the default text editor and displays an ASCII representation of the current disk quotas for the specified user or group name. To work with more than one user or group, specify two or more names in a space-separated list. To use disk quotas, you must first enable them by adding the required mount options (**usrquota** and **grpquota**) for each filesystem for which you wish to use quotas.

See also **quotacheck, quotaoff, quotaon.**

OPTIONS

Use This Option	To Do This
–g	Edit group quotas.
–p	Establish a quota for the specified user based on the prototypical value.

OPTIONS *(CONT.)*

Use This Option	To Do This
–t	Edit the soft time limits for each filesystem. If the time limits are zero, the default time limits in <linux/ quota.h> are used. Time units of sec(onds), min(utes), hour(s), day(s), week(s), and month(s) are understood. Time limits are printed in the greatest possible time unit such that the value is greater than or equal to 1.
–u	Edit the **userquota**. This is the default.

groupadd

groupadd [option] *group name*

Create a user group with the specified group name.

See also **groupdel**.

OPTIONS

Use This Option	To Do This
–g *gid*	Create the group with the specified group ID (*gid*)
–r	Create a system account
–f	Force creation of the group even if it already exists

groupdel

groupdel *group name*

Deletes the group with the specified group name. You cannot use this command to delete the primary group of an existing user.

See also **groupmod**.

groupmod

groupmod [option] *group name*

Modifies the settings for the user group specified by group name.

OPTIONS

Use This Option	To Do This
–g *gid*	Create the group with the specified group ID (*gid*)
–n *group name*	Change the group name to the specified group name

grpck

grpck [option]

Verifies the integrity of entries in the default group password files (/etc/group and /etc/gshadow). If errors are found, this utility prompts the user to delete improper entries.

See also **pwck**.

OPTIONS

Use This Option	To Do This
–r	Verify in read-only mode which changes cannot be made to the entries

insmod

insmod [option] *module* [argument]

Installs a loadable kernel module in the kernel that is currently running. This action affects the current kernel session only. You can optionally specify arguments (such as I/O ports and IRQ numbers) that affect the module's configuration. A more recent utility, **mod-probe,** provides a versatile front end to **insmod** and offers additional capabilities.

See also **rmmod.**

OPTIONS

Use This Option	To Do This
–f	Load the module even if the kernel version and architecture do not match.
–k	Remove modules that have not been used for a period of time. By default, the time is one minute.
–m	Output a load map for debugging.
–o	Name the module rather than deriving the name from the object file.
–p	Probe the module to determine whether it can be loaded safely.
–s	Send output to the kernel log (syslog).
–v	Display all messages.

install

install [option] [*source*] [*destination*]

Copies the source file to a destination file, or multiple source files to a destination directory, and enables you to specify permissions and ownership. Superuser status is required to use this command (see **su** in Chapter 1).

See also **cp, dd.**

OPTIONS

Use This Option	To Do This
–b, – –backup	Make a backup copy of existing destination files that will be deleted by the copying operation.

OPTIONS *(CONT.)*

Use This Option	To Do This
–d, **– –directory**	Create needed directories and subdirectories when copying and set the file permissions and ownership to the specified settings or to the default settings.
– –help	Display the available options.
–g *group name*, **– –group=***group name*	Set the group ownership of the copied files and directories to the specified group name. You can use the group name or a numeric group ID.
–o *owner name*, **– –owner=***owner name*	Set the file ownership of the copied files and directories to the specified owner name. You can use the owner name or a numeric owner ID.
–m *mode*, **– –mode=***mode*	Set the permissions of the copied files and directories to the specified mode. You can use octal numbers or symbolic mode specifications (see **chmod** in Chapter 5). The default mode is 0755.
–p, **– –preserve** *–timestamps*	Preserve the source file's timestamps when copying. By default, the last access and last modification times of the copied files are set to the time of installation.
–s, **– –strip**	Remove symbol tables from installed binary executables.
–S *extension*, **– –suffix=***extension*	When used with **–b**, apply the specified extension instead of the default backup suffix ~, which is appended to filenames.
– –version	Display the version number.
–V *type*, **– –version-control=***type*	Specifies the type of backup suffix to use with **–b**. The Available types are as follows: **t, numbered** Numbered backups. **nil, existing** Numbered if numbered backups exist.

EXAMPLE

This Command	**Does the Following**
`install -o mike -g users -m 0755 ballistic /home/ mike/games`	Installs the specified file (`ballis-tic`) in **/home/mike/games**, specifying the owner (`mike`), the group (`users`), and the permissions (`0755`).

klogd

klogd [option]

Launches the kernel log daemon. Normally, this daemon is launched by an initialization script. In most configurations, the daemon displays no messages by default. Use the –c option to change the default message level (see the Message Levels table in this section).

OPTIONS

Use This Option	**To Do This**
–c *n*	Set the default message level to *n*. (See the table Message Levels in this section.)
–f *filename*	Log messages to the specified filename instead of to the system log.
–n	Avoid auto-backgrounding.
–o	Read and log kernel messages and exit.
–p	Load kernel module symbol information whenever an error is encountered.
–s	Force **klogd** to use the system call interface to the kernel message buffers.
–k *filename*	Use the specified filename as the source of kernel symbol information.
–v	Display version information.

MESSAGE LEVELS

Message Level	Description
0	Show emergency messages only
1	Show alert messages
2	Show serious errors
3	Show errors
4	Show warnings
5	Show notices about situations that should be checked
6	Show information
7	Show debugging messages

ldconfig

ldconfig [option]

Configures shared program libraries by examining the libraries found in the default library directories (/usr/lib and /lib, as well as those specified in /etc/ld.so.conf). This command is normally executed by a startup script and requires root user status.

OPTIONS

Use This Option	To Do This
–C cache	Use the specified cache instead of /etc/ld.so.cache
–D	Run in the debugging mode
–f filename	Use the specified filename as the configuration file instead of /etc/ld.so.conf
–n	Process only those directories specified on the command line.
–N	Skip rebuilding the cache but update links unless **–X** is also specified
–p	Display the directories listed in the current cache
–q	Hide program messages

OPTIONS *(CONT.)*

Use This Option	To Do This
–r *directory*	Use the specified directory as the root directory
–v	Show all messages
–X	Skip link updating but update the cache unless **–N** is also specified

ldd

ldd [option] *program | library*

Displays the shared libraries required by the specified program or library.

OPTIONS

Use This Option	To Do This
–v	Display the version number
–V	Display the version number of the dynamic linker utility (**ld.so**)

logrotate

logrotate [option] [*filename*]

Launches a utility that makes backup files of system logs, which might otherwise become so voluminous that they would take up all available disk space. The rotation schedule involves moving logs to backup files, which are retained for a specified number of rotation cycles. At the conclusion of the rotation, the backup files are deleted. **logrotate** is normally run by commands specified in the root user's **crontab** file (`/etc/crontab`). (See the section "Scheduling Maintenance Processes with cron.") By default, **logrotate** performs the rotation based on the commands found in /etc/logrotate.conf. (See the section "Rotating System Logs.")

OPTIONS

Use This Option	To Do This
–d	Run **logrotate** in debug mode.
–f, – –force	Force the rotation, even if no changes are detected in the current log files.
–s *filename*, **– –state** *filename*	Use the specified filename instead of the default state file (/var/lib/logrotate.status).
– –usage	Display command options, version number, and copyright.

lpd

lpd [option]

Launches the print spooling daemon. Normally, this is done by a system initialization script, but it can also be launched by a user. When the daemon starts, it consults the default configuration file (usually /etc/printcap); subsequently, it runs in the background, waiting for print requests.

OPTIONS

Use This Option	To Do This
–L *log file*	Use the specified log file for error and debugging messages.
–F	Force the server to run in the foreground. By default, it runs in the background.
–V	Display version information.

make

make [option] [*target*]

Compiles a program from source code following the instructions in the specified target. If you omit the target, the command looks for a file named Makefile or makefile in the working directory. Most program authors supply a configuration script (usually called *configure*) that generates the needed target in accordance with the characteristics of your system. To install programs provided in source code form, you can usually complete the installation by following these instructions:

1. Use the **tar** utility to extract the files from the source code archive.

2. Switch to the directory that **tar** created when it extracted the files.

3. Type **./configure** and press Enter.

4. Type **make** and press Enter.

5. Switch to the root user by typing **su** and pressing Enter.

6. Type **make install** and press Enter.

TIP If these instructions do not work, make sure you have installed all the needed development tools. If you're not sure, run your Linux installation utility again and select the installation options that install the development support. Should these instructions fail even though your system is equipped with the needed development libraries, check the readme and install files to see whether the installation has special requirements.

OPTIONS

Use This Option	To Do This
–C *directory*	Change to the specified directory before reading the **make** file or undertaking any other actions.
–d	Display debugging information in addition to the usual messages.

OPTIONS *(CONT.)*

Use This Option	To Do This
–e	If possible, use the current environmental variables rather than those specified in the **make** file.
–f *filename*	Use the specified filename as a **make** file.
–i	Ignore errors generated by utilities launched by the **make** file and continue processing the **make** file.
–I *directory*	Search the specified directory for included **make** files.
–j *n*	Run *n* jobs simultaneously.
–k	If possible, continue after an error.
–l *n*	Delay new jobs if the load average exceeds the specified load level (*n*).
–n	Display but do not execute the commands that would be executed.
–p	Display the rules and variable rules and then execute them.
–q	Check to see whether the targets are up to date. If so, exit without making changes.
–r	Ignore the built-in implicit rules.
–s	Hide program messages.
–t	Mark the target files as up-to-date without actually altering them.
–v	Display the version number and continue processing.
–w	Display the working directory.

mkpasswd

mkpasswd [option] [*username*]

Generates a high-quality password consisting by default of nine characters, including at least two uppercase characters, two numbers, and two lowercase characters.

OPTIONS

Use This Option	To Do This
–2	Create a password that requires alternating the right and left hands when typing, thus providing some protection against snoopers who attempt to determine what the password is by watching the user type it in.
–c *n*	Create a password with at least *n* lowercase characters. The default is 2.
–C *n*	Create a password with at least *n* uppercase characters. The default is 2.
–d *n*	Create a password with at least *n* digits. The default is 2.
–l *n*	Create a password of *n* characters. The default is 9.
–v	Show the password-setting interaction on-screen. By default, it is hidden.

modprobe

modprobe [option] [*module* [option=value] | pattern]

Loads the specified module and any required dependencies indicated by the default module dependency file, modules.dep (see **depmod**). You can specify module options, such as IRQ or DMA settings. When used with a pattern, this utility attempts to load all the modules that match the specified pattern (or a module type, specified with the –t option) until one is found that works. If you specify a module name or alias that matches an entry in /etc/conf.modules (also called /etc/modules.conf), **modprobe** uses the options and commands found in this file.

See also **insmod**.

OPTIONS

Use This Option	To Do This
–r	Remove the specified module from the kernel
–l *pattern*	List all the modules that match the specified pattern

OPTIONS *(CONT.)*

Use This Option	To Do This
–t *type*	Load only those modules of the specified type
–c	Display the current module configuration
–l	List currently available modules
–v	Show all messages
–V	Display version information
–a	Load all modules until one is found that works

EXAMPLES

This Command	Does the Following
modprobe −c	Shows the current module configuration.
modprobe −a −t sound	Attempts to load all the modules of the type sound until one is found that works.
modprobe aha152x aha152x='0x340,12,7,5'	Loads the module named aha152x and sets the option (**aha152x**) to the specified values ('0x340,12,7,5').

---

passwd

passwd [option] *username*

Enables the user specified by *username* to change the password currently assigned to the account. A user with root privileges may use this command to change any user's password.

OPTIONS

Use This Option	To Do This
–k	Update the expired passwords only.
–l	Lock this account and make it accessible to the root user only. Requires root user status.

OPTIONS *(CONT.)*

Use This Option	To Do This
–u	Unlock the account so that it is open for use by a user without root privileges. Requires root user status.
–d	Disable the password for an account by removing the password. Requires root user status.
–S	Display the account status. Requires root user status.

pwck

pwck [–r]

Examines all the passwords in the default password files (/etc/passwd and /etc/shadow) to make sure they do not contain errors. If errors are found, the user is prompted to correct them. Use the –r option to run the command in a *test mode* (no changes are made to the password files).

pwgen

pwgen *length* [*count*]

Generates a high-quality password (one that combines uppercase and lowercase letters, as well as numbers) that may be pronounceable and, therefore, easy to remember. Specify the length by typing a number. You should create a password of at least six characters. Optionally, specify a count (a number) to generate more than one password. If **pwgen** is not installed on your system, you can obtain a copy from http://metalab.unc.edu/pub/Linux/system/security.

quota

quota [option] *name*

Displays the current disk usage and limits for the specified user or group name. Root user status is required to view other user's quotas. To view quota information, quotas must be enabled (see **edquota**).

See also **repquota, quotacheck, quotaoff, quotaon.**

OPTIONS

Use This Option	To Do This
–g	Display group quotas
–q	Use a concise display format
–v	Display quotas on filesystems where no storage is allocated

quotacheck

quotacheck [option] [*filesystem*]

Scans filesystems for which disk quotas are enabled in /etc/fstab and outputs the quota files for the specified filesystem. Or, with the –a option, it outputs all the quota-enabled filesystems. These files are named quota.user (for user quotas) and quota.group (for group quotas). They are positioned at the top-level directory for each of the enabled filesystems. To enable quotas for users, add **usrquota** to the fourth column (**mount** options) of /etc/fstab. To enable quotas for groups, add **grpquota**.

See also edquota, repquota, quotacheck, quotaoff, quotaon.

OPTIONS

Use This Option	To Do This
–g	Scan for group quotas and create quota.group. By default, **quotacheck** scans for only user quotas unless you use the **–a** option.
–a[R]	Scan all the filesystems for which user or group quotas are enabled in /etc/fstab and create quote.user and quote.group for each quota-enabled filesystem. To exclude the root filesystem, use the **–R** option.
–v	Show all available messages.

EXAMPLES

This Command	Does the Following
quotacheck -av	Scans for disk usage by all users and groups and creates `quota.user` and `quota.group` for each of the quota-enabled filesystems.
quotacheck -v /home	Scans the specified filesystem (`/home`) for disk usage by all users and creates `quota.user` for this filesystem if it is quota-enabled.

quotaoff

quotaoff [option] *filesystem*

Disables user and group file storage quotas for the specified filesystem. Requires root user status.

See also **repquota, quota, quotacheck, quotaoff, quotaon.**

OPTIONS

Use This Option	To Do This
−a	Disable quotas on all filesystems listed as read or write in `/etc/fstab`
−g	Disable group quotas only
−u	Disable user quotas only
−v	Show all messages

quotaon

quotaon [option] *filesystem*

Enables user and group file storage quotas for the specified filesystem according to the configuration information found in the binary configuration files, which are created with **edquota**. The required binary quota files (`quota.user` and `quota.group`) must be present within the root directory of the specified filesystem. Requires root user status.

See also **repquota, quota, quotacheck, quotaoff, quotaon.**

OPTIONS

Use This Option	To Do This
–a	Enable quotas on all filesystems marked as read or write in `/etc/fstab`.
–g	Enable group quotas only.
–u	Enable user quotas only. This is the default setting.
–v	Show all messages.

repquota

repquota [option] [*filesystem*]

Displays the disk usage and quotas for the specified filesystem. Or, with the –a option, displays all filesystems marked as read or write in `/etc/fstab`. Requires root user status to view quotas other than the user's.

See also **edquota, quota, quotacheck, quotaoff, quotaon.**

OPTIONS

Use This Option	To Do This
–a	Report on all read or write filesystems
–g	Report group quotas
–v	Display all quotas, even if there is no usage

rmmod

rmmod [option] *module*

Removes the specified module from the kernel.

OPTIONS

Use This Option	To Do This
−a	Remove all unused modules
−r	Remove the specified modules and all modules linked by the module dependency database
−s	Route output to the system log instead of the display

rpm

rpm [option] [*package*]

Launches the Red Hat Package Manager, a utility that can install, query, verify, update, and uninstall packages with the suffix .rpm that have been prepared with this utility. Although **rpm** is designed for use on Red Hat systems, the code is open source and is used on several other distributions. See the table "An Overview of the Basic Options" for a summary of the basic commands used to install, upgrade, query, and uninstall packages. Additional options are found in the General Options, Install Options, Query Options, Information Selection Options, Verify Options, and Uninstall Options tables. This utility can also be used to build RPM packages from source code (see the table Build Options). Version 3.04 is documented here. The utility's home page is located at http://www.rpm.org.

AN OVERVIEW OF THE BASIC OPTIONS

Use This Option	To Do This
−b, **−t**	Build a package
−e, **− −erase**	Uninstall the package
−F, **− −freshen**	Upgrade the package, but only if a previous version is already installed
−i, **− −install**	Install the package
−q, **− −query**	Query the package
−U, **− −upgrade**	Upgrade the package

AN OVERVIEW OF THE BASIC OPTIONS *(CONT.)*

Use This Option	To Do This
–v	Show messages while the program runs
–V, –y, – –verify	Verify the package

GENERAL OPTIONS

Use This Option	To Do This
– –dbpath *path name*	Use the RPM database in the path name.
– –ftpport *port*, **– –httpport** *port*	Use the specified port for an FTP or Web connection.
– –ftpproxy *host*, **– –httpproxy** *host*	Use the specified host for an FTP or Web connection.
– –help	Display the available options.
– –justdb	Update the database but not the filesystem.
– –pipe *command*	Pipe the output to the specified command.
– –quiet	Hide most messages.
– –rcfile *filename*	Obtain the configuration information from the specified filename. The default file list is `/usr/lib/rpm/rpmrc:/etc/rpmrc:~/.rpmrc`.
– –root *directory*	Use the system rooted at the specified directory for all operations.
– –version	Show the version number.
–vv	Show debugging information.

INSTALL OPTIONS

Use This Option	To Do This
– –allfiles	Install all the files in the package that are missing from the package.
– –badreloc	Force a relocation even if the package is not relocatable.
– –excludedocs	Exclude documentation files from the install.

INSTALL OPTIONS *(CONT.)*

Use This Option	To Do This
– –excludepath *path name*	Exclude files beginning with *path name*.
– –force	Force the install. This is the same as using **– –replacepkgs**, **– –replacefiles**, and **– –oldpackage**.
–h, **– –hash**	Show a progress bar.
– –ignorearch	Proceed with the installation even if the system architecture does not match.
– –ignoreos	Proceed with installation even if the package's operating system does not match the current system.
– –ignoresize	Omit the search for sufficient disk space.
– –includedocs	Install documentation files. This is the default setting.
– –nodeps	Skip the dependency check.
– –noorder	Skip re-ordering the files before the installation.
– –noscripts	Skip the pre-install and post-install scripts.
– –notriggers	Omit the execution of scripts included in the package.
– –oldpackage	Replace a newer package with an older one.
– –percent	Show progress as a percentage.
– –prefix *directory*	Install the package in the specified directory.
– –relocate *old directory new directory*	Install packages intended for the old directory in the new directory.
– –replacefiles	Replace files even if they already exist.
– –replacepkgs	Install all the packages even if some of them are already installed on this system.
– –test	Check for and report potential conflicts.
–U	Upgrade the package to a new version.

QUERY OPTIONS

Use This Option	To Do This
–a, **– –all**	Query all installed packages.
–c, **– –configfiles**	List only configuration files.
– –changelog	Display change information for the package.
–d, **– –docfiles**	List documentation files only.
– –dump	Show the following information: path name, file size, modification time, MD5 checksum, mode, owner, group, isconfig, isdoc, redev, and symlink. Used with one of these options: **–l**, **–c**, and **–d**.
–f *filename*, **– –file** *filename*	Query the package that owns the specified filename.
– –filesbypkg	List all the files in each package.
–g *group*, **– –group** *group*	Query packages with the specified group.
–l, **– –list**	List files in the package.
– –last	Install the latest packages first.
package	Query the package.
– –provides	List the capabilities that this package provides.
–p *package*	Query the specified package file.
– –querybynumber *n*	Query the *n*th database directory.
–R, **– –requires**	List the packages on which this package depends.
–s, **– –state**	Display the states of files in the package.
– –scripts	List the package-specific shell scripts that are used as part of the installation and uninstallation processes.
– –specfile *spec file*	Parse and query the specified spec file as if it were a package.
– –triggeredby *package*	Query the specified package.
– –triggers, **– –triggerscripts**	Display trigger scripts.

QUERY OPTIONS *(CONT.)*

– –triggerscripts	Show all the trigger scripts for the selected packages.
– –whatprovides *virtual*	Query all packages that provide the virtual capability.
– –whatrequires *capability*	Query all packages that require capability for proper functioning.

VERIFY OPTIONS

Use This Option	To Do This
– –nofiles	Ignore missing files when verifying
– –nomd5	Ignore MD5 checksum errors when verifying
– –nopgp	Ignore PGP checking errors when verifying
– –checksig *package*	Check the digital signature of the specified package

UNINSTALL OPTIONS (–e)

Use This Option	To Do This
– –allmatches *package*	Remove all versions of the package that match *package*
– –nodeps	Omit the dependency check
– –noscripts	Skip the pre-uninstallation and post-uninstallation scripts
– –notriggers	Skip scripts triggered by the package's removal
– –test	Test the uninstallation without actually removing files

BUILD OPTIONS (–b)

Use This Option	To Do This
–ba	Build binary and source packages
–bb	Build a binary package

BUILD OPTIONS (–b) *(CONT.)*

Use This Option	To Do This
–bc	Build the package based on the spec file
–bi	Install the package based on the spec file
–bl	Check to make sure all needed files exist
–bp	Execute the preparation stage from the spec file
–bs	Build the source package but not the binaries
– –buildroot *directory*	Use the specified directory instead of the default BuildRoot directory
– –clean	Remove the build tree after the packages are made
– –rebuild	Rebuild the source package
– –recompile	Install the source package with a complete recompile
– –rmsource	Remove the sources and spec file after the build
– –short-circuit	Skip straight to the specified stage
– –sign	Sign the package with a PGP signature
– –target *architecture vendor OS*	Create the package for the specified architecture, vendor, and OS (operating system)
– –test	Test without actually building
– –timecheck *n*	Specify the maximum age *n* (in seconds) of the file being packaged

REBUILD DATABASE OPTIONS

Use This Option	To Do This
rpm – –initdb	Build a new database
rpm – –rebuilddb	Rebuild an existing database

EXAMPLES

This Command	Does the Following
`rpm -ivh newpackage.rpm`	Installs the specified package (**newpackage.rpm**), which has never been installed before.
`rpm -Uvh newversion.rpm`	Upgrades the specified package (**newversion.rpm**) or installs the package if no previous version is found.
`rpm -Fvh newversion.rpm`	Upgrades the specified package (**newversion.rpm**) only if a previous version exists.
`rpm -ivh --nodeps new-package.rpm`	Installs the specified package (**newpackage.rpm**), ignoring package dependencies.
`rpm -ivh --force new-package.rpm`	Installs the specified package (**newpackage.rpm**), overwriting packages and files as necessary.
`rpm -e unwanted`	Uninstalls the specified package (**unwanted**).
`rpm -Uvh --oldversion installed-program oldpackage.rpm`	Upgrades the currently installed package (**installed-program**) to an earlier version (**oldpackage.rpm**)
`rpm -q installed-program`	Shows the version number of the specified installed package (**installed-program**).
`rpm -qa`	Shows a list of all installed packages.
`rpm -qa | grep -i string`	Shows a list of only those installed packages that contain the specified string.

rpmfind

rpmfind [option] *package*

Searches an Internet-accessible database of RPM packages for the specified package. By default, the utility searches http://rpmfind.org. You can specify a different server using the –s option. Version 1.4 is documented here. If this utility is not installed on your system, you can obtain the latest version from http://www.rpm.org.

OPTIONS

Use This Option	To Do This
– –apropos *keyword*	Browse through the RPM database looking for all packages that include the specified keyword in their description tag
– –auto	Perform the transfer without confirmation
–h	List all the available options
– –latest	Fetch the latest available package
– –source	Look for the source package
–s *URL*	Change the default server to the specified URL
– –upgrade	Suggest upgrades for the requested package and all dependencies
–v	Show available messages

EXAMPLES

This Command	Does the Following
`rpmfind --apropos gqview`	Shows all packages that contain the specified string (**gqview**) anywhere in their descriptions.
`rpmfind --latest ghostview`	Shows the latest available version of the specified package (**ghostview**).
`rpmfind --upgrade ghostview`	Finds an upgrade for the specified package (**ghostview**), if available.

runlevel

runlevel [*filename*]

Reports the current system run level, as disclosed by the default run level configuration file (/var/run/utmp) or the specified configuration filename.

tmpwatch

tmpwatch [option] [*n*] [*directory*]

Remove all the files in the specified directory if they have not been accessed in *n* hours. This command cleans up temporary directories, such as those in /tmp, and prevents them from consuming inordinate amounts of disk space.

OPTIONS

Use This Option	To Do This
–u, **– –atime**	Use the time of last access to decide whether to delete the file. This is the default setting.
–m, **– –mtime**	Use the time of last modification to decide whether to delete the file.
–a, **– –all**	Remove all file types not just regular files and directories.
–f, **– –force**	Remove files even if root doesn't have write access.
– –test	Display the files that would be removed without actually deleting them.
–v	Show all messages.

useradd

useradd [option] *username*

useradd – –D [option] *username*

Creates a new user (or updates an existing user) with the specified username. When you create a new user account, this command automatically configures the appropriate system files and copies the files found in /etc/skel. Use the **–m** option to create a new home directory (named /home/username). See the table Account Creation Options for the options you can use when you create a new account.

When used with the –D option, this command enables you to update existing user accounts. See the table Account Updating Options for the options you can use in this mode.

See also **userdel.**

TIP   To determine whether your system creates user's home directories by default, when you run **useradd**, examine /etc/login.defs. If you see the line CREATE_HOME yes, **useradd** will automatically create a new home directory for each new user and will copy all the files found in /etc/skel to this directory.

ACCOUNT CREATION OPTIONS

Use This Option	To Do This
–c *comment*	Insert the specified comment in the user's profile.
–d *directory*	Create the user's home directory with the specified directory name instead of the default (/home/**username**).
–e *date*	Expire the account on the specified date. The date is specified in the format *YYYY-MM-DD*.
–f *days*	Disable the account after the password has been inactive for the specified number of days.
–g *group*	Add the user to the specified initial login group.
–G *group*	Add the user to the specified supplementary group. To add the user to more than one group, type group names in a comma-separated list.
–m	If this option is not configured by default in /etc/login.defs, create the user's home directory and copy to this directory the files found in /etc/skel.
–M	Skip creating the home directory, even if automatic home creation is enabled by default in /etc/login.defs.
–n	Skip creating a group with the same name as the new user.

ACCOUNT CREATION OPTIONS *(CONT.)*

Use This Option	To Do This
–r	Create a system account with a numerical user ID lower than the minimum number for user account IDs specified in `/etc/login.defs`.
–p *password*	Use the specified password. If you omit this option, **useradd** will create the account but will not enable it.
–s *shell*	Assign the user the specified shell by default. If you omit this option, the account uses the systemwide default shell.
–u *uid*	Create the account with the specified numerical user ID (*uid*).

ACCOUNT UPDATING OPTIONS

Use This Option	To Do This
–b *prefix*	Create a new home directory for the user with the specified directory prefix.
–e *date*	Expire the account on the specified date.
–f *days*	Disable the account on the specified number of days after the password expires.
–g *group*	Add the user to the specified initial login group.
–s *shell*	Assign the user the specified shell by default. If you omit this option, the account uses the systemwide default shell.

userdel

userdel [–r] *username*

Deletes the user with the specified username. Use the –r option to delete the user's home directory and all the files within it.

See also **usermod.**

usermod

usermod [option] *username*

Modifies the settings of the user specified by *username*.

See also **userdel.**

OPTIONS

Use This Option	To Do This
– –**b** *prefix*	Create a new home directory for the user with the specified directory prefix.
–**c** *comment*	Insert the specified comment in the user's profile.
–**d** *directory*	Create the user's home directory with the specified directory name instead of the default (/**home**/**username**).
– –**e** *date*	Expire the account on the specified date.
– –**f** *days*	Disable the account on the specified number of days after the password expires.
– –**g** *group*	Add the user to the specified initial login group.
–**L**	Lock the user's password so that it cannot be used.
–**p** *password*	Use the specified password. If you omit this option, **useradd** will create the account but will not enable it.
– –**s** *shell*	Assign the user the specified shell by default. If you omit this option, the account uses the systemwide default shell.
–**U**	Unlock the user's password so that it can be used again.
–**u** *uid*	Create the account with the specified numerical user ID (*uid*).

CHAPTER 13

Configuring and Using
Networks and the Internet

This chapter covers the essential concepts and commands required to connect a Linux workstation to the Internet by means of dial-up PPP or Ethernet (LAN) connections. Also covered are the concepts and commands of Network File System (NFS) and Samba networking.

Although this chapter provides information on configuring Internet (TCP/IP) settings manually, be aware that Linux distributions vary in how they record essential configuration information. They also use varying scripts to launch the required networking daemons. For this reason, you should use your Linux distribution's network configuration utility, such as Red Hat's version of **linuxconf**, to configure your Internet connection. You may have already used this utility when you installed your Linux distribution. If not, consult your distribution's manual to determine how to run the utility after installation. Still, some of these utilities require some tweaking of the underlying configuration files in order to get the connection working properly. Even if you do not choose to configure your Internet connection manually, the information in this chapter should prove useful if such modifications are required.

NOTE Many of the commands in this chapter have especially voluminous lists of options, but many of these are of interest only to programmers or professional TCP/IP administrators. Accordingly, this chapter lists only the options useful for this book's intended audience, namely, a user running Linux on a single-user workstation that is connected to the Internet by means of a dial-up or LAN connection.

AT A GLANCE

How Do I	See This Entry	Example
View the current configuration for all active network interfaces?	**ifconfig**	ifconfig

AT A GLANCE *(CONT.)*

How Do I	See This Entry	Example
Display information about all the TCP/IP sockets currently in operation?	**netstat**	netstat -a
Look up the numerical address for a domain name?	**nslookup**	nslookup www.yahoo.com
Determine whether external Internet services are available?	**ping**	ping www.yahoo.com
Copy a file to a remote server (for which I have appropriate permissions)?	**rpc**	rcp essay1.doc essay1 .bak@lothlorien:/home/ suzanne/Documents/ Backup
Determine whether the NFS daemons are running?	**rpcinfo**	rpcinfo -p
View available NFS shares?	**showmount**	showmount -a
Mount a Samba share on a remote system?	**smbmount**	smbmount //lothlorien/ suzanne /home/suzanne/ lothlorien
Display the status of Samba networking?	**smbstatus**	smbstatus -d
Unmount a remote Samba share?	**smbumount**	smbumount //lothlorien/ suzanne /home/suzanne/ lothlorien
Connect to a remote Telnet service?	**telnet**	telnet lothlorien .mynetwork.org

Configuring Networking and Internet Settings

Linux includes a full implementation of the *TCP/IP protocol suite,* the communication standards that underlie the operation of the public Internet. You can also use TCP/IP to set up internal networks (called *local area networks* or LANs) that use the same protocols. To connect your Linux system to a computer network using TCP/IP, you need a network interface device, such as an Ethernet adapter or a modem. Fast Internet services, such as ISDN, cable services, and Digital Subscriber Line (DSL), frequently use adapters that present themselves as if they were Ethernet adapters. You can easily connect to these services by configuring your Linux system as if you were connecting to an Internet-enabled Ethernet.

This section begins with a brief explanation of the fundamental concepts of TCP/IP network. It then turns to the specifics of configuring TCP/IP networking on your system, including the use of the Network File System (NFS) to exchange files with other Linux or Unix systems, as well as the use of Samba (SMB networking) to exchange files with Microsoft Windows systems. The next section details the specifics of network interfaces.

TIP   Linux distributions configure basic TCP/IP settings in varying ways. Most enable you to supply TCP/IP network settings when you install the distribution. After installing Linux, you can modify the configuration using vendor-supplied tools, such as **netcfg** (a utility supplied with Red Hat Linux and other distributions). Consult your Linux distribution's documentation to learn which utility to use to configure TCP/IP networking on your system.

Essential TCP/IP Concepts

This section introduces the fundamental concepts of TCP/IP networking as they are implemented in the Linux environment, including IP addresses, address classes, netmasks and network addresses, broadcast and gateway addresses, the domain name system and DNS servers, network interfaces, services, and ports. The intention here is to provide a concise statement of this fundamental knowledge for the purpose of configuring a Linux workstation. For TCP/IP network administration, further study of TCP/IP routing and routing protocols is required.

IP Addresses

Every device that is fully connected to the Internet is called a *host,* and each such device must have a unique Internet address (also called an IP address). An IP address is a four-byte number, called a *dotted quad,* written using decimal equivalents, with each number separated by a dot, such as 192.168.100.44.

Each IP address begins with a portion that is shared by all the hosts within a network; this section is called the *network portion.* The remaining portion of the IP address identifies unique hosts within the network. This portion is called the *host portion.*

Address Classes

Internet addresses are divided into *classes* for administrative purposes. *Class A* networks have IP addresses that begin with a number that is less than 128. *Class B* networks have IP addresses that begin with 128 through 191. *Class C* networks have IP addresses that begin with 192 through 223. These networks vary in the number of hosts that they can accommodate. For example, class A networks can have millions of hosts, while class B networks can have a maximum of 65,534 hosts, and class C networks are limited to 254 hosts.

Some IP addresses are reserved for special uses. In all network classes, host number 0 is reserved for the network address, while host number 255 is reserved for the broadcast address. In addition, the following addresses are reserved:

127.0.0.1 This address, called the *loopback address,* is reserved so that a host can address itself.

10.0.0.0 This network address is reserved for private, internal networks that can accommodate millions of hosts.

172.16.0.0 This network address is reserved for private, internal networks that can accommodate thousands of hosts.

192.168.0.0 This network address is reserved for private, internal networks that can accommodate up to 254 hosts.

Netmasks and Network Addresses

Where does the network portion end, and where does the host portion begin? To determine this, you need to know the *netmask*. The netmask is another four-byte number; like an IP address, it is written with four decimal numbers, separated by dots. However, the netmask can contain only two numbers: 0 and 255. The number 255 is used to specify those portions of the address that make up the network portion, while the *0* is used to specify the portions of the address that make up the host portion. If the netmask is 255.255.255.0 and the IP address is 192.168.100.44, the network portion is 192.168.100, while the host portion is the last of the four numbers in the address. Additionally, the *network address* is the lowest possible address available for a host in the network. In the previous example, the network address is 192.168.100.0.

Broadcast Address

In addition to the addresses already mentioned, a given network has a *broadcast address*. This is the address that is monitored by every workstation on the network. By convention, the broadcast address is typically the network address with a final decimal value of 255. For the network with an address of 192.168.100.0, the broadcast address is 192.168.100.255.

Gateway Address

If your computer is connected to a local area network with access to the external Internet, or to another private network, you will need to know about yet another type of IP address: the *gateway address*. The gateway address is the IP address of the device that provides access to external networks. For example, suppose your local area network is connected to an ISDN adapter and router, which enables all the computers on your network to access the external Internet. The IP address of this device is 192.168.100.7. This is the *gateway address* for your network. To access the external Internet, you will need to configure each machine on the network so that it knows the gateway address. See the section "/etc/sysconfig/network" for more information about configuring Linux systems to use a gateway address.

Domain Name Service (DNS) and Domain Names

As the previous section explained, every host connected to a TCP/IP network has its own, unique IP address. However, IP addresses are difficult for people to work with. Moreover, a given machine's address may change if it is connected to a different network. The *domain name service (DNS)* solves this problem by mapping people-friendly *domain names*, such as www.yahoo.com, to specific IP addresses.

The domain name service is a worldwide service that involves the use of servers at many levels. However, the DNS server of greatest importance to you is the default DNS server for your network. If you connect to the Internet by means of a dial-up (modem) connection, you need to know the IP address of your Internet service provider's DNS server. If you are connecting to a private, internal network, you need to know the IP address of the computer that is running the DNS service locally.

Network Interfaces

To connect your Linux system to a TCP/IP network, you need to assign IP addresses to *network interfaces*. In brief, a network interface is a device, such as an Ethernet card or modem, that enables your computer to connect to a TCP/IP network. In Linux, network interfaces are created by the modules that support the device in question. For example, when **modprobe** detects an Ethernet card, it assigns the network interface *eth0* to the first detected card, *eth1* to the second detected card, and so on. Similarly, if you connect to the Internet by means of a modem running the PPP protocol, the software that supports your modem assigns the network interface *ppp0* to the first detected modem, *ppp1* to the second, and so on.

Although the software that supports networking peripherals assigns network interfaces automatically, you still need to associate each network interface with an IP address. Addresses can be assigned in two ways, *statically* or *dynamically*. In static addressing, you type the IP address that the network interface will use. In dynamic addressing, the IP address is automatically determined by services such as bootp or dhcp. If you plan to connect your Linux system to a local area network (LAN), ask the network administrator what type of address to use. If you are connecting to an Internet service provider using the PPP protocol, you will probably use dynamic addressing.

Network Services and Ports

TCP/IP uses a *client/server* design, in which network applications require two different types of programs. Users make use of a *client* program to obtain data of a particular type, such as FTP (for files located on the network), Web pages, or e-mail. *Servers* make a certain type of information available to clients. Although it's quite possible to run clients and servers on the same machine, the more usual arrangement is that users run clients on their machines and obtain data from the network by contacting servers running on other machines. Generally provided by means of a *daemon* running in the background, server software provides a distinctive type of TCP/IP service. If you are running FTP, Web, and mail servers, these three services are available from your computer.

So that TCP/IP can route incoming and outgoing signals to the various services correctly, TCP/IP associates a given type of networking service with a *well-known port,* a number that stands for a virtual electronic interface. For example, FTP is associated with port 21, while the Web servers are associated with port 80. The file called /etc/services lists all the ports that are defined for use on your system.

Disabling Unneeded Servers

Because Linux comes with a variety of powerful, built-in servers, it is deservedly popular among organizations looking for low-cost server solutions. However, most of the readers of this book have no need to run server software. Nevertheless, Linux distributions may install and enable a variety of servers, and these may be running without the user being aware of this fact. Poorly configured or out-of-date servers could present potential intruders with a means of gaining unauthorized access to a Linux system. For this reason, it is a good practice to determine which TCP/IP servers are running on your system. Furthermore, you should disable any services that you do not need.

To determine whether any TCP/IP services are running on your system, switch to superuser, type **ps −A**, and press Enter. You may find that certain server daemons are indeed running on your system, such as systat, netstat, ftpd (FTP), telnetd (Telnet), httpd (Web), sendmail (e-mail), or named (DNS). If you do not need these services, it is best to disable them. Some Linux distributions provide utilities for this purpose, such as the Control Center in Red Hat Linux.

Alternatively, you can disable individual network services by placing a hash mark (#) before their entries in /etc/inetd.conf, a portion of which is shown here:

```
#
# These are standard services.
#
ftp stream tcp nowait root /usr/sbin/
 tcpd in.ftpd −l −a
telnet stream tcp nowait root /usr/sbi/
n/tcpd in.telnetd
finger stream tcp nowait nobody /usr/sbin/
tcpd in.fingerd
```

Note that several TCP/IP services are enabled in this file, including Telnet, FTP, and finger. Should you wish to disable any of these services, type a hash mark at the beginning of the line on which the service's configuration is entered, save the file, and restart your system. To restart TCP/IP services after making this change, type **killall −HUP inetd** and press Enter.

Basic TCP/IP Configuration

As stressed in the beginning of this chapter, the best way to configure TCP/IP networking for your computer is to use the network configuration utility provided with your Linux distribution. If TCP/IP support is already enabled, you can configure TCP/IP manually by making changes to the configuration files that we will discuss next. You may also wish to configure TCP/IP manually if, for some reason, the configuration utility failed to configure your system properly. You may also wish to do so if your system has an unusual or unique configuration.

Required Information

To configure your computer properly, you should obtain the following information from your network administrator or your Internet service provider:

Domain name   This is the registered name of the domain to which you are connecting. For example, if you are connecting to an ISP named cstone.net, your domain name is cstone.net. If you are connecting to the University of Virginia's local area network, your domain name is virginia.edu.

Hostname   The name you should assign to your computer. The name should consist of two parts, separated by a dot. The first part is a unique name that is not taken by any other computer on the network to which you are connecting. The second part is the network *domain name*. An example of a valid domain name is bpmac.seas.virginia.edu.

IP address   If your computer requires a static IP address, obtain this address; you'll need to supply it to the various configuration files. If you're connecting via a modem to an Internet service provider, chances are that you'll be given a dynamic IP address each time you connect to the ISP's computer.

Gateway device   If you're connecting to a local area network that uses a gateway device (such as a bridge, router, ISDN router, or some other device), you'll need the device's IP address.

Search domain and DNS servers   The *search domain* defines the default domain to search for IP addresses. Generally, this is the same as the domain name. You'll probably be given two DNS server addresses, one IP address each for the *primary nameserver* and the *secondary nameserver*.

Netmask   If you are connecting to a Class C network, the default netmask is 255.255.255.0. The default for Class B networks is 255.255.0.0. On large local area networks that are professionally administered, you may be given a netmask other than the default. Such a netmask is used for internal purposes to set up a *subnet,* a portion of the network that has been differentiated as a separate unit.

Network Interfaces */etc/sysconfig*

In most Linux distributions, network interfaces are defined by scripts placed in the /etc/sysconfig/network-scripts directory. For example, the following script (called ifcfg-eth0) defines the network interface for eth0 (the first detected Ethernet card). It does so by specifying the boot protocol (the options are static, bootp, or dhcp), the broadcast address, the adapter's IP address, the default netmask, the network address, and the startup option (yes means that the interface is automatically activated when your system is booted):

```
DEVICE=eth0
   BOOTPROTO=static
   BROADCAST=192.168.100.255
   IPADDR=192.168.100.10
   NETMASK=255.255.255.0
   NETWORK=192.168.100.0
   ONBOOT=yes
```

Although you can edit such scripts manually, your best course of action lies in using your Linux distribution's default network configuration utility to define basic network interfaces.

/etc/sysconfig/network

The most basic TCP/IP configuration file, /etc/sysconfig/network, enables TCP/IP networking and defines basic networking settings. This file may be located in a directory other than /etc/sysconfig on some Linux distributions. A typical /etc/sysconfig/network file contains the following:

```
NETWORKING=yes
   FORWARD_IPV4=no
   HOSTNAME=lothlorien.mydomain.org
   GATEWAY=192.168.100.7
   GATEWAYDEV=
```

This first line in this file specifies that TCP/IP networking is enabled, but the second turns IP forwarding off. These settings are appropriate for a single-user workstation that is connected to a LAN or the external Internet. The HOSTNAME line specifies the name of this computer as it is defined for TCP/IP purposes. The GATEWAY line contains the IP address of the gateway device, if any, that is used to access the external Internet. This line is not needed if you are accessing the Internet by means of a modem.

/etc/hosts

One of several essential TCP/IP configuration files, /etc/hosts indicates the IP addresses of the computer's loopback interface and that of the default network interface. A typical /etc/hosts file looks like the following:

```
127.0.0.1    localhost.localdomain localhost
   192.168.100.10 lothlorien.mydomain.org lothlorien
```

For each line, the first column indicates the IP address (such as 127.0.0.1). The second indicates the *fully qualified domain name* (FQDN) of the host that is being defined (for the loopback interface, *localhost.localdomain* is the default). The third column indicates *aliases* that can be used to refer to this host.

If you are setting up a small, internal network and do not wish to run a DNS server, you can configure your network by adding to this file all the IP addresses, FQDNs, and aliases of the machines on your network. The following defines a network with five hosts in addition to the local host:

```
127.0.0.1    localhost.localdomain localhost
   192.168.100.10 lothlorien.mydomain.org lothlorien
   192.168.100.11 rivendell.mydomain.org rivendell
   192.168.100.12 gondor.mydomain.org gondor
   192.168.100.13 mordor.mydomain.org mordor
   192.168.100.14 laserjet.mydomain.org laserjet
```

/etc/HOSTNAME

This file should contain your computer's fully qualified domain name (FQDN), which should match the entry in /etc/hosts. For example, if /etc/hosts assigns lothlorien.mydomain.org to the machine located at 192.168.100.10, /etc/HOSTNAME must contain lothlorien.mydomain.org.

/etc/host.conf

Another essential TCP/IP configuration file, /etc/host.conf defines the order in which TCP/IP attempts to resolve domain names. In domain name resolution, the TCP/IP software tries to find the numerical IP address equivalent of a fully qualified domain name, such as www.yahoo.com, or an alias, such as rivendell. A typical /etc/host .conf file contains the following, which will suffice for most systems:

```
order hosts,bind
    multi on
```

These lines tell the TCP/IP software to check the /etc/hosts file first. If the needed information is not available there, the software uses the domain name service (DNS). In addition, the software retrieves all the available addresses for the requested host, not just the first one that is encountered.

/etc/resolv.conf

If your network will access the external Internet, or if you're connecting to a local area network that is running a domain name service, you need to tell your system the address of a domain name server. To do so, add the needed information to /etc/resolv.conf. For example, suppose you are connecting to the Internet by dialing your Internet service provider (ISP). Your ISP tells you that you should configure your system to access a *primary nameserver* (206.205.42.2) and a *secondary nameserver* (206.205.42.254). You're also told that your *search domain,* the domain TCP/IP uses to look for assistance in resolving IP addresses, is cstone.net. Your /etc/resolve.conf file will look like this:

```
domain cstone.net
    search cstone.net
    nameserver 206.205.42.2
    nameserver 206.205.42.254
```

/etc/hosts.allow and */etc/hosts.deny*

To help prevent unauthorized intrusions into your system, you should configure the file called /etc/hosts.allow so that only the hosts connected to your internal network, if any, are allowed to access TCP/IP services on your computer. You can do so by modifying /etc/hosts.allow and /etc/hosts.deny as explained in this chapter.

The file called /etc/hosts.allow lists the names of hosts that are allowed to access TCP/IP services on your computer. If you are connecting to a local area network in which all the other users are trustworthy, you can make your computer available to all the hosts on the network by typing the first three values of the network's IP address, followed by a period, as in the following example:

```
192.168.100.
```

Any of the machines connected to this network can access TCP/IP services on your computer. When you define /etc/hosts.allow, don't forget to grant access to the local host. To do so, type a space after the abbreviated network address, a colon, another space, and **127.**, as in the following example:

```
128.168.100. : 127.
```

The file called /etc/hosts.deny lists the hosts that are specifically denied access to TCP/IP services running on your computer. The safest way to configure this file is to type the following:

```
ALL:ALL
```

This configuration denies access to all hosts, except those specifically granted permission in /etc/hosts.allow.

Network File System (NFS) Configuration

The *Network File System (NFS)* is the native Linux networking system. NFS allows Linux systems to share directories and files over the network. The result, from the user's point of view, is a single, seamless filesystem, in which the remote directories seem like natural extensions of the filesystem that's physically present on the user's system. However, note that NFS has several disadvantages. Improperly configured, NFS can open security holes that a knowledgeable intruder could exploit. In addition, NFS does not provide a straightforward method to integrate Microsoft Windows 95/98/NT systems; if you would like to include Windows machines in your network, see the section "Configuring Samba Networking," later in this chapter.

Configuring NFS: An Overview

To get NFS working successfully, you must do the following:

1. Make sure that your user and group IDs match on the client and server systems.

2. On the server, modify /etc/hosts.allow and /etc/hosts.deny so that the server will accept portmap requests from clients on your network.

3. On the server, create or modify the file /etc/exports so that the server will make specified directories available to other machines on the network.

4. On the client, modify /etc/fstab so that the client will automatically load the exported directories when you start the client system.

User and Group IDs

NFS won't work smoothly (or at all) if the user and group names and numerical IDs aren't the same on both systems. If there are discrepancies, you must fix them before proceeding. See **usermod** (Chapter 12) for information on changing the UID and GID of users. Also see **chmod** (Chapter 5) for information on changing the ownership of files recursively throughout the user's directories.

TIP   If you change a user's IDs, all of the user's files must be modified (with **chmod**, discussed in Chapter 5) to match the new user and group IDs.

Portmap Security Restrictions

To use NFS safely, you should modify the /etc/hosts.allow and /etc/hosts.deny files so that you gain some measure of protection while using NFS. Modify /etc/hosts/deny by adding the following line:

```
portmap: ALL
```

Now, modify /etc/host.allow by adding a line such as the following:

```
portmap: 192.168.100.10/255.255.255.0
```

This line specifies that the indicated client (192.168.100.10) has permission to access the portmap utility. Note that the slash mark and netmask (/255.255.255.0) are required. If you are not sure what the IP address and netmask of the client are, go to the client, open a terminal window, type **ifconfig eth0**, and press Enter.

Required Daemons for NFS Service

To work with NFS, you will need the following *daemons* (memory-resident programs) running on both servers and clients:

portmap   Accepts remote requests for information and guides these requests to the appropriate port.

rpc.mountd   This daemon enables the system to mount and unmount remote NFS directories.

nfsd   This is the NFS daemon proper.

You should configure all the machines on your network so that they start these daemons at the beginning of each session. On Red Hat systems, you do this with the **/usr/sbin/setup** utility, a text-mode utility that enables you to specify which system services you want to run. Make sure that your system is running the following services: netfs, nfs, nfslock, portmap, rstatd, and ruserd. If any of these options aren't available on the Setup Program menu, you need to install the RPM packages for these services. Other distributions provide varying means to specify which services run automatically at startup; check your distribution's documentation to find out which utility to run.

To make sure you're running the needed utilities, you can run the startup scripts with the **status** option. Here's how to do this:

1. Switch to the directory where network scripts are stored. On Red Hat and kindred systems, this directory is /etc/rc.d/init.d.

2. Type **./portmap status** and press Enter. You should see a message stating that portmap is running. If not, type **./portmap startup** and press Enter.

3. Now, type **./nfs status** and press Enter. You should see a message informing you that rpc.mountd and nfsd are running. If not, type ./nfs start and press Enter.

4. Type **/usr/sbin/rpcinfo -p** and press Enter. You should see a list of all the running daemons, including their version numbers and the protocol they're using.

If you see an error message such as "Can't contact portmapper," "Connection refused," or "Prog not registered," portmap isn't running, or your /etc/hosts.deny and /etc/hosts.allow files aren't properly configured. Check your configuration, then restart your system and try the previous steps again.

Configuring */etc/exports*

The next step involves modifying the file /etc/exports on the server so that NFS knows which directories to "export," that is, make available to clients. To specify a directory to export, type the name of the directory you want to export, followed by a space, and the IP address of the client or clients to which you want to make the directory available. After the IP address, place the export options you want within parentheses. Here's an example:

```
/home/suzanne 192.168.100.33(rw)
   /mnt/cdrom 192.168.100.*(ro)
```

This example exports /home/suzanne, a directory owned by the user named suzanne on the server, to Suzanne's computer (192.168.100.33), where it will be available to her through NFS. The option (**rw**) specifes that this directory should be exported with read and write permissions

The second line exports the server's CD-ROM drive (/mnt/cdrom) to all the clients on my network, with read-only permission.

WARNING Before NFS can make use of the modifications you've made, you must use the **exportfs** utility to update the exported directory database, /var/lib/nfs/xtab. This database is needed by the remote mounting daemons; if it isn't accurate, clients won't be able to mount the exported directories. To synchronize /etc/exports with the database, type **exportfs –rv** and press Enter.

Configuring */etc/fstab* on the Client

Now you need to configure the clients so that they access the exported directories automatically. To do this, follow these steps:

1. On the client system, create the directories where you want to mount the remote directories. If you're creating mount points for a user's directories, be sure to do this from the user's account so that it will have the correct permissions.

2. Add mount information to /etc/fstab on the client system. The following examples load the directories /home/public and /home/suzanne, which are physically present on the server named rivendell:

   ```
   rivendell:/home/public /home/suzanne/
   public nfs rsize=8192,wsize=8192,user

   rivendell:/home/suzanne /home/suzanne/
   rivendell nfs rsize=8192,wsize=8192,user
   ```

These lines mount the specified directories to local directories named, respectively, /home/suzanne/public and /home/suzanne/rivendell. The additional options specify the filesystem type (nfs), read and write block sizes that are larger (and faster) than the default, and the all-important user option that enables ordinary users to mount and unmount the remote directories without switching to superuser (which, as you've already learned, would transform them into nobodies).

Make sure that the server is running, and restart the client. If you see an error messages such as "Program not registered," the needed NFS daemons aren't running on the client system. If you see a message such as "Permission denied," there's a problem on the server side. You may have forgotten to run **exportfs** (see the section "Configuring /etc/exports," earlier in this section).

Configuring Samba Networking

Samba is a Linux implementation of the Server Message Block (SMB) protocol used in Windows networking. With Samba, you can easily create peer-to-peer networks (akin to the Network Neighborhood concept in Windows 95/98/NT) that provide seamless file exchange between Linux and Windows systems. In peer-to-peer networking, users can choose to share certain directories on the network. A directory that is made available for network access is called a *share*. In addition, users can specify the level of access that is available for a given share. In *share-level access,* the share is made available to any network user, although it is possible to protect the share with a password. In *user-level access,* the share is made available only to a network user who has the same username as the local share's owner. In both share- and user-level access, the share can be made available read only, or with full read and write privileges.

In Windows-only environments, Microsoft Windows NT Server is required to make user-level access available to Windows users. However, it is possible to use Samba to mimic the behavior of Windows NT Server so that user-level access (and other advanced networking capabilities) become available to network users, even though Windows NT Server is not running on the network. However, considerably more expertise—including familiarity with Windows NT Server—is required to configure Samba to emulate Windows NT. In accordance with this book's focus on single-user Linux systems and small networks, this section focuses on configuring Samba for peer-to-peer networking for a small network of up to, say, a dozen computers.

To use Samba, you must configure your Linux system to start the Samba software automatically. The best way to do this is to choose the Samba option when you install your Linux distribution. If you did not enable Samba when you installed Linux, you may wish to do so by upgrading to a more recent version of your Linux distribution, which will ensure that you get the latest (and more secure) versions of the Samba software. Should you wish to keep using your current distribution, check your distribution's manual to determine how to enable Samba services on your system.

Configuring */etc/smb.conf*

Samba distributions typically include a sample `smb.conf` file, which is installed in the `/etc` directory. By making a few simple changes to this file, you can quickly enable peer-to-peer networking. After you do so, Windows users will be able to access files made available on a Linux system.

The following tables discuss the `smb.conf` options that need to be enabled to establish peer-to-peer networking between Linux and Windows systems.

TIP To enable user-level shares with Samba, you must establish user accounts on both systems—Windows and Linux—that share the same username. For example, suppose Suzanne uses a Windows 98 system with the username *suzanne*. To access her directories on a Linux system running Samba, the Linux system must recognize a user named suzanne. This is required because Windows systems automatically supply the current user's name when requesting an SMB connection. It is not necessary for both of these accounts to have the same password.

After you enable these necessary options in `smb.conf` and restart your system, the Samba server will make a Windows user's Linux directories available to a Windows user who has the same username. The Linux directories will show up in this Windows user's Network Neighborhood (a networking feature of Windows 95/98/NT). These same options enable Linux users to access their shares on Windows systems, as long as these shares have been made available for network sharing. (See your Windows manual for information on enabling file sharing with Windows.)

The Samba configuration file (/etc/smb.conf) is divided into several sections, including Global, Home, and Printers. The following tables (Global Section Configuration, Home Section Configuration, and Printers Section Configuration) discuss only those options that are pertinent to peer-to-peer networking. In the sample /etc/smb.conf, you may see additional options that are commented out with a semi-colon (;) or hash mark (#); leave these options unchanged.

Configuring the Global Section Options

The Global section includes options that govern the general behavior of the Samba server. You can quickly enable peer-to-peer networking by making a few simple changes to this section, as noted in the Global Section Configuration table. You may see additional options in the sample /etc/smb.conf configuration file; leave them commented out.

GLOBAL SECTION CONFIGURATION

Use This Option	To Do This
encrypt passwords=[**yes** | **no**]	Specify whether Samba should expect and send encrypted passwords. Note that encrypted passwords are enabled by default on Windows 98 and Windows NT 4.0 SP3 and later. If you are using Windows 95 or an earlier version of NT, choose **no**. To enable encrypted passwords with Samba, you must define the Samba users with the **smbpasswd** utility, discussed in this chapter.
hosts allow=*IP address*	Specify a comma, space, or tab-delimited list of the IP addresses of clients that have permission to access the Samba shares on this machine.
load printers=[**yes** | **no**]	Choose whether to make local printers available to Samba users.

GLOBAL SECTION CONFIGURATION *(CONT.)*

Use This Option	To Do This
security=[**user** | **share**]	Specify whether the Samba server enables user-level or share-level access. With user-level access, a remote user can access only those files on the Linux system that are owned by the same username. With share-level access, remote users can access shared directories even if they do not have the same username as the user who owns the Linux files. Choose user-level access to make a specific user's Linux directories available to that user, and that user only, via network connections. Choose share-level access to make the Linux directories available to all network users, provided they know the password required to access these directories. You should also choose share-level access if you want to enable guest accounts, which do not require a password.
server string=_string_	Use the specified string to describe the Samba server to network users.
smb passwd file=_/filename_	Specify the location of the Samba password file, which is required if encrypted passwords are used. (See **encrypt passwords** in this table.) The default is `/etc/smbpasswd`.
workgroup=_WORKGROUP_	Specify the name of the Windows workgroup. By convention, this is typed in capital letters. This setting must correspond to the workgroup name specified in the Network Control Panel in Microsoft Windows.

Homes Section Configuration

In the Homes section, you specify how the Samba server makes remote users' home directories available to them. By default, a remote user with a username corresponding to a valid username on the Linux system is granted access to that user's home directory.

HOMES SECTION CONFIGURATION

Use This Option	To Do This
available=[**yes** | **no**]	Make the service available (*yes*) or unavailable (*no*).
browseable=[**yes** | **no**]	Display (*yes*) or hide (*no*) this share in share lists generated by users other than the share's owner.
comment=*string*	Describe the share. This text is made available to users who are browsing available shares on the network.
writable=[**yes** | **no**]	Make the share available as read and write (*yes*) or as read only (*no*).

Printers Section Configuration

The Printers section defines network access to local printers.

PRINTERS SECTION CONFIGURATION

Use This Option	To Do This
browseable=[**yes** | **no**]	Specify whether to make local printers viewable when remote users browse available shares.
comment=*string*	Display the specified string in the comment column of network browsing utilities.
guest ok=[**yes** | **no**]	Specify whether guest access is enabled.
printable=[**yes** | **no**]	Enable (*yes*) or disable (*no*) printing.
public=[**yes** | **no**]	Permit the guest users to print (*yes*) or prohibit printing by the guest user.

Configuring PPP Dial-Up Connections

The Point-to-Point Protocol (PPP) is the standard method of establishing a dial-up connection between personal computers and Internet service providers (ISPs). Most Linux distributions rely on a utility called **wvdial** to establish PPP connections. Typically, Linux distributions are configured with scripts that launch this utility. They may also come with menu-based utilities that enable you to configure your PPP configuration easily.

If you would like to configure your PPP connection manually, you can do so by following these steps:

1. Run **wvdialconf** to detect your modem, determine its characteristics, and write the initial working copy of the **wvdial** configuration file, /etc/wvdial.conf.

2. Modify the **wvdial** configuration file (/etc/wvdial.conf) to dial your ISP and establish the connection.

The configuration file, /etc/wvdial.conf, has two or more sections. The first, Dialer Defaults, is generated automatically by **wvdialconf**. Do not alter the settings in this section. The second section, the name of which begins with Dialer, specifies the settings for a given PPP connection, including the phone number, username, and password. You can create two or more such sections, if you wish.

The following illustrates a typical **wvdial** configuration in /etc/wvdial.conf:

```
    [Dialer Defaults]
Modem = /dev/ttyS1
Baud = 115200
Init1 = ATZ
Init2 = ATQ0 V1 E1 S0=0 &C1 &D2 S11=55
SetVolume = 1
Dial Command = ATDT
```

```
[Dialer MyConnection]
Username = suzanne
Password = ilw2mfc
Phone = 555-1212
Dial Prefix = 9,,
Area Code = 800
```

This configuration dials 9, waits two seconds, and then dials 800-555-1212. When the ISP responds, it supplies the username *suzanne* and the password *il22mfc*, and establishes the connection using the ISP's preferred authentication method.

Alphabetical Command Reference

This section details the following:

- Working with the Network File System (**exportfs, rcp, rpcinfo, showmount**)

- Working with Samba networking (**smbclient, smbmount, smbstatus, smbumount**)

- Using e-mail (**fetchmail, fetchmailconf, mail**)

- Using FTP, the Web, and other Internet services (**ftp, lynx, telnet**)

- Accessing the Internet by means of dial-up (PPP) connections (**wvdial, wvdialconf**)

- Determining TCP/IP (Internet) information (**ifconfig, netstat, nslookup, ping**)

exportfs

exportfs [option] [*client:/path*]

Used after you have made modifications to the Network File System (NFS) export configuration file (/etc/exports), this utility creates the table of exported filesystems located in /var/lib/nfs/xtab. This file is read by the NFS mount daemon (rpc.mountd), and must be up to date if the mount is to succeed.

OPTIONS

Use This Option	To Do This
–a	Export all the filesystems listed in **/etc/exports**
–o *option*	Specify one or more mount options in the same way you would type them in **/etc/exports**
–i	Ignore the **/etc/exports** file
–r	Re-export all the filesystems listed in **/etc/exports** and make sure that the export database (**/var/lib/ nfs/xtab**) exactly duplicates **/etc/exports**
–u *directory*	Unexport the specified directory
–v	Show all messages

EXAMPLES

This Command	Does the Following
exportfs –av	Exports all the filesystems listed in **/etc/exports** and displays all messages.
exportfs –rv	Re-exports all the filesystems listed in **/etc/exports**, makes sure that the export database is correct, and displays all messages.

fetchmail

fetchmail [option] [*server*]

Starts a utility that runs in the background and retrieves mail and forwards it to the local (client) delivery system from the specified server, which can be a POP2, POP3, IMAP2bis, IMAP4, or IMAPPrev1 mail server. Before running **fetchmail**, use **fetchmailconf** to create the **fetchmail** configuration file (~/.fetchmailrc). If **fetchmailconf** is not available on your system, you can download a copy from Internet distribution sites such as http://www.freshmeat.net. The options available for basic **fetchmail** use are listed here. Many more options are available for intermediate and advanced functions.

OPTIONS

Use This Option	To Do This
–a, – –all	Get all messages from the server.
–b *n*, **– –batchlimit** *n*	Retrieve a maximum of *n* messages.
–B *n*, **– –fetchlimit** *n*	Retrieve a maximum of *n* messages in a single poll.
– –bsmtp *filename*	Append fetched mail to a BSMTP file.
–F, – –flush	Delete read messages from the POP3 or IMAP server.
–k, – –keep	Keep retrieved messages on the server instead of deleting them, which is the default behavior.
–l *n*, **– –limit** *n*	Specify the maximum size (in bytes) for messages to be downloaded. Messages larger than this size are skipped.
–p *protocol*, **– –protocol** *protocol*	Use the specified protocol when connecting to the mail server. If you do not specify a protocol, **fetchmail** attempts to detect the protocol automatically.
–s, – –silent	Hide program messages.
– –ssl	Use encryption if the server supports it.
–t *n*, **– –timeout** *n*	Set the server non-response time to *n* seconds.
–u *username*, **– –username** *username*	Log on with the specified username.
–v, – –verbose	Show all messages.

---

fetchmailconf

fetchmailconf

Launches an interactive editor that creates the configuration file (`~/.fetchmailrc`) for the **fetchmail** utility. If **fetchmailconf** is not available on your system, you can download a copy from Internet distribution sites such as http://www.freshmeat.net.

ftp

ftp [option] [*host*]

Establishes a File Transfer Protocol (FTP) connection with the specified host and launches an interactive utility that enables you to download (get) or upload (put) files from FTP servers (assuming that you have the appropriate permissions). See the Commands table for the commands that you can use in the interactive session.

OPTIONS

Use This Option	To Do This
–d	Enable debugging
–e	Disable command editing and history support
–g	Disable filename globbing
–i	Turn off interactive prompting during multiple file transfers
–n	Refrain from attempting auto-login upon initial connection
–p	Use passive mode for data transfers
–v	Show all responses from the remote server and report data transfer statistics

COMMANDS

Use This Option	To Do This
$ *macro* [*argument*]	Execute the macro that was defined with the **macdef** command.
? [*command*]	Display help for the specified command.
! [*command* [*argument*]]	Start an interactive shell on the local machine. Optionally, you can specify an argument.
account [*password*]	Start a supplementary login after the primary login has been successfully completed. You can optionally specify a password.

COMMANDS *(CONT.)*

Use This Option	To Do This
append *local filename* [*remote filename*]	Append the specified local filename to a file on the remote machine. If you do not specify a remote filename, a file is created on the remote machine with the same name as the local filename, but characters and line termination settings are changed according to the remote machine's settings, if any.
ascii	Set the file transfer type to ASCII. This is the default.
bell	Sound the bell after each file is successfully transferred.
binary	Set the file transfer type to binary.
bye	Close the FTP session and quit the **ftp** utility.
case	Toggle case mapping on or off. Case mapping is off by default. When case mapping is on, remote uppercase filenames are written to the local system in lowercase letters.
cd *directory*	Change to the specified directory.
cdup	Change to the parent directory.
chmod *mode filename*	Change the permissions of the remote filename to the specified mode.
close	Terminate the FTP session with the remote server but without quitting the **ftp** utility. *See also* **bye** in this table.
cr	Toggle ASCII-mode carriage return stripping on and off. The default is on.
delete *filename*	Delete the specified filename on the remote machine.
dir [*directory*] [*filename*]	Display the contents of the directory. Optionally, save to the specified filename.
disconnect	Terminate the FTP session with the remote server but without quitting the **ftp** utility. Same as **close**. *See also* **bye**.

COMMANDS *(CONT.)*

Use This Option	To Do This
form *format*	Set the file transfer type to the specified format. Options are **ascii** and **binary**.
get *remote filename* [*local filename*]	Retrieve the remote filename and optionally store it locally with the specified local filename.
glob	Toggle filename expansion for **mdelete**, **mget**, and **mput**. The default is on.
hash	Toggle hash signs for 1024-byte data block transfers.
help [*command*]	Show a list of all commands, or show help for the specified command.
idle [*seconds*]	Set the inactivity timer on the remote server to *seconds*.
lcd [*directory*]	Change the working directory on the local system to the specified directory or to the user's home directory if no directory is specified.
ls [*remote directory*] [*local filename*]	Display the contents of the specified directory and optionally save to the local filename.
mdelete *filename*	Delete *filename* on the remote machine.
mget *filename*	Get multiple files on the remote machine as specified by the filename, which can use filename expansion unless **glob** is toggled off.
mkdir *directory*	Make the directory on the remote machine.
mode *mode*	Set the file transfer mode to the specified mode. The default is stream.
modtime *filename*	Show the last modification time of the filename on the remote machine.
mput *filename*	Place multiple files on the remote machine as specified by the filename, which can use filename expansion unless **glob** is toggled off.
newer *remote filename* [*local filename*]	Get the remote filename only if the modification time of the remote file is more recent than the local filename.

COMMANDS *(CONT.)*

Use This Option	To Do This
open *hostname* [*port*]	Connect to the hostname. You can optionally use the specified port.
prompt	Toggle interactive prompting.
put *local filename* [*remote filename*]	Store the local filename on the remote machine, optionally using the remote filename.
pwd	Display the name of the current working directory on the remote machine.
quit	Close the FTP session and quit the **ftp** utility.
reget *remote filename* [*local filename*]	Resume the interrupted download of *remote filename* if the remote file is larger than the local filename.
remotehelp [*command*]	Request help from the remote FTP server.
remotestatus [*filename*]	Show the status of the remote machine. Optionally, show the status of the specified filename.
rename [*old filename*] [*new filename*]	Rename the old filename on the remote machine to the new filename.
reset	Clear the reply queue.
restart *marker*	Restart the **get** or **put** operation at the specified *marker*, a byte offset within the file.
rmdir *directory*	Delete the specified directory on the remote machine.
runique	Toggle file storage on the remote machine with unique filenames.
send *local filename* [*remote filename*]	Store the local filename on the remote machine, optionally using the remote filename.
sendport	Toggle the use of port commands, which can prevent delays when performing multiple file transfers.
size *filename*	Show the size of the specified filename on the remote machine.
status	Show the current status of the **ftp** utility.

COMMANDS *(CONT.)*

Use This Option	To Do This
struct [*structure*]	Set the file transfer structure to *structure*. The default structure is stream.
sunique	Toggle file storage on the remote machine with unique filenames.
system	Show the type of operating system running on the remote machine.
trace	Toggle packet tracing.
type [*mode*]	Set the file transfer type to the specified mode. The default is ASCII.
umask [*mask*]	Display the current **umask** on the remote system. Optionally, set the remote **umask** to the specified mask.
user [*password* [*account*]]	Log in to the remote system. Optionally, specify the password and the account.
verbose	Toggle verbose mode.

ifconfig

ifconfig [*interface*] [*option*] [*address*]

Displays information about network interfaces. This utility can also be used to configure network interfaces. It is used in this way by startup scripts to configure networking hardware when you boot your system. For users, **ifconfig** is most useful when invoked without options. It provides a quick way to view current network interface settings, including IP addresses and netmasks. The options available for basic **ifconfig** use are listed here. Many more options are available for intermediate and advanced functions.

OPTIONS

Use This Option	To Do This
broadcast *address*	Set the broadcast address of this interface
down	Deactivate the interface

OPTIONS *(CONT.)*

Use This Option	To Do This
io_addr *address*	Specify the interface device's I/O address
irq *address*	Specify the interface device's IRQ line
media *type* | *port*	Specify the physical port or medium type used by the device, if the device allows such a change to be made
mem_start *addr*	Set the start address for shared memory used by this device
mtu *n*	Set the Maximum Transfer Unit (MTU) of an interface
netmask *address*	Specify the netmask address for this interface
txqueuelen *length*	Set the length of the transmit queue of the device
up	Activate the interface

EXAMPLES

This Command	Does the Following
ifconfig eth0	Shows the current configuration for the specified network interface (eth0).
ifconfig	Shows the current configuration for all active network interfaces.

lynx

lynx [option] [*path* \| *URL*]

Launches a text-mode Web browser and optionally displays the specified path or URL. Once **lynx** starts, you can use commands (see the Commands table in this section) to control the browser. The options available for basic **lynx** use are listed here. Many more options are available for intermediate and advanced functions.

OPTIONS

Use This Option	To Do This
–accept_all_cookies	Accept all cookies.
–anonymous	Apply restrictions for anonymous account.
–assume_charset=_character set_	Use the specified character set for documents that do not specify a character set.
–assume_local_charset =_character set_	Use the specified character set for local documents.
–assume_unrec_charset =_character set_	Use the specified character set in place of character sets that are not recognized.
–auth=_login_:_password_	Use the specified login and password for password-protected documents.
–book	Start **lynx** with the bookmark page.
–cache=_n_	Cache _n_ documents in memory. The default is 10.
–case	Enable case-sensitive string searching.
–cfg=_filename_	Specify a configuration file other than the default.
–color	Use color mode if available.
–cookies	Toggle handling of Set-Cookie headers.
–cookie_file=_filename_	Store cookies in the specified filename.
–core	Toggle forced core dumps.
–dont_wrap_pre	Inhibit wrapping of text in <pre> tags.
–editor=_editor_	Use the specified editor for external editing.
–emacskeys	Enable **emacs**-like key movement.
–enable_scrollback	Toggle compatibility with communication programs' scrollback keys.
–error_file=_filename_	Write errors to the specified filename.
–force_html	Force the first document to be interpreted as HTML.

OPTIONS *(CONT.)*

Use This Option	To Do This
–help	Show on-screen help.
–homepage=*URL*	Use the specified URL as the page to display when home is selected.
–image_links	Toggle display of links for images.
–index=*URL*	Set the default index file to the specified URL.
–justify	Justify text on-screen.
–localhost	Disable URLs that point to remote hosts.
–mime_header	Show the MIME header of remote documents.
–nobold	Hide boldface text.
–nobrowse	Disable directory browsing.
–nocolor	Turn color mode off.
–nopause	Disable forced pauses for status-line messages.
–noprint	Disable most print functions.
–noredir	Prevent automatic redirection and print a message with a link to the new URL.
–noreferer	Disable transmissions of Referer headers.
–noreverse	Disable reverse video attribute.
–nostatus	Disable the retrieval status messages.
–nounderline	Disable underline video attribute.
–number_fields	Number links and form input fields.
–number_links	Number links but not form input fields.
–partial	Display partial pages while loading.
partial_thres=*n*	Render *n* lines before repainting the display.
–pauth=ID:*password*	Log on with the specified username and password.

OPTIONS *(CONT.)*

Use This Option	To Do This
–prettysrc	Show the HTML source with color tagging of HTML elements.
–use_mouse	Turn on mouse support if available.

COMMANDS

Use This Command	To Do This
–	View the previous page of the document
#	Go to toolbar or banner in the current document
*	Toggle handling of all images as links
+	View the next page of the document
<	Move up the page to a previous link
=	Display information on the current document and link
>	Move down the page to another link
****	Toggle source/presentation for the current document
`	Toggle minimal versus valid comment parsing
,	View the next page of the document
/	Search within the current document
;	View trace log if started in the current session
?	Display help on using the browser
?	Show available options
(	Go back half a page in the document
)	Go forward half a page in the document
1	Go to the end of the current document
2	Make the next link current
3	View the next page of the document
4	Go back to the previous document
6	Go to the document given by the current link
7	Go to the beginning of the current document

COMMANDS *(CONT.)*

Use This Command	To Do This
8	Make the previous link current
9	View the previous page of the document
a	Add to personal bookmark list
b	Go back
c	Send a comment to the author
Ctrl + A	Go to the beginning of the current document
Ctrl + B	View the previous page of the document
Ctrl + D	Quit the browser unconditionally
Ctrl + E	Go to the end of the current document
Ctrl + F	View the next page of the document
Ctrl + H	Display the stack of currently suspended documents
Ctrl + J	Go to the document given by the current link
Ctrl + K	View cookies
Ctrl + L	Refresh the screen
Ctrl + N	Go forward two lines
Ctrl + P	Go back two lines
Ctrl + R	Reload the current document
Ctrl + T	Toggle tracing of browser operations
Ctrl + V	Switch between two ways of parsing HTML
Ctrl + W	Refresh the screen to clear garbled text
d	Download the current link
Delete	Display a stack of currently suspended documents
Down arrow	Move to next hyperlink down
e	Edit the current document
E	Edit the current link
End	Go to the end of the current document
f	Display the file operations menu
F1	Display help
g	Go to the specified URL
G	Edit the current document's URL and go to the edited URL

COMMANDS *(CONT.)*

Use This Command	To Do This
h	Display help on using the browser
H	Show available options
Home	Go to the beginning of the current document
i	Display an index of potentially useful documents
j	Go to a target document or action
k	Display the current key bindings
K	Show keystroke mappings.
l	List the links in the current document
m	Return to the first screen
n	Go to the next occurrence
o	Display option settings
p	Print the current document
PgDn	View the next page of the document
PgUp	View the previous page of the document
q	Quit the browser
Q	Force browser exit
r	Delete the bookmark.
Return	Follow the selected hyperlink
Right arrow	Follow the selected hyperlink
s	Search the index
Space	View the next page of the document
t	Tag link for later action
Tab	Go to next link or text area
u	Go back to the previous document
Up arrow	Move to next hyperlink up
v	View the bookmark list
V	List links visited during the current session
x	Force submission of link or form without the cache
z	Interrupt the network connection

mail

mail [option] *address*

Launches an interactive utility that enables you to send or read e-mail. To send mail, specify the recipient's address, type your message, and press **Ctrl + d**. To read your mail, type **mail** with no options or addresses. Type **+** to move forward or **–** to move backward. To delete a message, type **d**. Type **u** to undelete the message. To reply to a message, type **r**. To quit the utility, type **q**.

OPTIONS

Use This Option	To Do This
–b *list*	Send blind carbon copies to the list, a comma-separated list of names
–c *list*	Send carbon copies to the list, a comma-separated list of names
–f	Read the contents of your mailbox
–i	Ignore **tty** interrupt signals
–I	Run in interactive mode
–n	Skip reading `/etc/mail.rc` upon startup
–N	Skip the initial display of message headers when reading mail or editing a mail folder
–s *subject*	Use the specified subject
–u	Read the user's default mailbox
–v	Show all the messages

netstat

netstat [option]

Displays information about the Linux networking subsystem. If you run **netstat** without options, you see a list of the current TCP/IP sockets. The options available for basic **netstat** use are listed here.

Many more options are available for intermediate and advanced functions.

OPTIONS

Use This Option	To Do This
–a, – –all	Show information about all sockets, including listening server sockets.
–c, – –continuous	Display continuous output until interrupted with **Ctrl + c**.
–e, – –extend	Display extended information.
–l, – –listening	Display information about the listening server sockets only.
–n, – –numeric	Show numerical IP addresses rather than trying to resolve domain names.
–p, – –programs	Display the process name and PID of each active process. Requires root user status.
–v, – –verbose	Show all messages.

EXAMPLE

This Command	Does the Following
`netstat –a`	Shows information about all the TCP/IP sockets currently in operation.

nslookup

nslookup [option][*host* [*server*]]

Looks up the numerical IP address of the specified host by querying the default Internet domain name server or the specified server. If you start **nslookup** without options or arguments, the utility enters an interactive mode in which you can use the commands listed in the Commands table in this section. In the interactive mode, you can obtain a wealth of information about Internet hosts (see the Query Types table later in this section). Values specified with the **set** option (see the Commands table) are saved to the user's `.nslookuprc` file.

COMMANDS

Use This Option	To Do This
host [*server*]	Look up information for the specified host. Optionally, obtain this information from the specified server.
lserver *server*	Change the default server.
root	Change the default server for the root of the domain name space. The default is ns.internic.com.
ls [option] *domain* [>*filename*]	List available host names and IP addresses for the specified domain. Optionally, append the output to the specified filename. You can use the following options: **–t** *querytype* List all the records of the specified query type. (See the table Query Types later in this section.) **–a** List aliases of hosts in the domain. **–d** List all records for the domain. **–h** List the CPU and operating system type for the domain.
help, **?**	Show available commands.
exit	Quit **nslookup**.
set *keyword*	Change the lookup method. Available *keyword = value* options are as follows: **all** Show the current values of set options. **class = *value*** Change the query class to IN (Internet classes), CHAOS (Chaos classes), HESIOD (MIT Athena class), or ANY (any of the options). **domain = *name*** Change to the specified default domain. The default is to use the current host's domain. **srchlist = *list*** Use the comma-separated list of domains to search. **port = *n*** Change the default DNS port to *n*. The default is port 53. **querytype = *query –type*** Use one of the query types listed in the Query Types table later in this section. The default is type **A** (Internet address). **recurse** Query other servers if the default server does not have the information. This is the default setting. Use **no recurse** to turn this feature off.

COMMANDS *(CONT.)*

Use This Option	To Do This
set *keyword*	**retry = *n*** Retry *n* times if the server is not available. The default is four retries. **root = *host*** Set the name of the root server to *host*. The default is ns.internic.net. **timeout = *n*** Set the timeout to *n* seconds. The default is five seconds.

QUERY TYPES

Use This Query Type	To View the Following Information
A	The host's Internet address
CNAME	The canonical name for an alias
HINFO	The host CPU and operating system type
MINFO	The mailbox or mail list information
MX	The mail exchanger
NS	The name server for the named zone
PTR	The host name if the query is an Internet address, otherwise, the pointer to other information
SOA	The domain's "start-of-authority" information
TXT	The text information
UINFO	The user information
WKS	The supported well-known services

EXAMPLES

This Command	Does the Following
`rcp essay1.doc essay1.bak@lothlorien:/` `home/suzanne/Documents/Backup`	Displays the numerical IP address for Yahoo.
`rcp essay1.doc essay1.bak@lothlorien:/` `home/suzanne/Documents/Backup`	Enters the interactive mode, in which you can use available commands.

ping

ping [option] *host*

Sends packets of Internet data to the specified host to see whether the host is online and capable of exchanging data. **ping** is frequently used to verify that a system is indeed connected to the Internet and capable of exchanging data with other Internet hosts.

See also **netstat, nslookup.**

OPTIONS

Use This Option	To Do This
–c *n*	Stop after receiving *n* packets.
–i *n*	Wait *n* seconds between sending each packet. The default is one second.
–l *preload*	Sends as many packets as possible. Requires root or superuser status.
–n	Show the numeric IP addresses only.
–p *pattern*	Pad the output with a specified pattern of up to 16 bytes.
–q	Hide messages.
–r	Ping the host directly without using routing tables.
–R	Record the route.
–s *n*	Send *n* bytes of data in each packet. The default is 56, which translates into 64 bytes when the header data is added.
–v	Show all messages.

EXAMPLES

This Command	Does the Following
ping 207.46.131.30	Pings the specified IP address.
ping www.yahoo.com	Pings the specified domain.

rcp

rcp [option] *source file destination file*

Copies the specified source file to the destination file. The source file or the destination file can be located on the local, or a remote, machine and can refer to a file or a directory. To indicate a local file, type the filename. You can also specify the path name if the file is not located in the working directory. To indicate a remote file, type the filename followed by @, the name of the host, and the path name on the host (see the Examples later in this section).

OPTIONS

Use This Option	To Do This
–p	Preserve the original modification times and permission modes of the source files if possible
–r	Copy the specified directory and all associated subdirectories (recursive mode)

EXAMPLES

This Command	Does the Following
`rcp essay1.doc essay1.bak @lothlorien:/home/suzanne/ Documents/Backup`	Copies the specified file (`essay1.doc`) to the remote machine (`lothlorien`) and writes it to the file named `/home/suzanne/ Documents/Backup/essay1.bak`.
`rcp -r Poems Poems@ lothlorien:/home/suzanne/ Documents`	Copies the specified directory (`Poems`) and all associated subdirectories to the remote machine (`lothlorien`). Creates a new directory called Poems, if necessary, within the `/home/suzanne/Documents` directory.

rpcinfo

rpcinfo [option] [host]

Displays information about the Network File System. This utility provides a useful way to check that all the required NFS daemons are installed and running properly.

OPTIONS

Use This Option	To Do This
–n *n*	Display information about the port number specified by *n*
–u *host n*	Display information about the program number *n* running on the specified host
–p [*host*]	Display information about the NFS daemons running on the current system or the specified host

EXAMPLE

This Command	Does the Following
rpcinfo –p	Displays a list of all the NFS daemons currently running, if any.

showmount

showmount [option] [*host*]

Displays the Network File System mounts available. Optionally, shows the mounts available on the specified host.

OPTIONS

Use This Option	To Do This
–a, – –all	List both the client hostname and mounted directory in *host:dir* format

OPTIONS *(CONT.)*

Use This Option	To Do This
–d, **– –directories**	List only mounted directories
–e, **– –exports**	Show the NFS server's export list
–h, **– –help** .	Show available options
–v, **– –version**	Display the version number

EXAMPLES

This Command	Does the Following
`showmount -a`	Displays all available NFS mounts.
`showmount lothlorien`	Displays the mounts available from the specified server (`lothlorien`).
`showmount -e`	Displays the exports made available from this system's NFS server.

smbclient

smbclient *service* [option]

Launches an interactive Samba utility that closely resembles **ftp**. With this utility, you can transfer files and perform other file-related operations on remote Samba directories. See the Commands table for the commands you can use in the utility's interactive mode.

See also **smbmount.**

OPTIONS

Use This Option	To Do This
–b *size*	Change the transmit/send buffer to the specified size in bytes.
–h	Show the available options.
–I *address*	Connect to the specified IP address.

OPTIONS *(CONT.)*

Use This Option	To Do This
–L	View options available on the server.
–l *filename*	Log operational data to the specified filename.
–N	Suppress the password prompt for services that do not require a password.
–n *name*	Use the specified name instead of the local machine's hostname.
–p *port*	Use the specified port to connect to the server. The default is 139.
–s *filename*	Use the specified filename as the Samba configuration file.
–T *option*	Create a **tar** backup. Available options are as follows: **c [*filename* | *device*]** Create a **tar** backup with the specified filename (or on the device) of the Samba share on a Unix machine. **x [*filename* | *device*]** Extract (restore) a local **tar** file back to a share. **X *filename*** Exclude the specified filename. **b *size*** Use the specified block size (512K by default). **g** Perform an incremental backup. **q** Hide **tar**'s messages. **N *date*** Back up only those files newer than the specified date. **a** Reset archive bit when files are backed up.
–U *username*	Use the specified username.
–W *WORKGROUP*	Use the specified WORKGROUP (typed in capital letters) instead of the default workgroup defined in `smb.conf`.

COMMANDS

Use This Command	To Do This
? [*command*]	Show help options or show help for the specified command.

COMMANDS *(CONT.)*

cd *directory*	Change to the specified directory.
del *filename*	Delete the specified filename. You can use shell pattern wildcards.
dir [*filename*]	Show the files in the current working directory. You can optionally show just the files that match the specified filename. You can use shell pattern wildcards.
exit	Terminate the connection with the server and exit from the program.
get *remote filename* [*local filename*]	Get the specified remote filename from the remote server and copy it to the system running the client. Optionally, write the file locally using the specified local filename.
help [*command*]	Show help options or show help for the specified command.
lcd *directory*	Change to the specified directory on the local system.
lowercase	Toggle automatic translation of filenames from upper- to lowercase when using the **get** and **mget** commands.
ls [*filename*]	Display the files in the working directory. Optionally, display only those files that match the specified filename. You can use shell pattern wildcards.
md *directory*	Create the specified directory on the remote system.
mget *filename*	Get multiple files matching the specified filename from the remote system and copy them to the local system. You can use shell pattern wildcards.
mkdir *directory*	Create the specified directory on the remote system.
mput *filename*	Copy multiple files matching the specified filename from the local system to the remote system. You can use shell pattern wildcards.
print *filename*	Print the specified filename.
printmode *graphics* | *text*	Use the specified printing mode (*graphics* or *text*).
prompt	Prompt for filenames during **mget** and **mput** operations.

COMMANDS *(CONT.)*

Use this Command	To Do This
put *local filename remote filename*	Copy the specified local filename from the local system to the remote system. Optionally, rename the copied file using remote filename.
queue	Display the print queue.
quit	Terminate the connection with the remote server and quit the program.
rd *directory*	Remove the specified directory on the remove server.
recurse	Toggle directory recursion for the commands **mget** and **mput**.
rm *filename*	Delete files in the remote working directory that match *filename*. You can use shell pattern wildcards.
rmdir *directory*	Remove the specified directory on the remove server.

smbmount

smbmount *service mountpoint* [*–o option*]

Mounts a remote Samba service at the specified mount point. You must create the mount point (a directory) before running this utility.

See also **smbumount**.

OPTIONS

Use This Option	To Do This
dmask=*mask*	Set the permissions mask for the remote directories mounted in the local filesystem. The default is based on the current umask.
fmask=*mask*	Set the permissions mask for remote files mounted in the local filesystem. The default is based on the current umask.

OPTIONS *(CONT.)*

Use This Option	To Do This
gid=*gid*	Set the group user ID (GID) for the mounted files. You can specify the group name or the numeric ID.
guest	Skip prompting for the password.
ip=*address*	Specify the destination hostname or IP address.
netbiosname=*string*	Specify the source NetBIOS name. This is set to the local host name by default.
password=*password*	Specify the password. If you omit this option, the utility will prompt you to supply the password, unless you have used the **guest** option.
port=*n*	Set the remote port number to *n*. The default is 139.
ro	Mount the share as read only.
rw	Mount the share as read and write.
uid=*uid*	Mount the files with the specified user ID. You can use a username or numeric user ID.
username=*username*	Connect with the specified username. The default is the current user.
workgroup=*n*	Specify the workgroup name.

EXAMPLE

This Command	Does the Following
smbmount //lothlorien/ suzanne /home/suzanne/ lothlorien	Mounts the share (//lothlorien/ suzanne) at the specified mount point (/home/suzanne/lothlorien).

smbstatus

smbstatus [option]

Displays the current Samba connections.

OPTIONS

Use This Option	To Do This
–b	Show concise output
–d	Show verbose output
–L	List locks only
–p	List running processes and exit
–S	List shares only
–s *filename*	Use the specified configuration filename
–u *username*	Show information for the specified username

EXAMPLE

This Command	Does the Following
smbstatus -d	Displays verbose status information concerning Samba networking.

---

smbumount

smbumount *mountpoint*

Unmounts the specified Samba mount point.

See also **smbmount.**

EXAMPLE

This Command	Does the Following
smbumount //lothlorien/ suzanne /home/suzanne/ lothlorien	Unmounts the share (//lothlorien/ suzanne) at the specified mount point (/home/suzanne/lothlorien).

telnet

telnet [option] *host*

Opens a terminal window on the remote host and starts an interactive session. See the Commands table in this section for selected commands you can use once the session begins.

OPTIONS

Use This Option	To Do This
–a	Attempt automatic login
–c	Disable use of the .telnetrc configuration file
–l *user*	Attempt to log in with the current user's username
–x	Turn on encryption of the data stream if possible

COMMANDS

Use This Command	To Do This
close	Close the session with the remote server, but without exiting **telnet** (see **quit**)
open *server*	Open a connection to the specified server
quit	Terminate the connection and exit the **telnet** utility
status	Show the current status of **telnet**

EXAMPLES

This Command	Does the Following
telnet lothlorien.mynetwork.org	Connects to the specified server (lothlorien.mynetwork.org).
telnet 192.168.100.10	Connect to the server specified by the numerical IP address.

wvdial

wvdial

Initiates a PPP dial-up connection using the settings specified in the utility's configuration file, /etc/wvdial.conf (see the section "Configuring PPP Dial-Up Connections" earlier in this chapter for more information on /etc/wvdial.conf).

See also **wvdialconf.**

wvdialconf

wvdialconf

Probes for a modem connected to your system and, if a modem is found, detects the port to which it is connected, its preferred initialization string, and its maximum data transfer rate. This information is automatically written to the file /etc/wvdial.conf. Requires root user or superuser status.

See also **wvdial.**

Index

Note to the reader: Throughout this index **boldfaced** page numbers indicate definitions or primary discussions of a topic.

X

Y

Z

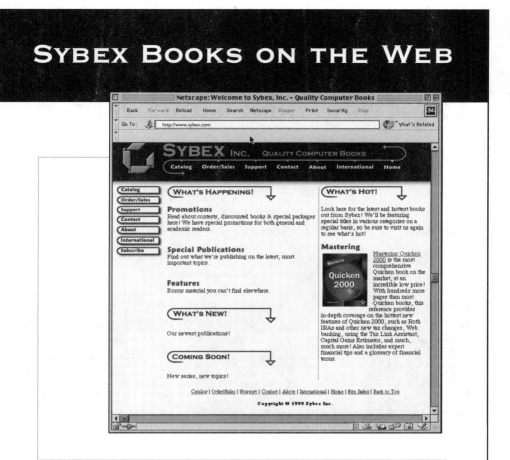